IFIP Advances in Information and Communication Technology 680

IFIP Advances in Information and Communication Technology

The IFIP AICT series publishes state-of-the-art results in the sciences and technologies of information and communication. The scope of the series includes: foundations of computer science; software theory and practice; education; computer applications in technology; communication systems; systems modeling and optimization; information systems; ICT and society; computer systems technology; security and protection in information processing systems; artificial intelligence; and human-computer interaction.

Edited volumes and proceedings of refereed international conferences in computer science and interdisciplinary fields are featured. These results often precede journal publication and represent the most current research.

The principal aim of the IFIP AICT series is to encourage education and the dissemination and exchange of information about all aspects of computing.

More information about this series at https://link.springer.com/bookseries/6102

Ibrahim (Abe) M. Elfadel ·
Lutfi Albasha
Editors

VLSI-SoC 2023: Innovations for Trustworthy Artificial Intelligence

31st IFIP WG 10.5/IEEE International Conference on Very Large Scale Integration, VLSI-SoC 2023
Sharjah, United Arab Emirates, October 16–18, 2023
Revised Extended Selected Papers

Springer

Editors
Ibrahim (Abe) M. Elfadel
Khalifa University
Abu Dhabi, United Arab Emirates

Lutfi Albasha
American University of Sharjah
Sharjah, United Arab Emirates

ISSN 1868-4238 ISSN 1868-422X (electronic)
IFIP Advances in Information and Communication Technology
ISBN 978-3-031-70949-4 ISBN 978-3-031-70947-0 (eBook)
https://doi.org/10.1007/978-3-031-70947-0

This Springer imprint is published by the registered company Springer Nature Switzerland AG
The registered company address is: Gewerbestrasse 11, 6330 Cham, Switzerland

Preface

This volume contains the extended versions of 15 papers that were presented at the 31st IFIP WG 10.5/IEEE International Conference on Very Large Scale Integration, (VLSI-SoC 2023) held at the American University of Sharjah, October 16–18, 2023. The title of the volume is inspired by the theme of the conference: VLSI Innovations for Trustworthy Artificial Intelligence.

VLSI-SoC 2023 received 77 regular papers from 24 countries across the various tracks. The number of double-blind reviews submitted for these papers was 306 for an average of 4 reviews per submission. Of these regular submissions, 43 were accepted for either a lecture or a poster. Only 15 papers out of the 43 accepted were invited to submit extended versions to the present volume. Additional reviews were conducted on the extended submissions to make sure they contain significant novelties above and beyond those published in the Proceedings of VLSI-SoC 2023.

This volume is organized in 4 parts, reflecting the breadth of contributions to the theme of the volume. These parts are:

1. Part 1: Architectures with 4 chapters.
2. Part 2: Accelerators with 3 chapters.
3. Part 3: Resiliency and Robustness with 5 chapters.
4. Part 4: Security and Privacy with 3 chapters.

We are pleased that the authors of the papers that were nominated for the best paper award at VLSI-SoC 2023 have all accepted our invitations to submit extended versions of their conference contributions. We are also pleased with the geographic distribution of the authors of this volume, a clear indication of the global character of this community and of the universality of its research endeavours. We hope the volume will serve as a stepping stone for the young members of the community, especially the graduate students who are striving to be at the cutting edge in their VLSI-SoC research.

We are deeply grateful to all those who contributed to the success of VLSI-SoC 2023, especially the Technical Program Committee members and the external reviewers who were instrumental in the conference paper selection. We are also grateful to the reviewers of the chapters of the present volume. Our warmest thanks go to our authors, without whose efforts and dedication, this volume would not have been possible.

July 2024

Ibrahim (Abe) M. Elfadel
Lutfi Albasha

Organization

General Chairs

Fadi Aloul	American University of Sharjah, UAE
Luis Miguel Silveira	INESC ID/IST Tecnico Lisboa, Universidade de Lisboa, Portugal

Program Chairs

Lutfi Albasha	American University of Sharjah, UAE
Abe Elfadel	Khalifa University, UAE

Finance Chair

Habib Ur Rehman	American University of Sharjah, UAE

Registration Chair

Usman Tariq	American University of Sharjah, UAE

Workshops and Tutorials Chair

Hasan Al-Nashash	American University of Sharjah, UAE

Special Session Chair

Said Hamdioui	Delft University of Technology, The Netherlands

General Relations Chair

Assim Sagahyroon	American University of Sharjah, UAE

PhD Forum Chair

Mahmoud H. Ismail	American University of Sharjah, UAE

Students Forum Chair

Amer Zakaria	American University of Sharjah, UAE

Industrial Chair

Fabrizio De Paolis	European Space Agency, UK

Local Arrangements Chair

Nasser Qaddoumi	American University of Sharjah, UAE

Publication Chairs

Hasan Mir	American University of Sharjah, UAE
Ricardo Reis	UFRGS, Brazil
Salvador Mir	TIMA Laboratory, France

Publicity Chairs

Sohaib Majzoub	University of Sharjah, UAE
Soliman Mahmoud	University of Sharjah, UAE
Anas Altarabsheh	University of Abu Dhabi, UAE
Fatih Uğurdağ	Özyeğin University, Turkey
Matthew Guthaus	UC Santa Cruz, USA
Graziano Pravadelli	University of Verona, Italy

Conference Manager

Shena Rosa	American University of Sharjah, UAE

Consulting

Mohamed Hassan	American University of Sharjah, UAE

On-Site Support

Dana Abdul Khaleq	American University of Sharjah, UAE
Khaled Obaideen	American University of Sharjah, UAE

Steering Committee

Chi-Ying Tsui	HKUST, China
Fatih Uğurdağ	Özyeğin University, Turkey
Graziano Pravadelli	Chair, University of Verona, Italy
Ian O'Connor	École Centrale de Lyon, France
Ibrahim Elfadel	Khalifa University, UAE
Luis Miguel Silveira	INESC ID, Portugal
Manfred Glesner	TU Darmstadt, Germany
Masahiro Fujita	University of Tokyo, Japan

Matthew Guthaus	UC Santa Cruz, USA
Ricardo Reis	UFRGS, Brazil
Salvador Mir	TIMA, France

Technical Program Committee

Hasan Al Nashash	American University of Sharjah, UAE
Mohammad Alhawari	Wayne State University, USA
Lilas Alrahis	NYU Abu Dhabi, UAE
Muhammad Awais Bin Altaf	Lahore University of Management Sciences, Pakistan
Hussam Amrouch	University of Stuttgart, Germany
Martin Andraud	Aalto University Finland
Mohamed Atef	United Arab Emirates University, UAE
Falah Awwad	United Arab Emirates University, UAE
Bevan Baas	University of California, Davis, USA
Amine Bermak	HBKU, Qatar
Alberto Bosio	Lyon Institute of Nanotechnology, France
Anupam Chattopadhyay	Nanyang Technological University, Singapore
Po-Hung Chen	National Chiao Tung University, Taiwan
Luc Claesen	Hasselt University, Belgium
Günhan Dündar	Boğaziçi University, Turkey
Nahla El-Araby	TU Wien, Austria and Canadian International College, Egypt
Ahmed Elwakil	University of Sharjah, UAE
Hector Gonzalez	SpinnCloud, Germany
Victor Grimblatt	Synopsys, Chile
Xinfei Guo	Shanghai Jiao Tong University, China
Matthew Guthaus	University of California, Santa Cruz, USA
Said Hamdioui	TU Delft, The Netherlands
İlker Hamzaoğlu	Özyeğin University, Turkey
Houman Homayoun	University of California, Davis, USA
Michael Huebner	Brandenburg University of Technology Cottbus, Germany
Mahmoud Ismail	American University of Sharjah, UAE
Haris Javaid	AMD, Singapore
Maksim Jenihhin	Tallinn University of Technology, Estonia
Srinivas Katkoori	University of South Florida, USA
Vinod Khadkikar	Khalifa University, UAE
Jinmyoung Kim	Samsung Advanced Institute of Technology, South Korea
Johann Knechtel	New York University Abu Dhabi, UAE
Ioannis Kouretas	University of Patras, Greece
Victor Kravets	IBM, USA
Martin Kumm	Fulda University of Applied Sciences, Germany
Aymen Ladhar	STMicroelectronics, France

Sohaib Majzoub	University of Sharjah, UAE
Piero Malcovati	University of Pavia, Italy
Wei Mao	Southern University of Science and Technology, China
Tiziana Margaria	Lero, Ireland
Mahmoud Meribout	Khalifa University, UAE
Hasan Mir	American University of Sharjah, UAE
Salvador Mir	TIMA Laboratory, France
Jose Miranda	EPFL, Switzerland
Baker Mohammad	Khalifa University, UAE
Jose Monteiro	INESC-ID, IST ULisboa, Portugal
Sami Muhaidat	Khalifa University, UAE
Kashif Nawaz	Technology Innovation Institute, UAE
Ian O'Connor	École Centrale de Lyon, France
Gaetano Palumbo	University of Catania, Italy
Sri Parameswaran	UNSW Sydney, Australia
Graziano Pravadelli	Università di Verona, Italy
Nasser Qaddoumi	American University of Sharjah, UAE
Bipin Rajendran	King's College London, UK
Wenjing Rao	UIC, USA
Mahmoud Rasras	New York University Abu Dhabi, UAE
Habibur Rehman	American University of Sharjah, UAE
Wala Saadeh	Western Washington University, USA
Mazen Saghir	American University of Beirut, Lebanon
Mihai Sanduleanu	Khalifa University, UAE
Atif Shamim	KAUST, Saudi Arabia
Kaveh Shamsi	University of Texas at Dallas, USA
Abdulhadi Shoufan	Khalifa University, UAE
Carlos Silva Cardenas	PUCP, Peru
Kostas Siozios	Aristotle University of Thessaloniki, Greece
Dimitrios Soudris	National Technical University of Athens, Greece
Thanos Stouraitis	Khalifa University, UAE
Mottaqiallah Taouil	Delft University of Technology, The Netherlands
Usman Tariq	American University of Sharjah, UAE
Theocharis Theocharides	University of Cyprus, Cyprus
Rasit Onur Topaloglu	IBM, USA
Chun-Jen Tsai	National Yang Ming Chiao Tung University, Taiwan
H. Fatih Uğurdağ	Özyeğin University, Turkey
Jaime Viegas	Khalifa University, UAE
Arnaud Virazel	LIRMM, France
Amer Zakaria	American University of Sharjah, UAE
Matthew Ziegler	IBM, USA

Contents

Resiliency and Robustness

Security and Privacy

Architectures

Synthesis of SFQ Circuits with Compound Gates

Rassul Bairamkulov, Alessandro Tempia Calvino(✉), and Giovanni De Micheli

Integrated Systems Laboratory, EPFL, Lausanne, Switzerland
{rassul.bairamkulov,alessandro.tempiacalvino,giovanni.demicheli}@epfl.ch

Abstract. Rapid single-flux quantum (RSFQ) is one of the most advanced superconducting technologies with the potential to supplement or replace conventional VLSI systems. However, scaling RSFQ systems up to VLSI complexity is challenging due to fundamental differences between RSFQ and CMOS technologies. Due to the pulse-based nature of the technology, RSFQ systems require gate-level pipelining. Moreover, logic gates have an extremely limited driving capacity. Path balancing and clock distribution constitute a major overhead, often doubling the size of circuits. Gate compounding is a novel technique that substantially enriches the functionality realizable within a single clock cycle. However, standard logic synthesis tools do not support its specific synchronization constraints. In this paper, we build first a database of minimum-area compound gates covering all the Boolean functions up to 4 variables and all possible input arrival patterns. Then, we propose a technology mapping method for RSFQ circuits that exploits compound gates using the database as a cell library. We evaluate our framework over the EPFL and ISCAS benchmark circuits. Our results show, on average, a 33% lower logic depth with 24% smaller area, as compared to the state of the art. We further extend our technology mapping framework to support the novel three-input SFQ gates, namely AND3, MAJ3, and OR3. We demonstrate the by using these gates, the area and logic depth of the logic networks are reduced, on average, by 11% and 30% respectively, indicating that developing the logic cells for these three-input gates can significantly improve the scalability of the SFQ technology.

Keywords: Single-Flux Quantum · logic synthesis

1 Introduction

Rapid Single-Flux Quantum (RSFQ) [1] is one of the most promising beyond-CMOS technologies. RSFQ systems consistently achieve operating frequencies on the order of tens of gigahertz [2–4], with particular cells operating at hundreds of gigahertz [5–7]. Furthermore, the operating power of the RSFQ systems is two to three orders of magnitude smaller than CMOS, even considering the refrigeration power [8].

Published by Springer Nature Switzerland AG 2024
I. (Abe) M. Elfadel and L. Albasha (Eds.): VLSI-SoC 2023, IFIP AICT 680, pp. 3–19, 2024.
https://doi.org/10.1007/978-3-031-70947-0_1

However, achieving the aforementioned advantages at scale remains a challenge. Unlike CMOS, most RSFQ logic gates operate as latches with one clock input and one or more data inputs [9]. Arrival of a *single-flux quantum* (SFQ) pulse at the data input changes the internal state of the gate. The presence or absence of an SFQ pulse within the clock period represents logical `1` or `0`, respectively. The clock pulse resets the gate to initial state, potentially releasing an SFQ pulse. This reliance on the clock signal requires SFQ circuits to be pipelined at the gate level. To ensure a correct data propagation, i.e., correct data arrives in the correct time frame, path balancing is required, as shown by the two path-balancing D-flip-flops (DFF) in Fig. 1b. Furthermore, due to the quantized nature of SFQ pulses, most RSFQ primitives have a maximum driving capacity of one gate. Consequently, a special cell called *splitter* is used to duplicate signals [9,10], as illustrated in Fig. 1.

Despite the advances in RSFQ technology mapping [11–13], the number of path-balancing DFFs and splitters can be prohibitively large, degrading the area and yield of an integrated system [14]. Different approaches have been proposed in the literature to tackle this fundamental issue. In [11], the number of path-balancing DFFs is reduced using dynamic programming, yielding, on average a 12% smaller area. Further reductions in path-balancing overhead is achieved by using dual clocking, where high- and low- frequency clock signals are used [15]. This technique however requires relatively expensive NDRO DFFs along with the duplication of the clock distribution network.

Different techniques to reduce the number of clocked elements are proposed in the literature [16,17]. In dynamic SFQ (DSFQ) the gates reset to the initial state after the specified period of time [18]. The design of DSFQ circuits is therefore similar to CMOS circuits where large combinational blocks can be synchronized using relatively few synchronous elements [10]. A similar approach based on clockless logic gates is proposed in [2]. Based on nondestructive readout (NDRO) flip-flops, two additional clockless cells, namely the `NIMPLY` ($\neg x_0 \wedge x_1$) and the `AND` functions, are efficiently realized using fewer clocked elements for synchronization. The advantages of these approaches are smaller area, lower clock network complexity, and simpler path balancing, as compared to conventional RSFQ. The timing constraints, however, constitute a major challenge. In DSFQ, the interaction between the input skew tolerance, clock frequency, and bias margins [10]

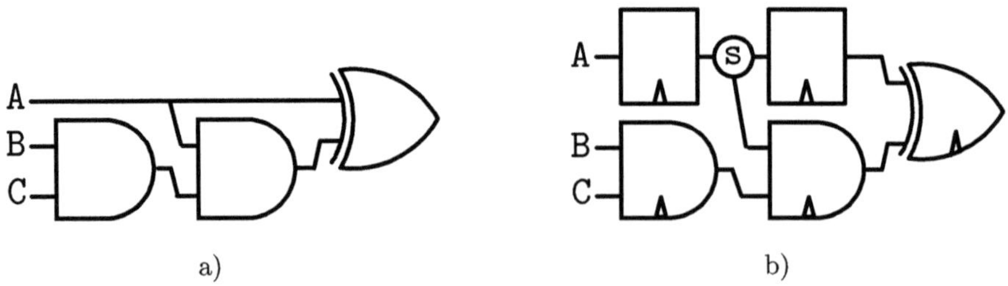

Fig. 1. a) An example of a CMOS circuit. b) Equivalent RSFQ circuit with a splitter and two path-balancing DFFs.

complicates the circuit design. The NDRO-based clockless gates are particularly sensitive to the arrival time of the inputs, necessitating careful timing analysis [19].

The *gate compounding* technique has been recently proposed as an alternative strategy to reduce the number of clocked elements [20]. Unlike DSFQ and clockless gates, *compound gates* (logic gates obtained by gate compounding) are not sensitive to the arrival of the inputs, reducing the complexity of the system design process. The functionality achievable within a single clock cycle is enriched by exploiting RSFQ synchronization mechanisms. Gate compounding can significantly reduce the pipeline depth and number of clocked elements, not only improving the latency and area of a functional circuit, but also reducing the size of the clock distribution network. However, due to complex synchronization requirements, traditional technology mapping tools are not directly applicable.

In this work, we first summarize a technology mapping method for SFQ compound gates based on a previous paper [21]. Inspired by [22–24], we create a database of compound gates using enumeration. We generate functionally correct and area-optimal compound gates for all functions up to four variables and all possible input arrival patterns. Next, we utilize these gates as library cells during technology mapping to synthesize large-scale SFQ circuits. Furthermore, we extend this framework to leverage three-input threshold SFQ gates (`AND3`, `MAJ3`, and `OR3`) as additional primitives for the creation of compound gates. In the experimental results, we show a drastic reduction in the area and logic depth by 24% and 33%, respectively, compared to the state-of-the-art, when using compound gates based on 2-input cell primitives. When extending compound gates to use 3-input cell primitives, the area and logic depth are further reduced by 11% and 30%, respectively, compared to compound gates generated using 2-input cells.

2 Gate Compounding Technique

The gate compounding technique exploits differences in pulse synchronization mechanisms to reduce the pipeline depth of an RSFQ circuit. In particular, RSFQ logic gates can be divided into three categories, namely, *AA*, *AS*, and *SA*, where the first letter denotes whether input signals should arrive (a)synchronously, while the second letter indicates whether the output is released (a)synchronously.

AA elements process the inputs immediately upon arrival and the output is released without a synchronizing signal (clock). For instance, a *merger* cell, often referred to as *confluence buffer* (CB), directs signals from multiple (typically two) input branches into one output branch, i.e., implements an `OR` function. Note that the merger produces two subsequent output pulses if input pulses are temporally separated, or a single pulse, if input signals arrive simultaneously.

AS elements process the input information immediately upon arrival and release the output synchronously after the arrival of the clock signal. The simplest RSFQ component of this type is *D-flip-flop (DFF)* that stores an incoming pulse and releases it upon the arrival of the clock signal. Other important AS elements are the *inverter* (*`NOT`*) and *exclusive-or* (*`XOR`*).

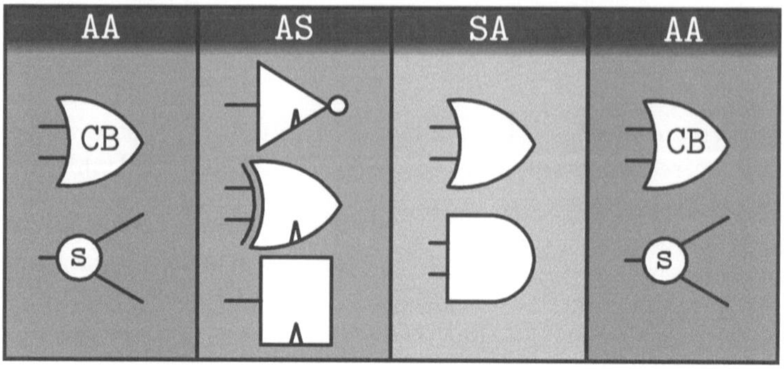

Fig. 2. Generic compound gate structure.

SA elements require the inputs to arrive simultaneously. The result of the computation is released immediately after processing. Assuming inputs arrive simultaneously, a CB can be tuned to produce at most a single output pulse, producing an *OR* element [25]. Furthermore, by adjusting the JJ size and bias current, the OR structure can be transformed into AND element. Note that, unlike conventional RSFQ, OR and AND elements are not clocked and require inputs to arrive simultaneously.

These three categories of components govern the flow of data within an RSFQ circuit. Most importantly, the SA components ensure simultaneous release of the SFQ pulses. Therefore, SA components can only be placed directly after the AS elements. To comply with these restrictions, the *gate compounding* technique was proposed in [20]. A compound SFQ logic gate can be produced by following the generic structure illustrated in Fig. 2. Inputs to a compound gate are initially processed by AA elements. The signals then flow towards the AS components where the result of a logical operation is stored until the arrival of the clock signal. The clock signal triggers the simultaneous release of the data towards the SA elements. Finally, the AA components complete the function.

The proposed structure offers two major advantages. Since the initial processing is handled by the AA or AS elements, arbitrary order of input arrival is supported, relaxing the timing constraints of the circuit. The proposed gate compounding technique significantly expands the set of functions realizable within a single clock cycle. Using compound gates, for example, all 16 two-input functions are realized within a single clock cycle, as compared to only 13 functions in conventional SFQ [20].

3 Background and Notation

A multi-output Boolean function $f : \mathbb{B}^k \mapsto \mathbb{B}^m$ maps k input signals to m output signals. A single output Boolean function ($m = 1$) $f : \mathbb{B}^k \mapsto \mathbb{B}$ can be represented as a truth table with 2^k rows. A truth table can be conveniently encoded as a

2^k-bit string $\mathtt{Y} = \overline{\mathtt{y}_{2^k-1}\cdots\mathtt{y}_0}$ where bit $\mathtt{y}_i$ denotes the output at the ith row in the truth table. For example, $f_1(\mathtt{x}_1, \mathtt{x}_0) = \mathtt{x}_1 \oplus \mathtt{x}_0$ is encoded as $\mathtt{Y}_1 = \mathtt{0110}_2$, since $f_1(\mathtt{1},\mathtt{1}) = \mathtt{0}$, $f_1(\mathtt{1},\mathtt{0}) = \mathtt{1}$, $f_1(\mathtt{0},\mathtt{1}) = \mathtt{1}$, and $f_1(\mathtt{0},\mathtt{0}) = \mathtt{0}$.

A *Boolean function*[1] f can be represented by a *Boolean network*[2] $\mathcal{N} = (\mathcal{V} = \mathcal{I} \cup \mathcal{O} \cup \mathcal{G}, \mathcal{E})$—a directed acyclic graph (DAG) representing the sequence of the Boolean operations applied to realize f. Set $\mathcal{G}$ is a set of gates, where each node $u \in \mathcal{G}$ applies a function f_u to its *fanins* $FI(u)$ and passes the result to *fanouts* $FO(u)$. Set $\mathcal{I}$ denotes the set of *primary inputs* (PI), i.e., nodes without fanins. Set $\mathcal{O}$ denotes the set of *primary outputs* (PO), i.e., nodes without fanouts.

3.1 Delay

In SFQ, the delay is typically expressed in terms of the number of clock cycles required to realize a function. In practice, input signals can often arrive at different clock cycles, as illustrated in Fig. 3a. We define the *input level pattern* $\boldsymbol{\ell}_\mathcal{N} = [\ell^0, \ldots, \ell^{k-1}]$ as a vector of integers describing the clock cycles during which the PI signals enter the network $\mathcal{N}$. Without loss of generality, we normalize the input patterns such that the earliest PI signal arrives at cycle 0, i.e., $\min(\boldsymbol{\ell}_N) = 0$. For example, an input level pattern $\boldsymbol{\ell}_\mathcal{N} = [0, 1]$ indicates that the data from the second PI is delayed by one clock cycle. A *level* l_u denotes the number of clock cycles between the earliest PI and node u. The *input arrival pattern* $\mathbf{d}_u = [d_u^0 \ldots d_u^{k-1}]$ is the number of clock cycles between u and each PI,

$$\mathbf{d}_u = [l_u - \ell^0, \ldots, l_u - \ell^{k-1}].$$

We define two operators to compare the delay patterns of any two nodes u and v:

$$\begin{aligned} \mathbf{d}_u = \mathbf{d}_v &\Leftrightarrow \forall i\ d_u^i = d_v^i, \\ \mathbf{d}_u < \mathbf{d}_v &\Leftrightarrow \exists i\ d_u^i < d_v^i \text{ and } \nexists i\ d_u^i > d_v^i. \end{aligned}$$

In the former case, corresponding delays are equal. In the latter case, the delays of u are not greater than the corresponding delays of v, but for at least one PI the delay of u is smaller.

3.2 Cost

The most common metric to evaluate the cost of an SFQ circuit is the JJ count, which directly correlates with the area of an SFQ circuit. Let q_u be the area cost associated with the logic primitive implemented by a node u. The area cost $c(\mathcal{N})$ of a circuit $\mathcal{N}$ is the sum of costs q_u for each node $u \in \mathcal{G}$. A transitive fanin cone $TFI(u)$ is defined as the set of all nodes having a path to u. The area cost c_u of a node u is defined as the cost of its TFI. Note that c_u differs from q_u,

[1] For brevity, we use the term *function* to represent a *Boolean function*.
[2] We use the terms *network* and *circuit* to represent a *Boolean network*.

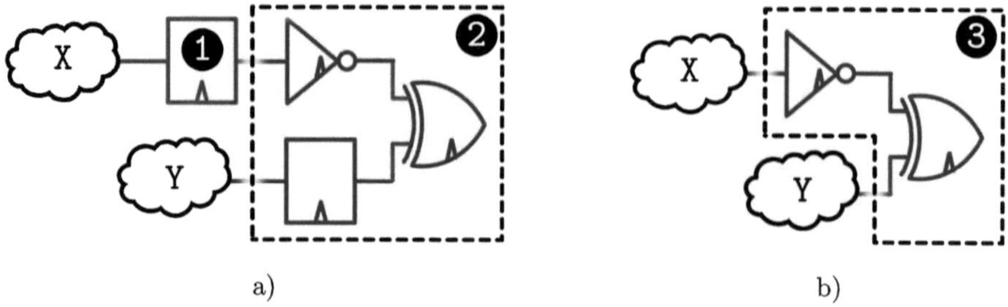

Fig. 3. Realization of an XNOR function between networks X and Y. The left network uses a path-balancing DFF (1) followed by an XNOR with equal delay pattern (2). This structure requires three clock cycles and 33 JJs. The right network uses an XNOR element with unequal delay pattern (3), requiring two clock cycles and 21 JJs.

since q_u defines the cost of a single primitive, while c_u is the sum of costs of all ancestors of u. Suppose nodes u, v are fanins of node w. The cost of the node w is,

$$c_w = q_w + S(u, v),$$

$$S(u, v) = \sum_{n \in TFI(u) \cup TFI(v)} \left[q_n + q_s \max\left(|FO(n)| - 1, 0 \right) \right],$$

where q_s is the cost of splitter.

An SFQ circuit should comply with specific technological constrains, such as path balancing and fanout constraints in SFQ. With SFQ gate compounding, gates also follow the structure described in Fig. 2 to avoid the data hazards described in the upcoming subsection.

3.3 Data Hazards

Double Pulse Hazard. If two pulses entering a CB are sufficiently spaced in time, two subsequent SFQ pulses are generated at the output, potentially producing an error. For instance, a double pulse produced by a CB entering a XOR may trigger unwanted switching, producing incorrect result. In particular, the internal storage loop within a XOR is toggled one additional time between 0 or 1 by the input pulses. Nevertheless, if the CB has its output pin connected to a DFF or an inverter, the second pulse has no effect on the system [9].

Consider the circuit implementing $(A \vee B) \oplus C$ shown in Fig. 4. The storage loop within the XOR element is correctly switched and reset with pulses A and C. The pulse B, however, sets the storage loop to state 1, producing an incorrect result. To avoid this data hazard, the XOR component is placed after a CB only if the CB is guaranteed to produce at most one SFQ pulse, i.e., the inputs to a CB are never simultaneously equal to 1.

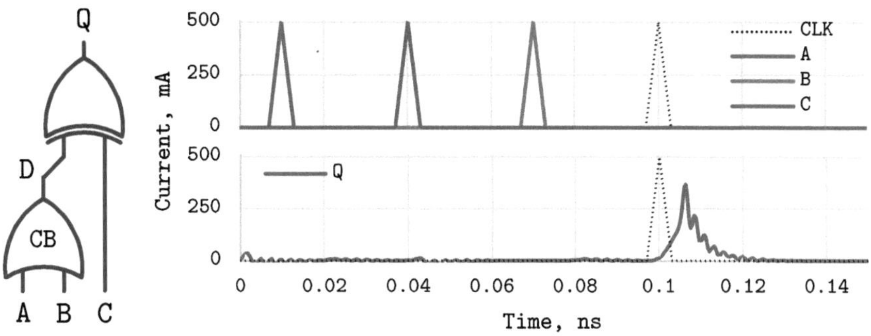

Fig. 4. Incorrect realization of $(\mathtt{A} \vee \mathtt{B}) \oplus \mathtt{C}$ function using a CB and an XOR. The main loop within an XOR element is set to 1 by A, reset to 0 by C, and subsequently set to 1 by pulse B, incorrectly producing an output pulse.

To identify the condition where a CB can produce two pulses, we assign a hazard flag $\mathtt{h}_n$ to each node n. If n is not a CB, $\mathtt{h}_n$ is 0; otherwise,

$$\mathtt{h}_n = \mathtt{h}_u \vee \mathtt{h}_v \vee \delta(\mathtt{Y}_u \wedge \mathtt{Y}_v),$$

where $u, v \in FI(n)$ and $\delta(\mathtt{Y}) = \mathtt{1}$ only if Y is nonzero.

For example, consider nodes u, v, w, with $\mathtt{Y}_u = \mathtt{1010}_2$, $\mathtt{Y}_v = \mathtt{0001}_2$, $\mathtt{Y}_w = \mathtt{1100}_2$, and $\mathtt{h}_u = \mathtt{h}_v = \mathtt{h}_w = \mathtt{0}$. Connecting u and v to a CB produces node p that can be used with XOR, since $\mathtt{h}_u = \mathtt{h}_v = \mathtt{0}$ and

$$\delta(\mathtt{Y}_u \wedge \mathtt{Y}_v) = \delta(\mathtt{1010}_2 \wedge \mathtt{0001}_2) = \delta(\mathtt{0000}_2) = \mathtt{0} \Rightarrow \mathtt{h}_p = \mathtt{0},$$

i.e., the u and v are never simultaneously equal to 1. In contrast, connecting u and w to a CB produces node q that cannot be used with XOR, since

$$\delta(\mathtt{Y}_p \wedge \mathtt{Y}_w) = \delta(\mathtt{1010}_2 \wedge \mathtt{1100}_2) = \delta(\mathtt{1000}_2) = \mathtt{1} \Rightarrow \mathtt{h}_q = \mathtt{1}.$$

Suppose node r is produced by connecting q and v to a CB. Although $\delta(\mathtt{Y}_q \wedge \mathtt{Y}_v) = \mathtt{0}$, node r cannot be used with XOR since $\mathtt{h}_q = \mathtt{1} \Rightarrow \mathtt{h}_r = \mathtt{1}$.

Desynchronization Hazard. The signal desynchronization is a timing hazard where the inputs cannot simultaneously arrive to an SA element. Consider for example the circuit illustrated in Fig. 5a. The splitter is placed between the AS (DFF) and SA (AND) components. Delays $a_0 \rightarrow a_1$ and $b_0 \rightarrow b_1$ are not equal. Therefore, pulses from A and B do not arrive simultaneously, violating the input timing requirement of the AND element. Thus, the AND operates as a constant 0.

A possible correction is shown in Fig. 5b. The splitter is placed before the DFFs to equalize delays $a_0 \rightarrow a_1$ and $b_0 \rightarrow b_1$. The timing violation is therefore avoided at the cost of an additional DFF.

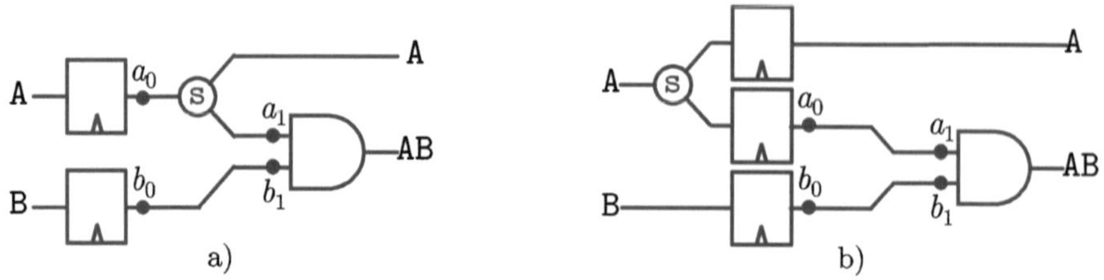

Fig. 5. a) A system violating the compound gate structure. Any AA element (splitter) between AS (DFF) and SA (AND) elements may desynchronize the input arrival. b) The issue is resolved by moving the splitter before the AS elements.

4 Library Construction

The fixed structure of the compound gates combined with the hazards described in the previous section complicates the technology mapping process. For example, AA elements should be prevented from being placed between AS and SA elements, an issue described in Sect. 3.3. Adapting the existing tools to consider these constraints requires to significantly modify the underlying algorithms, potentially degrading run time and quality of results.

Area- or delay-optimal SFQ circuits can be created using exact synthesis methods, such as Boolean satisfiability [26,27] and enumeration [22]. However, exact methods are limited to small sizes (≤ 16 nodes) and few variables (≤ 6), due to the computational intractability of the problem. Nevertheless, exact synthesis can be applied to create a database of optimal small-scale structures. Since the number of Boolean functions grows double exponentially with the number of variables (2^{2^k}), complete databases are typically limited to 4 variables. These locally-optimal networks are subsequently used to produce larger networks [22–24]. Library-driven approaches have been successfully applied to MIG resynthesis [23,24] and AQFP logic synthesis [22]. The database-driven mapping offers several advantages:

- *Functional correctness.* Each circuit block within a database describes a realization of a logic function complying with the specific technological constraints. Thus, technology mapping can safely proceed at the block level, since the technological requirements are satisfied during the database creation.
- *Local optimality.* The logic blocks in the database can be optimized for area or delay.
- *Performance.* The parameters of each logic block, such as area and delay, are computed in advance and can be accessed in constant time during mapping.
- *Reuse.* Once created, the database can be used multiple times to synthesize arbitrary SFQ circuits.

In this section, we present the procedure to create a database of area-optimal compound gate structures for each of the k-input, single-output Boolean function.

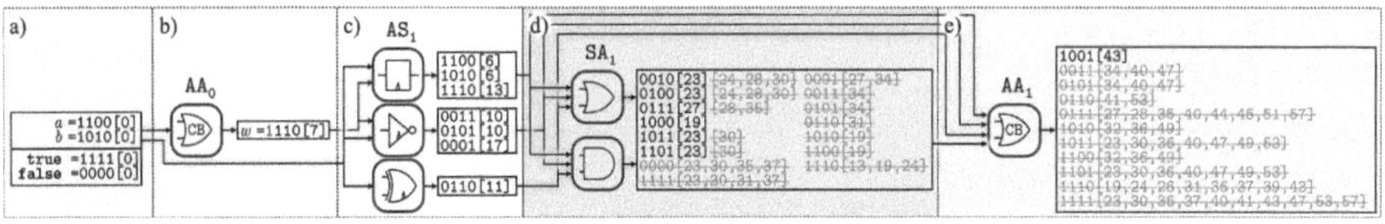

Fig. 6. Example of enumeration with 2 primary inputs represented by truth tables 1100 and 1010. The numbers in brackets represent the cost of a node (in JJ). The red 1 represents the double pulse hazard. The crossed grey numbers represent the discarded truth tables. (Color figure online)

4.1 Enumeration Procedure

The algorithm constructs a Boolean network $\mathcal{N} = (\mathcal{V}, \mathcal{E})$, where nodes represent a particular realization of a logic function using compound gates. Each node $u = (\mathtt{Y}_u, l_u, c_u, \mathtt{h}_u) \in V$ is a 4-tuple of a truth table, level, cost, and hazard flag. The procedure is initialized with k nodes representing the PIs. For example, Fig. 6a describes the initialization for $k = 2$:

$$a = (\mathtt{1100}_2, 0, 0, \mathtt{0}) \qquad b = (\mathtt{1010}_2, 0, 0, \mathtt{0})$$

For completeness, constant `true` and `false` are also included. After initialization, the algorithm cycles through three subroutines, following the compound gate structure in Fig. 2.

AA. The stage $\mathtt{AA}_i$ implements the addition of AA elements to a compound gate at level i. For each pair of nodes $u = (\mathtt{Y}_u, i, c_u, \mathtt{h}_u)$ and $v = (\mathtt{Y}_v, i, c_v, \mathtt{h}_u)$, a new node $w = (\mathtt{Y}_u \vee \mathtt{Y}_v, i, q_{\text{CB}} + S(c_u, c_v), \mathtt{h}_w)$ is produced. Consider the $\mathtt{AA}_1$ stage, illustrated in Fig. 6b, where the new node $w = (\mathtt{1110}_2, 0, 7, \mathtt{1})$ is discovered. The 7-JJ cost of the node is the cost of a CB used to realize this function.

AS. For each node $u = (\mathtt{Y}_u, i-1, c_u, \mathtt{h}_u)$, stage $\mathtt{AS}_i$ produces two new nodes,

$$p = (\mathtt{Y}_u, i, c_u + c_{\mathtt{DFF}}, \mathtt{0}) \quad \text{and} \quad q = (\neg\mathtt{Y}_u, i, c_u + c_{\mathtt{NOT}}, \mathtt{0}),$$

corresponding to addition of a DFF and `NOT` element. Note that the hazard flag is reset to 0, since only a single pulse is produced by the AS elements. In addition, for each pair of nodes $u = (\mathtt{Y}_u, i-1, c_u, \mathtt{0})$ and $v = (\mathtt{Y}_v, i-1, c_v, \mathtt{0})$, whose hazard flag is 0, a new node is produced

$$r = (\mathtt{Y}_u \oplus \mathtt{Y}_v, i, q_{\mathtt{XOR}} + S(c_u, c_v), \mathtt{0}).$$

In Fig. 6c, three new nodes are produced by a DFF, while four new truth tables are discovered by applying `NOT` and `XOR` operations. Note that the node w is not used with `XOR` due to the hazard flag $\mathtt{h}_w = 1$.

SA. After the AS stage, inputs are synchronized enabling the use of SA gates. At stage $\texttt{SA}_i$, each pair of nodes $u = (\texttt{Y}_u, i, c_u, 0)$ and $v = (\texttt{Y}_v, i, c_v, 0)$ produces 2 new nodes

$$p = (\texttt{Y}_u \wedge \texttt{Y}_v, i, q_{\texttt{AND}} + S(c_u, c_v), 0), \text{ and}$$
$$q = (\texttt{Y}_u \vee \texttt{Y}_v, i, q_{\texttt{OR}} + S(c_u, c_v), 0).$$

In Fig. 6d, the outputs of the $\texttt{AS}_1$ stage proceed to the $\texttt{SA}_1$ stage where the logical AND and OR are applied to the outputs of the previous stage. The 6 nodes implementing previously undiscovered functions with smallest cost are added to the network, while 36 nodes are discarded.

The algorithm repeats these three stages ($\texttt{AA}_{i-1} \rightarrow \texttt{AS}_i \rightarrow \texttt{SA}_i \rightarrow \texttt{AA}_i \rightarrow \ldots$) until all 2^{2^k} k-input functions are realized. In our example for $k = 2$, after stage $\texttt{SA}_1$ the algorithm proceeds to stage $\texttt{AA}_1$, where 78 nodes are produced, of which only a single node implements the remaining function $\texttt{1001}_2$. After this stage, all of the $2^{2^2} = 16$ two-input truth tables are discovered and the enumeration process is terminated.

4.2 Filtering

During the enumeration process, the size of the network grows rapidly with each additional stage. In Fig. 6, for example, only 7 nodes are produced at stage $\texttt{AS}_1$, while 62 nodes are produced at stage $\texttt{AA}_1$. The number of nodes considered during enumeration drastically increases with k, with several billions of nodes processed while enumerating four-input functions. To limit the number of nodes and prevent inferior nodes from being added to the database, the dominance relationship is used. Suppose, the node u implements a Boolean function f with input arrival pattern $\mathbf{d}_u$ and area c_u. Also, suppose another node v implementing the same function f with input arrival pattern $\mathbf{d}_v$ and area c_v has previously been discovered. The node v is said to *dominate* the node u in two cases,

- faster delay: $\mathbf{d}_v < \mathbf{d}_u$ and $c_v \leq c_u$;
- lower cost: $\mathbf{d}_v = \mathbf{d}_u$ and $c_v < c_u$.

In these cases, the node u is not created.

4.3 Input Arrival Patterns

During initial enumeration, all PIs are placed at equal levels $\boldsymbol{\ell} = (0, \ldots, 0)$. To consider different input arrival patterns, the enumeration process is repeated with PIs introduced at different levels $\boldsymbol{\ell} = (\ell^0, \ldots, \ell^{k-1})$. The number of input level patterns considered during the enumeration process can be reduced based on dominance relationship. Suppose that, while considering the pattern $\boldsymbol{\ell}_a = (\ell^1, \ldots, \ell^q, \ldots, \ell^k)$, all nodes were dominated by or equivalent to previously discovered nodes. The pattern $\boldsymbol{\ell}_b = (\ell^1, \ldots, \ell^q + 1, \ldots, \ell^k)$ is therefore unlikely to yield a non-dominated node, due to inferior delay and cost.

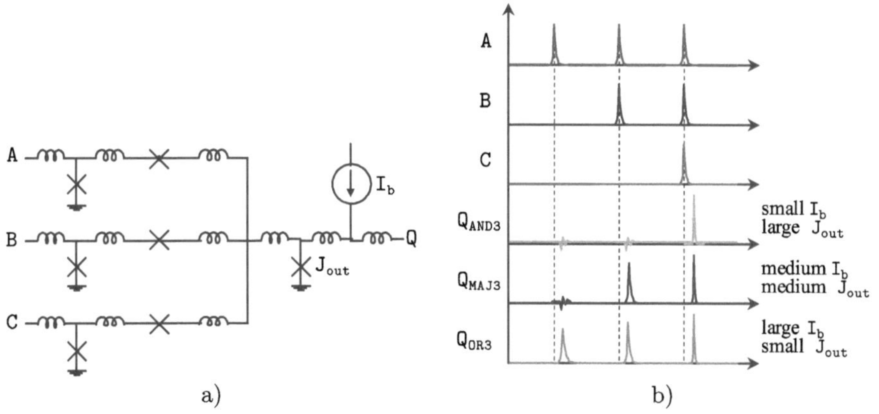

Fig. 7. Circuit and waveforms of the three-input threshold SFQ gates. a) Circuit diagram. b) Waveforms. By increasing the bias current and reducing the size of junction J_{out}, the AND3 gate can be turned into MAJ3 and OR3.

5 Extension to Three-Input Gates

Multiple works in the literature describe the use of the gates with fanin higher than two [28,29]. In the pioneering work [29], the ternary majority (MAJ3) function has been shown to provide greater expressive power, producing networks with superior area and delay. The high expressive power of the three input gates has been further investigated in [28]. Generally, three-input gates lead to a significant reduction in the number of necessary gates to implement a network, but it also increases the overall edge count. Multi-input gates in SFQ technology have been discussed in [30], where AND and OR gates with up to five inputs have been designed. Three-input majority gates for SFQ technology have been proposed in [31].

The topology of the SFQ AND3, MAJ3, and OR3 gates is a natural extension of the two-input AND2 and OR2 structures, as illustrated in Figs. 7a-b. The SFQ AND2 and OR2 gates can be viewed as threshold logic functions. In AND2 gate, the bias current is reduced while the size of the output junction is increased. Therefore, two pulses should arrive simultaneously from each input branch to produce and output pulse. By increasing the bias current and reducing the size, the output junction is made more sensitive, producing an OR2 gate. A single pulse is sufficient to switch the output junction.

By adding an extra input branch to the AND2/OR2 topology, the three-input threshold gates can be realized. The AND3 gate is produced by setting the small bias current and large output junction size. SFQ pulses from all three branches are necessary to switch the output junction. By increasing the bias current and reducing the size of the output the gate becomes MAJ3, and next OR3, requiring, respectively two and one pulse to switch the output junction, as shown in Fig. 7c.

To evaluate the impact of using the three-input gates in SFQ logic synthesis, we created a separate database incorporating the AND3, MAJ3, and OR3 gates. From the synchronization perspective, these gates belong to the SA category, since they require all inputs to arrive simultaneously. The enumeration process follows the same procedures outlined in Sects. 4.1–4.3.

6 Technology Mapping

We propose a three-stage technology mapping flow to synthesize arbitrary Boolean networks using SFQ compound gates, similarly to [13]. First, we employ a delay-driven technology mapper that uses the computed database as a cell library. Due to path balancing, delay optimization is essential for area reduction in SFQ circuits. Intuitively, longer critical paths require more DFF elements due to longer paths to balance [32].

Next, our flow inserts path-balancing DFFs and minimizes their number using minimum-area retiming [33], which provides an optimal solution. Note that retiming preserves the path-balancing constraint since each path traverses the same number of DFFs before and after retiming.

Finally, splitter cells are inserted to satisfy the driving capacity constraint. Our synthesis flow has been implemented using the open-source logic synthesis library `mockturtle` [34].

7 Experimental Results

7.1 Database Creation

We employed a computing cluster with 48 2.5 GHz Intel Xeon E5-2680 CPUs and 256 GB of RAM to create two databases. The original database only considers gates with up to two inputs. The extended database incorporates the three-input threshold gates, namely AND3, MAJ3, and OR3. Due to the computational complexity, we limited the number of inputs to four, i.e., $k = 4$. The enumeration process starts from pattern $\boldsymbol{\ell}_0 = (0, 0, 0, 0)$, i.e., all of the PIs are at the same level. During the subsequent iterations, the level of one of the PIs is incremented and the enumeration process is repeated. If the enumeration does yield to non-dominated nodes, a new PI level is incremented. Figure 8 illustrates possible level patterns considered by the enumeration process.

For the original database, the computation for the input level pattern $\boldsymbol{\ell}_0 = (0, 0, 0, 0)$ (without the three-input gates) required seven hours, evaluating over 13 billion nodes. Other delay patterns required between one to five hours. The resulting database was created in 52 h and consisted of 488,636 entries. Next, we filtered entries based on input-permutation equivalences (P-classes) [35]. Our final database contains 28,258 non-dominated implementations for all the 3,984 P-classes of Boolean functions up to 4 variables. Each entry represents a valid RSFQ compound gate. Note again that the considerable initial runtime for database creation is amortized by repeated use.

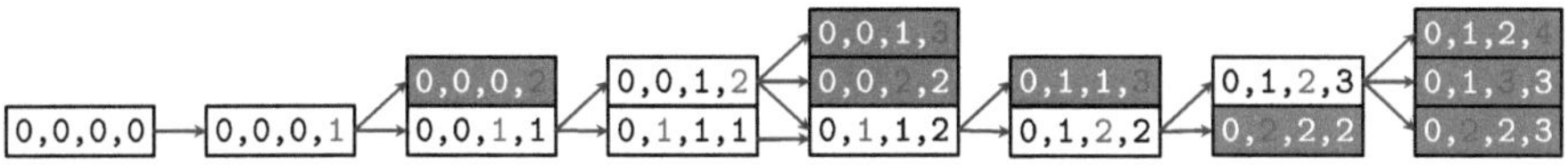

Fig. 8. Level patterns considered during enumeration. Due to permutation symmetry, only the sorted level patterns are considered. The process starts with the pattern $(0, 0, 0, 0)$. In subsequent iterations, the level of one of the PIs is incremented (marked red). If the iteration does not yield any cost- or area-optimal nodes, the pattern is not incremented (shaded gray). (Color figure online)

The process of calculating the extended database requires much smaller runtime as compared to the two-input database. The initial input level pattern $\ell_0 = (0, 0, 0, 0)$ required less than three hours while each remaining input arrival pattern was explored in 1–2 hours. This speedup is attributed to the high expressive power of the three-input gates. During the enumeration process, the depth-optimal implementations of all $2^{2^4} = 65,536$ functions are found with fewer logic levels and nodes to be explored.

7.2 Mapping with Original Database

We apply our original database to synthesize a subset of EPFL [34] and ISCAS [36] benchmark circuits. We compare our results against PBMap [11], the state-of-the-art dynamic programming algorithm for path balancing. The results are shown in Table 1. Compared to the state of the art, gate compounding technique drastically reduces logic depth by an average of 33%. Due to the use of more expressive compound gates, the area of the circuits (expressed as total JJ count) is reduced by an average of 24%, despite 53% larger number of path-balancing DFFs.

Despite substantial improvements in many benchmarks, our approach yields a weaker result in `dec` circuit. The increase in JJ count can be attributed to two factors. First, the logic depth of this circuit is only 4 cycles, limiting the impact of compound gates. Second, the JJ cost of each primitive in the RSFQ library used in [11] is not openly available at the reference. Likely, the CONNECT cell library [37] used in this work has a higher JJ cost for logic primitives compared to [11], contributing to the area increase.

We also compare our results with the dual clock methodology [15]. A logic circuit is partitioned into separate clocking domains using the NDRO flip flops. Subcircuits within each partition are clocked at high frequency, while the NDRO flip flops operate at a frequency 7 times smaller than the high frequency. The throughput of the system is therefore reduced by a factor of 7. The results are compared in Table 2. Despite 7 times smaller throughput and 64% fewer DFFs, the dual clocking method requires almost 2 times more JJs as compared to gate compounding. In addition, DCM systems require relatively expensive NDRO DFFs, pulse repeaters and an additional low-frequency clock distribution network, further degrading the area of the system.

Table 1. Number of path-balancing DFFs, JJs, and logic depth in a subset of EPFL [38] and ISCAS [36] benchmarks

Benchmark	#DFF			#JJ			Delay			Runtime, s
	Baseline	Ours	Ratio	Baseline	Ours	Ratio	Baseline	Ours	Ratio	
sin	13,666	17,627	1.29	215,318	126,694	0.59	182	86	0.47	0.399
cavlc	522	987	1.89	16,339	15,098	0.92	17	11	0.65	0.009
dec	8	16	2.00	5,469	6,324	1.16	4	4	1.00	0.006
int2float	270	443	1.64	6,432	5,616	0.87	16	10	0.63	0.004
priority	9,064	14,754	1.63	102,085	95,370	0.93	127	125	0.98	0.013
c499	476	512	1.08	7,758	5,593	0.72	13	8	0.62	0.040
c880	774	1,179	1.52	12,909	8,359	0.65	22	13	0.59	0.013
c1908	696	799	1.15	12,013	5,553	0.46	20	11	0.55	0.025
c3540	1,159	1,556	1.34	28,300	22,231	0.79	31	18	0.58	0.034
c5315	2,908	3,727	1.28	52,033	33,524	0.64	23	13	0.57	0.091
c7552	2,429	4,744	1.95	48,482	28,900	0.60	19	13	0.68	0.115
Average			1.53			0.76			0.67	

Table 2. Comparison with DCM [15] with 1/7 throughput on a subset of EPFL [38] and ISCAS [36] benchmarks

benchmark	DCM (1/7) [15]		Our Work			
	#DFF	#JJ	#DFF	Ratio	#JJ	Ratio
int2float	117	7,770	440	3.76	5,973	0.77
priority	8,562	257,252	14,754	1.72	68,177	0.27
voter	7,204	447,044	8,357	1.16	189,622	0.42
c432	224	10,734	1,180	5.27	6,905	0.64
c880	362	14,658	1,176	3.25	8,650	0.59
c1355	193	8,739	448	2.32	5,703	0.65
c1908	282	13,169	799	2.83	5,497	0.42
c3540	776	43,437	1,554	2.00	20,820	0.48
Average				2.79		0.53

7.3 Mapping Using Three-Input Gates

To evaluate the effect of using three-input gates in SFQ logic synthesis, we repeat our experiments using the extended database. The results are shown in Table 3. On average, the use of three-input gates reduces the number of DFFs by 43%, while reducing the area by 11%. These improvements can be attributed to two factors. First, the compound gates utilizing three-input elements, provide more logical expressive power with smaller area. Furthermore, the logic depth of the networks in reduced by 30%. With smaller logic depth fewer path balancing DFFs are needed to realize the same function.

Table 3. Synthesis of a subset of EPFL [38] and ISCAS [36] benchmarks using the original and extended (with three input-gates) databases

Benchmark	#DFF			#JJ			Delay		
	Original	Extended	Ratio	Original	Extended	Ratio	Original	Extended	Ratio
`sin`	17,627	11,988	0.680	126,694	105,377	0.832	86	69	0.802
`cavlc`	987	433	0.439	15,098	13,311	0.882	11	7	0.636
`dec`	16	2	0.125	6,324	8,848	1.399	4	2	0.500
`int2float`	443	182	0.410	5,616	4,521	0.805	10	6	0.600
`priority`	14,754	10,084	0.683	95,370	44,016	0.462	125	62	0.496
`c499`	512	430	0.840	5,593	4,847	0.867	8	7	0.875
`c880`	1,179	780	0.662	8,359	7,283	0.871	13	10	0.769
`c1908`	799	435	0.544	5,553	5,667	1.021	11	8	0.727
`c3540`	1,556	936	0.602	22,231	19,131	0.861	18	13	0.722
`c5315`	3,727	2,798	0.751	33,524	31,139	0.929	13	11	0.846
`c7552`	4,744	2,201	0.464	28,900	25,084	0.868	13	9	0.692
Average			0.564			0.891			0.697

8 Conclusions

RSFQ technology has the potential to enhance power and speed of the mainstream computing systems by several orders of magnitude. The gate compounding technique is a novel method to reduce the logic depth by exploiting the synchronization mechanisms of RSFQ technology. With more expressive logic gates, area of the circuits is considerably reduced. In this paper, we proposed a scalable technology mapping method that leverages SFQ compound gates. We generated a database of functionally correct and area-optimal compound gates for all functions up to 4 variables. Then, we applied a delay-driven technology mapping using the pre-computed database as a cell library. In the experimental results, we showed a substantial reduction in the area and logic depth by 24% and 33%, respectively, compared to the state-of-the-art.

We further extend our results to support the logic synthesis with three-input threshold gates, namely `AND3`, `MAJ3`, and `OR3`. By using the more expressive logic gates, the area and logic depth is further reduced by, respectively, 11% and 30%. These results indicate the great potential for the use of these three-input gate in SFQ logic synthesis, motivating the development of these logic cells in future SFQ cell libraries.

Acknowledgement. This research was supported by the SNF grant "Supercool: Design methods and tools for superconducting electronics", 200021_1920981, and Synopsys Inc.

References

1. Likharev, K., Mukhanov, O., Semenov, V.: Resistive single flux quantum logic for the josephson-junction digital technology. In: Proceedings of International Conference on Superconducting Quantum Devices, vol. 85, pp. 1103–1108 (1985)
2. Kawaguchi, T., Tanaka, M., Takagi, K., Takagi, N.: Demonstration of an 8-bit SFQ carry look-ahead adder using clockless logic cells. In: International Superconductive Electronics Conference (2015)
3. Gupta, D., Inamdar, A.A., Kirichenko, D.E., Kadin, A.M., Mukhanov, O.A.: Superconductor analog-to-digital converters and their applications. In: Proceedings of IEEE MTT-S International Microwave Symposium (2011)
4. Yang, S., Gao, X., Yang, R., Ren, J., Wang, Z.: A hybrid josephson transmission line and passive transmission line routing framework for single flux quantum logic. IEEE TASC **32**(9), 1–11 (2022)
5. Chen, W., Rylyakov, A., Patel, V., Lukens, J., Likharev, K.: Rapid single flux quantum t-flip flop operating up to 770 GHz. IEEE TASC **9**(2), 3212–3215 (1999)
6. Herr, Q.P., Smith, A.D., Wire, M.S.: High speed data link between digital superconductor chips. Appl. Phys. Lett. **80**(17), 3210–3212 (2002)
7. Akaike, H., et al.: Demonstration of a 120 GHz single-flux-quantum shift register circuit based on a 10 kA cm^{-2} Nb process. Supercond. Sci. Technol. **19**(5), S320 (2006)
8. Holmes, D.S., Ripple, A.L., Manheimer, M.A.: Energy-efficient superconducting computing-power budgets and requirements. IEEE TASC **23**(3), 1701610 (2013)
9. Bunyk, P., Likharev, K., Zinoviev, D.: RSFQ technology: physics and devices. Int. J. High Speed Electron. Syst. **11**(01), 257–305 (2001)
10. Krylov, G., Friedman, E.G.: Single Flux Quantum Integrated Circuit Design. Springer, Cham (2022)
11. Pasandi, G., Pedram, M.: PBMap: a path balancing technology mapping algorithm for single flux quantum logic circuits. IEEE TASC **29**(4), 1–14 (2019)
12. Kito, N., Takagi, K., Takagi, N.: Logic-depth-aware technology mapping method for RSFQ logic circuits with special RSFQ gates. IEEE TASC **32**(4), 1–5 (2021)
13. Calvino, A.T., De Micheli, G.: Algebraic and boolean methods for SFQ superconducting circuits. In: Proceedings of ASP-DAC (2024)
14. Bairamkulov, R., Jabbari, T., Friedman, E.G.: QuCTS - single-flux quantum clock tree synthesis. IEEE TCAD **41**(10), 3346–3358 (2022)
15. Pasandi, G., Pedram, M.: Depth-bounded graph partitioning algorithm and dual clocking method for realization of superconducting SFQ circuits. ACM JETCAS **17**(1), 1–22 (2020)
16. Yang, J.-H., et al.: Distributed self-clock: a suitable architecture for SFQ circuits. IEEE TASC **30**(7), 1–7 (2020)
17. Li, X., et al.: Optimization of delay time stabilization for single flux quantum cell library. IEEE TASC **30**(7), 1–5 (2020)
18. Rylov, S.V.: Clockless dynamic SFQ and gate with high input skew tolerance. IEEE TASC **29**(5), 1–5 (2019)
19. Kawaguchi, T., Takagi, K., Takagi, N.: Static timing analysis for single-flux-quantum circuits composed of various gates. IEEE TASC **32**(5), 1–9 (2022)
20. Bairamkulov, R., De Micheli, G.: Compound logic gates for pipeline depth minimization in single flux quantum integrated systems. In: Proceedings of GLSVLSI (2023)

21. Bairamkulov, R., Calvino, A.T., De Micheli, G.: Synthesis of SFQ circuits with compound gates. In: 2023 IFIP/IEEE 31st International Conference on Very Large Scale Integration (VLSI-SoC), pp. 1–6 (2023)
22. Marakkalage, D.S., Riener, H., De Micheli, G.: Optimizing adiabatic quantum-flux-parametron (AQFP) circuits using an exact database. In: Proceedings of NANOARCH (2021)
23. Amarú, L., et al.: Enabling exact delay synthesis. In: Proceedings of ICCAD, pp. 352–359 (2017)
24. Calvino, A.T., Riener, H., Rai, S., Kumar, A., De Micheli, G.: A versatile mapping approach for technology mapping and graph optimization. In: Proceedings of ASP-DAC, pp. 410–416 (2022)
25. Mukhanov, O., Semenov, V., Likharev, K.: Ultimate performance of the RSFQ logic circuits. IEEE Trans. Magn. **23**(2), 759–762 (1987)
26. Soeken, M., et al.: Practical exact synthesis. In: Proceedings of DATE, pp. 309–314 (2018)
27. Zhang, H.-T., Jiang, J.-H.R., Amarú, L., Mishchenko, A., Brayton, R.: Deep integration of circuit simulator and SAT solver. In: Proceedings of DAC, pp. 877–882 (2021)
28. Marakkalage, D.S., Testa, E., Riener, H., Mishchenko, A., Soeken, M., De Micheli, G.: Three-input gates for logic synthesis. IEEE Trans. Comput. Aided Des. Integr. Circuits Syst. **40**(10), 2184–2188 (2020)
29. Amarú, L., Gaillardon, P.-E., De Micheli, G.: Majority-inverter graph: a novel data-structure and algorithms for efficient logic optimization. In: Proceedings of the Design Automation Conference (2014)
30. Katam, N.K., Pedram, M.: Logic optimization, complex cell design, and retiming of single flux quantum circuits. IEEE TASC **28**(7), 1–9 (2018)
31. Krylov, G., Friedman, E.G.: Asynchronous dynamic single-flux quantum majority gates. IEEE TASC **30**(5), 1–7 (2020)
32. Calvino, A.T., De Micheli, G.: Depth-optimal buffer and splitter insertion and optimization in AQFP circuits. In: Proceedings of ASP-DAC, pp. 152–158 (2023)
33. Leiserson, C.E., Saxe, J.B.: Retiming synchronous circuitry. Algorithmica **6**(1–6), 5–35 (1991)
34. Soeken, M., et al.: The EPFL Logic Synthesis Libraries. arXiv:1805.05121v3 (2018)
35. Benini, L., De Micheli, G.: A survey of boolean matching techniques for library binding. ACM Trans. Design Autom. Electr. Syst. **2**(3), 193–226 (1997)
36. Hansen, M.C., Yalcin, H., Hayes, J.P.: Unveiling the ISCAS-85 benchmarks: a case study in reverse engineering. IEEE Des. Test Comput. **16**(3), 72–80 (1999)
37. Yorozu, S., et al.: A single flux quantum standard logic cell library. Physica C: Superconductivity **378–381**, 1471–1474 (2002)
38. Amarú, L., Gaillardon, P.-E., De Micheli, G.: The EPFL combinational benchmark suite. In: Proceedings of IWLS (2015)

Architecture-Compiler Co-design for ReRAM-Based Multi-core CIM Architectures

Rebecca Pelke(✉), Nils Bosbach, Niklas Degener, José Cubero-Cascante, Felix Staudigl, Rainer Leupers, and Jan Moritz Joseph

RWTH Aachen University, Aachen, Germany
{pelke,bosbach,degener,cubero,staudigl,leupers,joseph}@ice.rwth-aachen.de
https://www.ice.rwth-aachen.de

Abstract. Resistive Random-Access Memory (ReRAM)-based multi-core systems improve the performance of Convolutional Neural Network (CNN) inference. However, the potential speedup is limited by two factors, the interconnect of the cores and the workload itself. This paper investigates the impact of these factors on the inference latency of CNNs. The ReRAM-based Computing-in-Memory (CIM) architectures are modeled in a cycle-accurate SystemC Transaction-Level Modeling (TLM)-2.0-based simulator to analyze the impact of different architecture parameters. We further develop a compiler tailored to the architecture to execute and compare different CNN workloads. Depending on the architecture setup and workload, a CIM utilization of up to 95% can be achieved.

Keywords: CNN · ReRAM · CIM · SystemC · TLM · Simulation

1 Introduction

In recent years, the broad use of Convolutional Neural Networks (CNNs) yielded an ever-growing demand for efficient architectures to handle these compute- and data-intensive workloads. Due to the massive parallelism and reuse opportunities in CNNs, these applications are not only executed on classical von-Neumann architectures but also on specialized hardware including Graphics Processing Units (GPUs) and Tensor Processing Units (TPUs). Today, CNN accelerators exist in various form factors, from power-efficient edge devices to hyper-scaled compute clusters.

Despite the extensive innovation sparked by the ubiquitous use of CNNs, all these custom architectures suffer from one major performance limitation, namely, moving data from the system's main memory to the compute units, and vice versa [1]. In other words, CNN accelerators suffer from the von Neumann bottleneck [2]. Novel Computing-in-Memory (CIM) technologies promise to tackle this bottleneck by unifying memory and computation unit [3]. These designs offer a significant advantage over CMOS-based designs in terms of memory capacity, device

Published by Springer Nature Switzerland AG 2024
I. (Abe) M. Elfadel and L. Albasha (Eds.): VLSI-SoC 2023, IFIP AICT 680, pp. 21–44, 2024.
https://doi.org/10.1007/978-3-031-70947-0_2

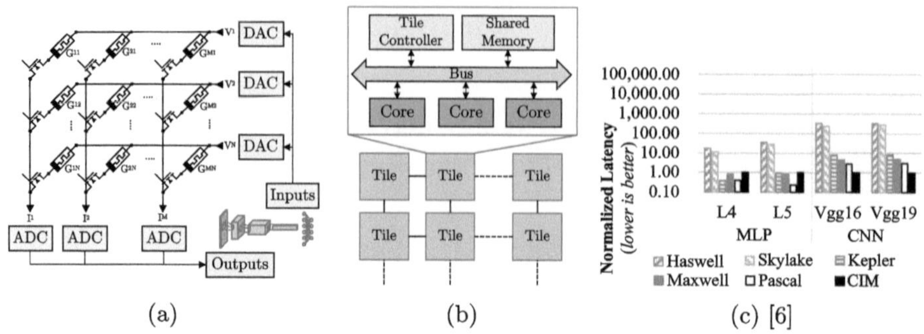

Fig. 1. ReRAM crossbars are used to perform MVMs in the analog domain in $\mathcal{O}(1)$ (a). Embedding ReRAM crossbars in cores of multi-core architectures (b) enables highly parallelized execution of CNN workloads (c)

density, and power consumption [4]. One CIM candidate is Resistive Random-Access Memory (ReRAM). ReRAM cells are arranged in crossbars (see Fig. 1a), that can execute Matrix-Vector Multiplications (MVMs) efficiently [5–8].

CIM-based architectures consist of multiple crossbars that are embedded in MVM cores. They are designed hierarchically to scale from single cores to complex multi-core systems (see Fig. 1b). In contrast to the execution of the MVM operation, programming the ReRAM cells requires a comparatively long time [5]. Hence, the accelerators aim at a weight stationary data flow, i.e., the weights of the CNN are statically assigned to ReRAM crossbars in a *setup* phase [9]. Ideally, weights can be reused an unlimited number of times during *inference*.

The authors of [6] showed that CIM-based architectures outperform Central Processing Units (CPUs) and GPUs especially for CNN workloads (see Fig. 1c). The performance of CIM-based architectures is measured in Tera Operations Per Second (TOPS) achieved by multiple parallel crossbars [6]. However, two important factors are often not considered: the impact of the interconnect system and the impact of the executed workload. An interconnected system, e.g., a bus or a Network-on-Chip (NoC), could potentially create a bottleneck, as inputs and intermediate results must be moved between different crossbars. Additionally, the workload may not be able to fully utilize the high parallelism of the architecture [10]. One possible reason could be data dependencies in the workload. This study aims to investigate the influence of these aspects in more detail.

Figure 2 illustrates our evaluation framework. The main components are a SystemC Transaction-Level Modeling (TLM)-2.0-based architecture simulator (I) and a CNN compiler (II). The simulated architecture is set up at runtime according to an architecture specification. This allows different architectures to be simulated without modifying the code. The simulator consists of individual components that can be connected in a modular way. Thus, the simulator is easily extensible. The focus is on modeling the communication between the components with sufficient detail. The compiler translates a pre-trained CNN layer by layer into instructions of the target Instruction Set Architecture (ISA),

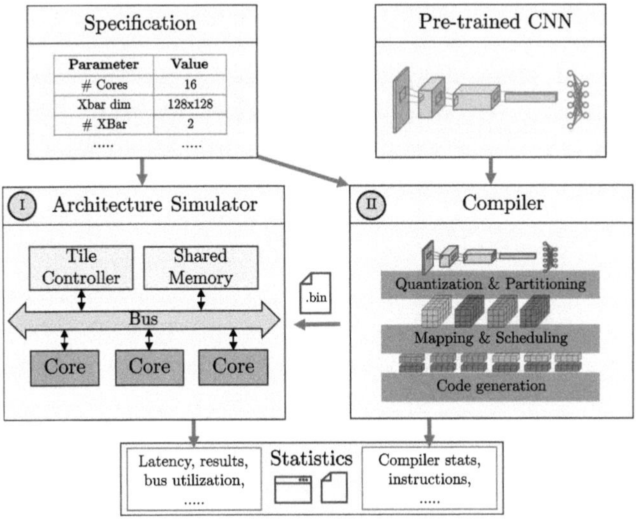

Fig. 2. Evaluation framework containing a simulator (I) and a compiler (II)

taking into account the architecture specification. The resulting binary file contains the instructions, CNN data like weights, and predefined memory regions for the Input Feature Map (IFM) and Output Feature Map (OFM). The file can be imported into the memory of the simulator at runtime. After executing the workload on the simulator, the captured tracing data can be analyzed. The tracing data enable predictions and understanding potential problems before the final CIM architecture is designed. The focus of the framework is to gain the following insights:

- Realistic inference latency predictions to determine if a workload fits a given CIM architecture configuration.
- Appropriate system parameters, e.g., bus width, number and size of cores, etc., so that the communication system does not induce a new bottleneck.

This work is an extension of the work presented in [9]. The previous work focuses on the compiler steps and inter-core communication, while this extension focuses on architecture modeling using TLM-2.0 (see Sect. 3). Additionally, the evaluation in this work includes an analysis of the crossbar utilization for various architecture configurations (see Sect. 5).

2 Background

2.1 ReRAM Crossbars

Multiple ReRAM devices can be arranged in crossbar structures to enable in-memory computing [11]. In the commonly used 1T1R crossbars, each ReRAM

Table 1. Integer vs. crossbar multiplication arithmetic

Signed Integer Multiplication		
in1	in2	out
−1	−1	+1
−1	+1	−1
+1	−1	−1
+1	+1	+1

Crossbar Multiplication		
in1	in2	out
0	0	0
0	1	0
1	0	0
1	1	1

cell consists of one transistor and one memristive device. The transistor is used as a switch to disconnect the memristor from the crossbar, which reduces sneak-path currents [12]. On ReRAM crossbars, MVMs can be performed in the analog domain in $\mathcal{O}(1)$ [13].

The CNN weights are represented as conductance values of the memristors. By applying the input values as voltages, currents are generated that correspond to the result of the MVM. Modern ReRAM crossbars have been fabricated in different sizes, e.g., 64×64 [6], and 128×128 [7].

2.2 Integer Arithmetic vs. Crossbar Arithmetic

To perform signed integer MVMs on ReRAM crossbars, activations and weights must be translated into voltages and conductances. This is not straightforward since the arithmetic of the signed integer multiplication differs from the crossbar arithmetic. This is illustrated in Table 1 for a binary multiplication. Signed integer multiplication follows `XNOR` logic, while crossbar multiplication follows `AND` logic. The two most common approaches to handle negative weights are *offset subtraction* [7] and *differential cells* [14]. In contrast to offset subtraction, differential mapping reduces the sensitivity to several categories of analog errors, such as state-independent errors, state-proportional errors, and quantization errors [15]. In the following, we will refer to the integer representation of the matrix (crossbar). The dimensions are labeled $M_{int} \times N_{int}$.

2.3 ReRAM-Based CIM Architectures

Several ReRAM-based CIM-based architectures have been presented [6–8,16]. They aim at efficient and parallel execution of MVMs. Besides different interconnect systems, they mainly differ in the design of the CIM cores. It ranges from simple MVM units to powerful ISA-based cores [17]. Simple MVM units are driven and synchronized by a central control unit. Autonomous cores, on the other hand, can execute workloads independently and do not need to be actively controlled [6]. Different abstract cores pose different challenges for simulators and compilers. Depending on the core, different models are required in the architecture simulation. In addition, the compiler must perform different tasks depending on the core. In the case of a generic core with its own ISA, the compiler has to perform significantly more tasks than, e.g., when the architecture can be accessed via an abstract interface and the cores cannot be addressed individually from the outside. To put it simply, any tasks that are not solved implicitly in the architecture must be solved on the software or compiler side. The modeled architectures are further explained in Sect. 3.

2.4 SystemC TLM-2.0

SystemC is a C++ class library used for the simulation of hardware components. It allows to model a system at different levels of abstraction: Register-Transfer Level (RTL), behavioral level, or system level [18]. SystemC is widely adopted in industry to enable HW/SW-codesign, enabling early exploration of system-level designs and early development and verification of software.

SystemC provides a concept of timing. A non-preemptive event-based scheduler keeps track of the simulation time. It allows scheduling pseudo-parallel processes by using coroutines. In SystemC, the suspending and resuming of a function at a later point in simulation time is realized by the function wait. When a wait statement is called, the function is suspended at that point, and the scheduler is triggered. The scheduler has a list of events and their corresponding time stamps. The list is sorted in ascending order by the timestamps. The event with the lowest timestamp gets computing time next. If the timestamp is greater than the global simulation time, the simulation time is increased. New events can be sorted into the list at any time. [19]

To divide complex systems into smaller parts, the basic component of SystemC, the SC_MODULE, can be used. It is allowed to nest modules hierarchically. Ports are the outward visible interfaces of the modules. Three types of ports are supported: sc_in<porttype>, sc_out<porttype>, and sc_inout<porttype>. An sc_in port is used to receive information, sc_out is used to send information, and sc_inout can be used for bidirectional communication.

Several modules can communicate with each other by connecting their ports by signals (sc_signal<signaltype>). The modeled system obtains functionality through processes. Processes are divided into methods (SC_METHOD) and threads (SC_THREAD). Threads are processes that can be suspended at any time by the wait function. They can also be synchronized by events (SC_EVENT). Unlike the SC_THREAD, an SC_METHOD can be called multiple times. Furthermore, it is not allowed to suspend a SC_METHOD. The wait function cannot be used. [18,19]

TLM-2.0 a SystemC extension that can be used to model memory accesses at a higher abstraction level. It abstracts the communication of SystemC by using *transactions* instead of signals.

The TLM manual [20] describes three different coding styles. Only two of them are potentially relevant for our application: *loosely-timed*, and *approximately-timed*. At the system level, the loosely-timed coding style in combination with *temporal decoupling* is typically used for fast and functional Instruction-Set Simulator (ISS) simulation [21,22]. In a loosely-timed communication, *blocking* transactions are used, while in approximately-timed communication, *non-blocking* transactions are used [20]. In the approximately-timed coding style, communication can be modeled more accurately at the expense of simulation speed. This style can be used for high-level architecture exploration and performance analysis. Since this work focuses on potential bottlenecks in the interconnect system, this coding style is used.

TLM-2.0 Non-blocking Interface. The timing of an individual transaction can be modeled more accurately with the non-blocking interface than with the blocking one. In the TLM base protocol, four phases are distinguished, which mark the beginning and the end of the request and the response, respectively. As depicted in Fig. 3, a transaction takes place between an initiator socket and a target socket.

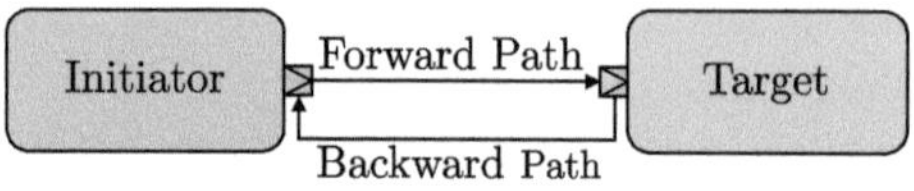

Fig. 3. Communication between initiator and target

Target and initiator communicate by sending messages, called payloads, through their sockets. The exchange of payloads is realized by two different functions: `nb_transport_fw`, and `nb_transport_bw`. When the initiator calls `nb_transport_fw`, a corresponding callback function is called in the target. In contrast, when the target calls `nb_transport_bw`, a callback function is called in the initiator. Besides a reference to the data, both callback functions require a phase and a timing annotation as an argument. There are three different return values: `TLM_ACCEPTED`, `TLM_UPDATED`, and `TLM_COMPLETED`. [23]

When a callback function is called, the callee must take a look at the timing annotation. The timing annotation specifies how long the callee must wait before modifying the data. In the non-blocking interface, the `wait` function cannot be used. Instead, there is a construct called Payload Event Queue (PEQ), which can be used to register the transaction object with the associated wait time. The PEQ has a callback function that is called when the wait time is exceeded.

The progress of the transaction is characterized by its phase: `BEGIN_REQ`, `END_REQ`, `BEGIN_RESP`, or `END_RESP`. The phase can be changed by both the initiator and the target. There are certain rules regarding phase changes. The allowed transitions between phases can be represented in a transition graph. The entire transition graph is illustrated in Fig. 4. The phases can only be passed through in one direction. However, it is possible to skip phases. As can be seen in the graph, not all combinations of return values and phase changes are allowed. During implementation, it is essential to catch combinations that are not allowed. [20]

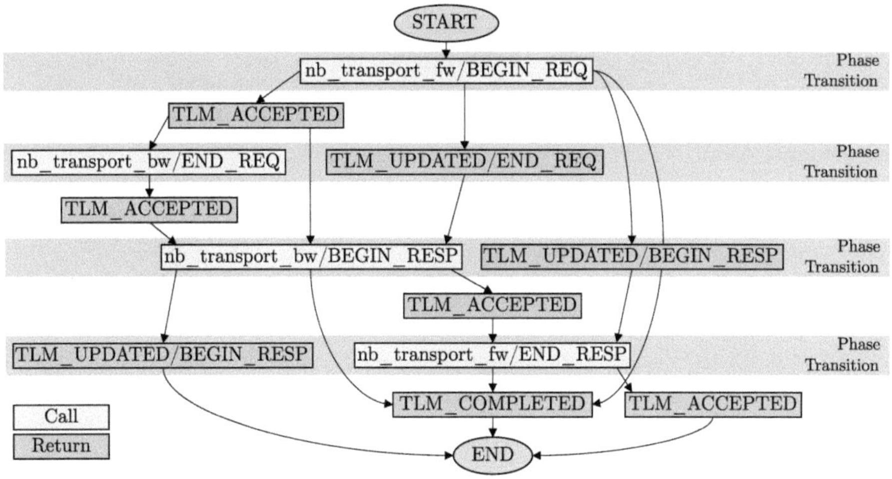

Fig. 4. TLM non-blocking transition graph of the base protocol

2.5 AMBA AXI4 Protocol Specification

The Advanced Microcontroller Bus Architecture (AMBA) bus protocols are a set of specifications that have been introduced by ARM in 1996 to ensure compatibility between Intellectual Property (IP) components. The Advanced eXtensible Interface (AXI) is part of the AMBA protocol specifications and targets high-performance systems [24]. As part of the architecture simulator of this work, a model of an AMBA AXI4-based interconnect is implemented.

AXI4 is well established in the industry and offers many features that are well suited for Machine Learning (ML) applications, such as *burst transactions* and *out-of-order-transaction completion*. These features are explained in more detail below, as well as the general functioning of the AMBA AXI4 protocol. Note that the protocol only specifies the communication between two components: an initiator and a target. In a multi-initiator-multi-target system, so-called *interconnects* are required. Details of the modeled interconnect can be found in Sect. 3.

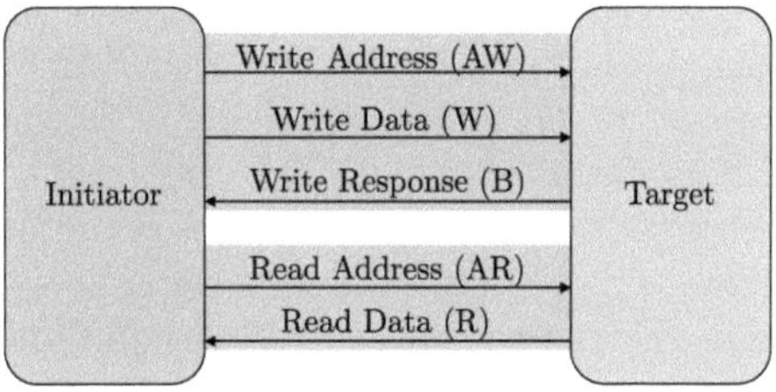

Fig. 5. Overview of AXI4 channels

AXI4 Channel. The AXI4 protocol describes five independent channels: `Write Address(AW)`, `Write Data(W)`, `Write Response(B)`, `Read Address(AR)`, and `Read Data(R)`. The channels are illustrated in Fig. 5. There are two types of transactions, the `write` transaction to write data from the initiator to the target, and the `read` transaction to read data from the target. Different sets of channels are used for the `write` and the `read` transactions. In a `write` transaction, the `AW`, `W`, and `B` channels are used (in that order). In a `read` transaction, the `AR` and `R` channels are used (in that order).

AXI4 Features. The initiator can request multiple transactions and does not have to wait for the transaction to complete before sending a new request. Even within a set, the channels are independent of each other: although each transaction must pass through the channels in the correct order, two different transactions, i.e., transactions with different IDs, can overtake each other. This is called out-of-order transaction completion.

AXI4 further supports burst transactions. The `W` and `R` channels only have a certain channel width. If the amount of data in the transaction exceeds the channel width, burst transactions can be used. New data can be read or written via the `R` and `W` channels in each bus cycle without the need to run through the other channels of the corresponding set again. As a result, burst transactions increase the throughput significantly. [25]

AXI4 Handshake. To synchronize communication, all channels use a handshake principle. The handshake is performed using two signals: `READY` and `VALID`. While the `VALID` signal is sent from the source to the target, the `READY` signal is sent from the target to the source. It depends on the channel whether the initiator or the target is the source or the destination. Setting the `VALID` signal to `HIGH` means that information is available in the source. Setting the `READY` signal to `HIGH` means that information can be received from the destination. Once the `VALID` signal has been set `HIGH`, it may not be set `LOW` again until the handshake is complete. It is not specified whether the `VALID` or the `READY` signal must be sent first. The control signal and the information flow are synchronized by a clock signal.

3 Architecture

As explained in Sect. 2.3, many different CIM core designs exist. Our simulator's configuration file allows for easy customization of parameters, including the crossbar dimension. However, this is not directly possible with different abstractions in the core design. For the framework, this means that we will focus on a more specific core design, namely ISA-based CIM cores. One advantage of these cores is their generality, which allows for flexibility in architecture and application. Additionally, they offer great potential for optimization on the software side. Similar designs can be found in [6,26].

3.1 CIM Architecture Model

Figure 6 illustrates the architecture model used in this work. Each tile contains a configurable number of CIM cores, a (volatile) shared memory, a tile controller, and an AXI4-based bus interconnect. The CIM cores use the shared memory to exchange their data. In this work, each tile executes one layer of the workload. Architecture parameters, e.g., the number of cores and the size of the crossbars, can be specified in an architecture specification to investigate their influence on the performance (see Sect. 5).

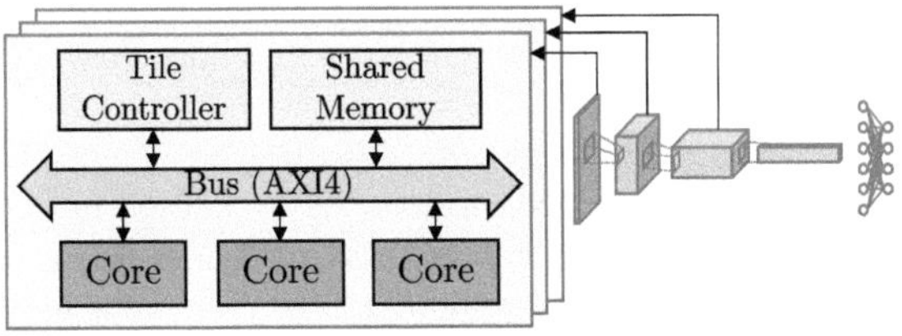

Fig. 6. The modeled multi-core CIM architecture

3.2 CIM Core Model

Figure 7 shows a schematic of the modeled CIM core including control and data flow. A Matrix-Vector Multiplication Unit (MVMU) contains control logic for the crossbar, input buffers, and output buffers. The buffer sizes depend on the matrix size that the MVMU can process. A core controller can execute 32-bit Reduced Instruction Set Computer (RISC)-like instructions. The ISA is limited to only 14 instructions, making it more streamlined compared to other well-known RISC ISAs. A data buffer, an instruction memory, and configuration registers are accessible from the outside through the interconnect. The configuration registers are programmed externally before the inference. They include, e.g., offsets of the shared memory and control flags. The CIM core can exchange data between shared memory and its data buffer via `LOAD` and `STORE` instructions. A `MOV` instruction can be used to exchange data between the MVMU and the data buffer. The CIM core includes an Arithmetic Logic Unit (ALU), allowing for operations that cannot be executed by the crossbar, such as activation functions or bias addition.

The cores operate in two phases. In the setup phase, the tile controller configures the CIM cores. The instructions are loaded and kernel values are programmed into the crossbar cells. In the inference phase, a CNN layer is executed. After all instructions are executed, an interrupt is signaled to the tile controller.

3.3 Implementation of AMBA AXI4 Protocol

ARM provides open-source header files and a precompiled library to define AXI4 payload types, signals, and sockets. The bus protocol itself or an interconnect is not implemented (open source), but all required signals are specified to ensure

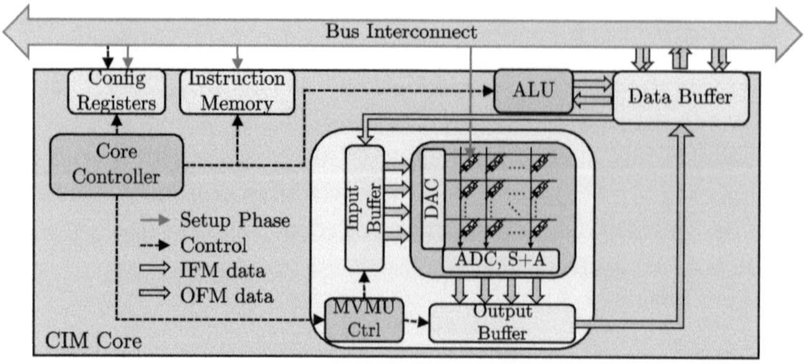

Fig. 7. CIM core architecture and data flow

compatibility with proprietary ARM models. As explained in Sect. 2.4, the TLM standard defines phases and return values used to model the state of each transaction, while the AXI4 protocol uses handshakes to synchronize a transaction. The ARM developer guide [27] defines how the handshakes can be integrated into the TLM phases. The TLM phases are replaced by the AXI4 related phases `ARM::AXI4::X_VALID` and `ARM::AXI4::X_READY`. Note that `X` is a placeholder for the abbreviation that defines the channel type (`AW`, `W`, ...). The original TLM return values are not changed. For each channel, a state machine has to be implemented. The transitions of the state machine can be seen in Fig. 8.

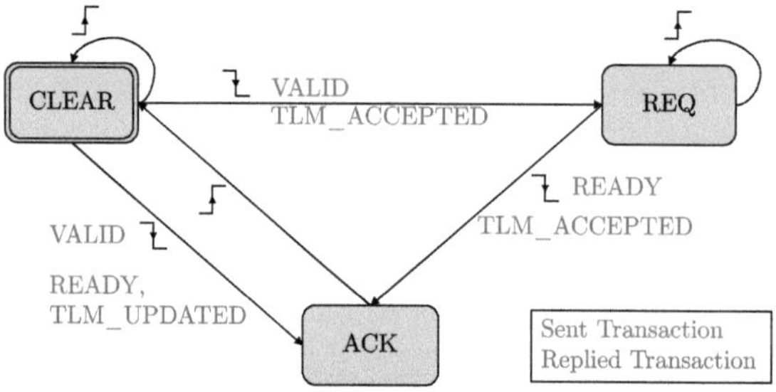

Fig. 8. Transition state machine for AXI4 channels

The valid transitions depend on the current state (`CLEAR`, `REQ`, `ACK`) and the clock state (rising edge, falling edge). The `CLEAR` state is the idle state. The sender of the transaction sets the phase (marked in blue). The recipient may respond with either `TLM_ACCEPTED` or `TLM_UPDATED`. The answer `TLM_UPDATED` requires a phase change from `VALID` to `READY`.

Note that the sender may not always be the initiator, and the replier may not always be the target. This depends on which of the five channels is being considered. It is important to note that not all combinations of phase and return values are allowed. All invalid combinations should be identified during implementation to prevent errors. The developer guide also specifies that the `READY` signal is always the response to `VALID` and that the `READY` signal cannot be sent first. This differs from the AXI4 protocol specification, where the order of the handshake signals is not defined. Our implementation uses two main classes to realize the bus protocol between the requester and responder. These classes have sockets to communicate with each other. The initiator socket is contained in the `BusRequesterComponent`, while the complementary target socket is contained in the `BusResponderComponent`. This is depicted in Fig. 9. The classes are purely virtual.

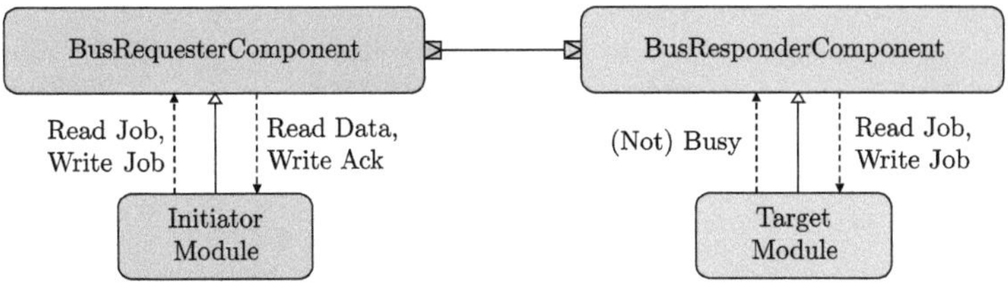

Fig. 9. Communication between initiator module and target module

An initiator module inherits from the class `BusRequesterComponent`, while a target module inherits from `BusResponderComponent`. This allows for communication between the initiator and target modules. The initiator module sends `READ` and `WRITE` jobs to the `BusRequesterComponent` through function calls. When data from the `READ` operation are available or when the `WRITE` operation is successful, a callback function is called in the initiator module. In the target module, a callback function is called when a `READ` or `WRITE` request is issued. The target module checks whether the request is permissible, e.g., whether the corresponding memory areas may be accessed, and then executes the operation. If the target module is busy, it can indicate this to the `BusResponderComponent` by setting a flag. As a consequence, the `BusResponderComponent` is unable to accept new jobs and will block the bus until the target module becomes available again. This is necessary to avoid deadlocks in this situation. Additionally, a module can inherit from both `BusRequesterComponent` and `BusResponderComponent`, allowing it to act as both a target and an initiator.

3.4 AMBA AXI4 in a Multi-initiator-Multi-target System

The AXI4 protocol only specifies the communication between one initiator and one target. However, the simulated architecture consists of multiple initiators and multiple targets. In addition to the implementation of the bus protocol, a so-called *interconnect* design is required. The interconnect system is not specified in the protocol. For an AXI4-based bus, there are several interconnects on the market. Among others, the companies Xilinx and Microchip have their own designs of a multi-initiator-multi-target AXI4 interconnect [28,29]. The main components of the designs are depicted in Fig. 10.

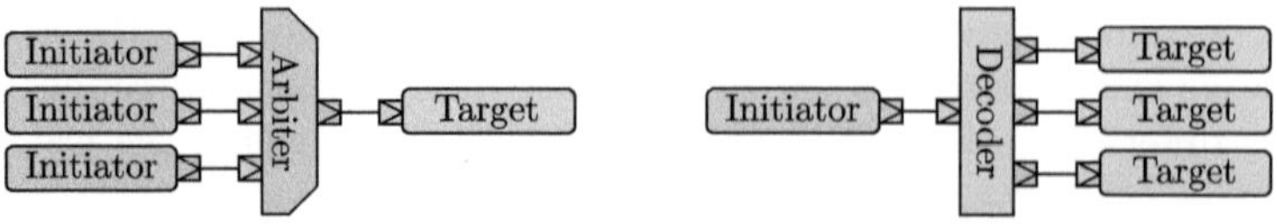

Fig. 10. Main components of AXI4 interconnect: arbiter and decoder

An arbiter is a N to 1 link. It connects N initiator modules to a single target module. The arbiter is responsible for controlling access to the target. Only one initiator can communicate with a target at a time. To ensure that the allocation of the communication time remains fair, *scheduling* algorithms are needed. Which scheduling algorithm is used is up to the architect. Common scheduling techniques are First In First Out (FIFO), round robin, or priority-based scheduling. A second task of the arbiter is to ensure that the target's response reaches the correct initiator. This is accomplished by providing certain control bits (initiator ID) of the transaction to uniquely identify the initiator. The arbiter sets these bits before a transaction is forwarded to the target and clears the bits when a response is returned to the initiator. The advantage of this is that the initiator module does not need to know its own ID.

A decoder is a 1 to N link. It connects a single initiator module to multiple target modules. Thereby, the decoder has to decode the target address and forward the transaction to the correct target. The initiator can only communicate with one target at a time. The arbiter and the decoder modules delay the transaction. The expected delays are listed in [29].

The connections of the arbiter and decoder modules are design-specific. One design is shown in Fig. 11. This design is derived from the SASD mode design from [28]. For each channel, there is one arbiter and one decoder connected in series. It is also possible to combine multiple channels or duplicate channels.

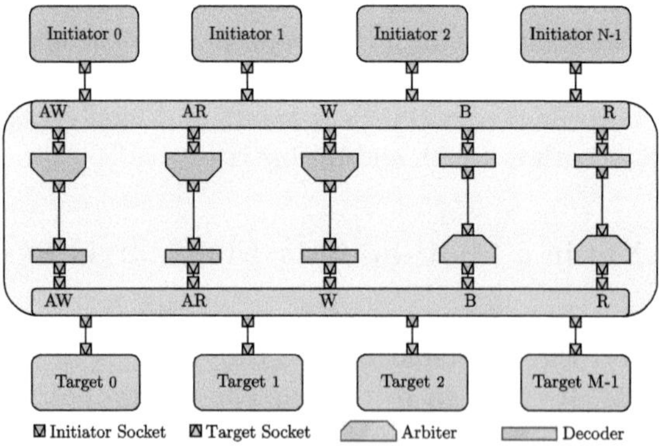

Fig. 11. N to M interconnect - Shared-Address Shared-Data (SASD) mode

4 Compiler

The compiler compiles the model layer by layer and generates a `bin` and a `cfg` file depending on the parameters in the architecture specification. The `cfg` file is interpreted by the tile controller to configure the CIM cores in the setup phase. The `bin` file is loaded into the shared memory (see Sect. 3.1). It contains an instructions section and a data section. In the data section, memory sections for the IFMs and OFMs are allocated.

Figure 12 shows a simplified overview of the steps in the compiler. It receives a pre-trained TensorFlow CNN and an architecture specification as input. First, Post-Training Quantization (PTQ) and layer fusion are performed (I). In layer fusion, the Batch Normalization (BN) layer can be merged with the previous operation, known as BN folding. Additionally, the Conv2D layer, bias addition and activation function are combined and considered as one operation. In the following, the steps (II) and (III) for the Conv2D operation are explained in more detail. In the last step (IV), the code is generated.

4.1 Partitioning and Loop Transformations

Partitioning means that the layers are divided into supported and unsupported layers. Only supported layers like Conv2D or Dense are executed on the architecture and therefore compiled for the architecture.

The idea behind loop transformations is that the original operation, e.g., Conv2D, is split into several smaller MVMs that are executed in parallel on the CIM cores. One of the first-published methods, im2col [30], assigns kernel values to crossbar cells with the densest ReRAM cell occupancy. Other approaches pack the crossbar more sparsely and duplicate kernel values to increase input

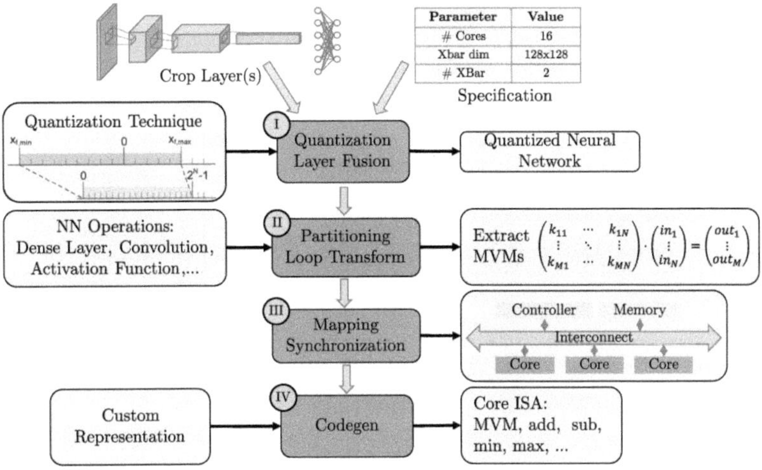

Fig. 12. Overview of the CNN compiler

reuse [31,32]. Since the im2col scheme requires the least number of ReRAM cells, this work uses an extended im2col method that splits the kernel values of a layer across multiple crossbars and extracts the MVMs [33,34].

Extracting MVMs. Figure 13a shows the main components of a Conv2D layer, i.e., an IFM of size $I_H \times I_W \times I_C$ (batch=1), an OFM of size $O_H \times O_W \times O_C$, and $K_H \times K_W \times I_C \times O_C$ kernel values. Figure 13b illustrates the im2col scheme [34]. The unrolled kernels form a matrix, which can then be multiplied by $O_H \cdot O_W$ unrolled vectors from the IFM. State-of-the-art CNN layers are often too big to be stored in a single crossbar. The kernel values of one layer have to be split over several CIM cores (red lines) [30,33].

In the setup phase, the CPU loads the IFM to the associated placeholder in the shared memory. Bias values are initially written to the placeholder of the OFM. The ALU is used to accumulate the bias values and to accomplish the activation function (see Sect. 3).

We extend the multi-core im2col scheme by assigning two group IDs to each core. All cores sharing the same Vertical Group (VG) ID operate on the same values of the IFM. All cores sharing the same Horizontal Group (HG) ID generate partial results for the same values in the OFM that have to be accumulated. In the following, the CIM cores are denoted as $C_{HG,VG}$. While the IFM is read-only, both, read and write accesses are performed on the OFM. Considering $M_{int} \times N_{int}$ crossbars and (K_H, K_W, I_C, O_C) Conv2D kernels (HWIO layout), the total number of needed cores C_{NUM} is

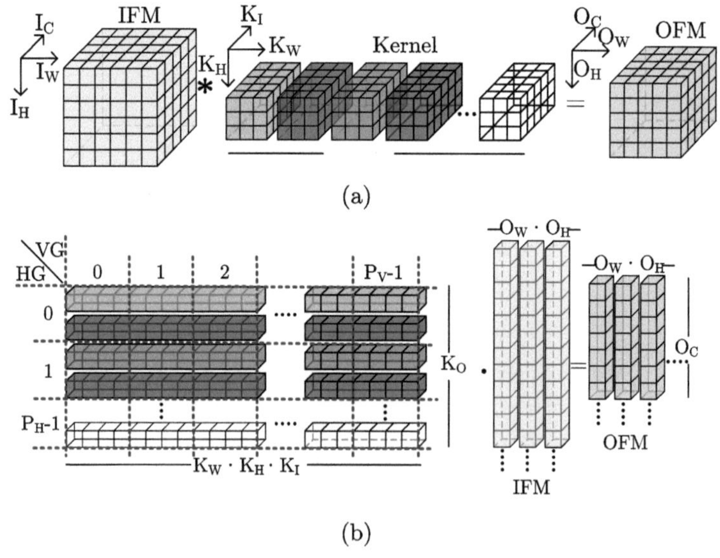

Fig. 13. Translation of a Conv2D operation into multiple MVMs

$$C_{NUM} = \underbrace{\left\lceil \frac{K_W \cdot K_H \cdot I_C}{N_{int}} \right\rceil}_{=:P_V} \cdot \underbrace{\left\lceil \frac{O_C}{M_{int}} \right\rceil}_{=:P_H}.$$

The area in the shared memory dedicated to the OFM is reused for the exchange of partial results. This keeps the CIM cores lean since the required buffer sizes and synchronization complexity remain minimal. As a consequence, all cores sharing the same HG ID operate on the same OFM locations in the shared memory. The access must be regulated to avoid race conditions. Hence, a synchronization technique is required to ensure that all partial results are accumulated correctly. This means P_H sets of P_V cores need to be synchronized for $O_{V,NUM} = O_W \cdot O_H$ different output vectors of size M.

4.2 Mapping and Synchronization

The parallel execution of layers causes critical data dependencies that can lead to incorrect results. This can be avoided at the cost of performance loss by executing the critical sections in sequence [32]. For parallel execution, synchronization methods are required that need to be supported by the architecture.

The authors of [6] introduced a central synchronization scheme. In their architecture, several *tiles* form the accelerator. A *tile* is structured similarly to the architecture in Fig. 6 and contains a controller, several CIM cores, and shared memory. The synchronization is solved centrally by extending the shared memory with an attribute buffer. This attribute buffer contains two attributes for each data entry, *valid* and *count*. A memory controller maintains the attributes to ensure the correct exchange of data. In this solution, a significant amount of memory is needed to store the attributes. For 64kB allocated the shared memory, 32K attributes are required [6]. We improve on this idea by proposing a decentralized synchronization scheme that requires significantly less memory.

Synchronization Schemes. All output vectors of the OFM stored in the shared memory can be treated as a resource that may only be owned by one core at any time. Figure 14 illustrates the proposed synchronization techniques for the example of three conflicting cores $C_{0,0}, C_{0,1}$, and $C_{0,P_V-1} = C_{0,2}$ ($P_H = 1, P_V = 3$) with 12 different output vectors, i.e., 12 different resources. To calculate correctly, each core must have owned each resource once to accumulate its partial results.

In the following, the different parallelization and synchronization schemes are presented. A red *sync* barrier means that the core that releases a resource notifies (`CALL`) its successor. That is the core that will receive the resource next. The successor must wait (`WAIT`) for the notification.

Sequential Synchronization. This scheme is the most basic one. It is used in [32,35]. Conflicting cores operate sequentially and not in parallel, which eliminates the need for complex synchronization procedures. In the example, $C_{0,0}$ gets

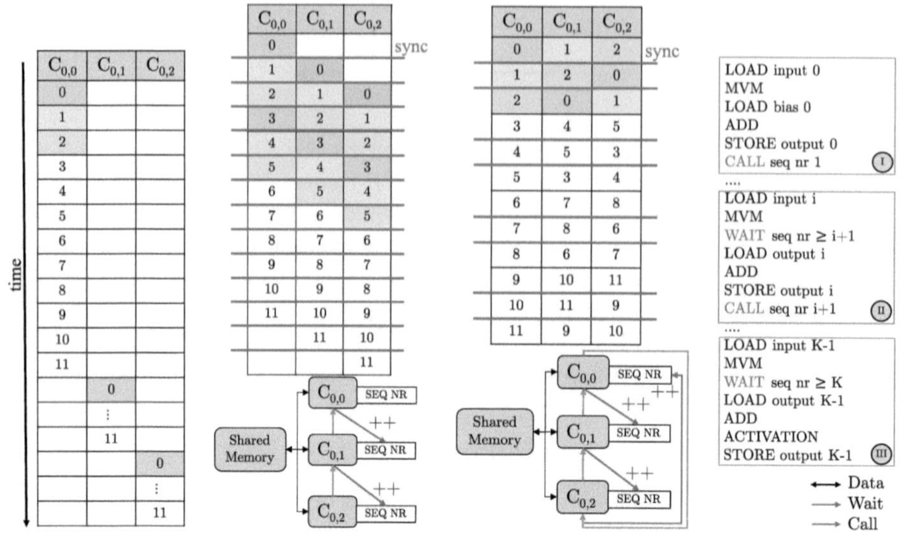

(a) No sync (b) Linear (c) Cyclic (d) Instructions

Fig. 14. Sequential computation of OFM without synchronization scheme (a), parallel computation of OFM with linear (b) and cyclic (c) synchronization for conflicting cores $C_{0,0}, C_{0,1}$ and $C_{0,2}$, generated pseudo instructions (d)

all resources first. After it has completed all calculations, the next core, $C_{0,1}$, is allowed to operate. The first core, $C_{0,0}$, accumulates the bias values and the last core, C_{0,P_V-1}, applies the activation function to all output vectors (see Fig. 14a). In the following, we propose two schemes, *linear* and *cyclic* synchronization, to achieve parallel processing, i.e., cores of the same HG can operate in parallel.

Linear Synchronization. The cores process the output vectors in the same order, starting from $C_{0,0}$ to $C_{0,2}$ in the example. Core $C_{0,0}$ has no predecessor and $C_{0,2}$ has no successor. Core $C_{0,0}$ accumulates the bias values and C_{0,P_V-1} applies the activation function for all output vectors (see Fig. 14b). In this case, the number of `CALL` and `WAIT` operations is

$$P_H \cdot O_{V,NUM} \cdot (P_V - 1)\,.$$

Cyclic Synchronization. In cyclic synchronization, tasks are distributed as fair as possible among the cores. Each core has exactly one predecessor and one successor. The output vectors are processed cyclically by the cores. The core that first gains access to an output vector accumulates the bias values to its partial results. The core that receives access to an output vector last executes the activation function (see Fig. 14c). As a result, the execution of the activation functions and the addition of the bias values are shared equally among all cores. In this case, the number of `CALL` and `WAIT` operations is

$$P_H \cdot \left\lceil \frac{O_{V,NUM}}{P_V} \right\rceil \cdot P_V \cdot (P_V - 1) \,.$$

4.3 Sequence Number

Each core has a sequence number `SEQ_NR`. The initial value is 0. A `CALL` operation increments the sequence number belonging to the successor core (blue line). When executing a `WAIT` operation, the core waits for its sequence number to reach at least a certain value.

Figure 14d shows pseudo instructions. Three cases are distinguished. In the first case, the core has no predecessor for the output it is working on. In the second case, the core has both, a predecessor and a successor. The last case describes the scenario in which a core is the last one operating on an output. Note that `CALL` and `WAIT` are alias instructions. `CALL` can be realized by a simple increment and store operation. `WAIT` can be realized through conditional branches.

The location of the `SEQ_NR` can be either in the core itself (e.g., as a register, as shown in Fig. 14b and Fig. 14c) or in the shared memory. The disadvantage of storing the `SEQ_NR` in the register rather than in shared memory is that a core must be able to write to another core's register. This must be allowed by the architecture. An advantage is that polling an address in shared memory would not be necessary. In the following, we will use the first variant for our simulations.

5 Results

In the following, we analyze the influence of various architecture parameters on inference latency and crossbar utilization. This is achieved using the framework developed in this work (see Fig. 2). The tracing tool NISTT [36] is used to capture the statistics during the architecture simulation (Sect. 3). Pretrained CNN layers of Mobilenet [37] and ResNet-18 [38] are used as workloads and compiled for the architecture (Sect. 4).

For each setup, our framework determines the inference latency and utilization per layer. We define utilization as the fraction of time that MVM operations are actually performed relative to the total inference latency of layer l:

$$Utilization_l := \frac{1}{\#Cores} \left(\sum_{c \in Cores} \frac{t_{MVM} \cdot \#MVM_c}{t_{layer,l}} \right) \tag{1}$$

The time t_{MVM} is the latency of one MVM operation and $\#MVM_c$ is the number of MVM operations for core c and layer l.

We have identified three main **architectural parameters** that potentially reduce utilization. These are the interconnect system (e.g., bus width and bus clock), the number of cores per bus (crossbar size), and the MVM latency. However, these parameters are difficult to evaluate individually. They can only be

Table 2. Overview of the benchmarked Mobilenet layers

Layer	Kernel $K_H \times K_W \times I_C \times O_C$	IFM $I_H \times I_W \times I_C$	Matrix Size $M_{int} \times N_{int}$	Cores #	MVM #Ops
L9	$1 \times 1 \times 128 \times 256$	$28 \times 28 \times 128$	32×32	32	784
L9	$1 \times 1 \times 128 \times 256$	$28 \times 28 \times 128$	64×64	8	784
L9	$1 \times 1 \times 128 \times 256$	$28 \times 28 \times 128$	128×128	2	784
L15	$1 \times 1 \times 256 \times 512$	$14 \times 14 \times 256$	32×32	128	196
L15	$1 \times 1 \times 256 \times 512$	$14 \times 14 \times 256$	64×64	32	196
L15	$1 \times 1 \times 256 \times 512$	$14 \times 14 \times 256$	128×128	8	196

evaluated in combination with the other parameters. Further details are provided in Sect. 5.1. Also, the workload itself can harm utilization. Data dependencies in the workload require **synchronization mechanisms** that lead to additional overhead (see Sect. 4.2). This is evaluated in Sect. 5.2.

5.1 Architectural Parameters

First, we analyze the influence of different architectural parameters. We use two Conv2D layers from Mobilenet for this. Table 2 shows the layer shapes. Depending on the matrix size $M_{int} \times N_{int}$ in integer arithmetic (see Sect. 2.2), different numbers of cores are required. Depending on the layer, 784 or 196 MVM operations are performed per core.

Figure 15 shows the inference latency and utilization for both layers. The bus width refers to the width of the data channels in bytes (see Sect. 2.5). All setups are simulated for 100 ns [6] and 1000 ns [5] as MVM latency. The bar color corresponds to the matrix size.

Bus Width. Figure 15 shows that the higher the bus width, the higher the utilization and the lower the inference latency. A large bus width goes hand in hand with higher energy consumption and more area. However, this trade-off is not in the scope of this work. If the MVM latency is high enough and the number of cores is low (maximum 32 cores in layer 9), the bus width has only little effect on performance. This can be seen in Fig. 15b and Fig. 15d.

Matrix Size. This is the most difficult parameter to interpret. A large matrix size means a small number of cores and therefore less synchronization and fewer competing bus accesses. Conversely, many cores with a small matrix process have shorter input and output vectors. The best matrix size depends heavily on the workload and other parameters. For example, Fig. 15f shows that smaller matrices are advantageous at 1000 ns and high bus widths. On the other hand, at 100 ns, the bus must be large enough. Otherwise, larger matrices are preferred (see Fig. 15a).

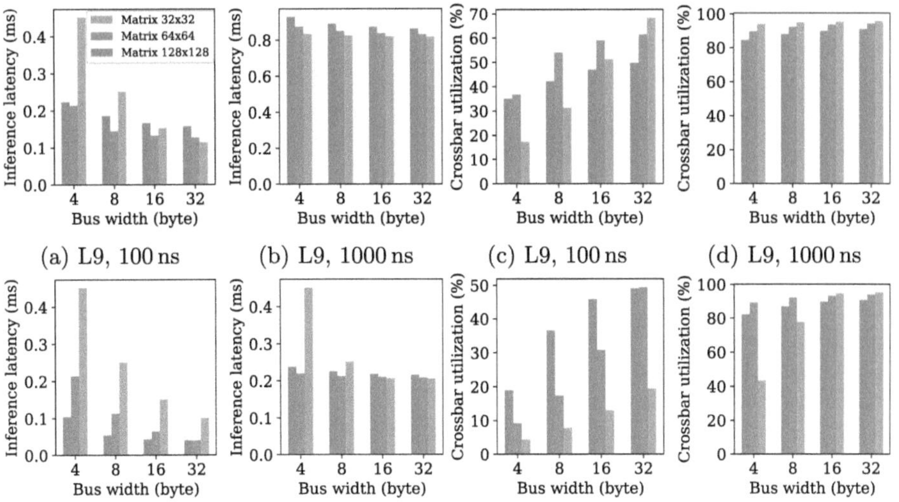

(a) L9, 100 ns (b) L9, 1000 ns (c) L9, 100 ns (d) L9, 1000 ns

(e) L15, 100 ns (f) L15, 1000 ns (g) L15, 100 ns (h) L15, 1000 ns

Fig. 15. Inference latency (a), (b), (e), (f) and crossbar utilization (c), (d), (g), (h) for different layers, MVM durations, data channel widths, and matrix sizes

MVM Latency. The latency of the MVM can also only be taken into account in combination with the other parameters. In principle, the lowest possible latency is desirable. However, low latency means that the interconnect system, i.e., the bus, quickly becomes congested because the cores are constantly requesting new data. The more cores, the worse the bottleneck. On the other hand, a latency of 1000 ns allows the system to cope well with smaller bus widths. For example, in Fig. 15d, utilization is between 85% and 95% for all bus widths.

5.2 Synchronization Mechanism

To evaluate the parallelization and synchronization methods (see Sect. 4.1, 4.2), we examine the speedup of the linear (Fig. 14b) and cyclic schemes (Fig. 14c). This makes it possible to understand the extent to which data dependencies can have an impact on performance. In the following, the speedup always refers to the latency of the corresponding sequential version [32,35] (Fig. 14a).

$$S_{LINEAR} = \frac{t_{SEQUENTIAL}}{t_{LINEAR}}, \qquad S_{CYCLIC} = \frac{t_{SEQUENTIAL}}{t_{CYCLIC}}$$

The variable t_X denotes the inference latency of a Conv2D layer using scheme X. An upper bound for the maximum achievable speedup is P_V, i.e., all conflicting cores run in parallel without synchronization overhead (see Sect. 4.2).

Figure 16 shows the speedup of the linear (blue) and the cyclic synchronization method (red) for different Conv2D layers of Mobilenet. The shapes of the used layers (Layer #) are listed in Table 3. The MVM latency is 200 ns. The

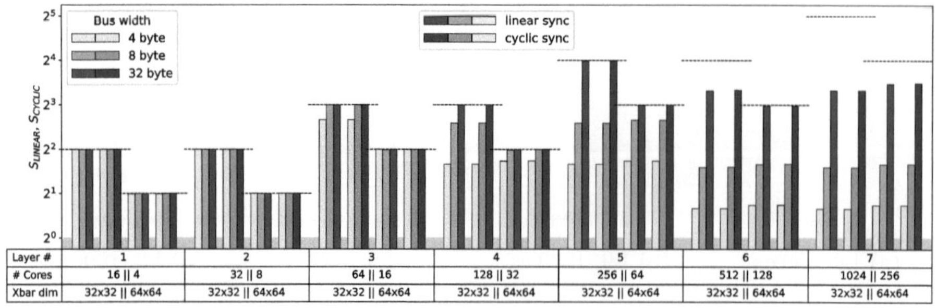

Fig. 16. Speedup vs. maximum achievable speedup (dashed lines) of the linear and cyclic synchronization for different layers, matrix dimensions, and bus widths. The number of cores depends on the layer and matrix dimension. It refers to 32×32 matrices (left entry) and 64 × 64 matrices (right entry). (Color figure online)

Table 3. Excerpt from Mobilnet's Conv2D Layers

#	kernel shape	matrix shape	input shape
1	1 × 1 × 128 × 128	128 × 128	56 × 56 × 128
2	1 × 1 × 128 × 256	256 × 128	28 × 28 × 128
3	1 × 1 × 256 × 256	256 × 256	28 × 28 × 256
4	1 × 1 × 256 × 512	512 × 256	14 × 14 × 256
5	1 × 1 × 512 × 512	512 × 512	14 × 14 × 512
6	1 × 1 × 512 × 1024	1024 × 512	7 × 7 × 512
7	1 × 1 × 1024 × 1024	1024 × 1024	7 × 7 × 1024

matrix dimensions are 32 × 32 and 64 × 64. This, in combination with the kernel shape of the layer, determines the number of needed cores. The upper bound for the maximum achievable speedup (P_V) is indicated by the dashed lines. The speedup increases when the matrix size is reduced.

A reduction from 64 × 64 to 32 × 32 crossbars results in a speedup of at most 2× referred to the corresponding sequential scheme. Up to 4× more cores are required which increases the bus utilization and synchronization complexity. This means that higher speedups can be achieved at the cost of higher numbers of cores and larger bus widths.

Figure 16 also reveals the speedup that can be achieved for Conv2D layers depending on the bus width and matrix dimension. The figure demonstrates that the speedup limit can be reached even for small bus widths (4B) when the total number of cores is small (≤ 32). Using a large bus width of 32B, up to 128 cores can operate in parallel. Beyond this, the speedup limit cannot be reached. Reaching the speedup limit for sufficiently high bus widths proves that the synchronization presented in this work does not cause long wait times. The highest speedup that is achieved is 16× for layer 5. The speedup of the cyclic method is slightly higher compared to the linear method because the instructions are distributed more evenly among the cores (see Sect. 4.2).

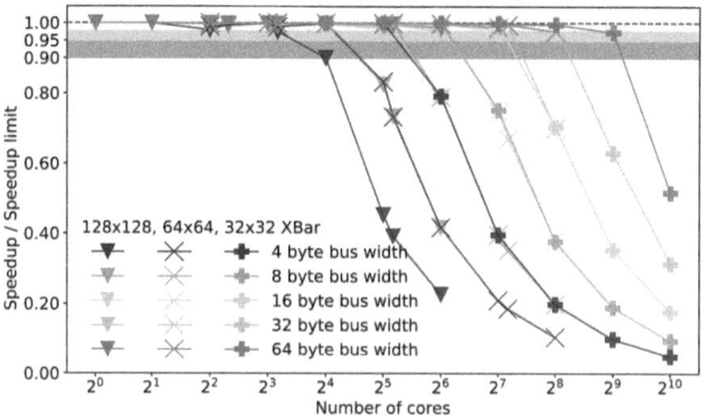

Fig. 17. Speedup divided by speedup limit of cyclic synchronization scheme for different layers, bus widths, and matrix dimensions. (Color figure online)

We previously demonstrated that the synchronization methods are very efficient as the speedup limit can almost be attained. However, this limit can only be achieved when the bus is sufficiently wide which prevents it from becoming a bottleneck. Figure 17 shows to which extent the speedup limit can be reached depending on the matrix dimension, bus width, and the number of cores. Each line represents one combination of matrix dimension and bus width. For every combination, Conv2D layers from the Mobilenet and ResNet-18 architecture were compiled and simulated. The data from Fig. 17 can be used to determine two things, the appropriate number of cores for a given matrix dimension and bus width, or a reasonable bus width for a given number of cores and crossbar dimension.

In general, the smaller the bus width, the lower the number of cores the bus can handle without becoming a bottleneck. For small bus widths (4B, red line), only a maximum of 16 cores are worthwhile to achieve more than 90% of the speedup limit, with 64B (blue line) the system can contain up to 512 cores. If the matrix dimension is halved, i.e., the number of required cores is quadrupled, then the bus width should at least be doubled to achieve similar performance. For a given number of cores, Fig. 17 can be used to determine a suitable combination of matrix dimension and bus width.

5.3 Synchronization Overhead

Synchronization requires additional operations. In contrast to the `WAIT` operation, the `CALL` operation must be transferred over the bus, which increases bus traffic. The smaller the matrix size, the more cores are needed, and the more `CALL` operations have to be executed.

Figure 18 shows that the bus traffic caused by `CALL` operations is small compared to the data values transferred over the bus. For `CALL` operations with a size of 4B and data values with a size of 1B, the overhead is less than 4% when using 32×32 matrices, less than 2% when using 64×64 matrices, and less than 1% when using 128×128 matrices.

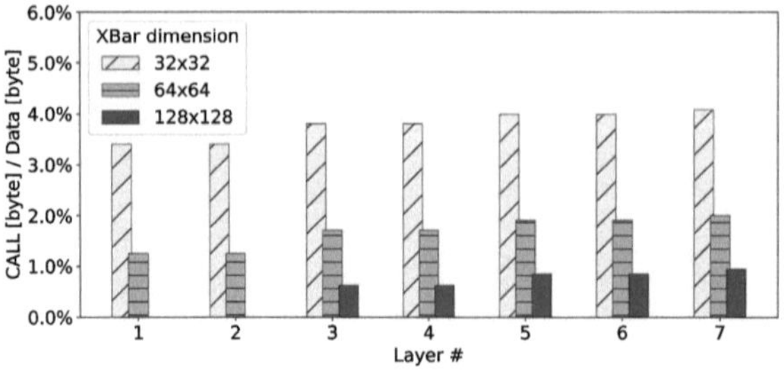

Fig. 18. Bus traffic caused by `CALL` operations (4% per operation) in relation to transferred data (1% per data value).

6 Conclusion

In this paper, we presented a framework for HW/SW co-design of ISA-based CIM accelerators. The framework comprises a SystemC TLM-2.0-based architecture simulator and a CNN compiler. We investigated the influence of various architectural parameters on inference latency and crossbar utilization. Using our framework, we simulated the impact of interconnect systems, the number and size of crossbars, and MVM latency on performance across different layers from Mobilenet and ResNet-18. In this architecture exploration, we were able to identify parameter combinations that allow for up to 95% crossbar utilization.

Furthermore, we investigated the impact of the workload, particularly data dependencies, on performance. Our findings demonstrate that the data dependencies within the workload necessitate synchronization mechanisms, resulting in additional overhead. The employed synchronization techniques achieved a speedup of up to 90% of the theoretical maximum, effectively reducing communication overhead to less than 4% of all bus transactions. In summary, our results highlight the intricate interplay of architectural parameters and workload optimization in shaping the efficiency of CIM accelerators.

Acknowledgement. This work was funded by the Federal Ministry of Education and Research (BMBF, Germany) in the project NeuroSys (Project 03ZU1106CA).

References

1. Jouppi, N.P., et al.: In-datacenter performance analysis of a tensor processing unit. In: ISCA (2017)
2. Zou, X., Xu, S., Chen, X., Yan, L., Han, Y.: Breaking the von neumann bottleneck: architecture-level processing-in-memory technology. Sci. China Inf. Sci. (2021)
3. Chang, Y.F., et al.: Memcomputing (memristor+ computing) in intrinsic sio x-based resistive switching memory: arithmetic operations for logic applications. IEEE (T-ED) **64**(7), 2977–2983 (2017)
4. Vetter, J.S., Mittal, S.: Opportunities for nonvolatile memory systems in extreme-scale high-performance computing. CiSE (2015)

5. Wan, W., et al.: A compute-in-memory chip based on resistive random-access memory. Nature **608**(7923), 504–512 (2022)
6. Ankit, A., et al.: Puma: a programmable ultra-efficient memristor-based accelerator for machine learning inference. In: ASPLOS XXIV (2019)
7. Shafiee, A., et al.: ISAAC: a convolutional neural network accelerator with in-situ analog arithmetic in crossbars. ACM SIGARCH Comput. Archit. News **44**(3), 14–26 (2016)
8. Chi, P., et al.: PRIME: a novel processing-in-memory architecture for neural network computation in ReRAM-based main memory. ACM SIGARCH Comput. Archit. News **44**(3), 27–39 (2016)
9. Pelke, R., Bosbach, N., Cubero, J., Staudigl, F., Leupers, R., Joseph, J.M.: Mapping of CNNs on multi-core RRAM-based cim architectures. In: 2023 IFIP/IEEE 31st International Conference on Very Large Scale Integration (VLSI-SoC). IEEE (2023)
10. Pelke, R., Cubero-Cascante, J., Bosbach, N., Staudigl, F., Leupers, R., Joseph, J.M.: CLSA-cim: a cross-layer scheduling approach for computing-in-memory architectures. arXiv preprint arXiv:2401.07671 (2024)
11. Cao, W., Zhao, Y., Boloor, A., Han, Y., Zhang, X., Jiang, L.: Neural-PIM: efficient processing-in-memory with neural approximation of peripherals. IEEE Trans. Comput. **71**(9), 2142–2155 (2021)
12. Mao, M., Cao, Y., Yu, S., Chakrabarti, C.: Optimizing latency, energy, and reliability of 1T1R ReRAM through cross-layer techniques. IEEE J. Emerg. Sel. Top. Circuits Syst. **6**(3), 352–363 (2016)
13. Li, B., Gu, P., Shan, Y., Wang, Y., Chen, Y., Yang, H.: RRAM-based analog approximate computing. IEEE TCAD **34**(12), 1905–1917 (2015)
14. Fouda, M.E., Lee, S., Lee, J., Eltawil, A., Kurdahi, F.: Mask technique for fast and efficient training of binary resistive crossbar arrays. TNANO **18**, 704–716 (2019)
15. Xiao, T.P., et al.: On the accuracy of analog neural network inference accelerators. IEEE CASS **22**(4), 26–48 (2021)
16. Song, L., Qian, X., Li, H., Chen, Y.: Pipelayer: a pipelined reram-based accelerator for deep learning. In: IEEE HPCA, pp. 541–552. IEEE (2017)
17. Mittal, S.: A survey of reram-based architectures for processing-in-memory and neural networks. Mach. Learn. Knowl. Extr. **1**(1), 75–114 (2018)
18. Panda, P.R.: Systemc: a modeling platform supporting multiple design abstractions. In: Proceedings of the 14th International Symposium on Systems Synthesis, pp. 75–80 (2001)
19. IEEE Standard for Standard SystemC Language Reference Manual. Technical report, IEEE ISBN: 9780738168012
20. Aynsley, J., et al.: OSCI TLM-2.0 language reference manual. Open SystemC Initiative (OSCI) (2009)
21. Bosbach, N., Pelke, R., Zurstraßen, N., Jünger, L., Weinstock, J.H., Leupers, R.: Work-in-progress: a generic non-intrusive parallelization approach for SystemC TLM-2.0-based virtual platforms. In: 2023 International Conference on Hardware/-Software Codesign and System Synthesis (CODES+ ISSS), pp. 42–43. IEEE (2023)
22. Zurstraßen, N., Brandhofer, R., Cubero-Cascante, J., Bosbach, N., Jünger, L., Leupers, R.: The optimal quantum of temporal decoupling. In: Proceedings of the 29th Asia and South Pacific Design Automation Conference, Incheon Songdo Convensia, South Korea, Association for Computing Machinery (2024)
23. Menard, C., Castrillon, J., Jung, M., Wehn, N.: System simulation with gem5 and systemc

24. Math, S.S., Manjula, R.: Design of AMBA AXI4 protocol for system-on-chip communication. Int. J. Commun. Netw. Secur. (IJCNS) **1**(3), 38–42 (2012)
25. ARM: Introduction to amba axi4
26. Ambrosi, J., et al.: Hardware-software co-design for an analog-digital accelerator for machine learning. In: 2018 IEEE International Conference on Rebooting Computing (ICRC), pp. 1–13. IEEE (2018)
27. ARM: ARM AMBA TLM 2.0 library developer guide (2019)
28. Microsemi: Hb0766 handbook coreaxi4interconnect v2.8
29. Xilinx: AXI interconnect v2.1 logicore IP product guide
30. Yanai, K., Tanno, R., Okamoto, K.: Efficient mobile implementation of a CNN-based object recognition system. In: Proceedings of the 24th ACM International Conference on Multimedia, pp. 362–366 (2016)
31. Zhang, Y., He, G., Wang, G., Li, Y.: Efficient and robust RRAM-based convolutional weight mapping with shifted and duplicated kernel. IEEE TCAD **40**, 287–300 (2020)
32. Rhe, J., Moon, S., Ko, J.H.: VWC-SDK: convolutional weight mapping using shifted and duplicated kernel with variable windows and channels. IEEE JETCAS **12**(2), 408–421 (2022)
33. Negi, S., Chakraborty, I., Ankit, A., Roy, K.: NAX: neural architecture and memristive xbar based accelerator co-design. In: Proceedings of the 59th ACM/IEEE Design Automation Conference (DAC), pp. 451–456 (2022)
34. Agrawal, A., Lee, C., Roy, K.: X-changr: changing memristive crossbar mapping for mitigating line-resistance induced accuracy degradation in deep neural networks. arXiv preprint arXiv:1907.00285 (2019)
35. Rhe, J., Moon, S., Ko, J.H.: VW-SDK: efficient convolutional weight mapping using variable windows for processing-in-memory architectures. In: DATE. IEEE (2022)
36. Bosbach, N., Joseph, J.M., Leupers, R., Jünger, L.: NISTT: a non-intrusive SystemC-TLM 2.0 tracing tool. In: 2022 IFIP/IEEE 30th International Conference on Very Large Scale Integration (VLSI-SoC). IEEE (2022)
37. Howard, A.G., et al.: Mobilenets: efficient convolutional neural networks for mobile vision applications. arXiv:1704.04861 (2017)
38. He, K., Zhang, X., Ren, S., Sun, J.: Deep residual learning for image recognition. In: IEEE CVPR, pp. 770–778 (2016)

A Leap of Confidence: A Write-Intensity Aware Prudent Page Migration for Hybrid Memories

N. S. Aswathy(✉), Aishwarya Gupta, and Hemangee K. Kapoor

Indian Institute of Technology Guwahati, Guwahati, India
{aswat176101002,hemangee}@iitg.ac.in, gupta.aishwarya@alumni.iitg.ac.in

Abstract. Hybrid memory composed of DRAM and PCM exploits the benefit of both types of memory. Due to the random page placement, write-intensive pages may end up in the PCM partition which could negatively impact memory performance because of the high write latency. Memory service time can be improved by moving write-intensive pages to DRAM. State-of-the-art techniques migrate pages whose write access count exceeds a set limit. These techniques do not examine the access pattern once the choice to migrate the page has been made, which might lead to unnecessary migrations because the page may have been hot before the decision, but the number of accesses may have dropped after migration. It is necessary to accurately identify page migration candidates to maximize the benefit of migration.

This chapter presents two page migration techniques AcPruMig and WiPruMig which prudently identify page migration candidates to improve memory service time. The first method AcPruMig is an access-based page migration technique which selects migration candidates based on write access count. The method uses an eDRAM buffer as a mediator for migration from PCM to DRAM. The hot pages which are migrated to eDRAM from PCM are prudently monitored by looking at the access pattern and performing migration either to DRAM or revoked back to PCM. This judicious identification of page migration candidates with the help of an eDRAM buffer reduces unnecessary migrations and improves memory service time.

The second method WiPruMig is a write-intensity-based page migration technique which maximizes the hits in DRAM by migrating write write-intensive page to DRAM. This method also uses an eDRAM buffer as a mediator for migration. WiPruMig looks into the write intensity of hot pages which crosses the set limit of write access count. The pages with write intensity greater than a predefined intensity threshold are migrated directly to DRAM to maximize the hits in DRAM. Both the proposed methods improve the memory service time by accurately selecting page migration candidates and early migrating write-intensive pages to DRAM. The proposed methods are implemented using a Gem5 [1] full system simulator integrated with NVMain [2] and evaluated using SPEC 2006 [3] and Parsec benchmarks [4]. AcPruMig and WiPruMig improve memory service time on average by 53% and 64% respectively.

Published by Springer Nature Switzerland AG 2024
I. (Abe) M. Elfadel and L. Albasha (Eds.): VLSI-SoC 2023, IFIP AICT 680, pp. 45–71, 2024.
https://doi.org/10.1007/978-3-031-70947-0_3

1 Introduction

Modern chip multi-processors include an increasing number of processing cores because of recent advances in semiconductor technology. The significant advancement in computing power offers an adequate basis for concurrent execution of modern data-intensive applications which require more memory to function at their best. Thus, developing fast and large-capacity main memory systems become increasingly essential at a rapid rate. Traditional DRAM memories are not capable of meeting the requirements demanded by such systems due to the low density and high leakage power demanded by such memories. Despite its performance and price, DRAM's limited scalability and frequent refresh requirements remain problems [5,6].

Emerging non-volatile memories such as Phase-Change Memory (PCM), Spin-Transfer Torque (STT-RAM), and Resistive RAM (RRAM), show great potential to replace DRAM in main memories. These NVMs offer fascinating characteristics like low-leakage energy, high density, and non-volatility, which are necessary for creating large-capacity, energy-efficient main memory systems.

However, drawbacks like poor cell endurance, high write latency, and high write energy prevent these NVMs from becoming the main memory standard. While the write endurance of DRAM-based memories is rather high ($>10^{16}$), that of PCM and ReRAM which is 10^8 and 10^{11} writes, respectively. NVMs have disparity in read and write latencies; that is, DRAMs have read and write latencies in the range of 50 ns. PCM has a read latency of 50 ns to 100 ns, but its write latency is approximately 350 ns [7], which is seven times longer than DRAM's write latency.

A hybrid memory system combines DRAM and NVM to deliver high density without compromising memory performance. The concept of a hybrid memory system with DRAM and NVM involves using both types of memory in a complementary manner to address the shortcomings of each while harnessing their respective advantages. By optimizing data placement and management, hybrid memory systems aim to balance between the speed of DRAM and the capacity and non-volatility of NVM. This can lead to improved overall system performance, lower power consumption, and better cost efficiency compared to systems that rely solely on DRAM or NVM.

A hybrid memory system allocates data randomly to either DRAM or NVM, with the option to move pages between the two types of memories to improve efficiency. Page migration in a hybrid memory system migrate memory pages between DRAM and NVM, in order to optimize memory utilization, performance, and energy efficiency. This method is used to reduce data access latency and maximize the utilization of the memory resources that are available. The important steps followed during page migrations are: (i)identifying data pages, (ii) classifying these pages based on their access patterns, (iii) migration decisions based on different policies, (iv) migration of data pages by copying the contents of the page from its current location to the destination memory, and (v) updates the page tables to reflect the new location of the data pages.

The two major concerns regarding migration decisions are figuring out which page to migrate and when to start the migration process. To identify the page migration candidates, the system continuously monitors the access patterns of pages in memory and classifies between frequently accessed pages (hot) and infrequently accessed pages (cold). These identified hot pages are migrated to DRAM to improve performance. Many works that migrate pages between DRAM and NVM depending on memory access patterns have been proposed [8, 9, 28–30] to improve the effectiveness of hybrid memory.

As the writes are costlier in NVM, it is beneficial to migrate write-intensive pages to DRAM to improve performance. Thus, the hot pages are selected based on the history of memory writes made while the page is stored in NVM. The migration happens either instantly when the page becomes hot, or it happens at regular intervals. State-of-the-art methods for page migration move pages according to either static or dynamic thresholds. That is when the write count of a page crosses a predefined threshold, the page is migrated immediately or when the interval boundary reaches. In the case of a dynamic threshold, the threshold gets updated after each migration based on the benefit of migration.

Attempts to migrate pages to DRAM are ineffective when the page's hotness is miscalculated or when the page almost finishes its write requests while in NVM. Also, some pages get relocated back to NVM when new hot pages are moved to DRAM due to the limited capacity of DRAM. The migration effort becomes futile if these redirected pages receive several writes in NVM. Therefore, improperly executed page transfers may lead to unsatisfactory system performance.

This chapter proposes effective techniques to identify page migration candidates which maximize migration benefits and thus improve system performance. Our first proposal is AcPruMig approach, an Access-based Prudent page Migration that uses an eDRAM buffer to verify the authenticity of the migration candidate. In particular, a page that has been designated as a hot page is moved to the temporary eDRAM buffer and remains there for a predetermined period. If the page receives enough write requests during this period, it is designated as a legitimate hot page and is migrated to DRAM. Otherwise, the page is redirected back to PCM.

To improve the benefit of migration further, the second method WiPruMig, a write intensity based prudent page migration, meticulously selects candidates for page migration using write intensity which is the number of write requests received per unit time. Before examining write intensity, a hotness threshold of migration must be crossed for the page i.e., the page is considered to be a possible migration candidate page and is ready to move to eDRAM. If the write intensity of this migration candidate page is greater than the predefined intensity threshold, instead of migrating to eDRAM, this page is directly migrated to PCM. The decision is based on the assumption that such highly intensive pages receive enough number of requests while being in eDRAM and certainly migrate to DRAM further. To avoid unnecessary migration to eDRAM such high-intensive pages are migrated directly to DRAM and maximizes the DRAM hits by early migrating the page. As the method, avoid migration via eDRAM for high-write-intensive pages, the method avoids revoking migration from eDRAM to PCM.

Our goal is to maximize the DRAM hits in order to increase the memory service time and energy-delay product (EDP). Using NVMain [2] integrated with the full system simulator Gem5 [1], we have evaluated our proposed migration policies.

2 Background

2.1 Phase Change Memory

Phase Change Memory (PCM) is a type of non-volatile memory technology that has gained research focus as an alternative to traditional DRAM systems. The basic component of PCM cell is a phase change material such as chalcogenide glass. This chalcogenide can switch between two stable states: crystalline (low electrical resistance) and amorphous (high electrical resistance) phases. These two resistance states are used to represent binary data '0' and '1'. One of the significant advantages of PCM is that it is non-volatile, which means it retains data even when the power is turned off. PCM has the potential for high-density storage making it suitable for future scalable devices. PCM can also store multiple bits per cell, Multi-Level Cell (MLC). This is achieved by encoding different resistance levels within the same cell to represent more than just 0 and 1.

2.2 Hybrid DRAM-PCM Memory

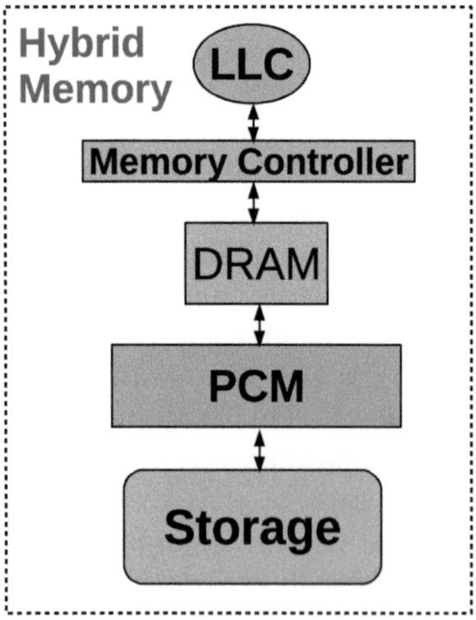

Fig. 1. Hybrid memory - Vertical organization

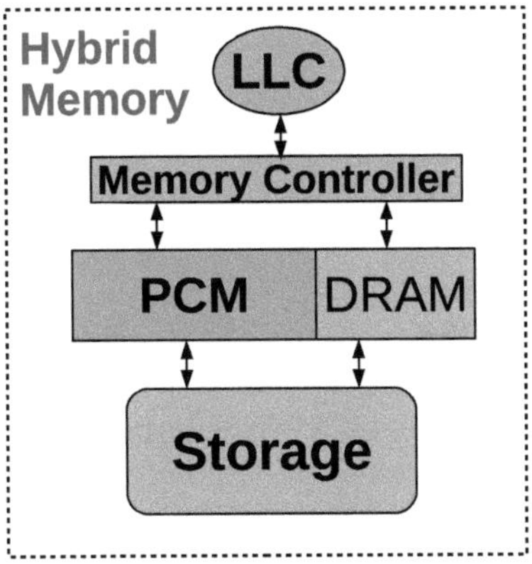

Fig. 2. Hybrid memory - Horizontal organization

In this work, we have considered hybrid memory with a combination of DRAM and PCM. Hybrid PCM and DRAM systems combine the strengths of both types of memory to optimize performance. The objective is to utilize the non-volatility and energy efficiency of PCM, while also leveraging the speed and low latency of DRAM for frequently accessed data. This can result in improved overall system performance.

The two organization for hybrid memory are horizontal method and vertical method. In vertical method shown in Fig. 1, smaller DRAM acts as a cache or write buffer for the larger PCM memory. We employ the horizontal method, which couples DRAM and PCM into a single physical address space. In the horizontal architecture depicted in Fig. 2, the operating system (OS) uses a proportionate distribution on a page fault and is aware of both memories for page allocation [10].

2.3 Page Migration in Hybrid Memory

Page migration aims to optimize the placement of data pages in these memory partitions based on access patterns. Page migration algorithms continuously monitor the access patterns of data pages. Designing efficient page migration algorithms is complex. Due to the high write latency of PCM memory, it is preferable to migrate write-intensive pages into the DRAM partition in order to improve memory performance. But it's crucial to precisely identify write-intensive hot pages in PCM and move them to DRAM because of the high migration overhead.

As the DRAM capacity is limited, it is possible that when migrating a page from PCM, no free space is available in the DRAM. Victim pages must be migrated from DRAM to PCM due to the limited DRAM capacity. If the selected victim page is write-intensive, migrating such page to PCM will negatively affect the performance. Also, this victim page migration doubles the overhead associated with migration. So, it is desirable to identify the victim page judiciously.

3 Related Works

The objective of hybrid memory is to utilize the advantages of NVM and DRAM technology to overcome the shortcomings of each. Hierarchical organizations employ DRAM as a cache or write buffer [11–15]. The goal behind these strategies is to use some cache management policies to limit the number of writes to PCM memories to get around PCM's write limitations. Qureshi et al. [11] presented a PCM-based hybrid memory the page at which a page fault occurs is stored in DRAM cache. The dirty blocks from a victim page are kept in a DRAM partition that functions as a write buffer in [12]. Khouzani et al. [13] present a conflict-aware page allocation technique that divides intensively written pages among distinct DRAM sets using segment information and conflict misses in DRAM. A novel PCM-MLC based memory storage architecture with a self-adaptive data filtering module and a DRAM buffer has been presented by the authors in [14]. Using data reusability and spatial and temporal localities, the method reduces the number of write operations in the PCM array and improves access latencies.

Since there is a limited amount of DRAM capacity available, the performance of these approaches is hindered by their inability to use the entire bandwidth of memory. The horizontal architecture share the address space and memory pages can be allocated exclusively to any partition. Due to the high write-latency of PCM, state-of-the-art methods [8,9,16–22] propose efficient page placement or migration strategies where the pages with the highest write count are either placed or migrated to DRAM.

In CLOCK-DWF proposed in [16], new pages for write requests are always loaded in DRAM. The pages in NVM will move to DRAM if a write request hits on memory. Prior to the migration from NVM to DRAM, a victim page with the lowest write access is moved to NVM if DRAM is full. To reduce energy consumption, the authors of [17] suggest a hybrid memory architecture that switches DRAM between a cache for NVM and a different DIMM for applications running on the core. Using a migration threshold, Double LRU [18] attempts to lower the migration cost brought on by CLOCK-DWF. While just the write count is evaluated with the threshold, refinery swap [19] is comparable to Double LRU in terms of determining the migration threshold.

UH-Mem [23] and UIMigrate [8] propose dynamic threshold-based policies to identify migration candidates in order to lower the amount of invalid migrations. The decision thresholds of both policies are updated in accordance with the costs and benefits of migration. In RAINBOW [15], short, hot, lightweight pages are stored in a DRAM cache and page migration is coordinated at a super granularity level. In [9], the authors propose on-the-fly page migration with periodical updates for the remap table. In the technique the page gets migrated immediately when it becomes write-intensive using a specialized hardware unit.

CAHRAM [21] maintains the low-referred pages in PCM and the high-referred pages in DRAM to enhance read performance of hybrid memory. To reduce the expense of page migration and the overhead of online page access monitoring, Liu et al. [20] suggest object-level memory allocation and migration. After selecting the candidate pages for migration, the correct instance for the migration is discussed in [24]. In the case if the selected migration candidate page is less effective, the page migration will be less beneficial. AcPruMig [25] proposes an eDRAM-based migration selection where the migration candidate pages are judiciously identified to maximize the hits in DRAM and thus improve performance. The authors of [22] suggest using AGDM to determine appropriate migration modes and granularity based on memory access patterns at run-time.

The process of migrating pages is expensive and energy and latency intensive. To guarantee that the benefits surpass any performance drawbacks, page migration must be carefully managed. Current page migration techniques are not able to precisely identify page migration candidates, which is more advantageous when migrated, despite their best efforts to decrease invalid migrations.

4 Proposed Page Migration Techniques

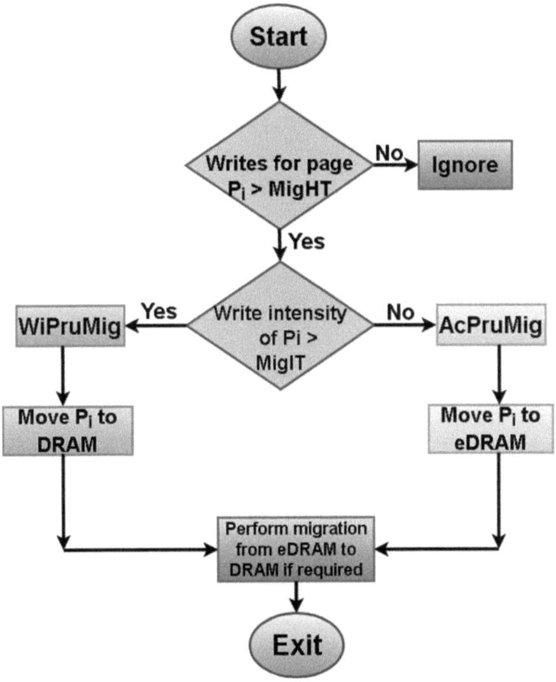

Fig. 3. Proposed prudent page migration techniques

This section discusses the motivation for our proposal, system model and both of our proposed techniques. The overview of the proposed techniques is depicted in Fig. 3. The first method is an Access-based Prudent page Migration, AcPruMig technique is from our prior work and is demonstrated and examined extensively in this chapter. The second method WiPruMig is a write intensity based migration selection.

4.1 Motivation

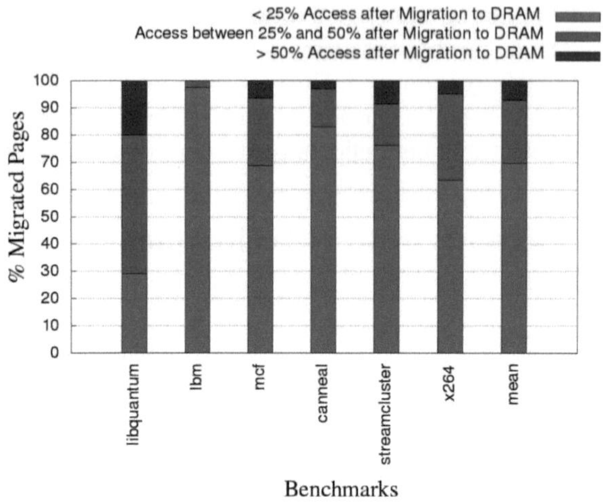

Fig. 4. Distribution of accesses to migrated pages using a generic threshold based policy. X-axis represents various benchmarks and Y axis represent percentage of access distribution

DRAM-PCM hybrid memory combines the advantages of both memory types. To enhance the memory performance, page migration move highest write count pages to DRAM due to the high write latency of PCM. It is expected that the memory access pattern follows the history of access, and maximize the hits in DRAM. Thus improves the memory performance due to the low access latency of DRAM compared to PCM. In cases where there are fewer accesses to the migrated page in DRAM, the benefits of migration are outweighed by the migration overhead.

The percentage of accesses to a set of migrated pages after migrating to DRAM using a generic threshold-based migration technique, Migrating on Surpassing Threshold (MoST) is shown in Fig. 4. This strategy is indicative of most of the approaches currently in practice. It is evident from the figure that after moving to DRAM, some of the migrated pages had less than 25% access. These pages can be considered as not really being hot to migrate to DRAM as the overhead of migration outweigh the benefit. The average number of pages with access below 25% is approximately 70%, between 25% and 50% is around 23%, and over 50% is just 7%. A meticulous choice of migration candidates should maximize the DRAM hits to the migrated page in order to optimize the benefit of migration and thus improve the memory performance.

4.2 System Model

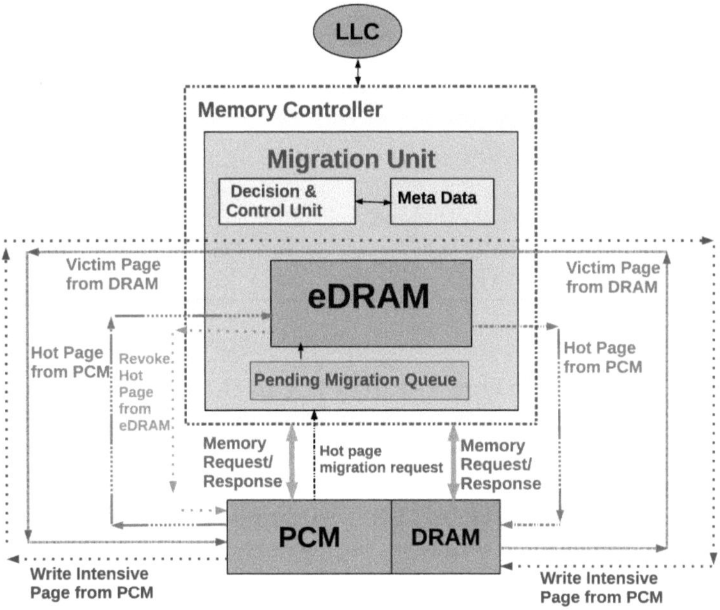

Fig. 5. Proposed hybrid memory controller

Hybrid memory composed of single DRAM channel and three PCM channels are considered for the proposed migration techniques. Figure 5 presents the proposed hybrid memory controller. The additional migration unit include an eDRAM buffer, a metadata unit, a decision and control unit, and a pending migration queue. A faster and smaller eDRAM buffer used to store fixed number of pages[1] at any point in time and will serve as a mediator for the migration of a page from PCM to DRAM. The write access count for every page is saved as metadata and is tracked by the decision and control unit, which then determines when to carry out a migration. The pages that are hot but cannot reside in eDRAM buffer because it is full are tracked by the pending queue.

4.3 Thresholds Used for Migration

The proposed policies use three threshold[2] to make decision about migration.

[1] We have selected the size of eDRAM as four pages to conduct our experiments.
[2] These threshold values are empirically determined by extensive experimental evaluation.

Algorithm 1: Write Intensity based Prudent Page Migration

```
MigHT: Migration Hotness Threshold; MigIT: Migration Intensity
  Threshold; MigCP: Migration Candidate Page;
Function WiPruMig
  if writes(MigCP) > MigHT then
    Compute the write intensity WI(MigCP)
    if WI(MigCP) > MigIT then
      /* New contribution                              */
      move_toDRAM(MigCP)
    else
      /* Earlier contribution AcPruMig                 */
      moveto_eDRAM(MigCP)
    move_eDRAMtoDRAM()
```

1. **Migration Hot Threshold (MigHT):** This threshold is used to quantize the hotness of the page in PCM. If the write access count of a page in PCM is greater than *MigHT*, the page is considered to be hot, and the proposed AcPruMig method migrates the page to eDRAM.
2. **eDRAM Hot Threshold (eHT):** This threshold is used for prudent identification of hot pages. In that, if the page residing in eDRAM gets more than eHT accesses within a short duration, it is considered genuinely hot and moved to DRAM.
3. **Migration Intensity Threshold (MigIT):** This threshold is used to identify the highly write-intensive pages in PCM. The write intensity of pages having write count greater than MigHT is calculated. WiPruMig consider such page as possible migration candidate and checks the write intensity of such pages against Migration Intensity Threshold (MigIT). If the intensity is greater than MigIT, the page is directly migrated to DRAM, otherwise the page migrated to eDRAM.

4.4 AcPruMig: Access-Based Prudent Page Migration

The existing page migration techniques only take into account the page's current access status when deciding whether or not to transfer a hot page to DRAM. However it is possible that after the migrated page is transferred to DRAM, access to it probably decreases dramatically. Therefore, the page cannot be characterized as a legitimately hot page. This incorrect migration may hinder the system's performance.

The proposed judicious page migration is explained in Algorithm 1. The write counter associated with each page is incremented each write access request made to the page. The page write counter is compared against the predefined Migration Hotness Threshold (*MigHT*). If the write count exceeds *MigHT*, the migration candidate page (*MigCP*) is either migrated to eDRAM or directly migrated to DRAM depending on the proposed policies (AcPruMig and WiPruMig).

Algorithm 2: Auxiliary Functions

```
1  MigPQ: Migration Pending Queue; eHT: eDRAM Hot Threshold; STime:
     Stipulated Time
2  Function move_toeDRAM(MigCP)
3      if eDRAM has space then
4          Add MigCP to eDRAM
5      else
6          if ∃ P_i | duration(P_i) > STime, where P_i ∈ eDRAM then
7              Move P_i back to PCM
8              Place MigCP in eDRAM
9          else
10             Add MigCP to MigPQ
11 Function move_eDRAMtoDRAM
12     ∀ P_i ∈ eDRAM
13     if duration(P_i) > STime then
14         Move P_i back to PCM
15     else
16         if writes(P_i) > eHT then
17             move_toDRAM(P_i)
18         else
19             Retain P_i in eDRAM
20 Function move_toDRAM(P_i)
21     if DRAM has space then Place P_i in DRAM
22     else
23         VicP_DRAM = VicP_LRU() or VicP_MRI()
24         if VicP_DRAM then
25             Move VicP_DRAM to PCM
26             Place P_i to DRAM
27         else Discard migration of P_i
```

The proposed AcPruMig method attempts to prevent threshold based page migrations by first moving the PCM hot page to a faster memory, like eDRAM, located in the memory controller, and then monitor the number of write requests the page receives in a specific period of time while the page resides in eDRAM. A page that is currently in eDRAM needs to be moved to DRAM, if it gets more write requests than a predefined eDRAM Hot threshold (eHT) and that too within a specific period of time, since it appears to be fairly hot.

For those pages which receives number of write requests greater than *MigHT* is either migrated to eDRAM or monitored by the pending queue. The function *move_toeDRAM* in Algorithm 2 describes the migration from PCM to eDRAM. This migration decision depends on the amount of eDRAM space available (lines 3–10 in Algorithm 2). The pages in eDRAM are checked by AcPruMig on a regular basis, and any page that remains in eDRAM for longer than a predetermined period of time (*STime*) is revoked and returned to PCM. Prudent decision making is aided by residence of the page in eDRAM and the number of write access

Algorithm 3: Victim Page Selection

```
Function VicP_LRU()
    Get the minimum write intensity page VicP_DRAM from the last k%
      pages in DRAM LRU list
    if writes(VicP_DRAM) < writes(MigCP) then
        return victim page VicP_DRAM
    else return NULL
Function VicP_MRI()
    Get the most read intensive page VicP_DRAM from DRAM MRI list
    return victim page VicP_DRAM
```

it receive while being in eDRAM. If accesses in eDRAM are more than *eHT*, it is promoted to DRAM; otherwise moves back to PCM. The proposed AcPruMig method ensures that the migration to DRAM will happen only through eDRAM, and there is no direct migration from PCM to DRAM.

The function *move_eDRAMtoDRAM* in Algorithm 2 describes the migration from eDRAM to DRAM. The function verifies the acquired write count for those pages which reside in eDRAM for a period shorter than the stipulated time *STime*. If the number of writes received for the page within *STime* is greater than *eHT*[3], the page appears to be write-intensive and moved to DRAM. Before shifting a page from eDRAM to DRAM, the size of DRAM is determined to find out if there is a free page in DRAM. To make room for new PCM hot pages, all pages that remain in eDRAM for longer than *STime* are revoked and returned to PCM. In order to minimize the amount of reward less migrations, the proposed AcPruMig prudently identifies that the page is actually hot by counting the number of write accesses within a given amount of time.

4.5 WiPruMig: Write Intensity Based Prudent Migration

The memory access behaviour varies across execution phases of applications. The cumulative write behavior of a page is shown by its write count. The current behavior of memory access may not be reflected if we take into account only the accumulated write count. Write intensity, which precisely adjusts to the run-time behavior, is defined as the number of write requests received per unit of time. Therefore, it is beneficial to scrutinize page migration candidates based on write intensity to maximize the benefit of migration. We propose WiPruMig an intensity based page migration which select page migration candidates based on write count as well as write intensity.

AcPruMig migrates highest write count pages to fixed eDRAM buffer and then migrated to DRAM if the page receive enough number of requests with in a specified period of time. The eDRAM act as a mediator and delay the migration for some time. If the pages are genuinely hot and are extremely write

[3] *eHT* is taken as *hot*% of *MigHT* to conduct our experiments. The value of *hot* is empirically found, and the analysis is given in Sect. 5.2.

intensive, this delay in migration may result in reduced memory performance as it unnecessarily migrated to eDRAM and then to DRAM. To overcome this problem, WiPruMig directly migrate such highly write-intensive pages to DRAM and maximize the hits while the page is in DRAM to improve memory service time.

WiPruMig method keeps track of the write count and write intensity of all PCM pages as shown in Algorithm 1. Similar to AcPruMig technique discussed in the previous section, the write count is incremented on each write request and is compared against *MigHT*. In AcPruMig, the pages with write count greater than *MigHT* are migrated to eDRAM if there is space available in eDRAM. Whereas WiPruMig compare the write intensity of such pages against Migration Intensity Threshold (*MigIT*). If the write intensity is greater than *MigIT*, the page is directly migrated to DRAM. Otherwise migrated to eDRAM. This write intensity based direct migration helps to maximize the access after migrating to DRAM and improve memory performance. The direct migration is based on the assumption that such highly write-intensive pages are legitimately hot and further receive enough number of write accesses to get migrated to DRAM.

As the PCM page is copied to eDRAM buffer, the original page is still available in PCM. The proposed WiPruMig make use of the availability of these pages. The write access received for the page while being in eDRAM page also update the original PCM page. Thus make sure that both the copied page in eDRAM and original page in PCM have the updated value at any point in time. By doing this, WiPruMig avoids the write back of revoke migration pages from eDRAM to PCM as the updated page is available in PCM. Instead of moving page from eDRAM to PCM, WiPruMig simply discard the migration and removes the page from eDRAM as it is not hot enough to migrate to DRAM.

As the DRAM size is limited while moving a page to DRAM, it is possible that the allocated capacity of DRAM for the particular application is full. We propose two victim page migration policies:

1. Least Recently Used (LRU) based: an LRU list of all DRAM pages together with associated write intensities is kept. A comparison is made between the write intensities of $k\%$ least recently used pages and the lowest write intensity page is chosen as a potential victim from this list. The page is designated as the victim if its write count is lower than the write count of migrating page. Function *VicP_LRU* explains the LRU-based victim page selection algorithm.
2. Most Read Intensive (MRI) based: Function *VicP_MRI* discusses victim selection strategy based on MRI. This technique monitors the DRAM's read-intensive pages and designate the page with the highest read count as the victim page.

4.6 Hardware Overhead

The proposed page migration policies maintain two 8-bit counters to store the write count and write intensity for each page. So in total the overhead associated with pages is 2.25 MB ($= 2*[8bit*(4GB/4\,\mathrm{KB})]$). The migration unit also include a pending queue with 32 entries, each of which is 2 bytes ($32 * 2B$), and an eDRAM buffer with a maximum capacity of four pages, each page of size 4 KB ($4 * 4$ KB). Therefore, the total storage overhead associated with the additional migration unit is 2.26 MB which is approximately 0.06% of total memory size of 4 GB.

5 Evaluation

5.1 Experimental Setup

The proposed page migration policies are implemented using Gem5 full system simulator integrated with NVMain. Three PCM and one DRAM channel hybrid memory is modeled using the memory simulator. To simulate such memory, we have used a large PCM chunk (3 GB) and a small DRAM component (1 GB) for our study. Table 1 displays the specifics of the system parameter that we employed in our experiments. The applications from multi-threaded PARSEC and the multi-programmed SPEC 2006 benchmark suites were used to analyze our results. We use Write-Back Per Kilo Instructions (WBPKI) to calculate the write intensity of applications and categorize the applications based on their write intensities as high, medium and low. We assume that the available DRAM capacity ranges from 20% to 30% for each application. For migration, we take 4KB pages with 32bytes of access granularity for each read/write.

The value of $MigHT$ and $MigIT$ are determined empirically based on their write intensities. The value of eHT is taken as 10% of $MigHT$. The stipulated time ($STime$), which determines the maximum amount of time a page can remain in eDRAM, is determined empirically. The sensitivity analysis for both $MigHT$ and $STime$ is given in Section.

To conduct a performance analysis of our proposed approach, we considered the following techniques:

1. **MoST:** Migrate on Surpassing Threshold is taken as the baseline technique which migrates a page when the write count surpasses a predefined threshold. This is a representation for all threshold-based techniques.
2. **UIMigrate** [8]**:** An existing page migration technique which dynamically update the threshold and migrate pages with write count greater than threshold in regular intervals.
3. **OntheFlyMig** [9]**:** An existing page migration policy that immediately migrates the pages when the write count exceeds a threshold and the threshold is updated with the highest access count on the start of each migration.
4. **AcPruMig:** Our proposed technique which accurately identifies the hot page by migrating the highest write count page to an eDRAM buffer and find the correctness the hot page by observing the write access within a stipulated time. We have considered two variations for *AcPruMig* based on the victim page selection policy: (a) *AcPruMig_LRU*, which uses LRU for DRAM victim selection (b) AcPruMig_MRI, which use MRI for DRAM victim selection.
5. **WiPruMig:** Our proposed technique which migrate write-intensive page directly to DRAM after comparing with a predefined intensity threshold.

Table 1. System Parameters

Components	Parameters
Processor	Quad-core, ALPHA,X86
L1 Cache	Private, 32 kB SRAM split I/D caches, 2-way associative, 64B block
L2 Cache	Private, 512 kB SRAM, 64B block, 8-way associative
Main Memory	PCM: 3 GB, 3 channels, 32 entry request queue Memory Controller: FR-FCFS DRAM: 1 GB, Single channel Memory Controller: FR-FCFS
Memory Latency [7,26]	PCM :: Read = 100 ns, Write = 350 ns DRAM:: Read = 50 ns, Write = 50 ns eDRAM:: Read = 15 ns, Write = 15 ns
Energy [26,27]	PCM :: Read = 0.2nJ/bit, Write=1 nJ/bit DRAM:: Read=0.1 nJ/bit, Write=0.1 nJ/bit eDRAM:: Read = 0.02 nJ/bit, Write = 0.02 nJ/bit
Benchmarks and their Classifications: SPEC2006: lbm (high), sjeng (high), mcf(medium) PARSEC: canneal (medium), x264 (low) SPEC-Mixes: **Mix-High**: gobmk,lbm,sjeng,libquantum; **Mix-Low**: namd,calculix,milc,gromacs;	

5.2 Results

Memory Service Time. Memory service time, or the average amount of time required to complete a memory request, is used to quantify memory performance. In Fig. 6, the normalized memory service time for the existing and proposed policies are shown. The memory service time has improved by 53%, 54% and 63% for AcPruMig_LRU, AcPruMig_MRI, and WiPruMig, respectively, over the baseline, while UIMigrate has only improved by 45% and OntheFlyMig has improved by 47%. The controlled migration results in a reduction of the total memory service time. Reducing the number of pointless migrations and, consequently, the memory service time is achieved by precisely identifying migration candidates by first migrating to eDRAM and subsequently to DRAM. The proposed WiPruMig achieves better improvement in memory service time over AcPruMig. This is by monitoring the present memory behavior by observing the write intensity of pages and identify high intensive migration candidate pages. These pages are directly migrated to DRAM to maximize the hits in DRAM. WiPruMig improves memory service time by 9% over AcPruMig technique. Among the proposed AcPruMig variants, AcPruMig_MRI performs better on read-intensive benchmarks such as *mcf, canneal.*

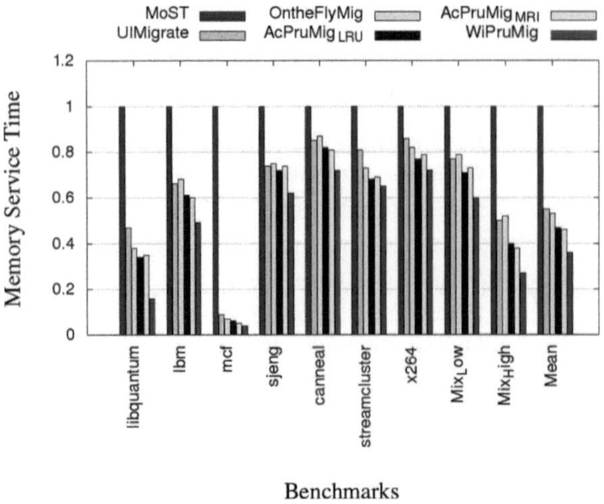

Fig. 6. Normalized Memory Service Time (lesser is better)

- Write intensive benchmarks such as *lbm*, and *sjeng* exhibits higher improvements in memory service time than the benchmarks with low write intensity (*streamcluster*, *x264*). The improvement in memory service time for WiPruMig is 51% for *lbm* and 28% for *x264*.
- For multi-programmed workloads, the memory service time improvement for WiPruMig is 72% for *Mix-High*, and 40% for *Mix-Low*.
- The multi-threaded workloads are medium or low write intensive and *canneal* performs better than the low intensive *x264*. For *canneal*, WiPruMig improves memory service time by 28% and AcPruMig improves memory service time by 19%. Similalry for *x264*, the improvement is 23% and 28% respectively for WiPruMig and AcPruMig.

Energy Delay Product (EDP). Energy Delay Product (EDP) is used to evaluate the energy-time trade off. A lower EDP value suggests that energy savings outweigh the proportional decrease in execution time. Figure 7 illustrates EDP obtained for existing and proposed policies normalized over MoST. While UIMigrate and OntheFlyMig only lower EDP by 32% and 39%, respectively, the proposed AcPruMig_LRU, AcPruMig_MRI and WiPruMig improve EDP by 53%, 54% and 62% over MoST.

Multi-threaded Workloads:
When compared to other multi-threaded workloads, *canneal* exhibits the highest EDP improvement of 51% for WiPruMig. This is due to the fact that *canneal* have a high WBPKI among multi-threaded workloads. Out of all the multi-threaded workloads, *streamcluster* exhibits the least improvement in EDP as 27%.

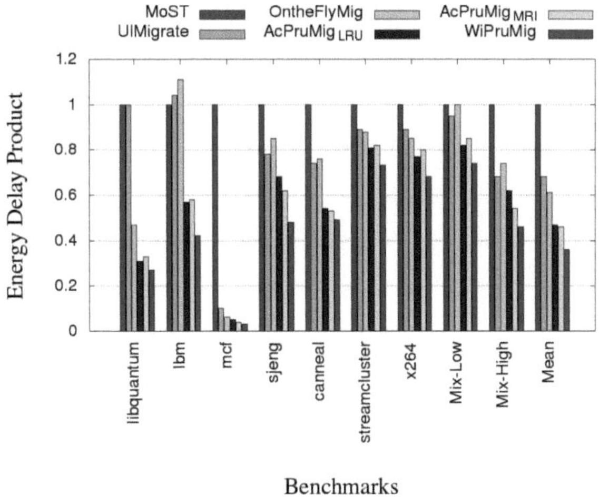

Fig. 7. Normalized Energy Delay Product (EDP) (lesser is better)

Multi-programmed Workloads:
Compared to low intensive benchmark, high intensive benchmark exhibits a significant improvement in EDP when multi-programmed workloads are seen. AcPruMig and WiPruMig improve EDP by 19% and 25% for *Mix-Low*, respectively. Further, the EDP improvement for *Mix-High* is 53% for WiPruMig and 46% for AcPruMig.

With the use of an eDRAM buffer and prudent migration candidate selection based on both write count and write intensity, the proposed AcPruMig and WiPruMig were able to enhance EDP significantly.

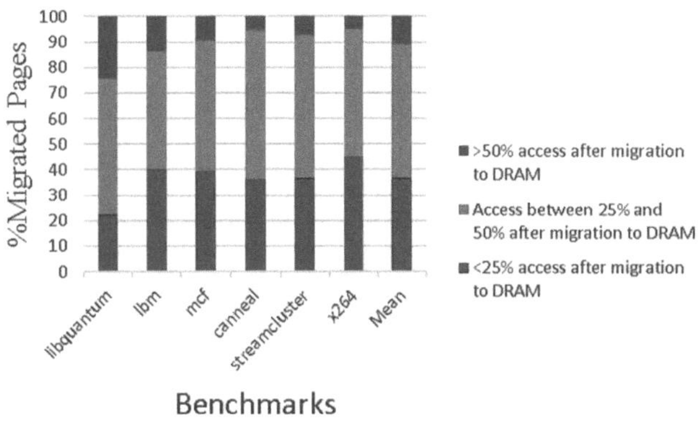

Fig. 8. For the pages migrated to DRAM, the distribution of accesses using **AcPruMig** to these pages: in the ranges of (i) <25%, (ii) 25%-50%, (iii) >50%

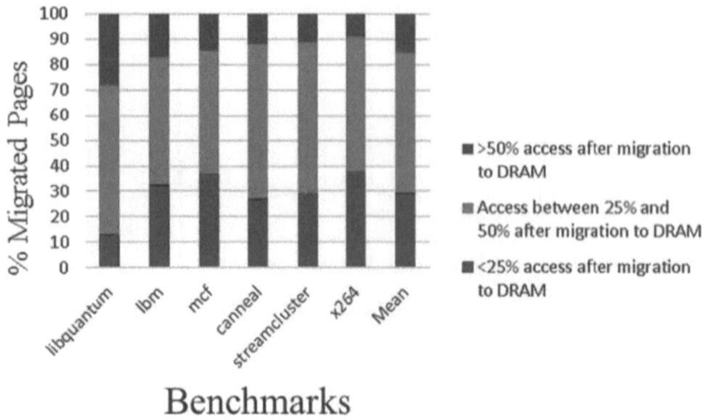

Fig. 9. For the pages migrated to DRAM, the distribution of accesses using **WiPruMig** to these pages: in the ranges of (i) <25%, (ii) 25%–50%, (iii) >50%

Distribution of Overall Accesses to Migrated Pages. As demonstrated in Fig. 4, when the migration is carried out via MoST, the number of pages with less than 25% access is large. With our proposed AcPruMig and WiPruMig, the access distribution for the migrated PCM pages is shown in Fig. 8 and 9. The figures show that both AcPruMig and WiPruMig could obtain a higher access percentage for all migrated pages by limiting the number of rewardless migrations. Our aim to reduce the percentage of pages receiving <25% accesses and increase those for higher access percentages.

For AcPruMig, the pages with access rate below 25%, between 25% and 50% and above 50% are respectively, 36%, 52% and 10%.

In WiPruMig, the pages with access rates below 25% reduce from 36% to 29.5%, those with access rates between 25% and 50% increase (as expected) from 52% to 55.5%, and those with access rates above 50% increase from 10% to 15%.

The judicious identification of page migration candidates based on write intensity and migrating pages through eDRAM helps both AcPruMig and WiPruMig to improve access percentage in DRAM. This leads to an improved memory service time.

Distribution of Accesses to Migration Candidate Pages. The proposed methods aim to optimize memory service time by prudently identifying the hot page to maximize DRAM hits. To demonstrate the effect of our method, Figs. 10 and 11 present the access count for migrated pages at different types of memory. The page's access count percentage is split into four categories: (i) when the page is loaded in PCM, (ii) when the page is in eDRAM, (iii) when the page is in DRAM and (iv) when the migrated page is returned back to PCM. The effectiveness of our selection of migration candidate pages is confirmed by the significant increase in access after moving to DRAM for the migrated pages.

The proposed AcPruMig method shows the access count of 48.21% after migrating to DRAM whereas the count is only 10.9% when the page is in eDRAM

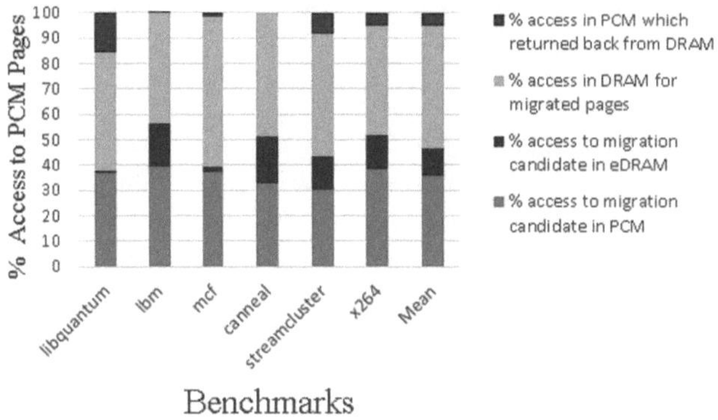

Fig. 10. Distribution of accesses using AcPruMig to migration candidate pages: (i) while in PCM, (ii) when moved to eDRAM, (iii) when migrated to DRAM, (iv) if returned back to PCM from DRAM.

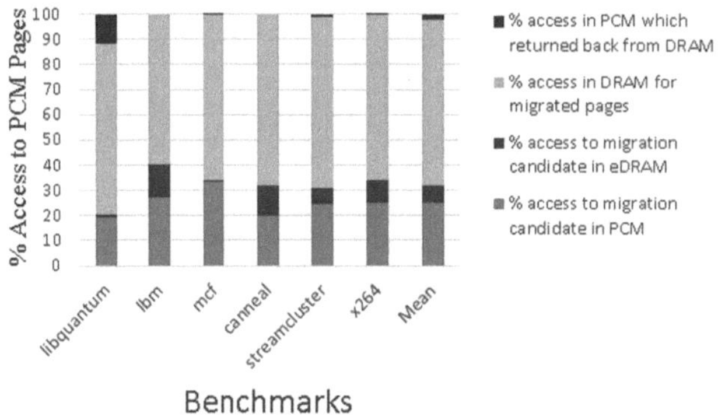

Fig. 11. Distribution of accesses using WiPruMig to migration candidate pages: (i) while in PCM, (ii) when moved to eDRAM, (iii) when migrated to DRAM, (iv) if returned back to PCM from DRAM.

and is 35.74% when the page is in PCM as shown in Fig. 10. This shows that hot pages are accurately identified by eDRAM and migrated to DRAM at the appropriate moment.

Similarly, proposed WiPruMig exhibits an access count of 65.89% after moving to DRAM, compared to only 7.03% while the page is in eDRAM and 24.86% when it is in PCM as depicted in Fig. 11. WiPruMig maximizes the access in DRAM by migrating write-intensive pages directly to DRAM as early as possible. Furthermore, after going back to PCM as a victim, the access count is only 5.15% for AcPruMig and is 2.2% for WiPruMig, demonstrating the effectiveness of our victim page selection technique.

Distribution of Migrated Pages. Figures 12 and 13 present the number of page migrations for both proposed AcPruMig and WiPruMig. The migrations are

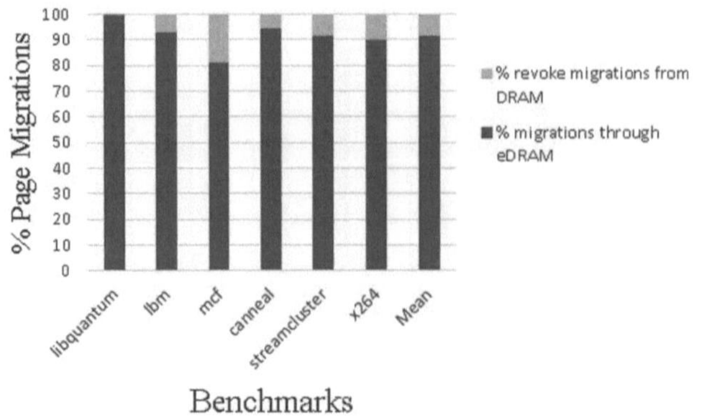

Fig. 12. Percentage distribution of migrated pages using AcPruMig: (i) through eDRAM to DRAM, (ii) Returning back to PCM from DRAM.

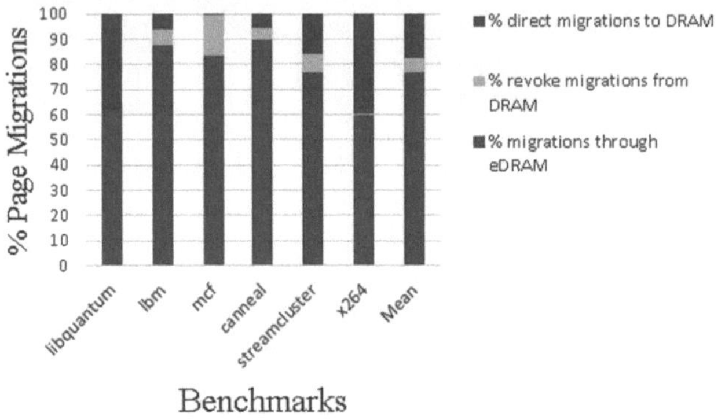

Fig. 13. Percentage distribution of migrated pages using AcPruMig: (i) through eDRAM to DRAM, (ii) Directly to DRAM, (iii) Returning back to PCM from DRAM.

classified to (i) migration to eDRAM, (ii) migration from eDRAM to DRAM, (iii) revoke migration to PCM and (iv) direct migration from PCM to DRAM. In the proposed AcPruMig, there is no direct migration from PCM to DRAM. All the hot pages will go through eDRAM before moving to DRAM. In contrast, write-intensive hot pages in WiPruMig are moved directly from PCM to DRAM under the presumption that they would receive sufficient access during the residency in eDRAM. This early migration of write-intensive pages maximizes the hits in DRAM and improve memory service time further.

From the figures we can observe that the percentage of direct migrations from PCM to DRAM is 0% for AcPruMig and 17% for WiPruMig. However, the proposed WiPruMig perform 76% migrations from eDRAM to PCM. Remaining 5% not enough hot pages are revoked to PCM from eDRAM. While AcPruMig perform 91% migrations from eDRAM to PCM and 8% revoke migrations from eDRAM to PCM.

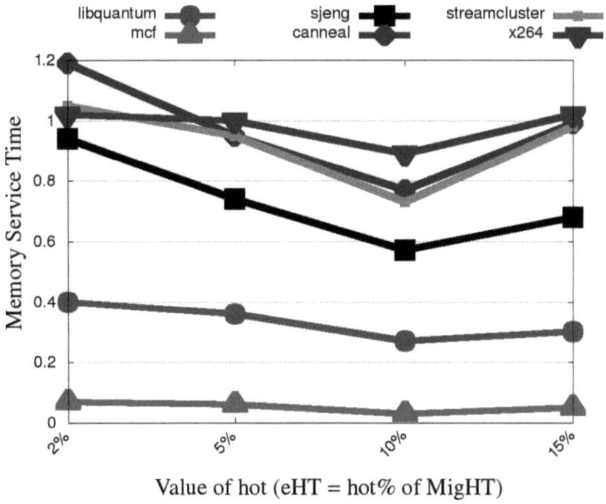

Fig. 14. Sensitivity Analysis for *hot* ($eHT = hot\%$ of $MigHT$)

5.3 Sensitivity Analysis

***1) Sensitivity Analysis for hot%*:** AcPruMig has adopted the eDRAM hot threshold (eHT) to accurately select the migration candidate page. Migration candidate pages to DRAM are selected as actual hot pages if they receive more writes than *eHT* during their residency in eDRAM within the allotted time. We use *hot%* of *MigHT* as the value of *eHT*. The proposed method tries to maximize the hits in DRAM and thus improve the memory service time due to smaller memory access latency for DRAM. Thus, the effectiveness of migration is indicated by the reduced memory service time and lower the memory service time better is the selection. The memory service time obtained for various values of *hot* is shown in Fig. 14.

Pages that are not hot enough also migrate when the value of *hot* is small as a small value of *hot* indicate a small value for *eHT*. Memory service time increases as a result of this pointless migration. If the value of *hot* is large, then we put harder restrictions on categorizing the eDRAM page as hot. Memory service time rises as a result of several revokes from eDRAM to PCM. Harder limitations are applied when classifying an eDRAM page as hot when *hot* is high. Memory service time rises as a result of several revokes from eDRAM to PCM. It can be observed from the figure that for the majority of benchmarks, $hot = 10\%$ yields better results. To accurately determine the migration candidate, AcPruMig choose $hot = 10\%$ to conduct the experiments.

2) Sensitivity Analysis for STime: The proposed AcPruMig technique stores the hot page from PCM in the eDRAM buffer for a predetermined amount of time (*STime*) in order to precisely determine the hotness of the page. The hot page is moved to DRAM if it receives more writes than *eHT* in a given time frame. It is revoked to PCM otherwise. The effect of *STime* on memory service time for different benchmarks is shown in Fig. 15. The advantage of migration can be seen by the decrease in memory service time, since migration maximizes hits in DRAM.

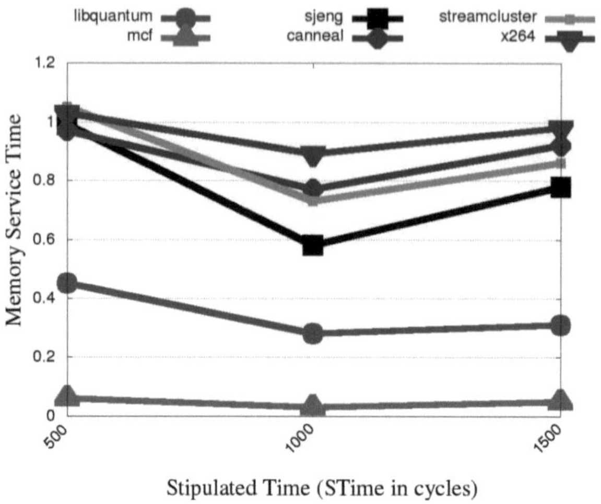

Fig. 15. Sensitivity Analysis for *STime*

If *STime* is large, PCM hot pages will stay in eDRAM for a long time, which will hinder hot page migration to DRAM. As the write-intensive pages cannot move to DRAM, this increases the memory servicing time. Furthermore, even if they are not actually hot enough to migrate to DRAM, the hot pages in eDRAM may cause the write access count to exceed *eHT* within the large value of *STime*.

If *STime* is small, a truly hot page, on the other hand, might be revoked to PCM, as it not reach *eHT* number of writes in *STime*. Moreover, a genuinely hot page will get migrated again to eDRAM in near future and lead to increase memory service time. The graph shows that for all benchmarks, $STime = 1000$cycles is yielding better results.

3) Sensitivity Analysis for eDRAM Size: To judiciously identify migrating pages, AcPruMig migrate hot pages initially to eDRAM buffer and then to DRAM. The pages reside in the eDRAM buffer for a predefined time (*STime*) and if they receive more than *eHT* number of writes it will migrate to DRAM. Otherwise the page is revoked to PCM. The number of pages which can reside in eDRAM at a time is dependent on the size of eDRAM.

If the size of eDRAM (*eSize*) is small, only less number of pages can reside in eDRAM, and cause some pages which have number of writes greater than *MigHT* to wait in the pending queue for migration. Therefore, some write-intensive hot pages still remain in PCM and increase memory service time due to the high write latency of PCM. If *eSize* is large, more number of pages can migrate to eDRAM. This may lead to large number of revoke migration as all pages which are migrated to eDRAM may not receive enough write requests to migrate to DRAM. Also, large *eSize* cause high storage overhead. The figure indicates that $eSize = 4$ is providing better results for all benchmarks (Fig. 16).

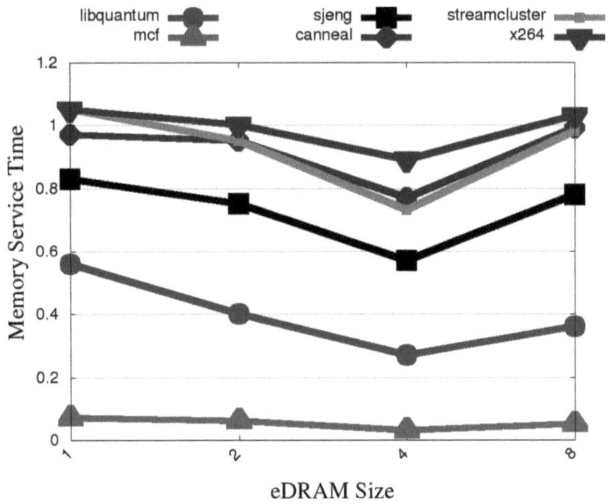

Fig. 16. Sensitivity Analysis for *eDRAM size*

Table 2. Advantage of write-intensity based direct migration from PCM to DRAM

Method	% Improvement in Memory Service Time	%Improvement in EDP
AcPruMig	54	54
WiPruMig	63	62

5.4 Discussion

The proposed AcPruMig and WiPruMig migrate pages through eDRAM based on write count. The optimized WiPruMig migrate write-intensive pages directly to DRAM to maximize the hits in DRAM. The advantage of selecting the page migration candidates based on write intensity and migrating the highest write-intensive page to DRAM helps to improve memory service time. The direct migration to DRAM is performed with the assumption that such write-intensive pages receive enough write requests during their stay in eDRAM and consequently migrate to DRAM. This avoids unnecessary migration through eDRAM

Table 3. Comparison of access percentage for proposed and baseline technique

Method	For the pages migrated to DRAM, the distribution of accesses		
	<25% lesser is better	Between 25% and 50% more is better	>50% more is better
MoST	70	23	7
AcPruMig	36	52	10
WiPruMig	29	55	15

and maximizes the hits in DRAM which leads to improved memory service time. Table 2 shows the improvement in memory service time, EDP and percentage of accesses while the PCM page is migrated to DRAM. The values are normalised with the MoST technique. From the table, we can infer that WiPruMig performs better than AcPruMig by directly migrating write-intensive pages to DRAM. The memory service time and EDP of WiPruMig are 9%, and 8% respectively, over AcPruMig.

Table 3 presents the access distribution of pages migrated to DRAM. The objective of the proposed prudent page migration technique is to maximize the access in DRAM. It can be observed from the table that both the proposed methods improve DRAM access percentage compared to the existing MoST technique. The reduction in average number of pages with access below 25% is 34 for AcPruMig and is 41 for WiPruMig. While the access between 25% and 50% is increased by 29% for AcPruMig and increased by 32% for WiPruMig. Similarly, the average access above 50% is improved by 3% and 8% respectively for AcPruMig and WiPruMig. The judicious selection of write-intensity based page migration candidate selection and migration through eDRAM helps to timely migrate pages and maximize hits in DRAM.

6 Conclusion

Traditional DRAM memory systems could be replaced with emerging non-volatile memories due to the limitation on scalability. These non-volatile memories offer low leakage power and high density, but they also have low write endurance, high write latency, and high energy consumption. In order to take advantage of both memory types, hybrid memory systems-a combination of DRAM and non-volatile memories-arose. It is better to place write-intensive pages in the DRAM memory partition since it has lower write latency than the non-volatile memory partition. This in turn improve the memory service time. To enhance the performance of a hybrid memory system, page migration is a technique that moves pages between the memory partitions. Two of the most significant challenges in page migration are choosing candidates for the migration and determining when it is best to move pages. Migrating write-intensive pages from NVM to DRAM helps to improve the execution time of applications.

To accurately identify the page migration candidate, the proposed prudent page migration techniques use eDRAM buffer as a mediator and also select candidate based on write-intensity. To migrate hot page from PCM to DRAM, the first method AcPruMig uses a faster eDRAM memory as a mediator to determine the correctness of hot page identification. The goal of our proposed AcPruMig approach is to minimize rewardless page migrations to DRAM by taking note of the hot page during its migration from PCM to eDRAM. The second method WiPruMig maximizes the benefit of migration by judiciously migrating write-intensive hot pages directly to DRAM. This direct migration of write-intensive pages avoid needless migration to eDRAM of those pages that will surely migrate to DRAM. This timely migration to DRAM maximizes the hits in DRAM and improves memory service time.

The results of the simulated-based studies show that, in comparison to the baseline technique, the proposed AcPruMig and WiPruMig method improve EDP by 54% and 62%, respectively. The improvement in memory service time is by 53% and 64% for the proposed AcPruMig and WiPruMig. The look-before-you-leap AcPruMig approach helps in avoiding unnecessary migrations whereas WiPruMig migrate write-intensive pages directly to DRAM to maximizes the hits in DRAM.

References

1. Binkert, N., et al.: The gem5 simulator. ACM SIGARCH Comput. Archit. News **39**(2), 1–7 (2011)
2. Poremba, M., Zhang, T., Xie, Y.: NVMain 2.0: a user-friendly memory simulator to model (non-) volatile memory systems. IEEE Comput. Archit. Lett. **14**(2), 140–143 (2015)
3. Henning, J.L.: SPEC CPU2006 benchmark descriptions. ACM SIGARCH Comput. Archit. News **34**(4), 1–17 (2006)
4. Bienia, C., Kumar, S., Singh, J.P., Li, K.: The parsec benchmark suite: characterization and architectural implications. In: Proceedings of the 17th International Conference on Parallel Architectures and Compilation Techniques, pp. 72–81 (2008)
5. Mittal, S.: A survey of architectural techniques for dram power management. Int. J. High Perform. Syst. Archit. **4**(2), 110–119 (2012)
6. Mutlu, O., Subramanian, L.: Research problems and opportunities in memory systems. Supercomput. Front. Innov. **1**(3), 19–55 (2014)
7. Salkhordeh, R., Mutlu, O., Asadi, H.: An analytical model for performance and lifetime estimation of hybrid dram-nvm main memories. IEEE Trans. Comput. **68**(8), 1114–1130 (2019)
8. Tan, Y., Wang, B., Yan, Z., Deng, Q., Chen, X., Liu, D.: Uimigrate: adaptive data migration for hybrid non-volatile memory systems. In: IEEE Design, Automation & Test in Europe Conference & Exhibition (DATE), pp. 860–865. IEEE (2019)
9. Islam, M., Adavally, S., Scrbak, M., Kavi, K.: On-the-fly page migration and address reconciliation for heterogeneous memory systems. ACM J. Emerg. Technol. Comput. Syst. (JETC) **16**(1), 1–27 (2020)

10. Kokolis, A., Skarlatos, D., Torrellas, J.: Pageseer: using page walks to trigger page swaps in hybrid memory systems. In: 2019 IEEE International Symposium on High Performance Computer Architecture (HPCA), pp. 596–608. IEEE (2019)
11. Qureshi, M.K., Srinivasan, V., Rivers, J.A.: Scalable high performance main memory system using phase-change memory technology. In: Proceedings of the 36th Annual International Symposium on Computer Architecture, pp. 24–33. ACM (2009)
12. Park, H., Kim, C., Yoo, S., Park, C.: Filtering dirty data in dram to reduce pram writes. In: 2015 IFIP/IEEE International Conference on Very Large Scale Integration (VLSI-SoC), pp. 319–324. IEEE (2015)
13. Khouzani, H.A., Yang, C., Hu, J.: Improving performance and lifetime of dram-PCM hybrid main memory through a proactive page allocation strategy. In: The 20th Asia and South Pacific Design Automation Conference, pp. 508–513. IEEE (2015)
14. Yoon, S.-K., Yun, J., Kim, J.-G., Kim, S.-D.: Self-adaptive filtering algorithm with PCM-based memory storage system. ACM Trans. Embed. Comput. Syst. (TECS) **17**(3), 1–23 (2018)
15. Wang, X., et al.: Supporting superpages and lightweight page migration in hybrid memory systems. ACM Trans. Archit. Code Optim. (TACO) **16**(2), 1–26 (2019)
16. Lee, S., Bahn, H., Noh, S.H.: Clock-DWF: a write-history-aware page replacement algorithm for hybrid PCM and dram memory architectures. IEEE Trans. Comput. **63**(9), 2187–2200 (2013)
17. Su, C., et al.: HPMC: an energy-aware management system of multi-level memory architectures. In: Proceedings of the 2015 International Symposium on Memory Systems, pp. 167–178. ACM (2015)
18. Salkhordeh, R., Asadi, H.: An operating system level data migration scheme in hybrid dram-NVM memory architecture. In: Design, Automation & Test in Europe Conference & Exhibition (DATE), pp. 936–941. IEEE (2016)
19. Chen, X., et al.: The design of an efficient swap mechanism for hybrid dram-nvm systems. In: International Conference on Embedded Software (EMSOFT), pp. 1–10. IEEE (2016)
20. Liu, H., Liu, R., Liao, X., Jin, H., He, B., Zhang, Y.: Object-level memory allocation and migration in hybrid memory systems. IEEE Trans. Comput. **69**(9), 1401–1413 (2020)
21. Fu, Y., Lu, Y., Chen, Z., Wu, Y., Xiao, N.: Design and simulation of content-aware hybrid dram-PCM memory system. IEEE Trans. Parallel Distrib. Syst. **33**(7), 1666–1677 (2021)
22. Peng, Z., Feng, D., Chen, J., Hu, J., Huang, C.: AGDM: an adaptive granularity data migration strategy for hybrid memory systems. In: 2023 Design, Automation & Test in Europe Conference & Exhibition (DATE), pp. 1–6. IEEE (2023)
23. Li, Y., Ghose, S., Choi, J., Sun, J., Wang, H., Mutlu, O.: Utility-based hybrid memory management. In: 2017 IEEE International Conference on Cluster Computing (CLUSTER), pp. 152–165. IEEE (2017)
24. Aswathy, N.S., Bhavanasi, S., Sarkar, A., Kapoor, H.K.: SRS-Mig: selection and run-time scheduling of page migration for improved response time in hybrid PCM-dram memories. In: 2022 Proceedings of the Great Lakes Symposium on VLSI, pp. 217–222 (2022)
25. Gupta, A., Aswathy, N.S., Kapoor, H.K.: Look before you leap: an access-based prudent page migration for hybrid memories. In: 2023 IFIP/IEEE 31st International Conference on Very Large Scale Integration (VLSI-SoC), pp. 1–6. IEEE (2023)

26. Manohar, S.S., Kapoor, H.K.: Dynamic reconfiguration of embedded-dram caches employing zero data detection based refresh optimisation. J. Syst. Architect. **100**, 101648 (2019)
27. Lee, B.C., Ipek, E., Mutlu, O., Burger, D.: Architecting phase change memory as a scalable dram alternative. In: Proceedings of the 36th Annual International Symposium on Computer Architecture, pp. 2–13 (2009)
28. Kotra, J.B., Zhang, H., Alameldeen, A.R., Wilkerson, C., Kandemir, M.T.: Chameleon: A dynamically reconfigurable heterogeneous memory system. In: 2018 51st Annual IEEE/ACM International Symposium on Microarchitecture (MICRO), pp. 533–545. IEEE (2018)
29. Vasilakis, E., Papaefstathiou, V., Trancoso, P., Sourdis, I.: LLC-guided data migration in hybrid memory systems. In: 2019 IEEE International Parallel and Distributed Processing Symposium (IPDPS), pp. 932–942. IEEE (2019)
30. Adavally, S., Islam, M., Kavi, K.: Dynamically adapting page migration policies based on applications' memory access behaviors. ACM J. Emerg. Technol. Comput. Syst. (JETC) **17**(2), 1–24 (2021)

Efficient Depth Optimization in Quantum Addition and Modular Arithmetic with Ling Structure

Siyi Wang(✉) and Anupam Chattopadhyay

College of Computing and Data Science, Nanyang Technological University, Singapore, Singapore
siyi002@e.ntu.edu.sg

Abstract. Improving the performance of quantum adder is an important technical challenge with major impact on the implementation of efficient, large-scale quantum computing. Continuing along this research direction, we propose a novel parallel-prefix quantum adder based on Ling expansion. We systematically explored classical structures for parallel-prefix adders assessing their suitability to be realized in quantum domain. Furthermore, Ling adder enforces Logical OR and large fan-out, which require innovative solutions. We addressed these challenges to realize the quantum Ling adder, which results in a T-depth of only $O(\log \frac{n}{2})$. This represents a substantial improvement over the previous quantum adders based on parallel prefix structure, which require $O(\log n)$ T-depth. Based on the proposed adder, an efficient quantum modular adder is also demonstrated in this paper, further extending the applicability of our approach. We present extensive theoretical and simulation-based studies to establish our claims.

Keywords: Quantum Computing · Quantum Arithmetic · T-depth Optimization · Carry-lookahead Adder · Ling Adder

1 Introduction

Addition is a fundamental operation in quantum computing, serving as a foundational component of various quantum circuits. It is necessary to explore more efficient and robust quantum adders since they play a crucial role in realization of computationally demanding kernels such as modular exponentiation, thereby improving efficiency of practically relevant quantum algorithms, such as Shor's algorithm [1].

In recent decades, significant research efforts have been devoted to the design and optimization of quantum adders. Initially, Vedral et al. [2] introduced a classical ripple-carry structure into the design of the first ripple-carry quantum adder. Afterward, quantum carry-lookahead adders based on parallel prefix structures were proposed to achieve significant reduction of the T-depth of quantum addition from the $O(n)$) required by ripple-carry adders to logarithmic

Published by Springer Nature Switzerland AG 2024
I. (Abe) M. Elfadel and L. Albasha (Eds.): VLSI-SoC 2023, IFIP AICT 680, pp. 73–89, 2024.
https://doi.org/10.1007/978-3-031-70947-0_4

complexity, i.e., $O(\log(n))$. However, there is an increasing demand for further improvements to reduce the resource requirements of quantum adders, which is being pursued actively [3].

In classical CMOS technology, arithmetic circuits have been studied for a long time. In a notable contribution, Ling [4] proposed a different expansion of the parallel prefix calculation, resulting in a reduced depth. However, this structure has not been exploited in quantum adders yet. This paper proposes a novel quantum adder based on Ling structure, which has the potential to outperform existing structures in T-depth. By thoroughly exploring the unique properties of Ling structure in the quantum world, we develop a quantum Ling adder and a quantum Ling modular adder that significantly reduce resource demands. We encountered several challenges in this research. One significant challenge is the noncopyability of qubits, which posed difficulties in directly translating Ling structure into quantum circuits. Hence, we modified the classical Ling structure, maximizing parallel structures while considering quantum circuit properties. Moreover, our building blocks are refined based on the parallel prefix adder design to address the strict requirements of OR logic in Ling structure.

This paper further extends the quantum ling adder design proposed in the conference paper [5] by introducing a novel quantum modular ling adder. The specific details, experimental results, and discussions are elaborated in Sect. 6. Our main contribution is the exploration of the effectiveness and potential advantages of Ling structure in the quantum world, compared to existing adder designs. Through a comprehensive evaluation of the proposed design by using T-depth (TD), Qubit Count (QC), and T-count (TC), we provide several valuable insights into the strengths and limitations of quantum Ling adder, thereby contributing to the continuous progress of quantum computing field.

2 Previous Works

In this section, we present a review of the relevant research.

In the quantum world, the quantum carry-lookahead adders (CLA) demonstrate superior efficiency by reducing the T-depth to $O(\log n)$ from $O(n)$. In 2004, Draper et al. [6] drew inspiration from classical Parallel Prefix structures and designed the first logarithmic T-depth quantum carry-lookahead adder. This design gained significant attention. Thereby, subsequent research such as several adders designed by Takahashi et al. [7,8] contributed to further optimization of Draper's adder. Moreover, Wang et al. [9] found the Brent-Kung structure [10] is the most efficient choice for quantum adders among all the parallel prefix structures, which we will briefly revisit in the next section.

Apart from parallel prefix structures, Ling structure [4] offers an alternative method to achieving high-speed addition in classical world. By altering the specific rules of propagation and summation in parallel prefix structures, Ling adders significantly decrease the logical levels required for addition, thereby demonstrating superiority over parallel prefix structures. However, currently there is a lack of research related to Ling structure in quantum world.

In this paper, we propose a novel quantum Ling adder and compare it with previous designs. The proposed adder has a T-depth of $O(\log(\frac{n}{2}))$, which is significantly lower than the T-depth of previous parallel prefix-based adders, making our approach a competitive candidate for implementing large-scale quantum addition. Additionally, we present a novel quantum modular Ling adder with reduced T-depth compared to existing modular adders.

3 Integrating Ling Into Parallel Prefix

In this section, the parallel prefix adders and Ling structure are introduced.

3.1 Parallel Prefix Structure

There are various Parallel Prefix structures, including Sklansky, Kogge-Stone, Ladner-Fisher, Brent-Kung, and Han-Carlson. Efficient quantum circuits require minimizing both fan-out and propagate operations, since both of them consume T-gate, which is a very expensive operation in quantum world. Hence, the Brent-Kung structure is frequently selected for quantum adders since its minimal number of propagate operations and low fan-out, making it an optimal choice for quantum propagation.

Draper et al. [6] proposed a quantum adder based on the Brent-Kung structure. For n-bit addition, two fundamental variables p and g are calculated firstly according to (1) and (2), respectively. Since it is impossible for p and g to be simultaneously equal to 1, XOR logic can be used instead of OR logic. In quantum world, XOR logic can be implemented with CNOT gate, which is cheaper than OR logic. Subsequently, the propagation which is denoted as $\circ$ is performed on p and g, based on (3). Then the carries are calculated using the propagated p and g according to (4). Based on the carries, it is straightforward to obtain the corresponding sum.

$$p_i = a_i \oplus b_i \tag{1}$$

$$g_i = a_i \cdot b_i \tag{2}$$

$$g_x, p_x \circ g_y, p_y = g_x + p_x \cdot g_y, p_x \cdot p_y \tag{3}$$

$$c_i = g_i + p_i \cdot c_{i-1} \tag{4}$$

As above, the basic building blocks of quantum Parallel Prefix adders are AND and XOR logics, which can be implemented using CNOT and Toffoli gates.

3.2 Ling Structure

Parallel prefix structure and Ling structure have notable similarities as they both require the pre-calculation of propagation variables and use the Brent-Kung structure for propagation to obtain the final sum. However, Ling structure requires different propagation variables, including pl, gl, and d, as shown in (5),

(6), and (7). After performing Ling precalculation on pl and gl, the corresponding propagation variables p and g can be obtained.

$$pl_i = a_i + b_i \tag{5}$$

$$gl_i = a_i \cdot b_i \tag{6}$$

$$d_i = a_i \oplus b_i \tag{7}$$

Moreover, there are differences in the propagation mechanisms between these two structures. In contrast to the parallel prefix structure, Ling structure uses two parallel Brent-Kung structures, as illustrated in Fig. 1(a) and Fig. 1(b).

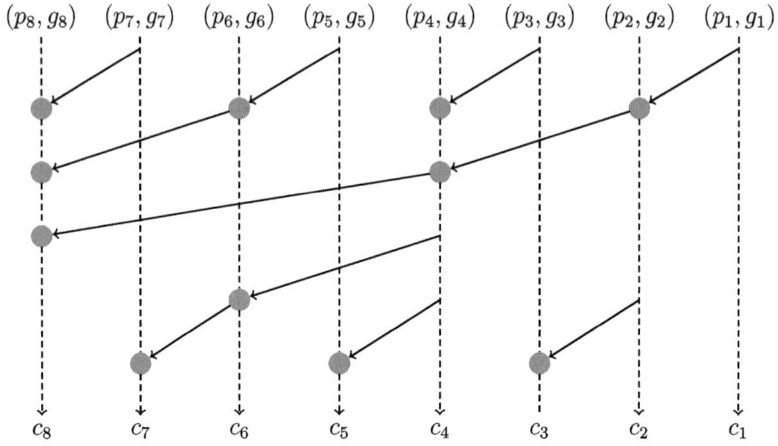

(a) Brent-Kung

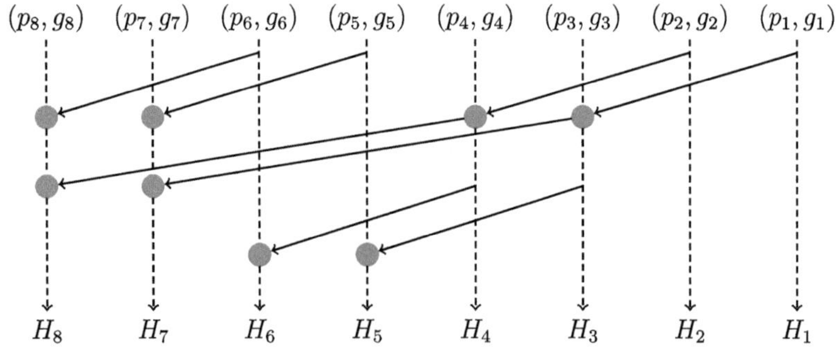

(b) Ling-based Brent-Kung

Fig. 1. Different Brent-Kung Structures

In this section, we only focus on the basic building blocks, whereas the subsequent section will cover other implementation details of the quantum Ling

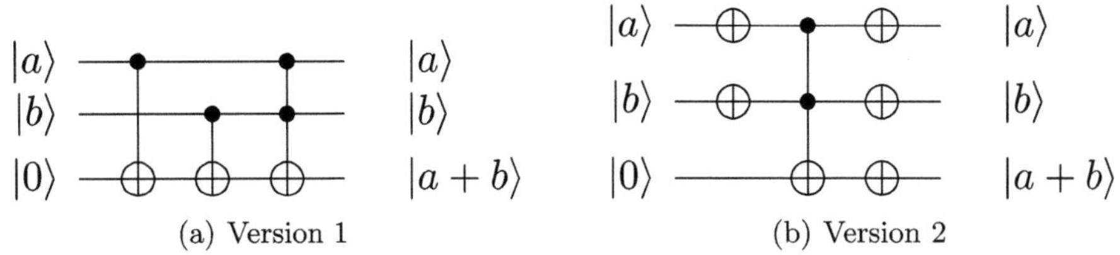

Fig. 2. Quantum Or Gate

structure. Compare with parallel prefix structure, Ling structure has stricter requirements on the OR logic. Specifically, the propagation variables p and g can take four possible values: '00', '01', '10', and '11'. Hence, the OR logic here cannot be simplified to XOR logic. As shown in Fig. 2(a) and Fig. 2(b), we propose two different quantum OR gates. Based on this paper [11], version 2 is used in our design considering the higher cost of two CNOT gates compared to five NOT gates. As mentioned above, apart from the AND and XOR logics, the basic building blocks of our adder also include the quantum OR logic, which is implemented using NOT and Toffoli gates in this paper. Most importantly, the Ling structure demonstrates the remarkable potential to outperform the standard parallel prefix structure both in classical and quantum implementation.

4 The Design of Quantum Ling Adder

In this section, we describe the proposed quantum Ling adder in detail. To begin with, we present the implementation details of each step, followed by a general overview of the entire design.

4.1 Step 1

Firstly, we construct few fundamental blocks for the quantum Ling adder, specifically targeting the computation of pl, gl, and d. It is one of the most basic subcircuits of our adder.

Taking a one-bit addition of a and b as an example, the quantum circuit shown in Fig. 3 uses two ancilla qubits. Specifically, we apply a Toffoli gate with a and b as control qubits and the first ancilla as the target bit to calculate and store the corresponding gl. To calculate and store the corresponding gl, a Toffoli gate is applied with a and b as control qubits and the first ancilla as the target qubit. Subsequently, employing three CNOT gates with the second ancilla as the target qubit and a, b, and gl as control qubits allows the computation of pl. The resulting value of pl is stored in the second ancilla. This approach eliminates the requirement for quantum OR operation, thereby avoiding the requirement for an extra Toffoli gate. Furthermore, d can be obtained by applying a single CNOT gate with a as the control qubit and b as the target qubit. The final state of d is stored in the qubit which initially stored b.

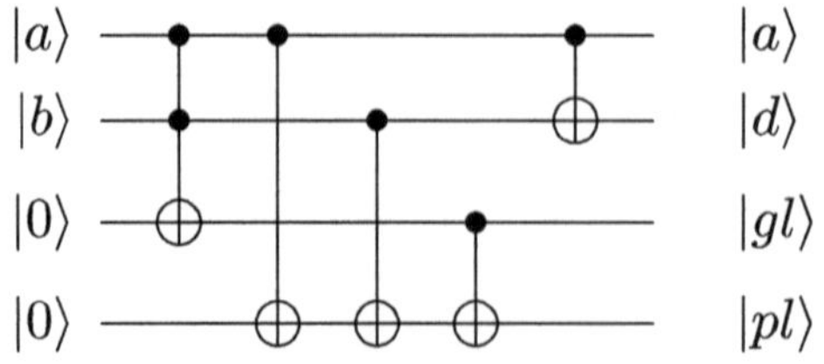

Fig. 3. Calculation of p, g and d.

4.2 Step 2

In this step, we perform a pre-calculation on pl and gl which are calculated in step 1 to obtain the propagation variables p and g. The corresponding equations are provided in (8) and (9).

$$g_i = gl_i + gl_{i-1}, \quad g_0 = gl_0 \tag{8}$$

$$p_i = pl_i \cdot pl_{i-1}, \quad p_0 = p_1 = 0 \tag{9}$$

As shown in Fig. 4(a), the classical Ling pre-calculation cannot be directly implemented in the quantum world since the inability to copy qubits as classical bits. Hence, the pre-calculation is divided into two parts, illustrated in Fig. 4(b) and Fig. 4(c), respectively. This design maximizes the parallel structure while accommodating the inherent properties of qubits, thereby enhancing the overall efficiency. The pre-calculation circuit in Fig. 5 is an example of performing pre-calculation to obtain p_{i-1} and g_i for the $i-th$ addend. It consists of two Toffoli gates and five NOT gates. It is noteworthy that the control and target qubits of these two Toffolis are nonoverlapping, allowing for simultaneous operations within a single time step.

4.3 Step 3

In the third step, the propagation operations are performed on p and g from the previous step to calculate the intermediate variable H, which is crucial in the summation process.

The circuits for P and G propagations are illustrated in Fig. 6. Following Ling-based Brent-Kung structure and using the propagation formulas described in (10), we obtain the propagation results which are denoted as P_{i-1} and G_i for the $i-th$ addend, representing the final values of p and g, respectively. Based on P_{i-1} and G_i, we proceed to calculate the intermediate variable H. Especially, H_0 equals to g_0 as shown in (11), while the formula for H in other positions is provided by (12).

$$g_x, p_{x-1} \circ g_y, p_{y-1} = g_x + p_{x-1} \cdot g_y, p_{x-1} \cdot p_{y-1} \tag{10}$$

$$H_0 = g_0 \tag{11}$$

$$H_i = G_i + P_{i-1} \cdot G_{i-2} \tag{12}$$

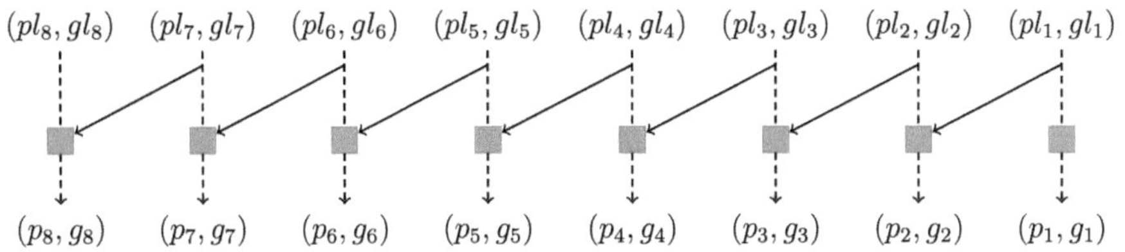

(a) Classical Ling Pre-calculation

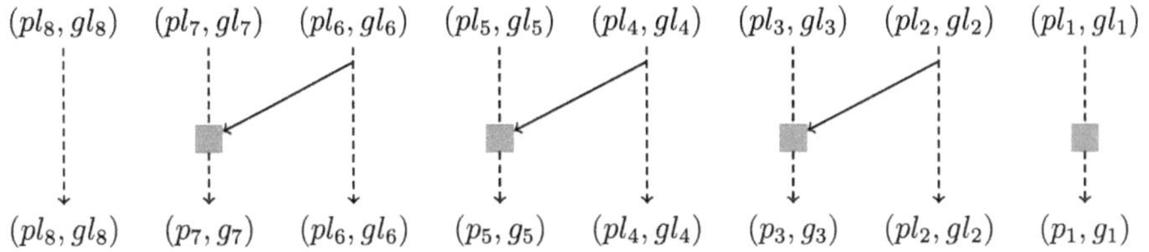

(b) The first part of Quantum Ling Pre-calculation

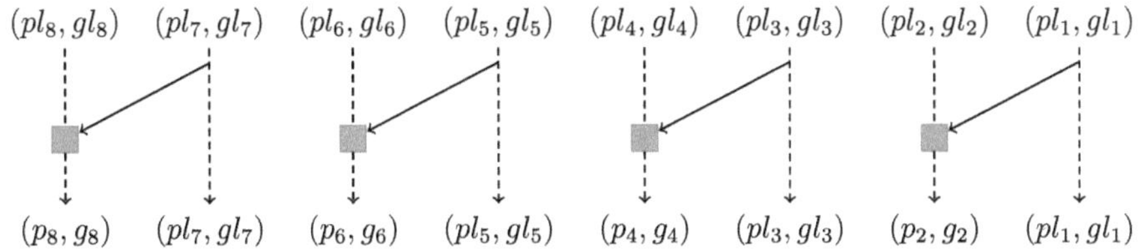

(c) The second part of Quantum Ling Pre-calculation

Fig. 4. Ling Pre-calculation

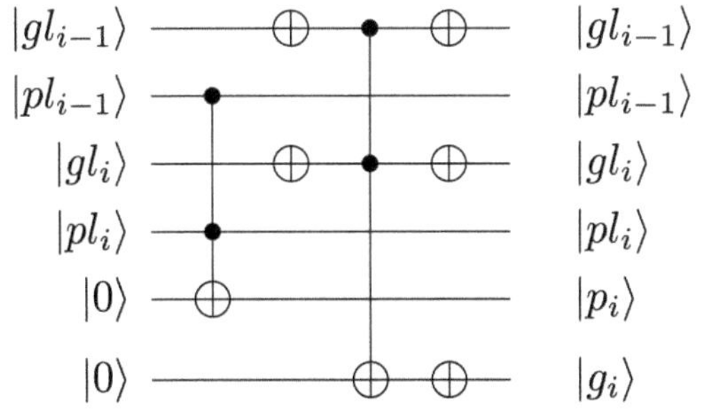

Fig. 5. Pre-calculation of quantum Ling adder

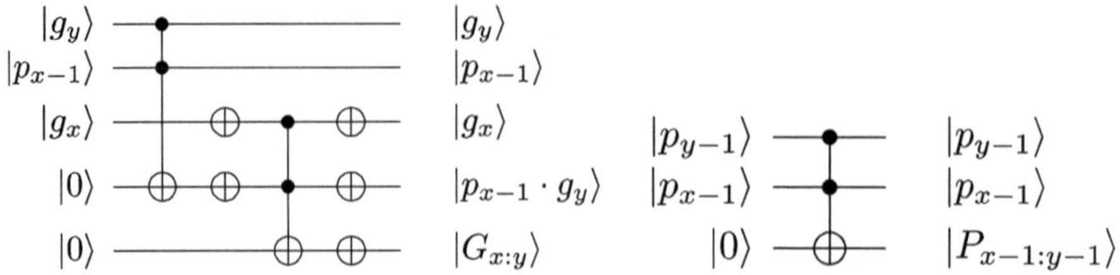

(a) Propagation of G (b) Propagation of P

Fig. 6. Ling Propagation

4.4 Step 4

In this step, we proceed to calculate the final sum, denoted as S. The calculation follows the formulas presented in (13), (14) and (15).

$$S_0 = d_0 \tag{13}$$

$$\begin{aligned} S_i &= \overline{H_{i-1}} \cdot d_i + H_{i-1} \cdot (d_i \oplus pl_{i-1}) \\ &= (H_{i-1} \cdot pl_{i-1}) \oplus d_i \quad ,if \quad 0 < i < n \end{aligned} \tag{14}$$

$$S_n = pl_{n-1} \cdot H_{n-1} \tag{15}$$

For the first bit of the sum S_0, it is equivalent to d_0. For the intermediate qubits of the sum, a circuit which serves as an illustrative example for comprehending the calculation process is provided in Fig. 7(a), only using a Toffoli gate. For the last qubit of S, as shown in Fig. 7(b), it is obtained by using only one Toffoli.

(a) Other bits (b) The last bit

Fig. 7. Summation Circuit

4.5 Uncomputation

In the fifth and sixth steps, we perform the uncomputation of the quantum circuit. This process is important for the resetting and subsequent reuse of ancilla qubits. We aim to maximize the number of uncomputation operations while preserving the final sum S.

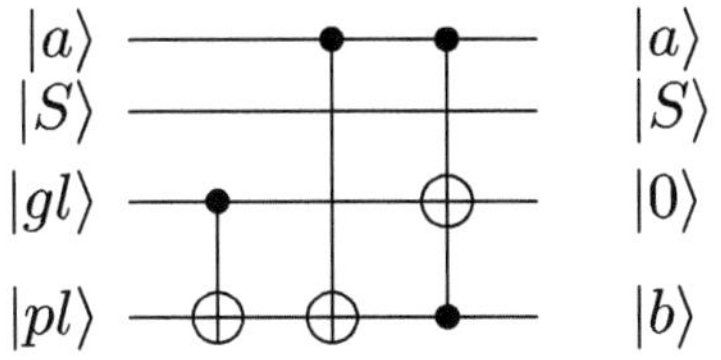

Fig. 8. Uncomputation of p, g and d.

In the fifth step, the circuit is constructed by simply reversing the order of the quantum gated applied in the second step. In the sixth step, as shown in Fig. 8, we perform the uncomputation operations for the first step. Particularly, the four qubits in this figure correspond one by one to the four qubits in Fig. 3, arranged from top to bottom.

4.6 Overall Structure of Quantum Ling Adder

Decomposition Methods.

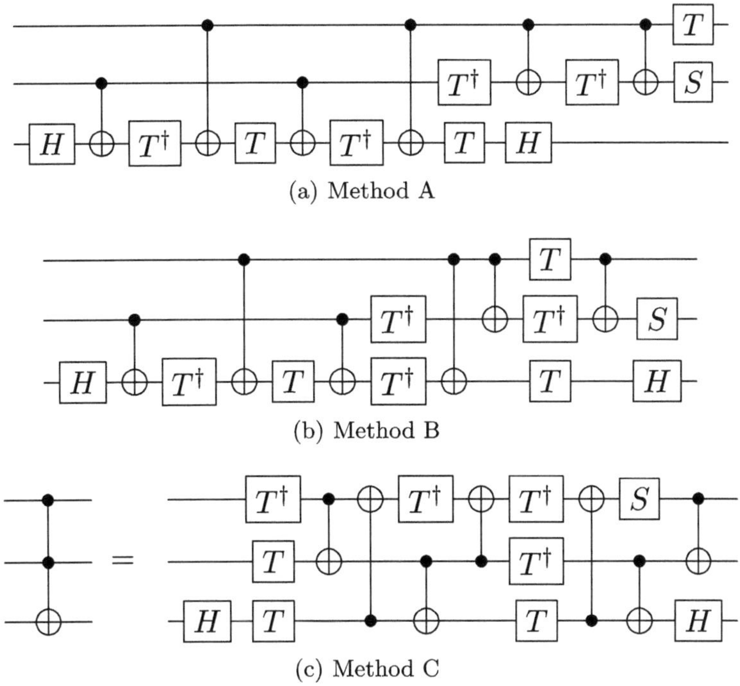

Fig. 9. Decomposition methods of Toffoli gate [12]

Before introducing the overall structure, it is necessary to highlight that the quantum Toffoli gate can be decomposed in various ways. In this work, we mainly took ideas from this work [12] that presented three decomposition methods without introducing extra ancilla qubits. As shown in Fig. 9, there are three general decomposition methods for the Toffoli gate. we can find that all decomposition methods use 7 T gates. Since the proposed quantum ling adder has a high QC, we do not wish to introduce more ancilla qubits by using decomposition methods with ancilla bits. Among Methods A(Fig. 9(a)), B(Fig. 9(b)), and C(Fig. 9(c)), Method C has the highest efficiency because it has the smallest T-depth. Hence, we choose Method C to decompose all the unpaired Toffolis in our work. However, it is essential to acknowledge that the decomposition method can be changed or modified according to specific requirements in other scenarios.

Overall Structure. Our work mainly focuses on the T gate, given its significantly higher cost compared to other quantum gates. Interestingly, Toffoli gate contains T gates. Consequently, a low-cost decomposition method is employed to effectively decompose all the Toffoli gates in our paper. For the decomposition, the method proposed by Selinger [12] is used in our paper. As shown in Fig. 9(c), the corresponding TD and TC are 3 and 7, respectively.

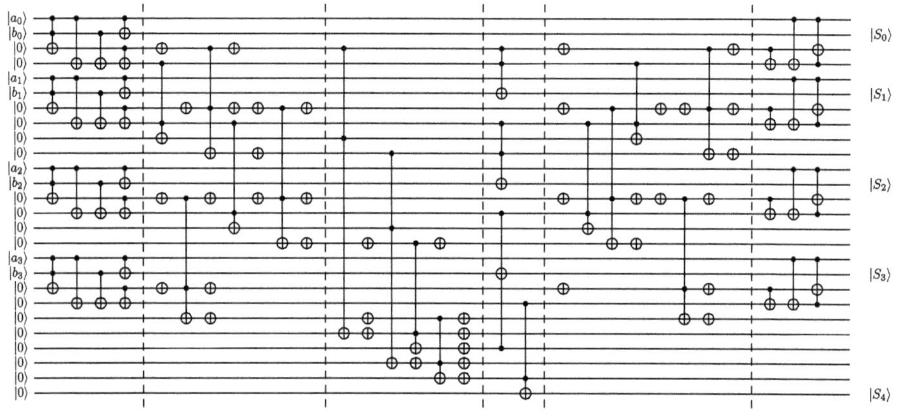

Fig. 10. 4-bit Quantum Ling Adder

By combining the six steps introduced previously, a comprehensive and general construction method is proposed for the quantum Ling adder. A comprehensive example of a complete 4-bit quantum Ling adder is depicted in Fig. 10. In the previous subsections, the specific quantum circuits for each step have been provided in detail. Here, a succinct overview of these steps will be presented, accompanied by a comprehensive cost analysis based on TD, TC, and QC.

Step 1 involves the calculation of pl, gl, and d. For n-bit binary addition, the corresponding TD is 3, TC is $7n$, and QC is $4n$. In Step 2, Ling pre-calculation is performed on pl and gl by using a specific method. For n-bit binary addition, the cost analysis indicates a TD of 6, TC of $14n-21$, and a requirement of $2n-3$ extra ancilla. Proceeding to Step 3, Ling propagation is implemented based on the Brent-Kung structure to obtain the intermediate variable H. The cost analysis is as follows: Initially, in the n-bit Brent-Kung structure, a total of $2n-1-\omega(n)-\lfloor\log(n)\rfloor$ propagation operations are performed with $\lfloor\log(n)\rfloor+\lfloor\log\frac{n}{3}\rfloor+1$ logical levels, where $\omega(n)$ represents $n-\sum_{y=1}^{\infty}\lfloor\frac{n}{2^y}\rfloor$; In Ling-based Brent-Kung structure, the initial structure is extended by incorporating two parallel Brent-Kung structures. $(2n-2-2\omega(\frac{n}{2})-2\lfloor\log(\frac{n}{2})\rfloor)$ propagation operations are executed, with $\lfloor\log\frac{n}{2}\rfloor+\lfloor\log\frac{n}{6}\rfloor+1$ logical levels; The proposed step 3 is designed based on Ling-based Brent-Kung tree structure. The corresponding TD is obtained by multiplying the logical levels of Ling-based Brent-Kung structure by 3 TD for each Toffoli, resulting in $6+6\lfloor\log\frac{n}{2}\rfloor+6\lfloor\log\frac{n}{6}\rfloor$; During propagation, the logical levels of P propagation are two less than those of G propagation. To simplify the formulas, we assume an additional layer of P propagation. Hence, upper bounds for TC and QC can be obtained. Specifically, the upper bound for TC is $42n-56-42\omega(\frac{n}{2})-42\lfloor\log\frac{n}{2}\rfloor$, and the number of extra ancilla is $6n-8-6\omega(\frac{n}{2})-6\lfloor\log\frac{n}{2}\rfloor$. In Step 4, the intermediate variable H is utilized to compute the final sum. For n-bit binary addition, the corresponding TD is 3, TC is $7n$, and one extra ancilla is required. Step 5 involves the uncomputation of Step 2. Similar to Step 2, the corresponding TD is 6, TC is $14n-21$, but no additional ancilla is needed. In the last step, the uncomputation of Step 1 is performed to reset certain ancilla to the initial state $|0\rangle$ with a TD of 3, TC of $7n$, and no extra ancilla requirement.

$$\begin{aligned}\mathrm{TD}=&\overbrace{3}^{\text{Step 1}}+\overbrace{6}^{\text{Step 2}}+\overbrace{6+6\lfloor\log\frac{n}{2}\rfloor+6\lfloor\log\frac{n}{6}\rfloor}^{\text{Step 3}}+\overbrace{3}^{\text{Step 4}}+\overbrace{6}^{\text{Step 5}}+\overbrace{3}^{\text{Step 6}}\\ =&27+6\lfloor\log\frac{n}{2}\rfloor+6\lfloor\log\frac{n}{6}\rfloor\end{aligned}\tag{16}$$

$$\begin{aligned}\mathrm{TC}=&\overbrace{7n}^{\text{Step 1}}+\overbrace{14n-21}^{\text{Step 2}}+\overbrace{42n-56-42\omega(\frac{n}{2})}^{\text{Step 3}}\overbrace{-42\lfloor\log\frac{n}{2}\rfloor}^{\text{Step 3}}+\overbrace{7n}^{\text{Step 4}}+\overbrace{14n-21}^{\text{Step 5}}+\overbrace{7n}^{\text{Step 6}}\\ =&91n-42\omega(\frac{n}{2})-42\lfloor\log\frac{n}{2}\rfloor-98\end{aligned}\tag{17}$$

$$\begin{aligned}\mathrm{QC}=&\overbrace{4n}^{\text{Step 1}}+\overbrace{2n-3}^{\text{Step 2}}+\overbrace{6n-8-6\omega(\frac{n}{2})-6\lfloor\log\frac{n}{2}\rfloor}^{\text{Step 3}}+\overbrace{1}^{\text{Step 4}}+\overbrace{0}^{\text{Step 5}}+\overbrace{0}^{\text{Step 6}}\\ =&12n-6\omega(\frac{n}{2})-6\lfloor\log\frac{n}{2}\rfloor-10\end{aligned}\tag{18}$$

As mentioned above, the total cost of these six steps can be obtained by summing the individual TDs, TCs, and QCs, as represented by (16), (17), and (18), respectively. For n-bit adder, the total TD, TC, and QC for the entire circuit are $27+6\lfloor\log\frac{n}{2}\rfloor+6\lfloor\log\frac{n}{6}\rfloor$, $91n-42\omega(\frac{n}{2})-42\lfloor\log\frac{n}{2}\rfloor-98$, and $12n-6\omega(\frac{n}{2})-6\lfloor\log\frac{n}{2}\rfloor-10$, respectively.

It can be observed that the quantum Ling adder has been extended and improved based on the quantum parallel prefix adder. In the next section, we will discuss the performance of our adder and compare it with other prominent works.

5 Experimental Results and Discussion

In this section, we describe the performance of the proposed quantum Ling adder and provide comprehensive discussions.

For the experimental implementation, the quantum Ling adder is implemented using Qiskit 0.23.3 and Qasm Simulator[1]. Our design exhibits remarkable scalability of the quantum Ling structure, which enables automatic construction of adders with large bit-sizes, while respecting the technology constraints such as limited fanout.

Table 1. Performance analysis of different quantum in-place adders. The formula for $\omega(n)$ is $\omega(n) = n - \sum_{y=1}^{\infty} \lfloor \frac{n}{2^y} \rfloor$, where n denotes the bit-width of the addend.

Adder	Year	TC	TD	QC
Draper In-place CLA [6]	2004	$70n - 21\omega(n) - 21\omega(n-1)$ $-21\lfloor \log n \rfloor - 21\lfloor \log(n-1) \rfloor - 49$	$24 + 3\lfloor \log n \rfloor + 3\lfloor \log(n-1) \rfloor$ $+3\lfloor \log \frac{n}{3} \rfloor + 3\lfloor \log \frac{n-1}{3} \rfloor$	$4n - \omega(n) - \lfloor \log n \rfloor$
Takahashi Adder [7]	2008	$196n$	$90 \log n$	$2n + \frac{3n}{\log n}$
Takahashi Combination [8]	2009	$49n$	$54 \log n$	$2n + \frac{3 \cdot n}{\log n}$
Higher Radix Adder [9]	2023	$56n - 7\frac{n}{r} - 7 \cdot (n-1) \pmod r$ $-21\omega(\frac{n}{r}) - 21 \log n + 21 \log r - 21$	$12 \log n + 9r - 6 \log r -$ $6 \log 3r + 6 \log(r-2) + 2$	$4n - \log n + \frac{n}{r}$ $-\omega(\frac{n}{r}) + \log r - 1$
Our Adder	–	$91n - 42\omega(\frac{n}{2}) - 42\lfloor \log \frac{n}{2} \rfloor - 98$	$27 + 6\lfloor \log \frac{n}{2} \rfloor + 6\lfloor \log \frac{n}{6} \rfloor$	$12n - 6\omega(\frac{n}{2}) -$ $6\lfloor \log \frac{n}{2} \rfloor - 10$

In Table 1, we present a comprehensive comparison of different quantum adders. The corresponding charts of these comparisons are presented in Fig. 11(b), Fig. 11(a), and Fig. 11(c). It is worth highlighting that the bit length of the addend, denoted as n in this paper, significantly influences the adder's performance. As n increases, the TC, TD, and QC of all the adders tend to increase accordingly. Draper In-place CLA based on parallel prefix structure initially achieves TD of $O(\log n)$, accompanied by TC complexity of $O(70n)$ and QC of $O(4n)$. Based on Draper In-place CLA, Takahashi Adder introduces specific modifications. Thereby, the corresponding QC decreases to $O(2n)$ while increasing TD and TC. Further enhancing the performance, Takahashi Combination Adder combines parallel prefix structure with ripple carry structure. This optimization allows it to maintain low QC of $O(2n)$ while significantly reducing TC and TD by nearly half compared to Takahashi Adder. Recently, Wang [9] et al. proposed a dynamic approach to finetune the quantum CLA, resulting in improved TD optimization. For the clarity of this paper, its performance is not shown in the figures, considering that the parameter r which denoted radix can

[1] The relevant code is available as a public repository (https://github.com/Siyi-06/Quantum_ling_adder).

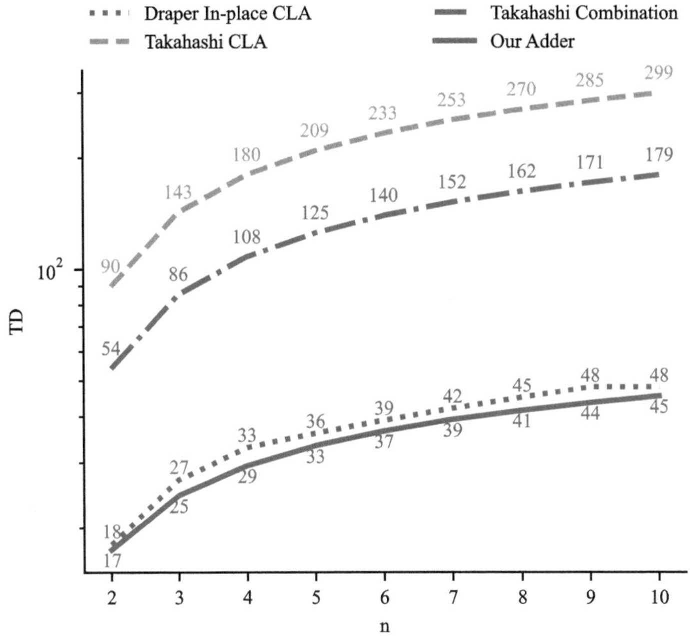

(a) TD Comparison

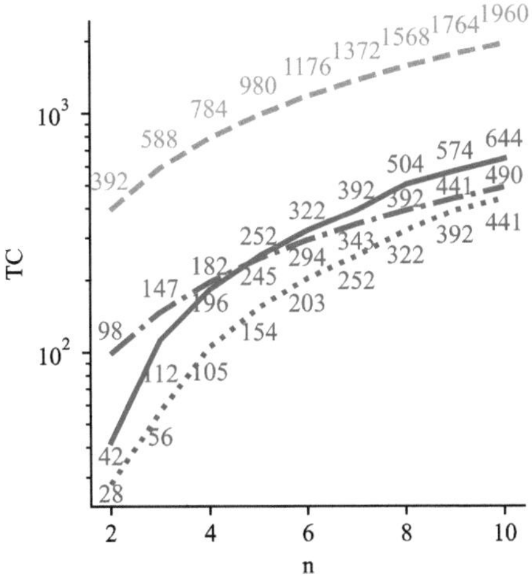

(b) TC Comparison

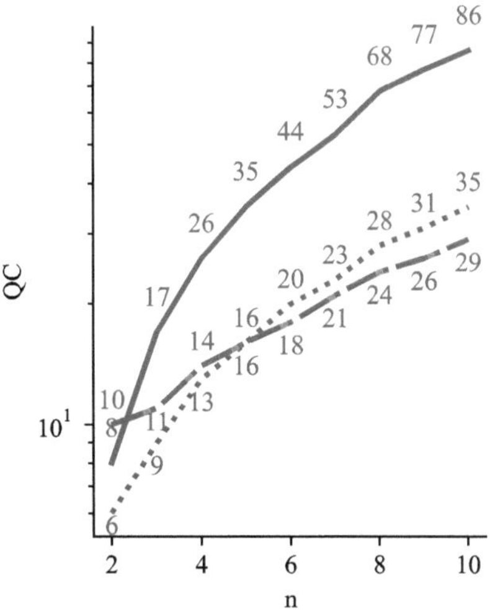

(c) QC Comparison

Fig. 11. Comparative Cost Analysis of Quantum Ling Adder and Other Prominent Quantum In-place Adders take various values. In contrast, our proposed adder offers a significant advantage over the other designs. It stands out with the lowest TD of $O(\log \frac{n}{2})$ while maintaining comparable QC and TC. Thus, especially when there is a strict requirement for low TD, our adder will become the obvious choice.

6 The Design of Quantum Ling Modular Adder

In this work, we also innovatively apply the modular framework by Vedral et al. [2] to propose a novel quantum modular adder. This modular design integrates the proposed quantum Ling adder, and is extensively illustrated in Fig. 12.

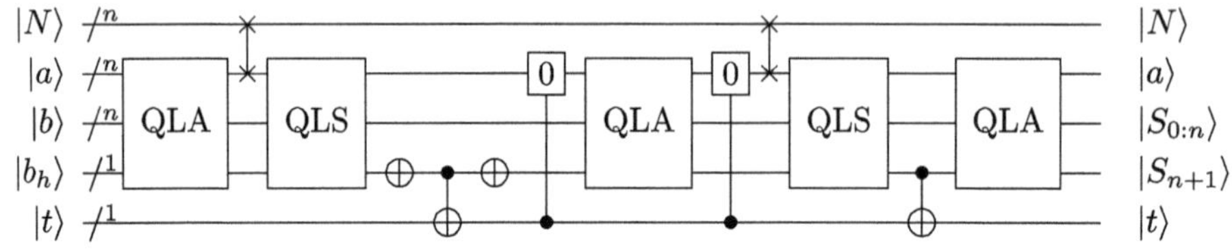

Fig. 12. Quantum Ling Modular Adder. Here we illustrate the overall design framework of the proposed modular adder, omitting ancillae for clarity. Consistent with the VBE Modular framework [2], the 'set 0' operation can be implemented using a series of CNOT gates.

Our quantum modular adder is essentially composed of two key components: the quantum Ling adder and the quantum Ling subtractor, the latter being a modified version of the former. These components are demonstrated in Figs. 13(a) and 13(b).

Specifically, as outlined in Formula (19), the subtractor is a straightforward application of our quantum adder. The process starts with the bit-wise complement of a, followed by adding b to it, thus calculating $a' + b$. Finally, we complement the bits of a and the output qubits. It is obvious that bit-wise complement can be easily implemented using quantum NOT gates. Therefore, the cost of a Quantum Ling subtractor is very close to the cost of the adder.

$$A - B = (A' + B)' \tag{19}$$

The effectiveness of our design is highlighted in Table 2, where it demonstrates an optimal TD in comparison to other relevant designs. However, this achievement comes at the cost of higher QC as shown in Fig. 14.

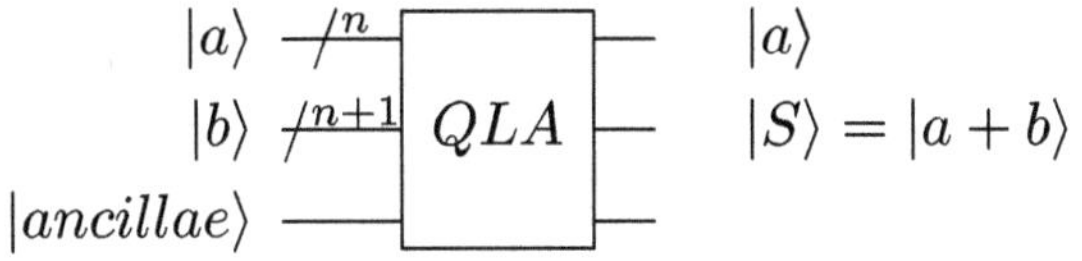

(a) Quantum Ling Adder

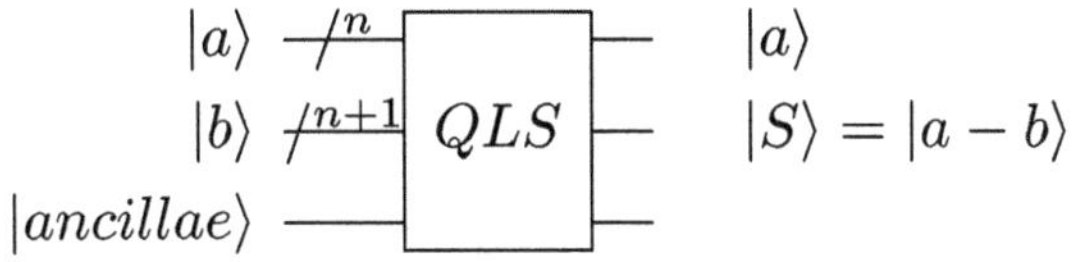

(b) Quantum Ling Subtractor

Fig. 13. Two sub-modules of our proposed modular adder

Table 2. Performance analysis of different VBE-based quantum modular adders. The formula for $\omega(n)$ is $\omega(n) = n - \sum_{y=1}^{\infty} \lfloor \frac{n}{2^y} \rfloor$, where n denotes the bit-width of the addend.

Modular Adder	Year	TC	TD	QC
VBE [2]	1995	$140n - 70$	$60n - 30$	$4n + 2$
Cucarro [13]	2004	$70n - 35$	$30n - 15$	$3n + 3$
Draper In-place [6]	2004	$350n - 105\omega(n) - 105\omega(n-1) - 105\lfloor \log n \rfloor - 105\lfloor \log(n-1) \rfloor - 245$	$120 + 15\lfloor \log n \rfloor + 15\lfloor \log(n-1) \rfloor + 15\lfloor \log \frac{n}{3} \rfloor + 15\lfloor \log \frac{n-1}{3} \rfloor$	$5n - \omega(n) - \lfloor \log n \rfloor + 1$
Our Design	–	$455n - 210\omega(\frac{n}{2}) - 210\lfloor \log \frac{n}{2} \rfloor - 490$	$135 + 30\lfloor \log \frac{n}{2} \rfloor + 30\lfloor \log \frac{n}{6} \rfloor$	$53n - 30\omega(\frac{n}{2}) - 49 - 30\lfloor \log \frac{n}{2} \rfloor$

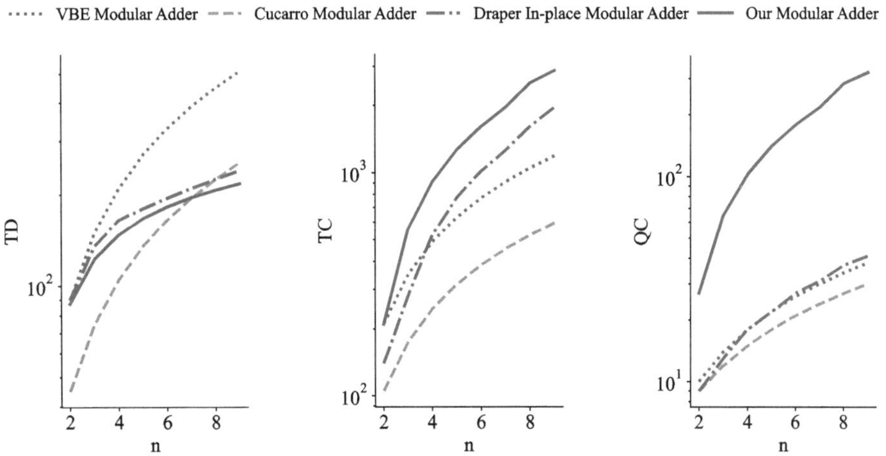

(a) TD Comparison (b) TC Comparison (c) QC Comparison

Fig. 14. Comparative Cost Analysis of Quantum Ling Modular Adder and Other Prominent Quantum Modular Adders

7 Conclusion

In conclusion, we propose a novel quantum adder based on Ling structure, which reduces depth compared to all the prior quantum adders based on parallel prefix structure. The presented quantum Ling adder achieves a T-depth of $O(\log \frac{n}{2})$. This represents a significant improvement compared to parallel prefix-based adders, including Draper carry-lookahead adder and Takahashi carry-lookahead adders, which has a T-depth of $O(\log n)$. Additionally, our research extends to the design of an efficient quantum Ling modular adder, which stands out by achieving a significantly lower T-depth compared to existing works.

In future, several research directions show great promise. For example, exploring circuit optimization techniques to minimize the number of qubits and quantum gates can significantly enhance the efficiency of our adder. Furthermore, considering Quantum Error Correction (QEC) is also vital for enhancing the fault tolerance and reliability of the adder.

Acknowledgement. This research is supported by the National Research Foundation, Singapore under its Quantum Engineering Programme Initiative. Any opinions, findings and conclusions or recommendations expressed in this material are those of the authors and do not reflect the views of National Research Foundation, Singapore.

References

1. Shor, P.: Algorithms for quantum computation: discrete logarithms and factoring. In: Proceedings of 35th Annual Symposium on Foundations of Computer Science (1996)
2. Vedral, V., Barenco, A., Ekert, A.: Quantum networks for elementary arithmetic operations. Phys. Rev. A **54**, 11 (1995)
3. Gidney, C.: Halving the cost of quantum addition. Quantum **2**, 74 (2018). https://doi.org/10.22331/q-2018-06-18-74
4. Ling, H.: High speed binary parallel adder. IEEE Trans. Electron. Comput. **EC-15**(5), 799–802 (1966)
5. Wang, S., Chattopadhyay, A.: Reducing depth of quantum adder using ling structure, pp. 1–6 (2023)
6. Draper, T., Kutin, S., Rains, E., Svore, K.: A logarithmic-depth quantum carry-lookahead adder. Quantum Inf. Comput. **6**, 07 (2004)
7. Takahashi, Y., Kunihiro, N.: A fast quantum circuit for addition with few qubits. Quantum Inf. Comput. **8**, 636–649 (2008)
8. Takahashi, Y., Tani, S., Kunihiro, N.: Quantum addition circuits and unbounded fan-out. Quantum Inf. Comput. **10**, 10 (2009)
9. Wang, S., Baksi, A., Chattopadhyay, A.: A Higher Radix Architecture for Quantum Carry-lookahead Adder. CoRR, vol. abs/2304.02921 (2023)
10. Brent, R., Kung, H.: A regular layout for parallel adders. IEEE Trans. Comput. **31**, 06 (2004)

11. Lee, S., Lee, S.-J., Kim, T., Lee, J.-S., Biamonte, J., Perkowski, M.: The cost of quantum gate primitives. J. Multiple-Valued Logic Soft Comput. **12**, 561–573 (2006)
12. Selinger, P.: Quantum circuits of T-depth one. Phys. Rev. A **87**, 10 (2012)
13. Cuccaro, S.A., Draper, T.G., Kutin, S.A., Moulton, D.P.: A new quantum ripple-carry addition circuit. arXiv preprint quant-ph/0410184 (2004)

Accelerators

Exploring Constrained-Modulus Modular Multipliers for Improved Area, Power and Flexibility

Mohammed Nabeel[1(✉)], Deepraj Soni[2], Ramesh Karri[2], and Michail Maniatakos[1]

[1] New York University Abu Dhabi, Abu Dhabi, UAE
mtn2@nyu.edu
[2] New York University, New York, USA

Abstract. Fully Homomorphic Encryption (FHE) promises complete input privacy by allowing computation on encrypted data at the expense of high computation. FHE hardware accelerators improve performance with large and densely packed computing units, which could potentially create thermal hot spots because of high power consumption. Therefore, it is necessary to reduce the area and power consumption of the accelerator and its most critical module, i.e., the modular multiplier. In this work, we use the fact that, for FHE computation, the modulus should be of a specific form with its lower bits constrained to a decimal value of one. We examine the impact on area and power of two popular modular multiplication algorithms, Barrett and Montgomery, with different constrained widths for different modulus sizes. Our experiment results show that modular multipliers with constrained width can reduce area by 20% and power consumption by 15%-to-25%. We also propose an approximation for the number of prime moduli available with such a constrained modulus.

Keywords: Modular Multiplier · Montgomery Reduction · Barrett Reduction · Low-power design · ASIC Design · Fully Homomorphic Encryption

1 Introduction

As the reliance on cloud computing is increasing rapidly, it raises concerns for the privacy of the input data, which needs to be decrypted before computation on the cloud server. The highest security guarantee is possible if the third-party server does not require data decryption. Fully Homomorphic Encryption (FHE) is a scheme that performs computation on the encrypted domain without needing decryption at the server. FHE schemes provide mathematical guarantees regarding the security and accuracy of the computed data. Thus, FHE can be applied to many applications where the input data is sensitive, e.g., privacy-protected machine learning, secure genome analysis, etc. [1–4].

Published by Springer Nature Switzerland AG 2024
I. (Abe) M. Elfadel and L. Albasha (Eds.): VLSI-SoC 2023, IFIP AICT 680, pp. 93–108, 2024.
https://doi.org/10.1007/978-3-031-70947-0_5

FHE schemes, such as CKKS [5] and BGV [6], are constructed based on the learning with errors problem, which requires modular arithmetic on large modulus sizes and resource-intensive computation on vast amounts of data. These FHE schemes exhibit tremendous performance overhead while running on a regular CPU. This hinders its mainstream adoption. FHE-specific hardware accelerators can resolve these issues. HEAX [7] introduced novel FPGA-based architectures for the CKKS scheme. F1 [8] and Craterlake [9] accelerators support all FHE operations. While RPU [10] supports all the FHE primitive operations and other ring processing operations. Prior work improves FHE performance using efficient modular arithmetic designs and parallel operations.

However, the clustered modular performing arithmetic operations at high frequency utilizes more power and correspondingly would dissipate a significant amount of heat [11]. Excessive heating and hotspots could cause faster aging of the chip, and it can also be self-damaging. The power consumption for FHE is as important as performance and functionality. Prior work on large FHE designs is synthesized with state-of-the-art tools and commercial memory compilers, but these designs are not yet fabricated on silicon. After these big designs are fabricated, the power consumption of these designs can potentially become a main issue.

There are two levels where power optimization is performed: (1) device-level optimization and (2) design-level optimization. As Moore's law is not applicable and it is challenging to transfer to lower technology nodes, improving power at the device level is nearly impossible. Thus, design-level optimization is the only option to reduce power. While looking at FHE designs, modular arithmetic operations turned out to be principal contributors to power utilization [10]. In arithmetic operations, modular adder/subtractor, modular multiplier, and modular comparator are the basic units. The modular multiplier consumes the majority of the total power. Therefore, the modular multiplier should be the primary focus of reducing power consumption.

As will be discussed in a later section, as a FHE primitive, the modular multiplier can function with only a subset of the moduli space. Recent work has implemented this design by constraining the modulus [8,12]. However, constrained width is selected without exploring the design for different constraints, and the impact of the constraint on the availability of prime moduli is not analyzed. Introducing the modulus constraint reduces the number of prime moduli available for higher-level FHE operations, which affects the usage of the Residue Number System (RNS) for FHE.

We derive an approximation function that can choose the constrained width for different modulus sizes. The approximation function assists in selecting the appropriate constrained width for target FHE applications with large modulus sizes, i.e., 64bit, 128bit, or 256bit. Based on the proposed approximation, a developer can analyze which constrained width to select based on the target application, security level, and the number of prime moduli required to support RNS. We report the area and power saving for different configurations of modulus size and constrained width. Finally, we run the optimized design on different low-level FHE primitives (NTT, iNTT, polynomial multiplication, and

Hadamard multiplication). Building upon the groundwork laid by Soni et al. [13], our contributions include:

- We evaluate the impact of constrained width on power consumption and area of two popular modular multipliers: the Barrett and the Montgomery multiplier.
- We compare the power and area impact with different modulus sizes on different FHE primitives.
- We propose two novel approximations to calculate the number of primes for any modulus size and constrained width. We evaluate the accuracy of the approximation with changes in input parameters.

2 Background

2.1 FHE Basics

Fully Homomorphic Encryption (FHE) offers cryptographic guarantees for data processing on private data in a third party server. The user encrypts the message m to a ciphertext $c = Enc(m)$. The remote server, an untrusted third party, receives the ciphertext and the evaluation key. It processes data on ciphertext c such that resultant ciphertext $c' = f(m)$. The untrusted third-party, who computes using ciphertexts, does not have the private key for decryption. As the input, output, and all the intermediate states are encrypted, FHE protects the private data from any attack on the third-party device used for computation. Only the authenticated user, the holder of the secret key, can decrypt and access the data. Gentry [14] presented the first blueprint of an FHE scheme. These schemes have been greatly improved over time [15–20].

The basic FHE operations –Key generation, Encryption, Decryption, Evaluation of addition and multiplication– require a set of Ring Learning-With-Errors (RLWE) parameters that define the computational properties of the ring and determine the level of security. The polynomial remains very large even for the lowest acceptable security level. Depending on these parameters and application requirements, each polynomial may have up to 65536 coefficients, where each coefficient is an n-bit integer where $n =$ several hundred bits.

FHE schemes, such as BFV, BGV, and CKKS, are based on the ring learning-with-errors (RLWE) problem and involve manipulation of ring objects as polynomials [5,6,21]. Every ciphertext has two polynomials, which are represented by an array of numbers–their coefficients. When ciphertexts are added or multiplied, a corresponding operation is required on polynomials including addition and multiplication on coefficients in modular arithmetic.

2.2 Number Theory Transform and the Constraint on the Modulus

FHE's ciphertexts are inherently large, represented as high-degree polynomials with big integer coefficients. Polynomial multiplication is the major operation in FHE, and Number Theory Transform (NTT) is deployed to do this as it brings down the runtime from $O(n^2)$ to $O(n\ logn)$. NTT is a generalized form of DFT. NTT is DFT on a ring over a finite field, where the ring is an integers modulo of a prime number p. Like the complex root of unity in DFT on a complex number field, for NTT, it is the primitive N^{th} root of unity w, so that $w^N = 1 \mod p$, where N is a polynomial degree. The primitive N^{th} of unity is also known as the twiddle factor. By Fermat's little theorem [22], a primitive root of unity exists if $p = 1 \ mod \ N$. All the popular FHE algorithms are based on lattice-based cryptography, and they work over ring $Z_p[x]/(x^N + 1)$, where N is the power of two and p is a prime modulus. Multiplication in such a ring requires negative wrapped convolution and requires extra computation compared to positive wrapped convolution, where one performs the NTT of two polynomials followed by a Hadamard multiplication of those NTT outputs, then followed by inverse NTT (iNTT). But as shown in [23], if $p = 1 \ mod \ 2N$, one can compute negative wrapped convolution efficiently by pre-processing and post-processing the inputs and outputs of positive wrapped convolution respectively. This constrains the modulus to $1 \ mod \ 2N$, where N is the polynomial degree and is a power of two. This is the baseline we take and propose how to optimize them further based on the design goals, to attain lower power and area.

2.3 Residue Number System

The Homomorphic Encryption Standard [24], which provides recommended parameters, shows that modulus size can go up to a few hundred bits depending on the application, security level, and error distribution. However, FHE hardware accelerators are typically designed to support a fixed modulus size and cannot natively support polynomials with a coefficient modulus size larger than the size supported by the hardware. The popular way this problem is tackled is by using the residue number system (RNS) [22]. Using RNS, polynomials with larger modulus sizes are split into multiple polynomials with modulus sizes matching the size supported by the FHE hardware accelerator. In order to split polynomials using RNS, there should be enough prime modulus availability, and the number of prime modulus requirements also depends on the target application. This factor also decides how much one can constrain the modulus supported by the FHE accelerator.

2.4 Montgomery Modular Multiplier

Montgomery algorithm replaces division operation with multiplication operation. As Algorithm 1 describes, Montgomery multiplication requires three multipliers, three barrel shifters ($mod \ 2^n$ is implemented using barrel shifter to select least n bits), one adder, and one subtractor. The size of each multiplier is the same as the maximum modulus size the multiplier supports. However, the algorithm works only in the Montgomery domain. At least one of the inputs must be transformed to this domain before being multiplied. If both the inputs are in the Montgomery domain, the output should be transformed back. A number is transformed to the Montgomery domain by multiplying with R defined in the Algorithm 1. To exit from the Montgomery domain, multiply by its inverse, i.e., $R^{-1} mod \ q$.

When modulus M has the form described in Sect. 2.2, i.e., $q = 1 \bmod 2N$, the multiplier at the line 5 and the adder at the line 7 will get optimized. The greater optimization is achieved when the constrained width is large. However, this might restrict the number of prime moduli. In [8], the authors claim a reduction of area of the multiplier by 19% and power by 30% using only 16-bit digits in 32-bit moduli. With such restrictions, plenty of prime numbers in excess of 6000 are still to be chosen for FHE parameters. This work extends this constraint on modulus and studies the area and power savings for different constrained widths for different modulus sizes.

Algorithm 1. Montgomery Modular Multiplication

Input: A, B, q; μ
Conditions: $A, B \in \mathbb{Z}_q$, $q \in [0, 2^n)$, $\mu = q^{-1} mod\ 2^n$, $R = 2^n mod\ q$
Output: $Y = ((A * B * R^{-1}) \bmod q) \in \mathbb{Z}_q$

1: $Y \leftarrow A * B$ ▷ Mult1
2: $t \leftarrow Y \bmod 2^n$
3: $t \leftarrow t * \mu$ ▷ Mult2
4: $t \leftarrow t \bmod 2^n$
5: $Y \leftarrow (Y - t * q)/2^n$ ▷ Mult3
6: **if** $Y \leq 0$ **then**
7: $\quad Y \leftarrow Y + q$
8: **end if**
9: **return** Y

2.5 Barrett Modular Multiplier

Modular multiplication needs costly division operations to perform modular reduction after regular multiplication. Modular reduction algorithms like

Algorithm 2. Barrett Modular Multiplication

Input: q, A, B, R, n
Conditions: $q \geq 3$, $q \neq 2^i$; A, B $\in \mathbb{Z}_q$; $n = \lceil \log_2 q \rceil$; $R = \lfloor 4^n / q \rfloor$
$q = q_H * 2^w + 1$; if constrained modulus where w = constraint-width
Output: $t = (A * B) \bmod q \in \mathbb{Z}_q$

1: $s \leftarrow (A * B)$ ▷ Mult1
2: $s_h \leftarrow s \gg n - 1$
3: $c \leftarrow (s_h * R) \gg n + 1$ ▷ Mult2
4: $t' \leftarrow S - c * q$ ▷ Mult3
5: **if** $t' > 2 * q$ **then** $t \leftarrow t' - 2 * q$
6: **else if** $t' > q$ **then** $t \leftarrow t' - q$
7: **else** $t \leftarrow t'$
8: **end if**
9: **return** t

Barrett-reduction optimize this cost by avoiding division operation by approximating the modulus q to R = 2^n/q. This approximation removes costly division operations and replaces them with bit-shift and multiplication.

Algorithm 2 presents the Barrett reduction algorithm optimized for hardware implementation. When used in the context of Number Theory Transform (NTT), modulus q should be a friendly prime, satisfying the condition $q = 1 \ mod \ 2N$, where N is the polynomial degree. This means that the value of lower $1 + log_2N$ bits of the modulus is one, i.e., after the least significant bit (lsb), at least the next log_2N bits should be 0s. We make use of this fact to optimize the multiplier design during RTL synthesis and extend it by constraining more than the aforementioned number of bits 0s.

In Algorithm 2, post regular multiplication, there are two additional multiplication operations required for the modular reduction operation. Line 4 shows that the second multiplication is with the modulus q itself. This operation can be optimized significantly by the proposed constrained modulus.

2.6 Prime-Counting Function (PCF)

Prime-counting function counts the number of prime less than or equal to input integer. It is denoted as $\pi(x)$. For example, $\pi(15) = 16$ because there are seven prime numbers (2, 3, 5, 7, 11, and 13) less than or equal to 16. The prime counting function is a crucial idea in number theory, applied across math in prime number distribution, theorems, cryptography, and analyzing algorithms. It's central for understanding prime number characteristics in math and related disciplines.

$$\lim_{x \to \infty} \frac{\pi(x)}{x/ln(x)} = 1 \tag{1}$$

Gauss and Lagrange hypothesized prime-counting function as $\pi(x) \sim \frac{x}{ln(x)}$. The Prime Number Theorem asserts that $\frac{x}{ln(x)}$ provides a reliable estimate for $\pi(x)$. It mathematically defines the concept that as prime numbers grow larger, their occurrence diminishes, by precisely gauging the speed of this decrease. Error between prime-counting function and approximation is unbounded, and it grows with large x. However, the relative error reduces, which is defined by Eq. 1. Equation 1 mentions that the approximation becomes accurate with increase in x. This equation is known as Prime Number Theorem (PNT). PNT provides the rate of prime number occurrence. PNT states that the average distance between first x prime numbers is $\frac{1}{ln \ x}$. The probability of any integer x being a prime number is $\frac{1}{ln \ x}$. Consequently, PNT infers that prime numbers are less common for larger integer values.

For RNS, FHE requires a prime number as a modulus. Modulus size is denoted as $|q|$. Approximate numbers of possible modulus is $\frac{2^{|q|}}{ln \ 2^{|q|}}$. FHE requires 10 s of prime modulis, as described in [25]. If $|q| = 16$, the prime-counting function $\pi(2^{10}) = 6542$ which is sufficient for RNS in terms of the number of required prime numbers.

3 Methodology

In this section, we explain design parameter selection to evaluate the impact of the constrained modulus on design. We explain the impact of the constrained modulus on the count of prime numbers as the total count of prime numbers has an impact on RNS and the functionality of the design. Finally, we sketch out the details of the experimental setup. For the rest of the paper, q denotes the prime used as modulus; where $q = q_H * 2^w + 1$. $|q|$ denotes the modulus size or modulus width. w denotes the constraint-width that applies on modulus; where $0 < w < |q|$.

3.1 Parameter Selection

We evaluate the modular multiplier on different $|q|$ and w. Popular FHE accelerators use 28-bit [8] and 32-bit [9] modular multiplier design. Latticed-based PQC algorithms work on 16-bit [26] or 32-bit [27] modular multipliers. Higher modulus size is also utilized for FHE accelerators [28]. To understand the impact on all kinds of designs, we study the design for modulus sizes of 16, 20, 24, 28, 32, 64, 128, and 256. For each modulus size, we vary w from 1 to $|q| - 1$. As w increases, we can further optimize $Mult3$ in Algorithms 1 and 2. This is the main source of optimization for the modular multiplier, along with the subtractors for the final modular reduction operation. We analyze the impact of the constrained width on different modulus sizes; this can help the designers choose the right modulus size and the constrained width depending on the application, security parameters, and the availability of the hardware resources.

3.2 Modulus-Counting Function (MCF)

When constraint width puts a limitation on prime numbers, the prime-counting function (PCF) will not show the total number of prime numbers for a given range. We are defining the prime number counting with constraint as a Modulus-Counting Function (MCF). We denote MCF as $\pi'(|q|, w)$. For example, $\pi'(4, 2)$ = 2. Even though there are 6 prime numbers less than or equal to 16 ($|q| = 4$, here), only two moduli (5 and 13) satisfy the condition where the last two digits (w = 2, here) in the binary is "01". However, it takes years to calculate MCF for large numbers. The proposed MCF approximations provide the number of moduli with a mathematical formula within a fraction of a second instead of traditionally counting the moduli for large bitwidth, which takes a long time. MCF is critical to select the constraint based on FHE security and application. For example, if a particular FHE application requires 1000 prime numbers, we cannot select the constrained width such that the total number of primes is less than 1000.

Looking at the importance of MCF, we propose two novel conjectures for MCF approximation as:

$$A_l(|q|, w) = \frac{2^{|q|-(w-1)}}{ln\ 2^{|q|}} \tag{2}$$

$$A_h(|q|, w) = \frac{1}{2^{(w-1)}} \int_{2}^{2^q} \frac{1}{ln\ 2^x} dx \tag{3}$$

Here $0 < w < |q|$. MCF approximations are a generalized form of modulus-counting function approximation. If there is not a constraint (i.e., $w = 1$), the MCF is the same as PCF. $A_h(|q|, w)$ approximation shows mostly the upper limit of the number of moduli while $A_l(|q|, w)$ approximation shows mostly the lower limit of the number of moduli. $A_l(|q|, w)$ indicates that the average distance between two prime numbers are $ln\ 2^{|q|}$ for the range $2^{(|q|-(w-1))}$.

$$\lim_{(|q|,w)\to(\infty,1)} \frac{\pi'(|q|, w)}{A_l(|q|, w)} = \lim_{(|q|,w)\to(\infty,1)} \frac{\pi'(|q|, w)}{2^{(|q|-(w-1))} / \ ln\ 2^{|q|}} \approx 1 \tag{4}$$

$$\lim_{(|q|,w)\to(\infty,1)} \frac{\pi'(|q|, w)}{A_h(|q|, w)} = \lim_{(|q|,w)\to(\infty,1)} \frac{\pi'(|q|, w)}{\frac{1}{2^{(w-1)}} \int_{2}^{2^q} \frac{1}{ln\ x} dx} \approx 1 \tag{5}$$

To measure the accuracy of the approximation, we take the ratio of the MCF and its approximation. This ratio reaches to one as modulus size increases and constraint-width decreases. As defined in Eq. 4 and Eq. 5, the ratio of MCF and its approximation tends to 1 as w tends to one, and $|q|$ tends to infinity. The relative error between the actual count of prime modulus and its approximation becomes less. We run the MCF approximation for different values of two inputs; $|q|$ and w. Section 4 shows the ratio of total moduli and MCF approximation to check the accuracy of the approximation.

3.3 Experimental Setup

Synthesis: All the designs are synthesized using Synopsys Design Compiler (DC) with TSMC 22 nm Ultra Low Leakage (ULL) technology library. This library is characterized for the worst corner; worst temperature of 125 °C, worst voltage of 0.81V, and worst process/parasitic (resistance and capacitance). This library ensures that we achieve the operational frequency at the voltage of 0.9 V $\pm$ 10% and at a temperature less than 125 °C. We synthesize the multipliers to be as fast as possible (250ps clock period) for block-level analysis. Once we know the critical path of the design based on this synthesis result, we rerun the synthesis with the corrected frequency so that the design is not over-optimized.

Verification: Multiplier design is functionally verified for one million test cases. Synopsys VCS is used for functional simulation. Our verification strategy injects one million random numbers in the range from 0 to $2^n - 1$ for two operands and one million weighted random numbers from 1 to $2^n - 1$ for modulus, where n is the size of the multiplier. The two operands are smaller than the modulus.

Power Measurement: We use the Synopsys PrimePower tool for accurate power measurement. PrimePower measures the power of each switching activity of every node within the netlist. The switching activity file is generated from gate-level functional simulation(GLS) in value change dump (VCD) format. For GLS, the design under test is a post-synthesis netlist and is run for 1000 test vectors. For these testcases, we choose the modulus value as $2^N - 1$, the highest value of modulus, for which the multiplier requires more power. Hence, the power results report the pessimistic power consumption.

We take advantage of scaling to compare our design (22 nm) to Previous work runs on 16/12 nm technology nodes. We report power and area estimates using foundry-reported scaling factors. Specifically, we scale 0.4× power and 0.65× area from 22 nm to 16/12 nm [29,30].

4 Experimental Results

In this section, we show the impact of the constrained modulus on the modular multipliers. First, we evaluate the area and power utilization of the multipliers with a change in constraint width (w) for different modulus sizes ($|q|$). Second, we show the MCF and accuracy of the MCF approximations. Third, we run the different FHE primitives with an optimized Barrett design. Finally, we compare the result with state-of-the-art FHE modular multiplier implementation.

4.1 32-Bit Optimized Modular Multipliers

Figure 1 shows the effect of the constrained-width w on Barrett Multiplier and Montgomery Multiplier while keeping the constant bitwidth $|q| = 32$. All the design points are normalized to the unoptimized design, i.e., the designs where the constrained bit is only the least significant bit (LSB) of the modulus, i.e.,

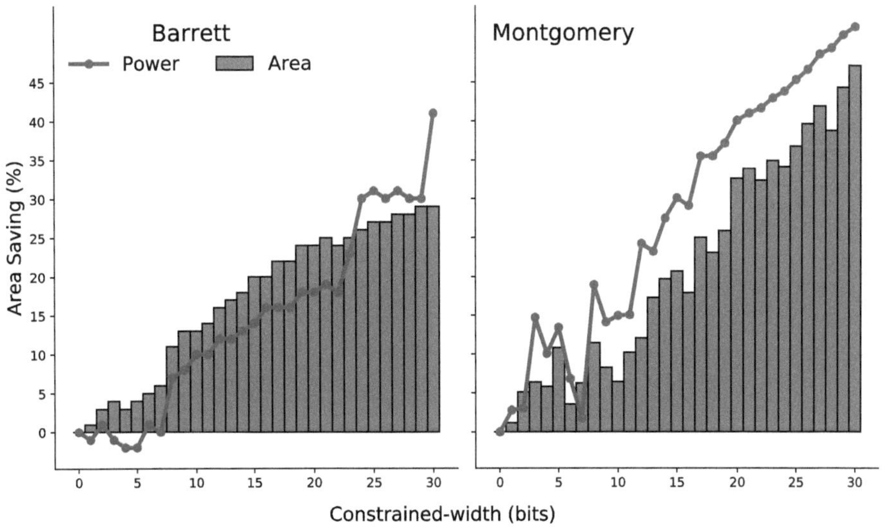

Fig. 1. Percent change of area and power vs constraint width (w) for 32-bit modulus size ($|q|$).

$w = 1$. For each of these design points, we evaluate area and power optimization. As the w increases, the area utilization and power utilization improve. For $w = |q|/2$, the area saving is ~20% for both the multipliers, the power saving is ~15% for the Barrett Multiplier and ~25% for the Montgomery Multiplier. For $w = |q| * 3/4$, the area saving and power saving is ~25% for Barrett Multiplier. For Montgomery Multiplier, area and power savings are ~35% and ~45%, respectively. Hence, the Montogmery Multiplier's area and power saving figures are better compared to that of Barrett Multiplier. However, Montogmery Multiplier inputs and the output require domain conversion as discussed in Sect. 2.4, which needs additional hardware or additional execution time.

4.2 Multiplier with Different Bitwidth

Figures 2 and 3 show the area and power consumption improvement for the Barrett and Montgomery multipliers by changing both the variables; modulus-size ($|q|$) and the constrained-width (w). Previous research reports that area and power increase with an increase in modulus ($|q|$) [11]. Hence, we run the designs for all the constrained widths and show the utilization for three different moduli. Figure 2 shows the area improvement for three different constraint-width compared to traditional design with $w = 1$. For example, if the modulus size is 32bit, Fig. 2 shows the design point for $w = 8$, 16, and 24. As w increases, the area reduces for all the modulus sizes. For $w = |q|/2$, the median area improvement is ~20%. The area saving is higher if we constrain the modulus for a high bit width. Power follows a similar trend as area, as shown in Fig. 3. The median power saving is ~17% for $w = |q|/2$ for the Barrett Multiplier, and it is also

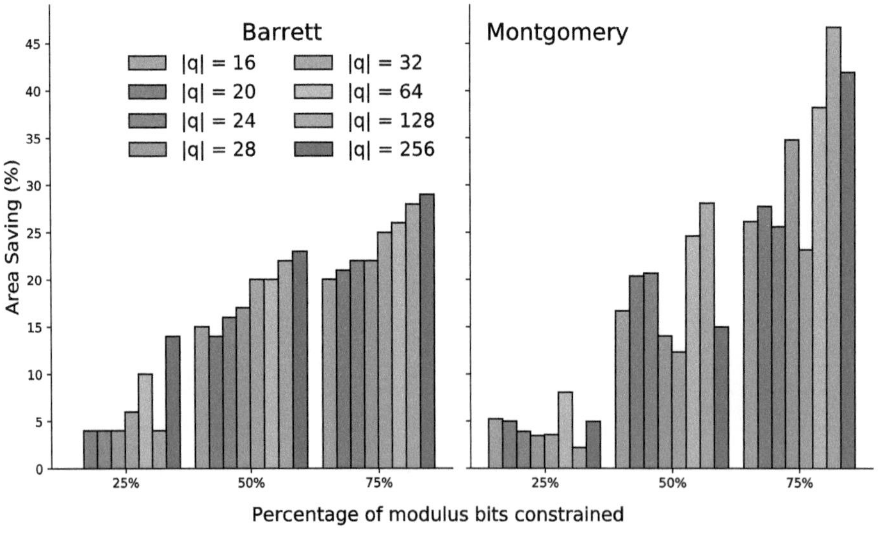

Fig. 2. Area Saving.

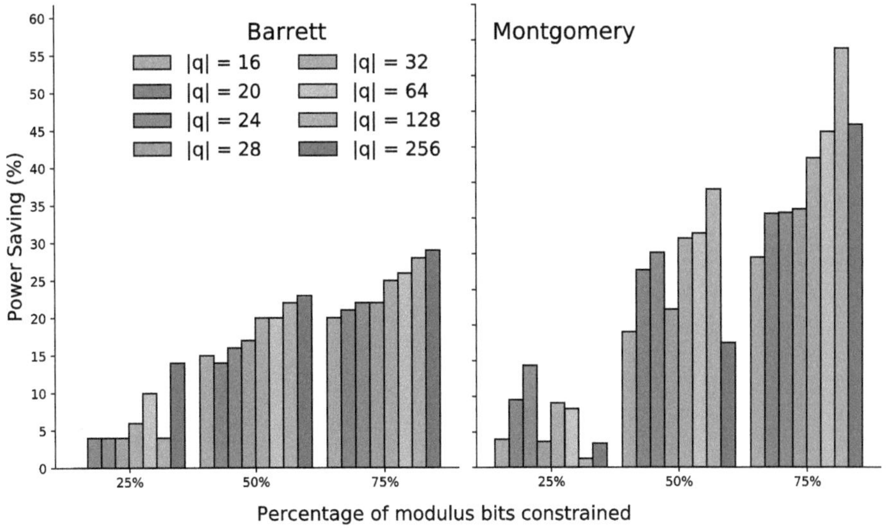

Fig. 3. Power Saving.

Table 1. Modulus size and constraint-width for fixed number of modulis ($\pi'(|q|, w)$)

Modulus size	$\pi'(\lvert q\rvert, w) \approx 100$		$\pi'(\lvert q\rvert, w) \approx 500$		$\pi'(\lvert q\rvert, w) \approx 1000$		$\pi'(\lvert q\rvert, w) \approx 10000$	
	A_l, w	A_h, w	A_l, w	A_h, w	A_l, w	A_h, w	A_l, w	A_h, w
16	92, 7	102, 7	369, 5	411, 5	738, 4	822, 4	-	-
28 [9]	105, 18	111, 18	422, 16	446, 16	844, 15	892, 15	13506, 11	14288, 11
32 [8]	92, 22	96, 22	369, 20	387, 20	748, 19	775, 19	10505, 15	10965, 15
64	92, 53	94, 53	369, 51	378, 51	738, 50	756, 50	11818, 46	12907, 46
128 [28]	92, 116	93, 116	369, 114	373, 114	738, 113	747, 113	11818, 109	11954, 109
256	92, 242	92, 242	369, 240	371, 240	738, 240	742, 240	11818, 236	11885, 236

~17% for the Montgomery Multiplier. and the power saving increases to ~25% for Barrett and ~35% for Montgomery Multiplier when $w = |q| * 0.75$. The area has a limited impact on power. The power depends on the switching activity, and these designs have higher switching activity as the input values are random. For large $|q|$, we achieve higher power savings with an increase in w. For $w = |q|/2$, 15% area is saved for 16bit modulus, and ~22% area is saved for 256bit modulus. For $w = |q|/2$, ~11% power is saved for 16bit modulus and ~23% power is saved for 256bit modulus. The power saving increases with an increase in $|q|$ and w.

4.3 Modulus-Counting Function (MCF)

Based on Fig. 2 and Fig. 3, we need to select high w. However, we do not have sufficient numbers of moduli for the high value of w as shown in Fig. 4. Figure 4 shows the value of the modulus-counting function $\pi'(|q|, w)$ with a change in $|q|$ and w. For a fixed modulus size, the number of moduli is approximately double with a single decrement in constraint-width. As we increase modulus size, the number of moduli also increases exponentially. The modulus-counting function is proportional to modulus size ($|q|$) and inversely proportional to constraint-width (w).

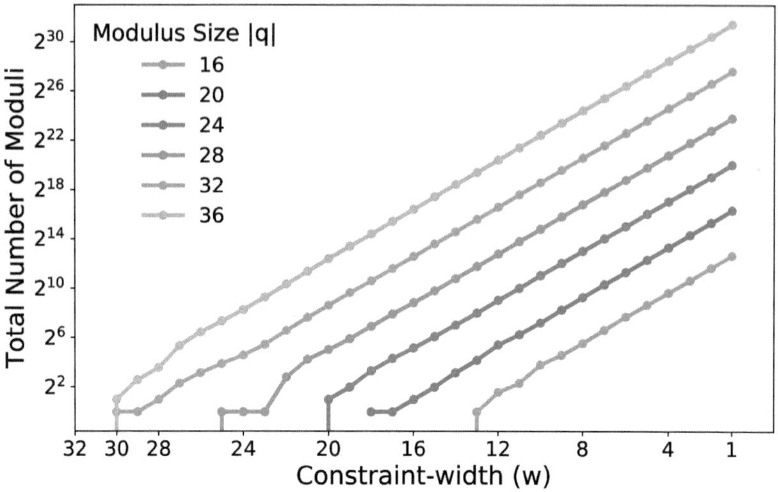

Fig. 4. Total Number of Moduli vs Constraint width(w) for different modulus size where each modulus q = $q_H * 2^w + 1$

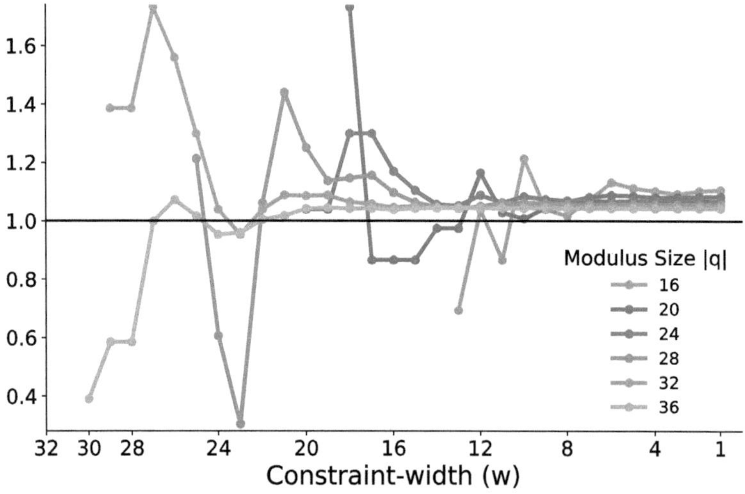

Fig. 5. Ratio of the MCF to its higher approximation A_l.

For large $|q|$, we cannot find $\pi'(|q|, w)$. We approximated MCF in Eq. 4. To confirm the approximation, we run ratio of MCF and its approximation for different $|q|$ and w as shown in Fig. 5. Figure 5 shows that ratio reaches to one for each modulus size as we reduce the w. When w closer to $|q|$, the ratio varies drastically. However, when w reduces, it converges to 1. For higher modulus size, there are more w which follows this ratio. Modulus-counting approximation is a generalized form of prime-counting approximation. Figure 5 and Fig. 6 confirm the validity of Eq. 4 and Eq. 5. A_l approximation is closer to the actual moduli count than compared to A_h approximation majorly. A_l generally provides the lower bound of the MCF and A_l provides the upper bound of the MCF. It is likely that, for large constraint width (w), the $A_l < \pi'(|q|, w) < A_h$.

Using the MCF approximation, Table 1 reports the approximation values and w for different $|q|$. If we need around 1000 moduli for $|q| = 32$, we can choose $w = 19$ where A_h and A_l would be 775 and 748, respectively. For $|q| = 256$, we can constrain the last 239 bits if FHR primitives need around 10000 moduli.

4.4 Power Saving for FHE Primitives

In this section we present the result when the constrained-width Barrett multiplier is used as the modular multiplier for the hardware accelerator for FHE primitives. We perform NTT, iNTT, Polynomial Multiplication, and pointwise multiplication (Hadamard multiplication) on 8192° polynomials. The Table 2 reports the power utilization for these primitives for different optimization of 32bit multiplier. For NTT, power improvement of ~1%, ~15%, and ~21% are reported for constraint-width of 8, 16, and 24, respectively. We observe a similar trend for other primitives. This power optimization further improves with higher modulus size.

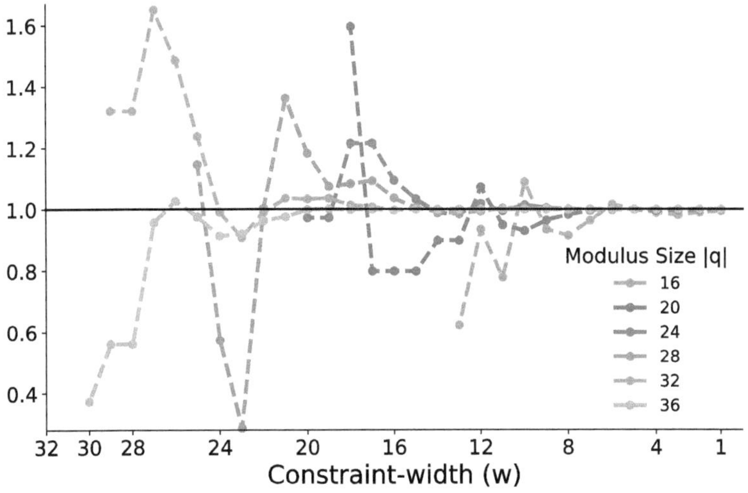

Fig. 6. Ratio of the MCF to its lower approximation A_h.

Table 2. Power and area for FHE primitives using 32-bit Barrett multiplier.

Algorithm	For $w = 0$	For $w = 8$	For $w = 16$	For $w = 24$
	Power (mW)	Power (mW)	Power (mW)	Power (mW)
PolyMul	10.16	10.04	8.63	8.03
Hadamard	10.7	10.5	9	8.31
NTT	10.11	10	8.6	7.98
iNTT	10.17	10.05	8.64	8.05

Table 3. Related work of ASIC designs of FHE accelerators.

	Node	$\|q\|$	w	Area (μm)	Power (mW)	Delay (ns)	Area Saving	Power Saving
F1 [8]	16/12 nm	32	-	5,271	18.4	1.317	-	-
This work			0	5,225	4.28	0.41	0.9%	76.7%
			8	4,915	4.28	0.41	6.8%	76.7%
			16	4,176	3.68	0.43	20.8%	80%
			24	3.907	3.31	0.46	25.9%	82%

4.5 Comparison

Understanding the need for the FHE accelerators, several cryptographic designs have been developed. However, a thorough search of the relevant literature yielded only the F1 [8] that shares the ASIC area and power utilization of the core computation unit of FHE, i.e., modular multiplier. Table 3 compares the area and power utilization of F1 accelerator to the proposed design with different modulus size. Our Barrett multiplier with wallace-tree implementation requires ~6% more area and ~65% less power compared to prior design. If we constrain modulus with 16bit and 24bit, we achieve 68% and 70% power saving, respectively. We achieve an area saving of 9.5% and 13.3% for w = 16 and w = 24, respectively.

5 Conclusion

In this paper, we deep dive into optimizing the area and power of modular multiplier, a critical module used in FHE hardware accelerators, using constrained modulus. We showed that the Barrett and Montgomery multipliers offer area and power optimization based on the constraint-width selection. We presented the area and power optimization trend for a different configuration of modulus size and constraint width. We demonstrated that with 50% of the modulus size constrained, it provides ~80% power improvement and ~20% area improvement compared to prior designs. Furthermore, when compared to the same base design not optimized for the constrained width, for 32-bit modulus, our approach with 50% of the modulus size constrained reduces area by 20% and power consumption by 15% for Barrett and 25% for the Mongtomery multiplier. Importantly, this optimization retains a sufficient number of prime numbers for Residue Number System (RNS) operations. Finally, we proposed a novel approximation equation to count prime numbers in the modulus range, where modulus $q = q_H * 2^w + 1$. This equation helps us select the constraint width for a large modulus ($\geq$ 128-bit) within a fraction of a second, which might take years to calculate the number of moduli for a large biwidth.

References

1. Chen, H., Laine, K., Rindal, P.: Fast private set intersection from homomorphic encryption. In: Proceedings of the 2017 ACM SIGSAC Conference on Computer and Communications Security, CCS 2017, pp. 1243–1255 (2017)
2. Han, K., Hong, S., Cheon, J.H., Park, D.: Logistic regression on homomorphic encrypted data at scale. In: Proceedings of the AAAI Conference on Artificial Intelligence, vol. 33 (2019)
3. Juvekar, C., Vaikuntanathan, V., Chandrakasan, A.: GAZELLE: a low latency framework for secure neural network inference. In: 27th USENIX Security Symposium (USENIX Security 2018) (2018)
4. Kim, M., Song, Y., Li, B., Micciancio, D.: Semi-Parallel logistic regression for GWAS on encrypted data. BMC Med. Genomics **13**, 99 (2020)
5. Cheon, J.H., Kim, A., Kim, M., Song, Y.: Homomorphic encryption for arithmetic of approximate numbers. In: Takagi, T., Peyrin, T. (eds.) ASIACRYPT 2017. LNCS, vol. 10624, pp. 409–437. Springer, Cham (2017). https://doi.org/10.1007/978-3-319-70694-8_15
6. Brakerski, Z., Gentry, C., Vaikuntanathan, V.: Fully homomorphic encryption without bootstrapping. Cryptology ePrint Archive, Report 2011/277 (2011)
7. Riazi, M.S., Laine, K., Pelton, B., Dai, W.: HEAX: an architecture for computing on encrypted data. In: Proceedings of the Twenty-Fifth International Conference on Architectural Support for Programming Languages and Operating Systems, pp. 1295–1309 (2020)
8. Feldmann, A., et al.: F1: A Fast and Programmable Accelerator for Fully Homomorphic Encryption (Extended Version). arXiv:2109.05371 (2021). arXiv: 2109.05371
9. Samardzic, N., et al.: Craterlake: a hardware accelerator for efficient unbounded computation on encrypted data. In: ISCA, pp. 173–187 (2022)
10. Soni, D., et al.: RPU: the ring processing unit. In: 2023 IEEE International Symposium on Performance Analysis of Systems and Software (ISPASS), pp. 272–282. IEEE (2023)
11. Soni, D., et al.: Design space exploration of modular multipliers for ASIC FHE accelerators. In: 2023 24th International Symposium on Quality Electronic Design (ISQED), pp. 1–8 (2023)
12. Mert, A.C., Ozturk, E., Savas, E.: Design and implementation of a fast and scalable NTT-based polynomial multiplier architecture. In: 2019 22nd Euromicro Conference on Digital System Design (DSD), pp. 253–260 (2019)
13. Soni, D., Nabeel, M., Karri, R., Maniatakos, M.: Optimizing constrained-modulus barrett multiplier for power and flexibility. In: 2023 IFIP/IEEE 31st International Conference on Very Large Scale Integration (VLSI-SoC), pp. 1–6. IEEE (2023)

14. Gentry, C.: Fully homomorphic encryption using ideal lattices. In: Proceedings of the Forty-First Annual ACM Symposium on Theory of Computing, STOC 2009, New York, NY, USA, pp. 169–178 (2009)
15. Bos, J.W., Lauter, K., Loftus, J., Naehrig, M.: Improved security for a ring-based fully homomorphic encryption scheme. In: Stam, M. (ed.) IMACC 2013. LNCS, vol. 8308, pp. 45–64. Springer, Heidelberg (2013). https://doi.org/10.1007/978-3-642-45239-0_4
16. Brakerski, Z.: Fully Homomorphic Encryption without Modulus Switching from Classical GapSVP (2012)
17. Brakerski, Z., Gentry, C., Vaikuntanathan, V.: (leveled) fully homomorphic encryption without bootstrapping. ACM Trans. Comput. Theory (TOCT) **6**(3), 1–36 (2014)
18. Fan, J., Vercauteren, F.: Somewhat Practical Fully Homomorphic Encryption. Report Number: 144 (2012)
19. Gentry, C.: Computing arbitrary functions of encrypted data. Commun. ACM **53**, 97–105 (2010)
20. Gentry, C., Halevi, S., Smart, N.P.: Fully homomorphic encryption with polylog overhead. In: Pointcheval, D., Johansson, T. (eds.) EUROCRYPT 2012. LNCS, vol. 7237, pp. 465–482. Springer, Heidelberg (2012). https://doi.org/10.1007/978-3-642-29011-4_28
21. Fan, J., Vercauteren, F.: Somewhat practical fully homomorphic encryption. Cryptology ePrint Archive, Report 2012/144 (2012)
22. Pommersheim, J.: Number Theory: A Lively Introduction with Proofs, Applications, and Stories. Wiley, Hoboken (2010)
23. Longa, P., Naehrig, M.: Speeding up the number theoretic transform for faster ideal lattice-based cryptography. In: Foresti, S., Persiano, G. (eds.) CANS 2016. LNCS, vol. 10052, pp. 124–139. Springer, Cham (2016). https://doi.org/10.1007/978-3-319-48965-0_8
24. Albrecht, M., et al.: Homomorphic encryption standard (2018)
25. Gentry, C., Halevi, S., Smart, N.P.: Homomorphic evaluation of the AES circuit. In: Safavi-Naini, R., Canetti, R. (eds.) CRYPTO 2012. LNCS, vol. 7417, pp. 850–867. Springer, Heidelberg (2012). https://doi.org/10.1007/978-3-642-32009-5_49
26. Ducas, L., Lepoint, T., Lyubashevsky, V., Schwabe, P., Seiler, G., Stehlé, D.: Crystals–dilithium: digital signatures from module lattices (2018). https://pq-crystals.org/dilithium/index.shtml
27. Bos, J., et al.: CRYSTALS - Kyber: a CCA-secure module-lattice-based KEM. In: 2018 IEEE European Symposium on Security and Privacy (EuroS P), pp. 353–367 (2018)
28. Nabeel, M., et al.: CoFHEE: a co-processor for fully homomorphic encryption execution. In: Design, Automation and Test in Europe (DATE) Conference (2023)
29. TSMC Limited: 1612nm technology. https://www.tsmc.com/english/dedicatedFoundry/technology/logic/l_16_12nm. Accessed 19 Nov 2022
30. TSMC Fights back Intel in Terms of 16nm FinFET - CTIMES News. https://en.ctimes.com.tw/DispNews.asp?O=HJY1GE204OGSAA00NK. Accessed 19 Nov 2022

Accelerating Large Kernel Convolutions with Nested Winograd Transformation

Jingbo Jiang[1], Xizi Chen[2(✉)], and Chi-Ying Tsui[1]

[1] Department of Electronic and Computer Engineering, Hong Kong University of Science and Technology, Clear Water Bay, Hong Kong
jjiangan@connect.ust.hk, eetsui@ust.hk
[2] College of Informatics, Huazhong Agricultural University, Wuhan, Hong Kong
xchenbn@mail.hzau.edu.cn

Abstract. Recent literature has shown that convolutional neural networks (CNNs) with large kernels outperform vision transformers (ViTs) and CNNs with stacked small kernels in many computer vision tasks, such as object detection and image restoration. The Winograd transformation helps reduce the number of repetitive multiplications in convolution and is widely supported by many commercial AI processors. Researchers have proposed accelerating large kernel convolutions by linearly decomposing them into many small kernel convolutions and then sequentially accelerating each small kernel convolution with the Winograd algorithm. This work proposes a nested Winograd algorithm that iteratively decomposes a large kernel convolution into small kernel convolutions and proves it to be more effective than the linear decomposition Winograd transformation algorithm. Experiments show that compared to the linear decomposition Winograd algorithm, the proposed algorithm reduces the total number of multiplications by 1.4 to 10.5 times for computing 4×4 to 31×31 convolutions.

1 Introduction

Deep neural networks have been widely applied to various computer vision tasks over the past decade. While popular neural networks use vision transformers or convolution with stacked small kernels (e.g., 3×3) as their backbone, recent literature [6,9,12,14] has found that by incorporating training techniques such as re-parameterization, convolution with large kernels such as 31×31 achieves comparable or superior results to state-of-the-art ViTs in many typical downstream computer vision tasks, with lower computational complexity. Literature has also found that large kernel convolution captures more detail than stacked small kernel convolution in applications requiring per-pixel prediction, such as semantic segmentation [17] and image super-resolution [16]. As a result, there has been increasing interest in applying large kernel convolution to different scenarios [4,15].

Convolution is typically compute-bound [10] because it requires sliding through the entire input feature map to perform repetitive multiplication-and-

Published by Springer Nature Switzerland AG 2024
I. (Abe) M. Elfadel and L. Albasha (Eds.): VLSI-SoC 2023, IFIP AICT 680, pp. 109–125, 2024.
https://doi.org/10.1007/978-3-031-70947-0_6

accumulation (MAC) operations. The Winograd transformation [11] is commonly used to reduce the computational complexity of convolution by replacing some of the expensive multiplications with cheaper operations such as additions or constant multiplications to improve computational throughput. The Winograd algorithm reduces the number of multiplications by using larger transformation matrices for the input feature map, kernel, and output feature map. However, it also introduces numerical instability and computational overhead during data transformation between spatial and Winograd domains [2]. As a result, the common practice for modern ASIC AI processors is to implement a fixed set of Winograd transformation matrices on-chip and only accelerate fixed small kernel (e.g., 3×3) convolution.

Yang et al. [21] and Huang et al. [8] have proposed different accelerator architectures to compute convolution with arbitrary size and stride based on a single set of fixed Winograd transformation matrices. For large kernel convolution operations, they linearly decompose them into a sequence of 3×3 convolution operations by slicing the large input feature maps and kernels into multiple small input tiles and 3×3 kernel tiles, respectively, and then performing 3×3 Winograd convolutions on each pair of input and kernel tiles. However, it has been found that this linear decomposition method does not fully utilize the Winograd transformation to reduce repetitive multiplications between different input tiles, thus not yielding the best multiplication efficiency.

In this work, we propose a *nested Winograd transformation algorithm* that iteratively decomposes a large convolution into a sequence of small (e.g., 3×3) convolutions and prove that it reduces more multiplications than the linear decomposition Winograd algorithm. Intuitively, this is achieved because one small Winograd transformation reduces a certain number of multiplications, and nested Winograd applies fixed small Winograd transformations more times to the data than the linear decomposition Winograd transformation. To demonstrate the effectiveness of the proposed algorithm, we propose an accelerator architecture and a runtime for utilizing nested Winograd transformation to accelerate large kernel convolution and verify its effectiveness using FPGA. We also demonstrate the way to support stride convolution by incorporating the stride Winograd algorithm onto the accelerator. We observe that nested Winograd reduces the number of multiplications by 1.4 to 10.5 times compared to the linear decomposition Winograd algorithm when running convolution with kernel sizes ranging from 4×4 to 31×31. We also show that compared to a previous linear decomposition Winograd accelerator running FSRCNN-s for image super-resolution [18], our proposed nested Winograd accelerator achieves an overall 1.27 times throughput improvement. In summary, the contributions of this paper are as follows:

- A nested Winograd transformation algorithm is proposed to accelerate the execution of convolution with large kernel sizes and proved to outperform the state-of-the-art linear decomposition Winograd algorithm.

- An accelerator architecture and runtime are proposed to accelerate native convolution with arbitrary kernel sizes using nested Winograd transformation.

2 Background

2.1 Winograd Algorithm

A 2D stride-1 native convolution correlates M channels of input feature maps x of size $H \times W$ with N groups of M-channel kernels w of size $R \times C$ to produce N channels of output feature maps y. For each channel of the $R \times C$ kernel, "“the native convolution takes an $R \times C$ tile from the input feature map, performs a MAC operation on it, and produces one output pixel. The input feature map window then slides by 1 to take the next input tile.

In contrast, Winograd convolution takes a larger $l \times l$ input tile x from the input feature map, transforms it along with the kernel into the Winograd domain to produce two $l \times l$ tiles, and then performs element-wise matrix multiplication (EWMM) between these two $l \times l$ tiles to create an $l \times l$ output tile. Finally, the output tile is transformed back into the spatial domain to produce an $m \times m$ output tile. Stride m is used to sample the next input tile from the input feature map. This procedure is denoted as $F(m \times m, r \times r)$ [11], where $r \times r$ is the kernel size of the native convolution (in this example $R = C = r$) and $l = m + r - 1$. This process is illustrated in Fig. 1. Let B, G and A denote the input, kernel, and output transformation matrices, respectively, and let $\odot$ represent the EWMM. The 2D Winograd convolution can be formulated as

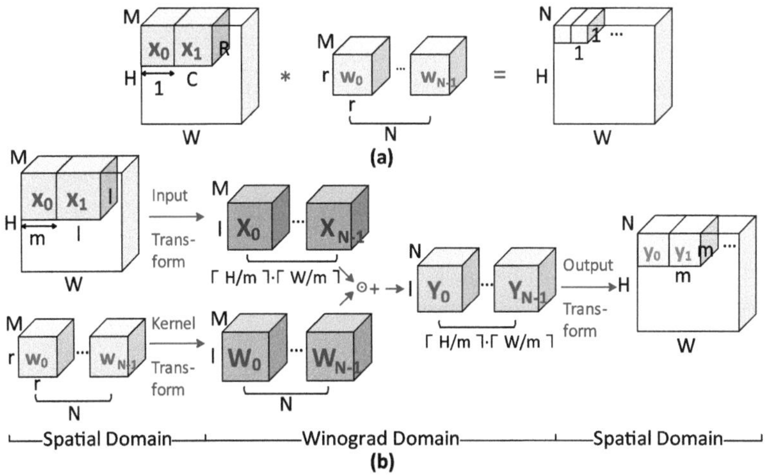

Fig. 1. The computation flow of (a) the native convolution and (b) the Winograd convolution $F(m \times m, r \times \ r)$.

$$y = A^T \left(B^T x B \odot G w G^T\right) A \tag{1}$$

For 1D Winograd convolution applied to the input vector x and kernel vector w, (1) reduces to

$$y = A^T \left(B^T x \odot \mathrm{G} w\right) \tag{2}$$

and is represented as $F(m, r)$. By comparing (1) and (2), it can be seen that multi-dimensional Winograd convolution is constructed by applying the 1D Winograd transformation to each axis of the input tensor, kernel, and output tensor, respectively. Therefore, $F(m, r)$ is referred to as the *Winograd base*, reflecting its role as the base operator for constructing the multi-dimensional Winograd algorithm. The transformation matrices of a commonly used Winograd base $F(2, 3)$ is

$$B^T = \begin{bmatrix} 1 & 0 & -1 & 0 \\ 0 & 1 & 1 & 0 \\ 0 & -1 & 1 & 0 \\ 0 & 1 & 0 & -1 \end{bmatrix} \; G = \begin{bmatrix} 1 & 0 & 0 \\ 1/2 & 1/2 & 1/2 \\ 1/2 & -1/2 & 1/2 \\ 0 & 0 & 1 \end{bmatrix} \; A^T = \begin{bmatrix} 1 & 1 & 1 & 0 \\ 0 & 1 & -1 & -1 \end{bmatrix} \tag{3}$$

The Winograd algorithm reduces the number of multiplications by exploiting data overlaps between adjacent input tiles in native convolution [20], which would otherwise require computing repetitive multiplications on the same data. The Winograd algorithm transforms the MAC operation from the real number field to a finite field, allowing it to explore the data overlaps and use additions and constant multiplications to replace some of the repetitive multiplications. If there are no data overlaps between adjacent input tiles, the Winograd algorithm reduces to $F(1, r)$ and converges to native convolution.

2.2 Linear-Decomposition Winograd Algorithm

Accelerating convolutions with different kernel sizes $r \times r$ requires using different Winograd bases. However, instantiating multiple Winograd bases on-chip reduces area efficiency. Linear-decomposition Winograd algorithm provides a solution for accelerating convolution with $R > r$ on a fixed $F(m, r)$.

Figure 2 illustrates the procedure for accelerating a 3×3 convolution using the linear-decomposition Winograd algorithm with $F(m = 2, r = 2)$. The $R \times R$ kernel is divided into $\lceil R/r \rceil^2 = 4$ groups of non-overlapping sub-kernel tiles, each with a size of $r \times r$ and can be accelerated with $F(m = 2, r = 2)$. The input tile, sized $h \times w$ where $h = w = l + (\lceil R/r \rceil - 1) \cdot r = 5$, is also divided into the same number of sub-input tiles. Unlike sub-kernel tiles, adjacent sub-input tiles have a size of $l \times l$ and are sliced using a stride-r sliding window, creating data overlap between them. EWMM is then performed between these sub-input tiles and sub-kernel tiles to produce $\lceil R/r \rceil^2$ groups of sub-output tiles. These sub-output tiles are further summed together to produce an $l \times l$ output tile. Note that in this step, M input channels are accumulated into one output channel. Finally, the $l \times l$ output tile is transformed back into the spatial domain

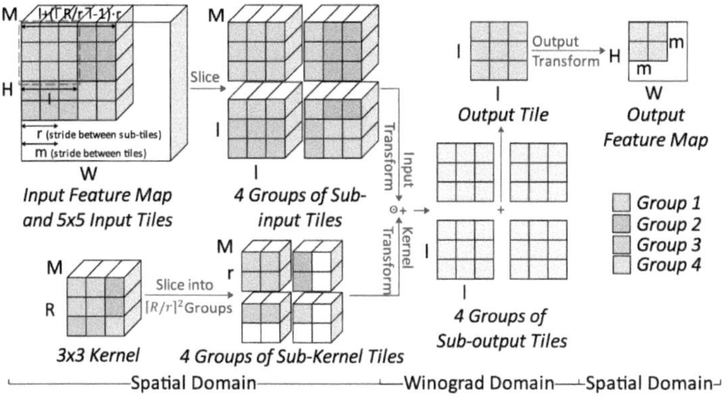

Fig. 2. Accelerating the convolution of a 5×5 input tile with a 3×3 kernel using linear-decomposition Winograd $F(2 \times 2,\ 2 \times 2)$.

to produce an $m \times m$ output tile. The sliding window on the input feature map slides by m to generate the next input tile.

Although the Winograd algorithm is applied to each pair of sub-input and sub-kernel tiles to reduce the number of multiplications, the linear decomposition algorithm does not explore the data overlap between sub-input tiles. Methods exist to apply additional Winograd transformations on these overlapped data to further reduce the number of repetitive multiplications.

2.3 Stride Winograd Algorithm

Stride Winograd [20] is an algorithm that accelerates stride convolution with the Winograd transformation. It can be used in harmony with the nested Winograd algorithm to compute convolution with arbitrary size and stride with only one Winograd base. The stride Winograd algorithm states that a stride-s convolution with length-r weight, denoted as $F(m, r; s)$, can be decomposed into s separate computations of $F(m, r')$, where $r' = \lceil r/s \rceil$. The expression is symbolically expressed as

$$\begin{gathered} F(m, r; s) = s \cdot F(m, r') \\ r' = \lceil r/s \rceil \end{gathered} \tag{4}$$

For 2D convolution, the equation becomes

$$\begin{gathered} F(m \times m, r \times r; s) = s^2 \cdot F(m \times m, r' \times r') \\ r' = \lceil r/s \rceil \end{gathered} \tag{5}$$

Data re-arrangement on input feature map and weight is required for the stride Winograd algorithm: data are fetched from the input tile and weight with stride-s in both horizontal and vertical directions. The fetched data are concatenated to form s^2 groups of sub-input tiles and sub-weights, respectively. Then, EWMM is performed on each sub-input tile and sub-weight group, generating s^2

groups of results. Finally, the results are summed into one group and transformed back to the space domain. An example of performing stride-2 3×3 convolution using $F(2 \times 2, 2 \times 2)$ is shown in Fig. 3. The edge length of the output tile is m, and the edge length of the input tile is calculated as

$$l = (m + r - 1) \cdot s \tag{6}$$

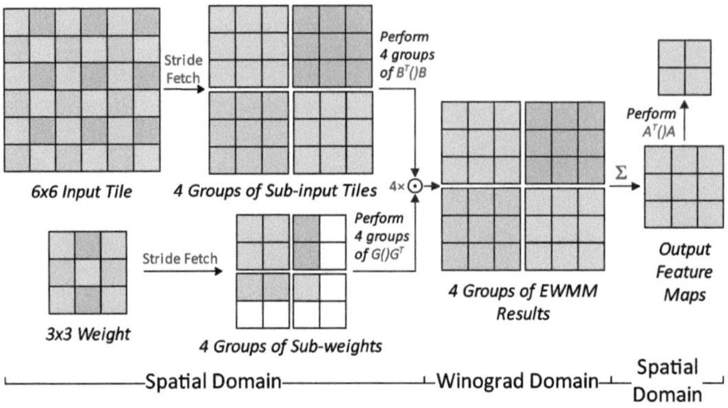

Fig. 3. Computing 3×3 stride-2 convolution with $F(2, 2)$ using stride Winograd algorithm.

3 The Nested Winograd Algorithm

3.1 The Nested Decomposition Algorithm

Nested decomposition is a general method that uses high-dimensional fast algorithm transformations, such as 2D Winograd or 2D fast Fourier transformation (FFT), to accelerate low-dimensional convolution (e.g., 1D). This is achieved by re-expressing the input vector x with length $N = N_1 \cdot N_2$ into a matrix X of size $N_1 \times N_2$. Then, a 1D fast algorithm transformation is applied to each column followed by each row of X. This procedure can be formulated as

$$(A \cdot X) \cdot A^T \tag{7}$$

where A represents the transformation matrix of the 1D fast algorithm. Note that (7) has a similar form to the 2D Winograd transformation shown in (1) but is used to accelerate 1D convolution. Different data pre-processing procedures, such as padding and repeating, must be applied to X to align it with the corresponding re-expressed kernels for various types of long convolution problems.

Nested decomposition has been applied to various types of convolution problems throughout history. For example, in 1964, Cooley and Tukey applied nested decomposition to accelerate discrete Fourier transform (DFT) [5]. Later, in 1977,

Agarwal and Cooley applied nested decomposition with Winograd algorithm to the cyclic convolution [1]. These prior works inspired us to develop a method for applying nested decomposition with Winograd algorithm to convolution in machine learning.

3.2 The Proposed Nested Winograd Algorithm

We begin by using an example to illustrate how to apply our proposed nested Winograd transformation to 1D convolution and then extend it to 2D convolution. Figure 4 illustrates the process of using nested Winograd with $F(m = 2, r = 2)$ to accelerate a 1D convolution with kernels of length $R = 4$.

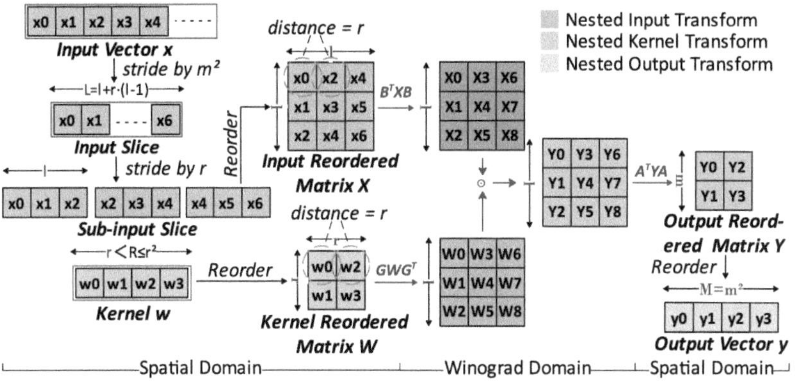

Fig. 4. Example of accelerating 1D convolution with a length-4 kernel using nested Winograd algorithm based on $F(2, 2)$.

The first step is to perform the *nested input transformation*. This involves applying a stride-m^2 sliding window to slice the long input vector into length-L input slices, where $L = l + r \cdot (l - 1)$ and $l = m + r - 1$. Then, a stride-r sliding window is applied to further slice the input slices into length-l sub-input slices, which are arranged column-by-column to form the *input reordered matrix* X of size $l \times l$. The 2D Winograd input transformation $B^T \cdot () \cdot B$ is then applied to X to transform it into the Winograd domain. The second step is to perform the *nested kernel transformation*. This is achieved by reshaping the length-R kernel into a $r \times r$ *sized kernel reorder matrix* W and using the 2D Winograd kernel transformation $G \cdot () \cdot G^T$ to transform W into the Winograd domain.

The nested Winograd algorithm requires data alignment between the input data and the kernel. This means that adjacent columns in the input reordered matrix must have the same *index distance* as the kernel matrix. For instance, as illustrated by the dashed yellow circle in Fig. 4, the horizontal elements in the kernel reordered matrix have index distance $r = 2$. This necessitates that the sliding window applied to the input slice has a stride equal to r. Given that $F(2, 2)$ requires the sub-input slice to have a length of l, the window length of the input slice is calculated as $L = r \cdot (l-1)+l$. Finally, the input vector x should stride by m^2 because nested Winograd produces m^2 output data elements when convolving kernel with one input slice.

The final step involves performing an EWMM between the input and kernel reordered matrices. This is followed by a *nested output transformation*, where a 2D Winograd output transformation $A^T \cdot () \cdot A$ is applied to produce the output reordered matrix Y. Finally, the output reordered matrix is flattened into a length-m^2 output vector.

Winograd algorithm specifies that the kernel transformed by $F(m, r)$ must have a length no greater than r. Similarly, the kernel transformed by $F(m \times m, r \times r)$ used in nested Winograd must have a length R no greater than r^2. To accelerate convolution with a kernel length greater than r^2, the kernel should first be reshaped into a tensor and then be transformed with a multi-dimensional Winograd algorithm [3]. If R is not equal to an integer power of r (i.e., $r, r^2, r^3, \ldots$), zero-padding should be performed at the end of kernel x. In general, if an n-dimensional Winograd transformation is used, the nested Winograd algorithm can accelerate convolution with a kernel length no greater than r^n, consume l^n multiplications, and produce m^n output data elements for computing one input slice.

The above description outlines the general procedure for aligning data between the input and kernel reordered matrices for all $F(m, r)$. However, it is recommended to use $F(m, r)$ with $m = r$ when possible. Otherwise, the output vector y may include redundant data elements that should be discarded, potentially reducing the computational efficiency.

The procedure for accelerating 2D native convolution using the nested Winograd algorithm is illustrated in Fig. 5. First, the previously described nested input and kernel transformations are applied to all rows followed by columns of the input tiles and kernels, respectively. Then, EWMM is performed between the transformed input and kernel, and produces the transformed output matrix. Finally, the first row of the transformed output matrix is transformed back to the space domain using the nested output transformation. The result is then reshaped to form the output vector. This process is iteratively performed on all rows followed by all columns of the transformed output matrix to produce the final output tile.

3.3 Multiplication Complexity Analysis

We provide an algorithm analysis to demonstrate the advantages of using nested Winograd. The multiplication complexity is defined as the number of multiplications required to produce one output data element in a convolution. Similar to the multiplication complexity analysis of the vanilla Winograd algorithm [20], the number of additions and constant multiplications incurred by the Winograd transformation are considered as overhead and are not included in this analysis.

To derive the multiplication complexity, consider a convolution of a length-R kernel with an infinite length input vector using $F(m, r)$. The linear decomposition Winograd algorithm slices the length-R kernel into R/r sub-vectors and

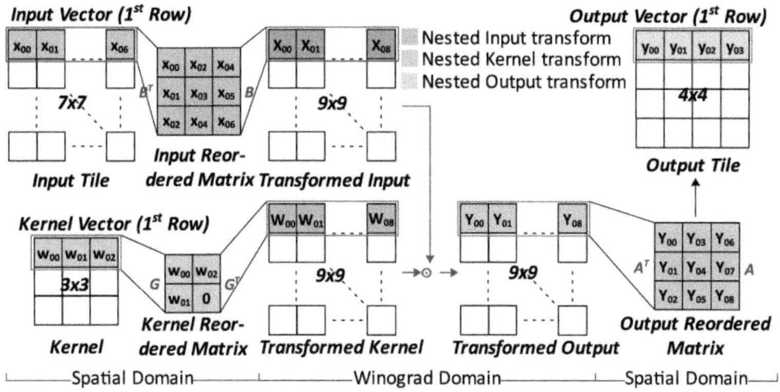

Fig. 5. Accelerating a 2D convolution with a 3×3 kernel using nested Winograd algorithm based on $F(2,2)$.

applies $F(m,r)$ to them individually to produce a length-m output kernel. Since each $F(m,r)$ transformation requires $l = m + r - 1$ multiplications, the overall multiplication complexity is

$$\mathcal{O}((l/m) \cdot (R/r)) \tag{8}$$

For nested Winograd, we only analyze Winograd base with $m = r$ to simplify the discussion, the $m \neq r$ case can be derived similarly. Assuming the reordered tensor of nested Winograd has $b = \log_r R$ dimensions. Since applying $F(m,r)$ to one length-r kernel consumes l multiplications and produces m output elements, the overall algorithm complexity for nested Winograd is the product of the multiplication complexity in all dimensions, given by

$$\mathcal{O}\left((l/m)^{\log_r R}\right) \tag{9}$$

It is hard to directly compare the complexity of (9) and (8) at this stage. Thus, we further approximate (9) with the order-1 Taylor expansion at point r and we get

$$\mathcal{O}\left(\frac{l}{m \cdot r} \cdot \log_r\left(\frac{l}{m}\right) \cdot R + \alpha\right) \tag{10}$$

where α represents the constant term. If we apply $l = m + r - 1$, then divide (10) by (8) and let the result smaller or equal to 1, we get $m + r - 1 \leq m \cdot r$, which is valid for m and r belongs to any positive integer. It means that nested Winograd almost always has a gentler slope than the linear decomposition Winograd algorithm. However, as (10) also has a constant term which may let nested Winograd be less efficient than OLA-Winograd, a simulation on some common cases is performed and the performance difference between these two algorithms is summarized in Sect. 5.

4 The Accelerator Design

4.1 Overview of the Accelerator Design

We designed an accelerator architecture and implemented it with Xilinx ZYNQ FPGA to evaluate the effectiveness of the nested Winograd algorithm. The accelerator is composed of two parts: an on-chip Arm processor that implements a runtime for decomposing a large kernel convolution into multiple fixed $F(m, r)$ Winograd convolutions, and a fabric logic array that implements a convolution engine for executing fixed $F(m, r)$ Winograd convolutions.

The accelerator is programmed by calling self-defined C++ functions such as *Conv2d()* in the Xilinx Software Development Kit. When the *Conv2d()* function is called, the Arm processor decomposes it into a sequence of $F(m, r)$ Winograd convolution instructions and sends them to the convolution engine via the AXI-LITE bus through the Xilinx General Purpose (GP) port. Upon receiving an instruction, the convolution engine decodes it into multiple micro-operations which are then dispatched to different compute pipelines for execution. Once input data is streamed in and all executions are completed, the convolution engine streams the output data from its on-chip buffer to the external DRAM via the AXI-MM bus through Xilinx High Performance (HP) port. The Winograd convolution instruction is then retired and this process is repeated until all layers of a CNN have been processed.

4.2 The Convolution Engine

The micro-architecture of the convolution engine is illustrated in Fig. 6, which majorly contains the following modules: an instruction FIFO buffering the instruction sent from the Arm processor; a Controller decoding the instruction into micro-operations and dispatching them to the compute pipelines; four multi-stage compute pipelines including the forward transformation pipeline (p0), the general matrix multiplication (GEMM) pipeline (p1), the backward transformation pipeline (p2), and the post-processing pipeline (p3); scratchpad memories (SPMs) including InBuf, WBuf, Acc.Buf, OBuf isolating the compute pipelines; AXI-InFIFO, AXI-WFIFO, and AXI-OFIFO exchanging data between the Arm processor and the convolution engine; a Line Buffer unrolling input tensor into overlapped input tiles; pipelined Input, kernel and output 2D Winograd transformation units implementing fixed Winograd base; matrix transpose blocks (.T) implemented as a shift-register based buffer to perform Winograd transformations in a loop for accelerating 2D convolution with nested Winograd; a processing element (PE) containing G_{ch} channels of $G_w \times G_{in}$ number of MACs connected with a 2D broadcast network to perform output stationary GEMM; $G_w \times G_{in}$ number of adders accumulating the ELWW outputs for the stride Winograd algorithm; fixed-functional units including Relu, Bias, and Quantization for post-processing.

The total number of execution cycles required to complete one instruction varies among the four compute pipelines (p0-p3). This variation can be

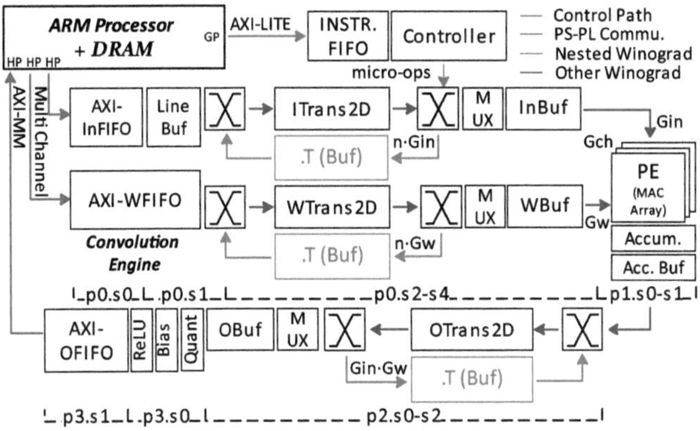

Fig. 6. The architecture of the accelerator and the convolution engine.

attributed to the fact that the nested Winograd transformation in p0 can require multiple iterations of $F(m \times m, r \times r)$. During each iteration, data is transposed by the .T block and returned to the Trans2D block until completed. p1 consumes the transformation results while p0 produces and writes them to InBuf, WBuf, and OBuf. The production and consumption throughput do not need to be equal. p1 is often the throughput bottleneck of all compute pipelines due to the limited number of power-hungry MACs imposed by the thermal design power (TDP) requirement. Multiple Winograd convolution instructions can be pipelined naturally to maximize the resource utilization rate of p0 to p3.

We designed a unified 6D data layout $(HW_{in}, C_{in}, g, G_{in}, H', W')$ to represent the feature map and the intermediate data for nested Winograd, stride Winograd, and the direct Winograd $F(m, r)$. The meanings of H' and W' are not the same for different types of Winograd convolutions: for the nested Winograd, it represents the height and width of the input tile, which equal to l^2; for stride Winograd, H' represents the total number of groups and W' represents the flattened input tile size which has the size l^2; direct Winograd performs $F(m, r)$ on an (l, l) input tile, thus $H' = 1$ and $W' = l^2$. $HW_{in} = \lceil H/m^b \rceil \cdot \lceil W/m^b \rceil$ represents the total number of input sliding windows, where we have $b = 2$ for nested Winograd and $b = 1$ for other cases. g represents the number of groups for stride Winograd. C_{in} represents the number of input channels. The data layout for the weight and the output feature maps are constructed similarly.

4.3 Theoretical Performance Modeling

Different types of convolutions require different computation-to-communication ratios, which affects the selection of the architectural parameters of an accelerator [19]. In this section, a theoretical performance model for the proposed accelerator is derived, providing intuition to designers adopting the accelerator to different SoC projects or FPGA platforms. The most prominent factor that affects the computation throughput is the number of MAC units, which is calculated as

$$MAC = G_{ch} \cdot G_{in} \cdot G_w \tag{11}$$

When the bandwidth is sufficient and the utilization rate of MAC is full, the execution time T of a convolution layer is

$$T = C_{in} \cdot g \cdot H' \cdot \left\lceil \frac{\lceil H/m^b \rceil \cdot \lceil W/m^b \rceil}{G_{in}} \right\rceil \cdot \left\lceil \frac{C_{out}}{G_w} \right\rceil / f \tag{12}$$

where f denotes the frequency of the accelerator.

The computation throughput can be bounded by the bandwidth of transferring data and weight from the off-chip DRAM to the accelerator. The accelerator is normally designed to have sufficient bandwidth to fully utilize the MAC unit, which means the data transfer time should be smaller than T. Denote the total bandwidth between the DDR and accelerator as BW (Gb/s), we have

$$BW \geq \frac{16bit \cdot (HW_{in} \cdot C_{in} \cdot g \cdot G_{in} \cdot H' \cdot W' + H \cdot W \cdot C_{out} + R \cdot C \cdot C_{in} \cdot C_{out})}{T} \tag{13}$$

The proposed accelerator utilizes SRAM (or BRAM in FPGA) to synchronize the data between pipelines. We provide a simple theoretical model to measure the size of SRAM

$$\begin{aligned} SRAM(bit) = 16bit \cdot (G_{ch}^2 \cdot (G_{in} + G_w + G_{in} \cdot G_w) + C_{in} \cdot C_b \cdot G_in \cdot l^4 \\ + C_w \cdot C_b \cdot G_w \cdot r^4 + G_{in} \cdot G_w \cdot m^4) \end{aligned} \tag{14}$$

It is also important to model the Winograd transformation units since they consume non-negligible hardware resources. The area modeling is done in a gray-box fashion: we synthesize the hardware of three Winograd transformation units to obtain their area as S_{in}, S_w, and S_o. Then, if n-channels of the Winograd transformation matrices are implemented on-chip, the total area of the Winograd transformation unit S_{wino} is estimated as

$$S_{wino} = n \cdot (G_{in} \cdot S_{in} + G_w \cdot S_w + G_{in} \cdot G_w \cdot S_o) \tag{15}$$

4.4 The Decomposition Algorithm

The decomposition algorithm running in runtime on the Arm processor decomposes a $Conv2d()$ function that executes a convolution with arbitrary kernel size and stride into a stream of $F(m, r)$ Winograd convolution instructions. Alg. 1 shows the procedure of this algorithm.

An example of using Algorithm 1 to decompose a 31×31 stride-2 convolution, which is represented as $F(M, R = 31; S = 2)$, into a stream of $F(m = 3, r = 3)$ Winograd convolution instructions is shown below. Algorithm 1 iteratively checks if the given $F(M, R; S)$ has $S > 1$ or $R > r$, and checking $S > 1$ has higher priority than checking $R > r$. The first round of checking finds that $F(M, R = 31; S = 2)$ has $S > 1$. Thus, it is decomposed with the stride Winograd algorithm and gives

$$F(M = 3, 31; 2) = 2 \cdot F(3, 16) \tag{16}$$

Algorithm 1. Decomposition Algorithm

Input: $F(M, R; S)$ to be decomposed
Output†**:** ET containing $\{F(m,r), \wedge, \cdot, Const.\}, M$
Initialize ET and M
$ET = [F(M, R; S),]$
$M = m$
Procedure to decompose $F(M, R; S)$:
while For loop not ended **do**
  for (F in ET) and (F is a Winograd base) **do**
    if F has $S > 1$ **then**
      F_{out}, s = StrdWinoDecompose(F)
      Replace F in ET with $[s, F_{out}, \cdot]$
    else if F has $R > r$ **then**
      F_{out}, b = NestedWinoDecompose(F)
      Replace F in ET with $[b, F_{out}, \wedge]$
      Let $M = M^b$
    end if
  end for
end while

function NestedWinoDecompose($F(m, r)$)
$b = 0$, $r_{tgt} = 3$, $r_{tmp} = r$
while $r_{tmp} > r_{tgt}$ **do**
  $r_{tmp} = float(r_{tmp}/r_{tgt}); b = b + 1;$
end while
return $F(m, r_{tgt})$, b
end function

function StrdWinoDecompose($F(m, r; s)$)
return $F(m, \lceil r/s \rceil)$, s
end function
return ET, M

† ET denotes expression tree, M denotes output length, $Const.$ denotes constants represented with letter in lower case.

The second round of checking finds that $F(3, 16)$ has $R > r$. Thus, it is decomposed with the nested Winograd algorithm and gives

$$F(M = 27, 31; 2) = 2 \cdot F(3, 3)^3 \tag{17}$$

In the above equations, $F(m, r)^b$ represents the procedure of nested Winograd with a nesting order of b, and $s \cdot F(m, r)$ represents the procedure of stride Winograd with a group number of s. In the runtime C++ program, (17) is implemented as an *expression tree* in *reverse polish notation* (RPN)

$$F(M = 27, 31; 2) = [2, 3, F(3, 3), \wedge, \cdot] \tag{18}$$

The expression tree can be then evaluated to construct the instruction stream sent to the accelerator.

5 Experiments

5.1 Multiplication Complexity Simulation

To compare the multiplication complexity between nested Winograd and linear decomposition Winograd algorithm, we simulated 2D convolutions with different kernel sizes ranging from 3×3 to 31×31 with $F(3,3)$, $F(4,3)$ and $F(4,4)$. Winograd base larger than $F(4,3)$ is rarely used due to the increased transformation overhead [2].

The simulation results summarized in Fig. 7 demonstrate that the nested Winograd algorithm reduces 1.17 to 10.56 times more multiplications than the linear decomposition Winograd algorithm and reduces 2.07 to 44.25 times more multiplications than the native convolution. The gap increases as the kernel size becomes larger, and the zig-zag shaped multiplication reduction curve results from the fact that nested Winograd based on $F(m,r)$ requires padding the kernel height and width to the power of r.

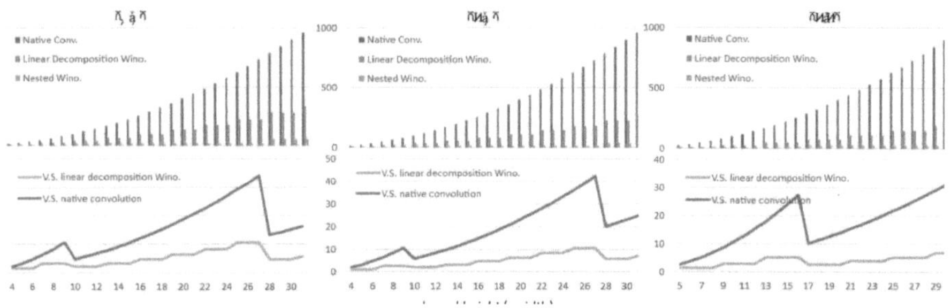

Fig. 7. Multiplication complexity comparison between the native convolution, linear decomposition Winograd and nested Winograd algorithm.

5.2 End-to-End Performance Evaluation

We compare the throughput of running nested Winograd and linear decomposition Winograd algorithm on the accelerator designed in Sect. 4 with CNNs that have kernel size ranging from 5×5 to 9×9. The accelerator is implemented on the Xilinx ZCU102 board containing an Arm dual-core A53 processor with a DDR4-2666 providing sufficient bandwidth in off-chip data accessing. The convolution engine is implemented to run at 200MHZ which is consistent with [14]. The convolution engine is implemented with $F(3,3)$ and the G_{ch}, G_{in}, G_w are set to be 25, 6, 6.

We compared the throughput of running the nested Winograd algorithm and the linear decomposition Winograd algorithm on the accelerator designed in Sect. 4 with different CNNs. The accelerator was implemented on a Xilinx ZCU102 board containing an Arm dual-core A53 processor with DDR4-2666, providing sufficient bandwidth for off-chip data access. The convolution engine is implemented to run at 200 MHZ with 16-bit data path. The Winograd base is set to $F(3,3)$ and the G_{ch}, G_{in}, G_w are set to be 25, 6, 6.

The acceleration results of four single convolution layers are demonstrated in Table 1. The 5×5 and 9×9 convolution layers were chosen from the acceleration result of SRCNN [7], while the 7×7 depthwise convolution layer is chosen from PNasNet [13]. We further compare the end-to-end acceleration results with a previous work [18], which design an FPGA accelerator running FSRCNN-s to upscale an image from 1920×1080 to 3840×2160. They propose an FTConv algorithm to decompose all the layers in FSRCNN-s to 5×5 convolutions, then use linear decomposition Winograd to accelerate it. The decomposed FSRCNN-s has 86.1% MACs coming from the 5×5 convolution. The results summarized in Table 2 show that our accelerator achieves 1.27 times end-to-end speed up compared with [18] with around the same number of DSPs. We did not observe a PSNR drop by adopting nested Winograd in this experiment.

Table 1. GOPs Speed Up on Different Convolution

Conv. Type	From	Conv. Shape in (Cout, Cin, H, W)	GOPs[b] Nested Win.	GOPs L.D.[c] Win.	Speed up
Conv2D 9×9[a]	SRCNN Layer-1	(64,1,256,256)	3503	1063	3.29
Depth-wise 7×7	PNasNet	(54,54,83,83)	540	384	1.41
Conv2D 5×5[a]	SRCNN Layer-2	(32,64,256,256)	991	692	1.43
Conv2D 5×5[a]	SRCNN Layer-3	(1,32,256,256)	186	130	1.43

[a.] These three layers concludes all the layers of the SRCNN.
[b.] GOPs = (#multiplication + #addition)/execution time when using native convolution.
[c.] L.D. is short for linear decomposition.

Table 2. Throughput Comparison on FSRCNN-s Network

	#LUT	#DSP	BRAM (Mb)	Frame Rates
[18]	172K(63%)	746(30%)	10.9(34%)	120.4(fps)
Ours	184K(67%)	748(30%)	9.8(30%)	153.1(fps)

6 Conclusion

In this work, a nested Winograd algorithm is proposed for accelerating convolution with large kernel size. The multiplication complexity is reduced when comparing with existing linear decomposition Winograd algorithm. Furthermore, an accelerator combining the stride Winograd algorithm and the proposed nested Winograd algorithm is designed to accelerate convolution with arbitrary kernel sizes and stride. Simulation results show 1.4 to 10.5 times speed-up in executing convolution with kernel size from 4×4 to 31×31 using $F(3,3)$ Winograd transformation.

Acknowledgment. We would like to extend our sincere gratitude to the Hong Kong AI Chip Center for Emerging Smart Systems (ACCESS) for their pivotal support to our work.

References

1. Agarwal, R., Cooley, J.: New algorithms for digital convolution. IEEE Trans. Acoust. Speech Signal Process. **25**(5), 392–410 (1977)
2. Andri, R., Bussolino, B., Cipolletta, A., Cavigelli, L., Wang, Z.: Going further with winograd convolutions: Tap-wise quantization for efficient inference on 4x4 tiles. In: 2022 55th IEEE/ACM International Symposium on Microarchitecture (MICRO), pp. 582–598. IEEE (2022)
3. Budden, D., Matveev, A., Santurkar, S., Chaudhuri, S.R., Shavit, N.: Deep tensor convolution on multicores. In: International Conference on Machine Learning, pp. 615–624. PMLR (2017)
4. Chen, Y., Liu, J., Qi, X., Zhang, X., Sun, J., Jia, J.: Scaling up kernels in 3D CNNs. arXiv preprint arXiv:2206.10555 (2022)
5. Cooley, J.W., Tukey, J.W.: An algorithm for the machine calculation of complex Fourier series. Math. Comput. **19**(90), 297–301 (1965)
6. Ding, X., Zhang, X., Han, J., Ding, G.: Scaling up your kernels to 31×31: revisiting large kernel design in CNNs. In: Proceedings of the IEEE/CVF Conference on Computer Vision and Pattern Recognition, pp. 11963–11975 (2022). https://doi.org/10.1109/cvpr52688.2022.01166
7. Dong, C., Loy, C.C., He, K., Tang, X.: Learning a deep convolutional network for image super-resolution. In: Fleet, D., Pajdla, T., Schiele, B., Tuytelaars, T. (eds.) ECCV 2014 Part IV. LNCS, vol. 8692, pp. 184–199. Springer, Cham (2014). https://doi.org/10.1007/978-3-319-10593-2_13
8. Huang, D., et al.: A decomposable winograd method for n-d convolution acceleration in video analysis. Int. J. Comput. Vision **129**(10), 2806–2826 (2021)
9. Huang, T., Chen, J., Jiang, L.: Ds-unext: depthwise separable convolution network with large convolutional kernel for medical image segmentation. SIViP **17**(5), 1775–1783 (2023)
10. Jouppi, N.P., Young, C., Patil, N., Patterson, D.: A domain-specific architecture for deep neural networks. Commun. ACM **61**(9), 50–59 (2018)
11. Lavin, A., Gray, S.: Fast algorithms for convolutional neural networks. In: Proceedings of the IEEE Conference on Computer Vision and Pattern Recognition, pp. 4013–4021 (2016)
12. Lee, H.H., Bao, S., Huo, Y., Landman, B.A.: 3D UX-Net: a large kernel volumetric convnet modernizing hierarchical transformer for medical image segmentation. arXiv preprint arXiv:2209.15076 (2022)
13. Liu, C., et al.: Progressive neural architecture search. In: Proceedings of the European Conference on Computer Vision (ECCV), pp. 19–34 (2017)
14. Liu, S., et al.: More convnets in the 2020s: scaling up kernels beyond 51x51 using sparsity. arXiv preprint arXiv:2207.03620 (2022)
15. Luo, P., Xiao, G., Gao, X., Wu, S.: LKD-Net: large kernel convolution network for single image dehazing. In: 2023 IEEE International Conference on Multimedia and Expo (ICME), pp. 1601–1606. IEEE (2023)
16. Luo, W., Li, Y., Urtasun, R., Zemel, R.: Understanding the effective receptive field in deep convolutional neural networks. In: Advances in Neural Information Processing Systems, vol. 29 (2016)

17. Peng, C., Zhang, X., Yu, G., Luo, G., Sun, J.: Large kernel matters–improve semantic segmentation by global convolutional network. In: Proceedings of the IEEE Conference on Computer Vision and Pattern Recognition, pp. 1743–1751 (2017)
18. Shi, B., Tang, Z., Luo, G., Jiang, M.: Winograd-based real-time super-resolution system on FPGA. In: 2019 International Conference on Field-Programmable Technology (ICFPT), pp. 423–426. IEEE (2019)
19. Williams, S., Waterman, A., Patterson, D.: Roofline: an insightful visual performance model for multicore architectures. Commun. ACM **52**(4), 65–76 (2009). https://doi.org/10.1145/1498765.1498785
20. Winograd, S.: Arithmetic Complexity of Computations, vol. 33. Siam (1980)
21. Yang, C., Wang, Y., Wang, X., Geng, L.: WRA: A 2.2-to-6.3 tops highly unified dynamically reconfigurable accelerator using a novel winograd decomposition algorithm for convolutional neural networks. IEEE Trans. Circ. Syst. I: Regular Papers 66(9), 3480–3493 (2019)

A Unified and Energy-Efficient Depthwise Separable Convolution Accelerator

Yi Chen(✉), Jie Lou, Christian Lanius, Florian Freye, Johnson Loh, and Tobias Gemmeke

Chair of Integrated Digital Systems and Circuit Design, RWTH Aachen University, Aachen, Germany
{chen,lou,lanius,freye,loh,gemmeke}@ids.rwth-aachen.de
https://www.ids.rwth-aachen.de/

Abstract. Lightweight convolutional neural networks (CNNs) reduce computational workloads, making them suitable for embedded devices with limited hardware resources compared to conventional CNNs. Depthwise separable convolution (DSC) serves as the fundamental convolution unit of lightweight CNNs. This paper introduces a hardware accelerator tailored for DSC in Application-Specific Integrated Circuit (ASIC), featuring a unified engine supporting both depthwise convolution (DWC) and pointwise convolution (PWC) with high hardware utilization. It ensures 100% processing element (PE) array utilization for DWC and achieves up to 98% utilization for PWC while minimizing latency. By partitioning the input feature map (ifmap) Static Random-Access Memory (SRAM) into three banks, memory access is streamlined. Furthermore, a data scheduling strategy, along with a multiplexed registers (MR) bank based First-In-First-Out (FIFO) system between adjacent PEs, is implemented to maximize data reuse and reduce latency. This work is implemented in a 22 nm FDSOI technology and validated on the CIFAR10 dataset using the MobileNetV1 architecture. The proposed DSC accelerator can operate at 1 GHz, exhibiting an energy efficiency of 5.07 (3.96) TOPS/W and an area efficiency of 519.2 (461.52) GOPS/mm^2 for DWC (PWC) at 0.8 V. Scaling the supply voltage down to 0.5 V increases the energy efficiency to 13.64 TOPS/W for DWC and 10.64 TOPS/W for PWC.

Keywords: depthwise separable convolution · unified engine · hardware accelerator · PE utilization · energy-efficient design · memory access

1 Introduction

In recent years, the use of convolutional neural networks (CNNs) has increased dramatically in a variety of fields such as image recognition, natural language processing, and object detection. Nevertheless, the growing complexity of CNNs presents challenges, particularly in finding efficient mappings of network model to the computing architecture and related need for low power consumption.

I. (Abe) M. Elfadel and L. Albasha (Eds.): VLSI-SoC 2023, IFIP AICT 680, pp. 127–146, 2024.
https://doi.org/10.1007/978-3-031-70947-0_7

To tackle above challenges, lightweight CNNs have emerged as a promising solution. An increasing number of networks are incorporating layers of better computational efficiency, such as Inception [1], Xception [2], MobileNet series [3–5], ShuffleNet [6], EfficientNet [7], Transformer [8] and Conformer [9]. These architectures leverages depthwise separable convolution (DSC), which comprises two components: depthwise convolution (DWC) and pointwise convolution (PWC).

There exists a significant demand for processors or accelerators that can efficiently execute such CNN models. There are several hardware optimization methods, such as row-stationary (RS) dataflow introduced by Eyeriss [10], that significantly reduce data movement and increase data reuse in CNNs processors. Diverse optimization methods [11–13] further enhance data reuse efficiency. Some CNNs accelerators have incorporated systolic arrays to reduce processing time and improve throughput by leveraging data parallelism [14,15]. Nevertheless, these accelerators are tailored for standard convolution (SC) and cannot be directly applied to lightweight CNNs architecture.

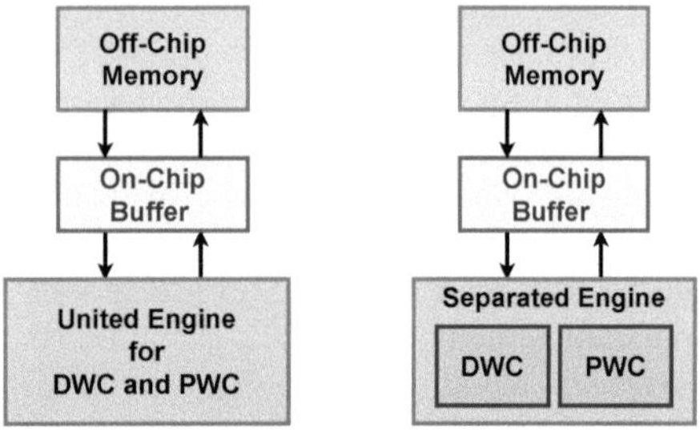

Fig. 1. Architecture of unified and separated engines [17].

While DSC effectively reduces the computational complexity, it diminishes at the same time opportunities for data reuse. This results in inefficient utilization of processing elements (PEs) and poses a challenge in achieving the desired performance improvements [16]. Current DSC hardware accelerators can be classified into two categories: unified and separated engines, which are shown in Fig. 1. Unified engines often demonstrate suboptimal performance, especially in the case of DWC. In contrast, separated engines utilize a pipelined architecture, requiring meticulous allocation of multiply-accumulate (MAC) units to achieve a balanced performance between the two components [17]. To optimize PE utilization and promote data reuse, a unified reconfigurable PE array was independently proposed by [18] and [19]. Separable PE arrays were implemented by [20] and [21] to facilitate parallel data processing. Nevertheless, these designs are predominantly implemented on Field Programmable Gate Arrays (FPGAs), and the shift towards Application-Specific Integrated Circuits (ASICs) remains a significant challenge. The optimization of lightweight CNNs on ASICs requires further exploration.

To address the current gap in ASICs, we introduce a unified DSC accelerator. It balances high PE utilization in both DWC and PWC while minimizing memory accesses. It is worth noting that this paper is an extension of [22]. Compared to [22], this paper provides detailed MobileNetV1 layerwise parameters, serving as a reference for selecting the PE array and tiling size. Besides, we conduct a more detailed power analysis to provide insights into circuit optimization. Furthermore, in the circuit simulation, we present results on simulated frequency, dynamic energy and leakage power at varying voltages. Those data are crucial for understanding how system performance scales under different voltages. The main contributions of this work are highlighted as follows:

- We introduce a Convolution (Conv) unit featuring a four-stage pipeline within the PE array, leading to 56% latency improvement compared to the systolic array [23] featuring a nine-stage pipeline. Additionally, it can enables 100% utilization for DWC and up to 98% utilization for PWC.
- To optimize performance, we present a tailored dataflow and timing scheme for the proposed accelerator. We partition the ifmap Static Random-Access Memory (SRAM) for DWC into three banks to enable one-time access. Furthermore, a multiplexed registers (MR) based First-In-First-Out (FIFO) is implemented within the Conv unit to facilitate efficient data reuse. This design minimizes the necessity of reloading activations and weights for both DWC and PWC.
- The unified Conv unit demonstrates compatibility with both DWC and PWC, providing scalability through column expansion without compromising PE utilization. The layout design in a 22 nm Fully-Depleted Silicon-on-Insulator (FDSOI) technology demonstrates remarkable energy efficiency of 5.07 (3.96) TOPS/W for DWC (PWC) at 0.8V. The analysis of voltage scaling indicates that the energy efficiency of the DSC accelerator can reach 13.64 (10.64) TOPS/W for DWC (PWC) at 0.5 V, emphasizing its potential for low-power applications.

The article is organized as follows. Section 2 provides an introduction to SC, DSC and the MobileNetV1 architecture. Section 3 presents the proposed hardware architecture, dataflow, and timing. Section 4 shows the circuit simulation results, followed by a conclusion in Sect. 5.

2 Background

2.1 Standard Convolution Versus Depthwise Separable Convolution

CNNs comprise multiple layers, with the convolution layer serving as the fundamental building block. The operation of SC is shown in Fig. 2, where each kernel convolves with the input feature map (ifmap), producing a single channel output feature map (ofmap). This convolution process is iterated across multiple weight kernels, utilizing the same ifmap and resulting in a multi-channel ofmap. In SC, the dimensions of the ifmap are R×C×D. There exist K kernels, each with dimensions H×W×D. The result is an ofmap with dimensions M×N×K.

The total number of MAC operations O_{SC} in SC can be computed using Eq. 1, whereas the count of weights W_{SC} can be determined using Eq. 2.

$$O_{\mathrm{SC}} = H \times W \times D \times M \times N \times K \quad (1)$$

$$W_{\mathrm{SC}} = H \times W \times D \times K \quad (2)$$

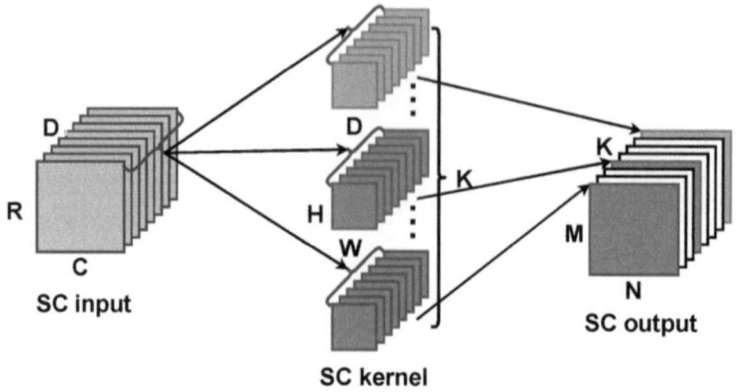

Fig. 2. Standard convolution.

In contrast, the DSC operation can be decomposed into two components: DWC and PWC, as illustrated in Fig. 3. DWC involves convolving each input channel individually with a kernel of channel size of one [24]. It is a channel-wise convolution, preserving the resolution and number of channels for input channels, output channels, and kernels. The ifmap has dimensions R×C×D, and the kernel dimensions are H×W×D. The total number of MAC operations required for DWC is H×W×M×N×D. DWC involves a two-dimensional (2D) convolution to extract spatial features in one 2D map, followed by PWC. The output of DWC, subsequently processed through batch normalization (BN) and rectified linear unit (ReLU), serves as the input for PWC. PWC can be considered as a SC with a kernel size of 1 × 1, involving element-wise multiplication between the ifmap and the kernels [25].

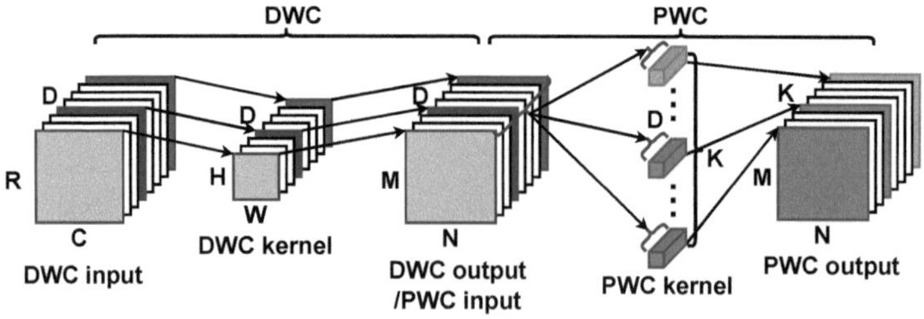

Fig. 3. Depthwise separable convolution.

The total number of MAC operations O_{DSC} and weights W_{DSC} in DSC can be determined using Eq. 3 and Eq. 4.

$$O_{\mathrm{DSC}} = O_{\mathrm{DWC}} + O_{\mathrm{PWC}} = H \times W \times M \times N \times D + M \times N \times K \times D \tag{3}$$

$$W_{\mathrm{DSC}} = W_{\mathrm{DWC}} + W_{\mathrm{PWC}} = H \times W \times D + D \times K \tag{4}$$

The ratio of DSC to SC operations can be expressed using Eq. 5 [24]. When the value of K is large and the kernel size H and W are set to 3, the computational complexity of DSC is around one-ninth of SC [26].

$$\frac{O_{\mathrm{DSC}}}{O_{\mathrm{SC}}} = \frac{H \times W \times D \times M \times N + M \times N \times K \times D}{H \times W \times D \times M \times N \times K} = \frac{1}{K} + \frac{1}{H \times W} \approx \frac{1}{9} \tag{5}$$

2.2 MobileNetV1 Architecture

DSC is used as building block in lightweight CNNs. The distribution of DSC layers varies across different networks, but their contribution is consistently significant, typically accounting for more than 50%. MobileNetV1 [3] was the pioneering network to incorporate DSC, and its DSC layer is illustrated in Fig. 4. In MobileNetV1, a total of 13 DSC layers are employed. The details of the first 6 DSC layers utilizing the CIFAR10 dataset, with the layer0 input size specified as 32 × 32, are presented in Table 1.

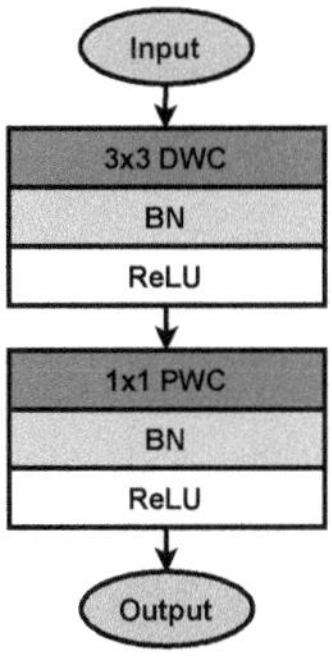

Fig. 4. DSC layer in MobileNetV1 architecture.

Table 1. Layerwise parameter of MobileNetV1.

Layer	Type	Kernel	Input	Padding	Stride
0	DWC	3 × 3 × 32	32 × 32 × 32	1	1
0	PWC	1 × 1 × 32 × 64	32 × 32 × 32	0	1
1	DWC	3 × 3 × 64	32 × 32 × 64	1	2
1	PWC	1 × 1 × 64 × 128	16 × 16 × 64	0	1
2	DWC	3 × 3 × 128	16 × 16 × 128	1	1
2	PWC	1 × 1 × 128 × 128	16 × 16 × 128	0	1
3	DWC	3 × 3 × 128	16 × 16 × 128	1	2
3	PWC	1 × 1 × 128 × 256	8 × 8 × 128	0	1
4	DWC	3 × 3 × 256	8 × 8 × 256	1	1
4	PWC	1 × 1 × 256 × 256	8 × 8 × 256	0	1
5	DWC	3 × 3 × 256	8 × 8 × 256	1	2
5	PWC	1 × 1 × 256 × 512	4 × 4 × 256	0	1

3 Proposed Hardware Architecture

3.1 Overall Architecture

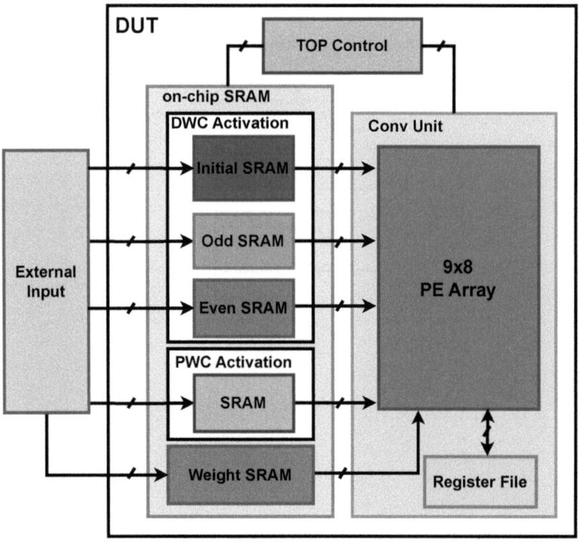

Fig. 5. Proposed DSC overall architecture.

The overall architecture of the proposed DSC accelerator is depicted in Fig. 5, which comprises three main components: top control, on-chip SRAM, and Conv unit. The unified Conv unit is equipped with a 9 × 8 PE array and a register file. The PE array is utilized to execute DWC and PWC operations, while the register file is employed to store intermediate results, facilitating efficient processing. The on-chip SRAM plays a crucial role in connecting external data with the Conv unit under the control of the top control unit. Before the Conv unit initiates computation, ifmaps and weights are loaded into on-chip SRAM. The Conv unit generates ofmaps, which are then written to the register file before being sent back to external memory. To provide an appropriate tiling size for initial layers and efficient utilization for subsequent layers, we select the 4th layer as the basis. This results in an ifmap size of 10 × 10 × 256 for DWC and 8 × 8 × 256 for PWC, as indicated in Table 1.

The PE array comprises 8 columns, enabling it to process data from eight channels in parallel. To fulfill the minimum on-chip memory requirements, we opt to store the same number of ifmap data in the on-chip memory. Both activations and weights are quantized to 8 bits, while the partial sum (Psum) is represented with 32 bits. As illustrated in Fig. 5 and Table 2, the DWC activation SRAM is partitioned into three banks: initial, odd, and even, with a total size of 6.25 Kb. The PWC has a dedicated SRAM of 4 Kb to store its computed activations. The weight SRAM is shared between DWC and PWC, with a size of 18 Kb.

Table 2. SRAM size distribution.

DWC activation SRAM			PWC activation SRAM	Weight SRAM
Initial	Odd	Even		
1.875 Kb	2.5 Kb	1.875 Kb	4 Kb	18 Kb

3.2 Unified Convolution Unit

Figure 6 depicts the proposed Conv unit, which is organized in a weight-stationary format with 9 rows and 8 columns. Each column can store one channel weight for DWC or one portion kernel weight for PWC. The Conv unit utilizes four-stage pipelines, with each block comprising three parallel-operating PEs. Each PE is equipped with a multiplier capable of executing within a single clock cycle. The products from multipliers within the same block are summed together and propagated for subsequent cycle addition. In each column of the Conv unit, a FIFO is inserted between adjacent PE units within each PE block to enhance ifmap reuse in DWC. These FIFOs are designed as MR banks to maintain low dynamic switching activity. Each PE unit is equipped with an activation register and a weight register. The activation register refreshes its value in each cycle, while the weight register preserves its value until the subsequent loop cycle. This Conv unit features a shallower pipeline compared to the systolic array of [23], achieving a 56% reduction in latency. Specifically, it requires 4 cycles instead of 9 cycles, assuming each PE takes one cycle.

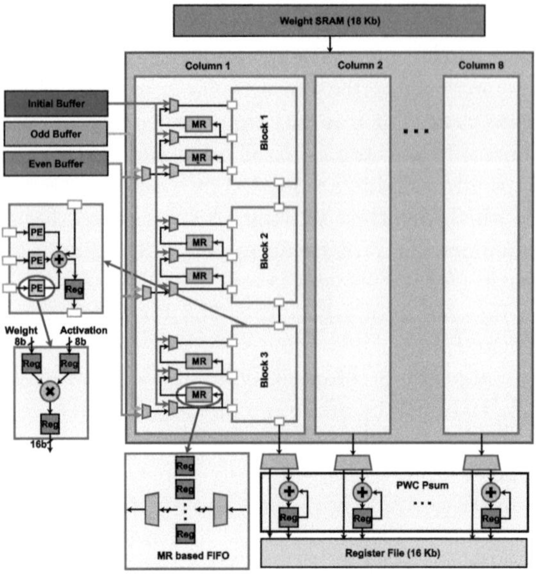

Fig. 6. Proposed Conv unit, consisting of a 9 × 8 PE array.

For DWC, the 3 × 3 kernel size enables the direct output of an ofmap by a single column, with 8 columns concurrently processing 8 channels. However, for PWC, one column computes 9 channels of a single kernel, while 8 columns simultaneously process 8 different kernels. Due to the larger channel size in the PWC kernel, an additional accumulator is necessary for accumulating the Psum. The number of rows of the Conv unit is determined by the kernel size H×W (cf. Fig. 3, 3 × 3 here), but it can be extended to larger values.

3.3 Loop Tiling and Data Reuse

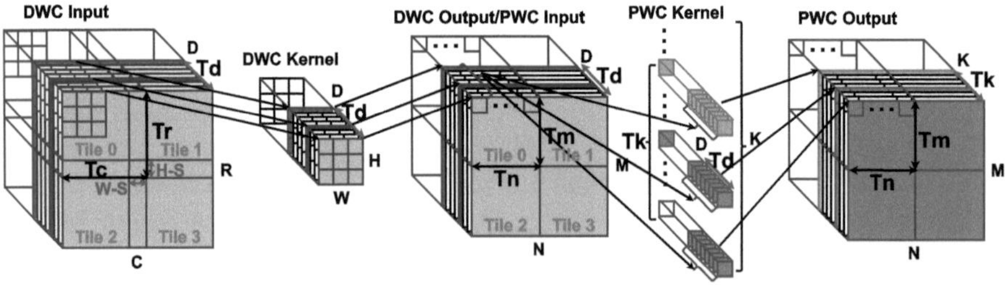

Fig. 7. The DWC and PWC data direction.

This section introduces the dataflow and data reuse pattern utilized by DSC. To tackle the limited storage of the accelerator, loop tiling [13] is employed for both DWC and PWC, as illustrated in Fig. 7. Specifically, the ifmap and ofmap of DWC are partitioned into tiles with dimensions of $T_{\mathrm{c}} \times T_{\mathrm{r}} \times T_{\mathrm{d}}$ and $T_{\mathrm{n}} \times T_{\mathrm{m}} \times T_{\mathrm{d}}$, respectively. The tile sizes T_{n} and T_{m} are determined by Eq. 6 and Eq. 7, respectively, where S denotes the stride size.

$$T_{\mathrm{n}} = \frac{T_{\mathrm{c}} - W}{S} + 1 \tag{6}$$

$$T_{\mathrm{m}} = \frac{T_{\mathrm{r}} - H}{S} + 1 \tag{7}$$

The tiling order should follow the sequence of columns, rows, and channels, which optimizes activation and weight accesses by loading the ifmap and kernel only once. However, the overlapping area has to be reloaded between two adjacent tiles. This issue can be addressed by increasing the tile size, which can reduce the number of tiles and overlapping regions. However, this also necessitates increasing the on-chip SRAM as well as the PE size. Weight tiling is straightforward for DWC as it operates channel-wise and utilizes weight stationary. The total number of activation tiles N_{adwc} and weight tiles N_{wdwc} in DWC can be calculated using Eq. 8 and Eq. 9:

$$N_{\mathrm{adwc}} = \lceil \frac{D}{T_{\mathrm{d}}} \rceil \times \lceil \frac{C}{T_{\mathrm{c}} - (W - S)} \rceil \times \lceil \frac{R}{T_{\mathrm{r}} - (H - S)} \rceil \tag{8}$$

$$N_{\mathrm{wdwc}} = \lceil \frac{D}{T_{\mathrm{d}}} \rceil \tag{9}$$

The ifmap of PWC uses the same column-row-channel tiling order as DWC. Since the kernel size is 1×1, there is no overlapping area between adjacent tiles. To maximize activation reuse, the weight loading order should be kernel before channel, as the activation of a channel can be shared by all kernels of the same channel. The weights remain stationary until the activation moves to the next tiled T_d channel. To calculate the tile numbers N_{apwc} and N_{wpwc} for activation and weight in the PWC, Eq. 10 and Eq. 11 can be employed:

$$N_{\mathrm{apwc}} = \lceil \frac{D}{T_{\mathrm{d}}} \rceil \times \lceil \frac{N}{T_{\mathrm{n}}} \rceil \times \lceil \frac{M}{T_{\mathrm{m}}} \rceil \tag{10}$$

$$N_{\mathrm{wpwc}} = \lceil \frac{D}{T_{\mathrm{d}}} \rceil \times \lceil \frac{K}{T_{\mathrm{k}}} \rceil \tag{11}$$

The above loop tiling equations (Eq. 8, 9, 10 and 11) can also be applied to all other layers.

3.4 Timing

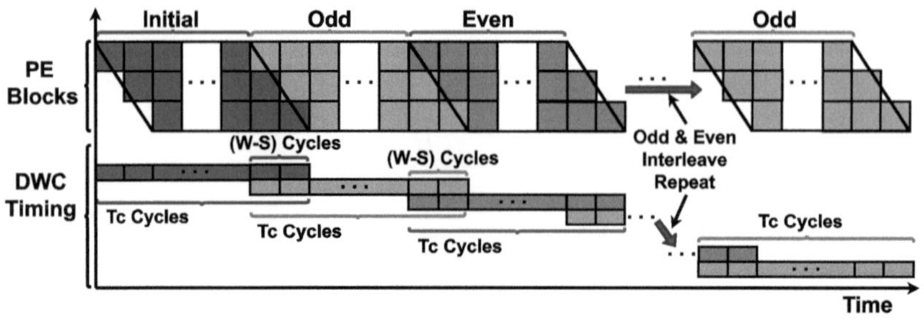

Fig. 8. DWC Timing from SRAM to Conv unit.

Figure 8 illustrates the data reading process from SRAM to Conv unit for DWC. Tiled activations are stored in three SRAMs: initial, odd, and even. Each column is sequentially read from the initial SRAM per cycle. In total, it requires T_c cycles to completely read the tiled ifmap into the PE array. An overlap of (W-S) cycles occurs when transitioning from the penultimate column of the initial SRAM to the first column of the odd SRAM. Similar overlaps exist between the odd and even SRAMs. Unlike the initial SRAM, which reads three rows concurrently, the odd and even SRAMs read only one row per cycle. Previously read activations are temporarily stored in MR based FIFOs for reuse in each PE block. For our proposed design, the baseline layer4 has a tiled data size of $10 \times 10 \times 8$, and T_c is 10, W is 3 and S is 1. Assuming the reading of 8 channels data each time, it would take 10×10 cycles to read the ifmap data. Consequently, with the new reading sequence, the required cycle count has been reduced from 100 to 66, with a 34% reduction in latency.

For PWC, activation data is consolidated in a single SRAM, streamlining the column-wise, then row-wise data reading process. Similarly, the weights of each DWC and PWC tile undergo a single read operation from SRAM to PE.

4 Results and Discussion

The proposed DSC accelerator is implemented in a 22 nm FDSOI technology from GlobalFoundries, employing both low and super-low threshold voltage cells. The synthesis is performed using Synopsys Design Compiler, and layout is done using Cadence Innovus. We run the simulation with real data to obtain the switching activity from the value change dump file by using Mentor QuestaSim. Synopsys Primetime is used to estimate power consumption. The MobileNetV1 was trained on the CIFAR10 dataset using PyTorch. The weights and activations were quantized to 8 bits using LSQ [27] technique through quantization aware training.

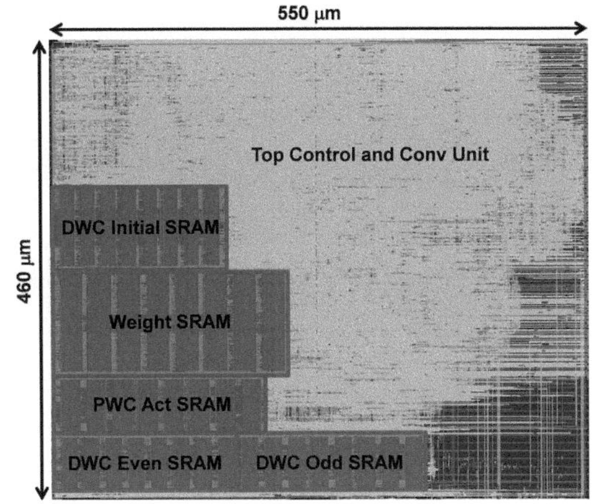

Fig. 9. Layout view of the DSC accelerator.

The layout of the proposed DSC accelerator is illustrated in Fig. 9, featuring dimensions 460 μm × 550 μm. The accelerator integrates an 18 Kb weight SRAM and a 7.5 Kb DWC activation SRAM (comprising 3 Kb initial SRAM and 2 Kb even SRAM, accounting for discrete sizes available from the memory compiler), and a 4 Kb PWC activation SRAM. The DSC accelerator can achieve a peak frequency of 1 GHz, utilizing high-performance SRAM at 0.8V and TT corner.

4.1 Area and Power Breakdown

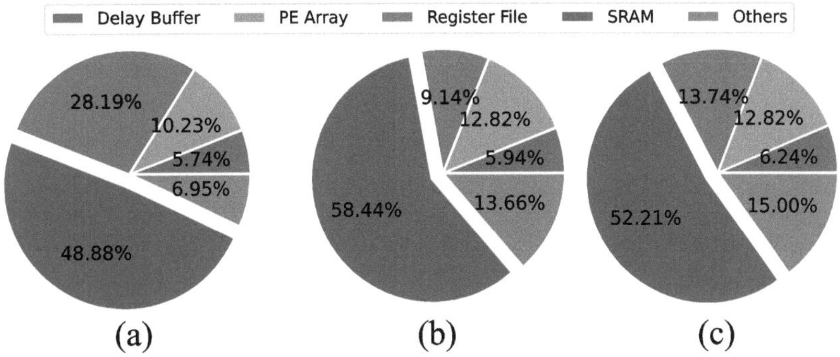

Fig. 10. (a) Area breakdown; (b) DWC power breakdown; (c) PWC power breakdown.

Figure 10(a) illustrates the area breakdown of the DSC accelerator, where SRAM occupies 48.88% of the total area, followed by the register file (28.19%) and

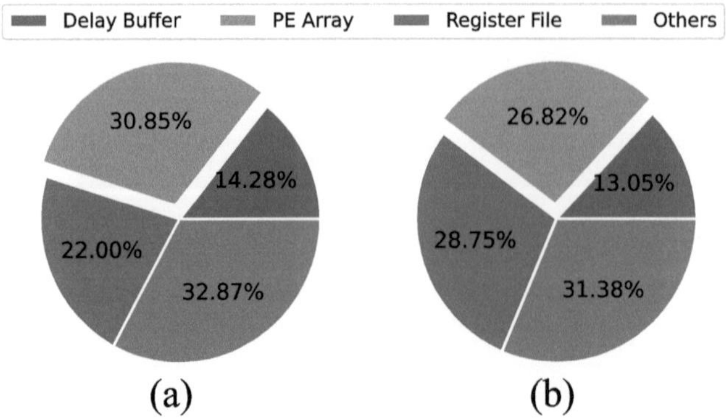

Fig. 11. Power breakdown without SRAM (a) DWC (b) PWC.

PE array (10.23%). The power breakdown for DWC and PWC is depicted in Fig. 10(b) and (c), with comparable total powers of 61.6 mW and 61 mW, respectively. The DWC's SRAM exhibits higher power consumption as it needs to read more data than PWC within the same timeframe. Conversely, the PWC's register file consumes more power due to Psum accumulation. The power breakdown for DWC and PWC without SRAM is shown in Fig. 11, with the corresponding power dissipation illustrated in Fig. 12.

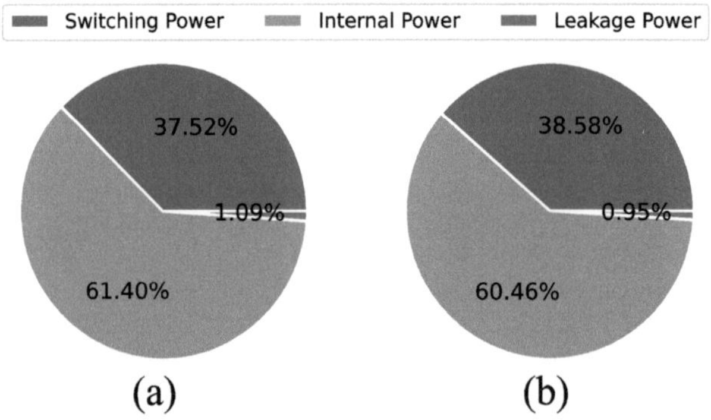

Fig. 12. Power dissipation without SRAM (a) DWC (b) PWC.

4.2 Memory Access

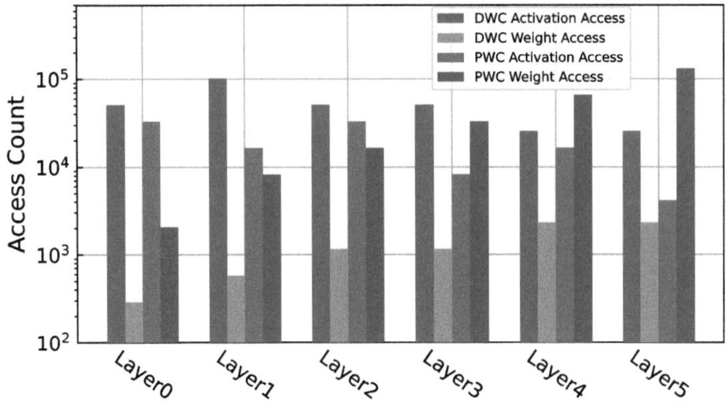

Fig. 13. Activation and weight memory access count on different layers.

Figure 13 illustrates the memory access requirements from SRAM to PE for different layers based on the proposed DSC architecture and dataflow. The output memory access is excluded here, as the potential direct use of quantized DWC output as PWC input can provide more benefits. Based on the proposed dataflow and timing scheme, DWC activation access overhead occurs only during loop tiling, whereas DWC weight access, PWC activation, and PWC weight need to be loaded only once from SRAM to PE, minimizing data access. Figure 13 indicates that DWC requires more activation access count than PWC, while weight access count in PWC is more significant due to the increased number of weight parameters.

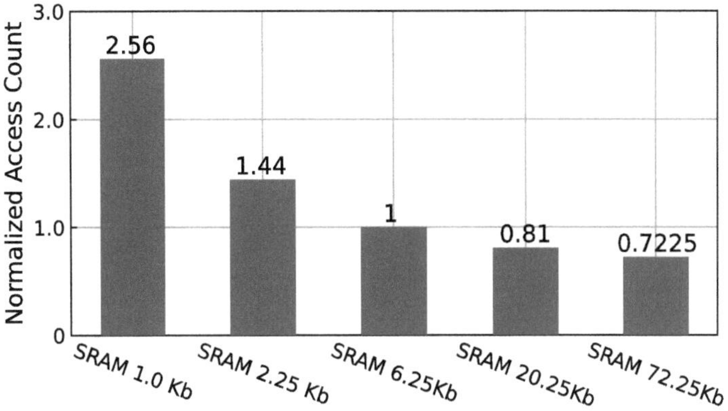

Fig. 14. Normalized access count of DWC layer0 for varying SRAM sizes.

The overhead from DWC activation tiling can be reduced by enlarging the tiling size, albeit at the expense of an increase in the SRAM size. Figure 14 demonstrates how activation access count vary with different SRAM sizes in layer0, with tiling sizes set to 4 × 4, 6 × 6, 10 × 10, 18 × 18 and 34 × 34, respectively. For the proposed design, we utilize an SRAM size of 6.25 Kb with the Conv unit size of 9 × 8. The Conv unit size is adjustable by increasing its columns, while the number of rows is constrained by the utilization, primarily determined by the DWC kernel size. However, for PWC, increasing the number of rows is advantageous for reducing the Psum access count. For the proposed architecture, increasing the Conv unit linearly increases the SRAM size, subsequently reducing memory access count.

4.3 Throughput and Energy Efficiency

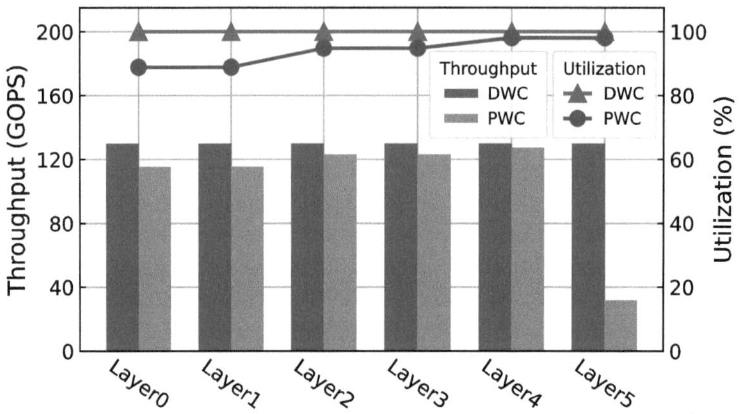

Fig. 15. Throughput and utilization on different layers.

The proposed DSC accelerator runs at 1 GHz with a back-annotated netlist. Notably, DWC and PWC differ in their channel processing approach. DWC processes channels through columns, computing 8 channels simultaneously, and can consistently achieve 100% utilization. PWC assigns channels of each kernel to a column, allowing it to compute 9 channels of 8 kernels concurrently. However, this distinction may result in under-utilization during the last fetch in PWC. Figure 15 shows average throughput for different layers. DWC maintains 129.8 GOPS throughput with 100% utilization, while PWC achieves the highest throughput of 127.3 GOPS with 98.08% utilization on layer4. The sudden drop in PWC layer5 is due to its input being only 25% of the baseline (cf. Table 1), leading to PE under-utilization. However, the throughput of deeper layers can be improved by using a smaller tiling size. Expanding the column count by an integer factor can increase the throughput and enable consistent utilization for DWC and PWC.

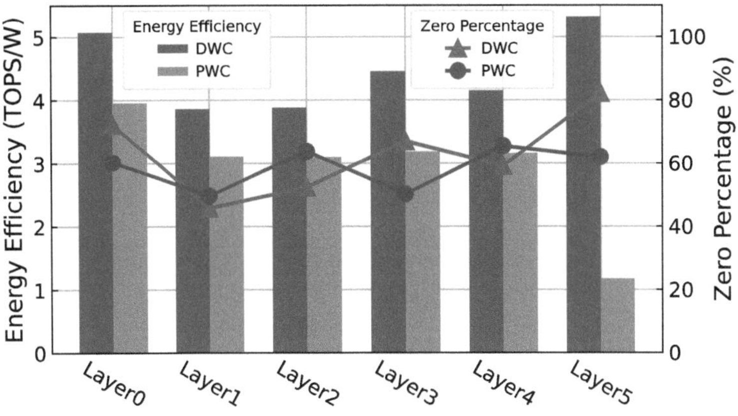

Fig. 16. Energy efficiency and activation zero percentage on different layers.

Figure 16 illustrates the energy efficiency of DWC and PWC across different layers, excluding SRAM power consumption. The corresponding activation zero percentage is displayed on the right. The highest energy efficiency is observed for DWC in layer5 and PWC in layer0, with corresponding zero percentages of 82.3% and 60.3%, respectively. The decline in PWC energy efficiency at layer5 is attributed to under-utilization. For the same layer, the energy efficiency of PWC is lower than that of DWC. This is due to DWC consistently achieving 100% utilization, while PWC's utilization is lower. Additionally, PWC needs to accumulate the intermediate Psum, requiring frequent accesses to the register file.

4.4 Circuit Simulation

To analyze the behavior of the circuit at different voltages, we extracted the netlist of the critical path using Innovus and performed SPICE simulations. To account for the increased impact of statistical outliers due to mismatch at reduced voltages, we ran a Monte Carlo simulation with 50 iterations at the TT corner.

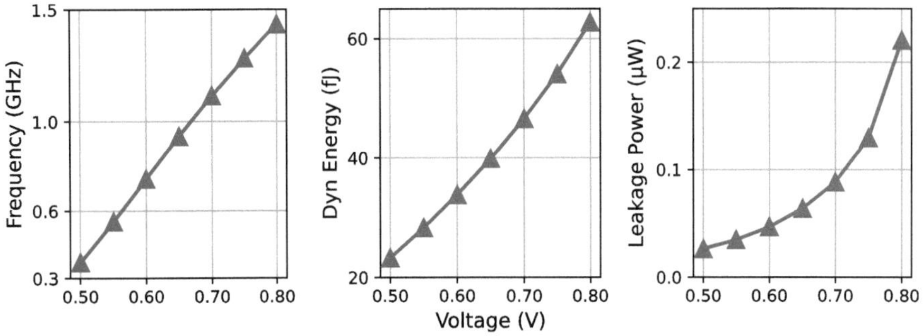

Fig. 17. Circuit simulated frequency, dynamic energy and leakage power.

Figure 17 shows the simulated frequency, dynamic energy and leakage power under different voltages. The scaling factors depicted in Fig. 17 are used to estimate the throughput and energy efficiency at different voltages for the DSC accelerator. The key circuit simulation results are highlighted in Table 3.

Table 3. Key circuit simulation results.

Voltage (V)	Frequency (GHz)	Dynamic energy (fJ)	leakage Power (μW)
0.8	1.433	62.71	0.2203
0.5	0.370	23.26	0.0264

Figure 18 illustrates the throughput across different voltages, with a throughput difference of 3.9X observed between 0.8 V and 0.5 V. The trend of the energy efficiency across different voltages is depicted in Fig. 19, and the energy efficiency

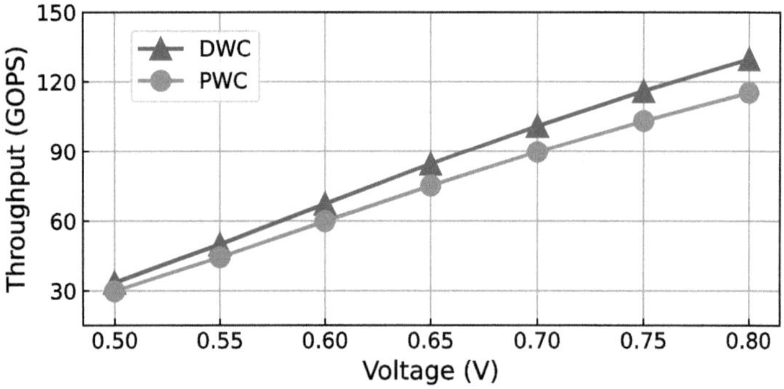

Fig. 18. Impact of voltage scaling on throughput.

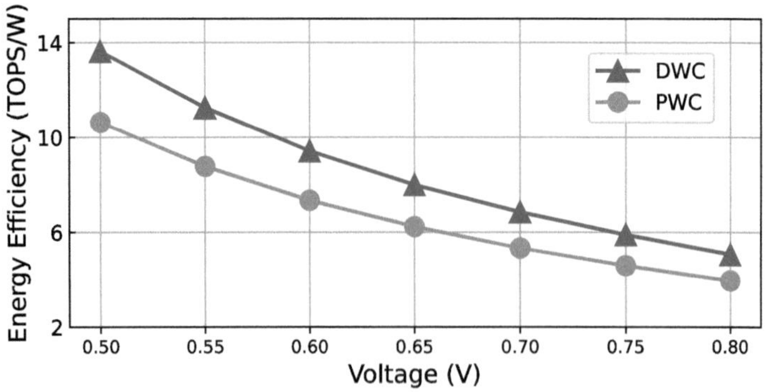

Fig. 19. Impact of voltage scaling on energy efficiency.

for DWC (PWC) increase from 5.07 (3.96) TOPS/W at 0.8 V to 13.64 (10.64) TOPS/W at 0.5 V.

4.5 Comparison with Prior Art

The selection of memory type and size can significantly influence the performance and power of an accelerator. To ensure a fair comparison with state-of-the-art works, we evaluate our approach in Table 4 and Fig. 20, disregarding the costs of memory access. It is important to note that the work [28] exclusively considers the power from PE array while disregarding the buffer and control logic power.

Before technology scaling, our approach demonstrates a remarkable improvement in energy and area efficiency compared to previous works. Specifically, this work achieves approximately 1.62X to 11.14X improvement in energy efficiency for DWC and 1.27X to 8.7X improvement for PWC. Our Conv unit can efficiently balances high PE utilization between DWC and PWC, achieving high energy efficiency. In terms of area efficiency, our approach achieves approximately 2.76X to 32.86X improvement for DWC, and 2.46X to 29.21X improvement for PWC. To provide a more comprehensive figure of merit, we analyze the energy-delay product. The energy-delay product improvements are 3.1X to 55.73X for DWC and 2.42X to 43.52X for PWC, respectively. When scaling the supply voltage down to 0.5 V, the energy efficiency is significant improved, increasing from 5.07 TOPS/W to 13.64 TOPS/W for DWC and from 3.96 TOPS/W to 10.64 TOPS/W for PWC, respectively. Although technology scaling is less favorable for advanced technology nodes, as depicted in Fig. 20, employing the technology scaling methodology outlined in [32,33], we can still outperform previous works in either energy efficiency, area efficiency, or both.

Table 4. Comparison with State-of-the-Art Works Considering the Workload of Layer0.

	ISCAS'21 [28]	ISVLSI'19 [29]	TCAS-I'22 [30]	ICCE-TW'21 [31]	This Work
Technology	40 nm	65 nm	28 nm	40 nm	22 nm
Flow	Synth	Layout	Layout	Layout	Layout
Supply Voltage (V)	0.85	1.08	0.72	0.9	0.8
PE Count	1024	256	288	128	72
Benchmark	MobileNet	MobileNet	VGG16	MobileNet	MobileNet
Power (mW)	25.3	55.4	186.6	112.5	25.6/29.16
Frequency(MHz)	100	100	700	200	1000
Area (mm^2)	1.03	3.24	2.145	2.168	0.25
Throughput (GOPS)	79.3	51.2	403	51.2	129.8/115.38
Energy Efficiency (TOPS/W)	3.13	0.92	2.16	0.455	5.07/3.96
Area Efficiency (GOPS/mm^2)	76.99	15.8	187.89	23.62	519.2/461.52
Energy Delay Product EDP (pJ·ps)	3195†	10870	611.4	10989	197.2/252.5
Normalized Energy Efficiency (TOPS/W)	8.86†	7.73	2.71	1.44	5.07/3.96
Normalized Area Efficiency (GOPS/mm^2)	349.8	266.86	501.16	95.71	519.2/461.52

Only considers power from CONV unit

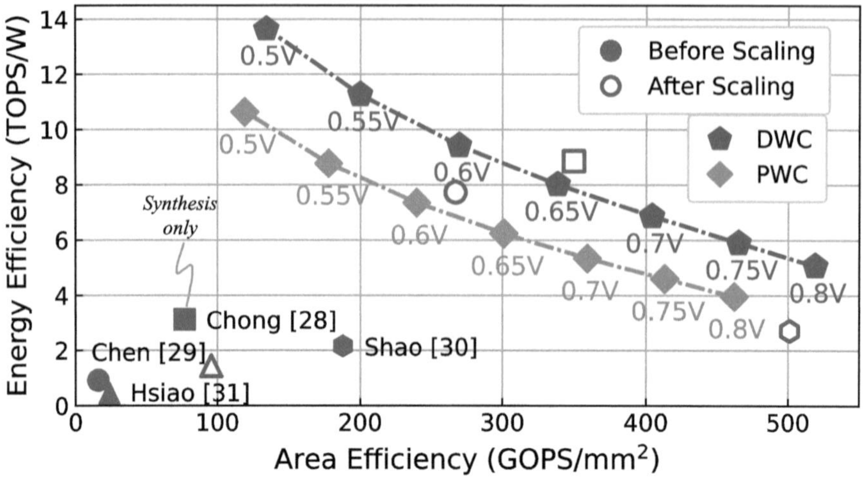

Fig. 20. Comparison with state-of-the-art works.

5 Conclusion

In this paper, we introduce a unified and energy-efficient DSC accelerator implemented in 22 nm technology, achieving 100% utilization for DWC and up to 98% utilization for PWC. This work analyzes how the proposed architecture can be mapped to different layers and and how to enlarge the PE array without sacrificing its benefits. We evaluate its extensibility for various layers of the network and optimize the memory access and data reuse. Our results indicate promising energy and area efficiency compared to state-of-the-art works, with 5.07 TOPS/W and 519.2 GOPS/mm^2 for DWC, and 3.96 TOPS/W and 461.52 GOPS/mm^2 for PWC at 0.8 V. Furthermore, we investigate the potential of the accelerator operating at lower voltages and found that it can achieve an energy efficiency of 13.64 TOPS/W for DWC and 10.64 TOPS/W for PWC at 0.5 V. These findings demonstrate the potential of the proposed DSC accelerator in achieving high energy and area efficiency. For future work, we will focus on optimizing intermediate data movement between DWC and PWC.

Acknowledgments. This work is partially funded by the Federal Ministry of Education and Research (BMBF, Germany) under the project NEUROTEC II (project number 16ME0399) and NeuroSys (project number 03ZU1106CA).

References

1. Szegedy, C., et al.: Going deeper with convolutions. In: IEEE Conference on Computer Vision and Pattern Recognition (CVPR), pp. 1–9. Boston, MA, USA (2015)
2. Chollet, F.: Xception: Deep learning with depthwise separable convolutions. In: IEEE Conference on Computer Vision and Pattern Recognition (CVPR), pp. 1800–1807. Honolulu, HI, USA (2017)
3. Howard, AG., et al.: MobileNets: efficient convolutional neural networks for mobile vision applications (2017)
4. Sandler, M., Howard, A., Zhu, M., Zhmoginov, A., Chen, L.: MobileNetV2: inverted residuals and linear bottlenecks. In: IEEE/CVF Conference on Computer Vision and Pattern Recognition (CVPR), pp. 4510–4520. Salt Lake City, UT, USA (2018)
5. Howard, A., et al.: Searching for MobileNetV3. In: IEEE/CVF International Conference on Computer Vision (ICCV), pp. 1314–1324 (2019)
6. Zhang, X., Zhou, X., Lin, M., Sun, J.: ShuffleNet: an extremely efficient convolutional neural network for mobile devices. In: IEEE/CVF Conference on Computer Vision and Pattern Recognition, pp. 6848-6856. Salt Lake City, UT, USA (2018)
7. Tan, M.X., Quoc, V.Le.: EfficientNet: rethinking model scaling for convolutional neural networks (2019)
8. Vaswani, A., et al.: Attention is all you need. In: 31st Conference on Neural Information Processing Systems, Association of Computational Machinery (2017)
9. Gulati, A., et al.: Conformer: convolution-augmented transformer for speech recognition. In: Proceedings of Annual Conference on International Speech Communication Association, pp. 5036–5040 (2020)
10. Chen, Yu-Hsin., et al.: Eyeriss: an energy-efficient reconfigurable accelerator for deep convolutional neural networks. IEEE J. Solid-State Circ. (JSSC), 127–138 (2017)
11. Yue, J.S, et al.: A 3.77 TOPS/W convolutional neural network processor with priority-driven kernel optimization. IEEE Trans. Circ. Syst. II: Express Briefs, 277–281 (2019)
12. Chang, K.W., et al.: VWA: hardware efficient vectorwise accelerator for convolutional neural network. IEEE Trans. Circu. Syst. I: Regular Papers, 145–154 (2020)
13. Tu, F.B., et al.: Deep convolutional neural network architecture with reconfigurable computation patterns. IEEE Trans. Very Large Scale Integr. (VLSI) Syst. 2220–2233 (2017)
14. Anders, M.A., et al.: 2.9 TOPS/W reconfigurable dense/sparse matrix-multiply accelerator with unified INT8/INTI6/FP16 Datapath in 14NM Tri-Gate CMOS. In: IEEE Symposium on VLSI Circuits, pp. 39–40 (2018)
15. Kim, H., et al.: Row-streaming dataflow using a chaining buffer and systolic array+ structure. In: IEEE Computer Architecture Letters, pp. 34–37 (2021)
16. Wu, X., Ma, Y., Wang, Z.: Efficient inference of large-scale and lightweight convolutional neural networks on FPGA. In: 2020 IEEE 33rd International System-on-Chip Conference (SOCC), pp. 168–173. Las Vegas, NV, USA (2020)
17. An, F., et al.: A high performance reconfigurable hardware architecture for lightweight convolutional neural network. Electronics (2023)
18. Huang, J., Liu, X., Guo, T., Zhao, Z.: A high-performance FPGA-based depthwise separable convolution accelerator. Electronics (2023)
19. Xuan, L., et al.: An FPGA-based energy-efficient reconfigurable depthwise separable convolution accelerator for image recognition. IEEE Trans. Circuits Syst. II Express Briefs **69**(10), 4003–4007 (2020)

20. Wu, D., et al.: A high-performance CNN processor based on FPGA for MobileNets. In: 29th International Conference on Field Programmable Logic and Applications (FPL), pp. 136–143. Barcelona, Spain (2019)
21. Xiao, C.H., et al.: FGPA: fine-grained pipelined acceleration for depthwise separable CNN in resource constraint scenarios. IEEE (ISPA/BDCloud/SocialCom/SustainCom), pp. 246–254 (2021)
22. Chen, Y., Lou, J., Lanius, C., Freye, F., Loh, J., Gemmeke, T.:An energy-efficient and area-efficient depthwise separable convolution accelerator with minimal on-chip memory access. In: IFIP/IEEE 31st International Conference on Very Large Scale Integration (VLSI-SoC), pp. 1–6. Dubai, United Arab Emirates (2023)
23. Kung, H.T.: Why Systolic Architectures? Computer, pp. 37–46 (1982)
24. Lin, Y., Zhang, Y., Yang, X.: A low memory requirement mobilenets accelerator based on FPGA for auxiliary medical tasks. In: Bioengineering, Basel (2022)
25. Fan, Z., Hu, W., Guo, H., Liu, F., Xu, D.: Hardware and algorithm co-optimization for pointwise convolution and channel shuffle in ShuffleNet V2. In: 2021 IEEE International Conference on Systems. Man, and Cybernetics (SMC), pp. 3212–3217. Melbourne, Australia (2021)
26. Ou, J., Li, X., Sun, Y., Shi, Y.: A configurable hardware accelerator based on hybrid dataflow for depthwise separable convolution. In: 4th International Conference on Advances in Computer Technology. Information Science and Communications (CTISC), pp. 1–5. Suzhou, China (2022)
27. Esser, S.K., McKinstry, J.L., Bablani, D., Appuswamy, R., Modha, D.S.: Learned Step Size Quantization. ArXiv (2019)
28. Chong, Y.S., et al.: An energy-efficient convolution unit for Depthwise separable convolutional neural networks. In: IEEE International Symposium on Circuits and System (ISCAS), pp. 1–5 (2021)
29. Chen, W., Wang, Z., Li, S., Yu, Z., Li, H.: Accelerating compact convolutional neural networks with multi-threaded data streaming. In: 2019 IEEE Computer Society Annual Symposium on VLSI (ISVLSI), pp. 519–522 (2019)
30. Shao, Z., et al.: Memory-efficient CNN accelerator based on interlayer feature map compression. IEEE Trans. Circ. Syst. I: Regular Pap. 668–681 (2021)
31. Hsiao, S., Tsai, B.: Efficient computation of Depthwise separable convolution in MoblieNet deep neural network models. In: 2021 IEEE International Conference on Consumer Electronics-Taiwan (ICCE-TW), pp. 1–2 (2021)
32. Stillmaker, A., Baas, B.M.: Scaling equations for the accurate prediction of CMOS device performance from 180 nm to 7 nm. Integration **58**, 74–81 (2017)
33. Latotzke, C., Gemmeke, T.: Efficiency versus accuracy: a review of design techniques for DNN hardware accelerators. IEEE Access **9**, 9785–9799 (2021)

Resiliency and Robustness

Analyzing the Reliability of TCUs Through Micro-architecture and Structural Evaluations for Two Real Number Formats

Robert Limas Sierra(✉), Juan-David Guerrero-Balaguera, Josie E. Rodriguez Condia, and Matteo Sonza Reorda

Department of Control and Computer Engineering (DAUIN), Politecnico di Torino, Corso Duca degli Abruzzi, 24, 10129 Turin, TO, Italy
{robert.limassierra,juan.guerrero,josie.Rodriguez, matteo.sonzareorda}@polito.it
https://cad.polito.it

Abstract. Modern Graphics Processing Units (GPUs) include in-chip hardware accelerators (*Tensor Core Units*, or TCUs) to increase the performance of machine learning applications. Unfortunately, cutting-edge semiconductor technologies are increasingly prone to suffer from faults and affect devices during their operation. Moreover, the execution of safety-critical and High-Performance Computing (HPC) applications in GPUs strongly stresses crucial resources, such as TCUs, which increases the likelihood of different kinds of failures. Thus, the resilience analysis of GPUs and their critical units (TCUs) are vital in safety-critical domains, e.g., in automotive, space, and autonomous robotics, to develop effective countermeasures or improve designs. Recently, new arithmetic formats have been proposed, particularly suited to neural network processing. However, an effective reliability characterization of TCUs supporting different arithmetic formats was still missed.

In this work, we propose a hierarchical multi-level strategy to assess the reliability of permanent faults arising in TCUs inside GPUs when using two number formats, i.e., *Floating Point* (FP) and *Posit*. The proposed strategy combines a fine-grain micro-architectural characterization of hardware faults in TCUs with a higher-level structural evaluation to observe the interactions with other GPU structures and the error propagation effects. The micro-architectural characterization resorts to two representative descriptions of the main components in TCUs (Dot-Product Units) for both formats (FP and Posit). Then, the fine-grain findings feed a structural TCU model (PyOpenTCU) to propagate and observe the principal error effects. The experimental results show the advantages in performance and accuracy of using clever methods for the reliability assessment of large hardware accelerators, such as TCUs, and identified a relation between the corrupted spatial areas in the output matrices and the TCU's scheduling policies. Finally, the results demonstrate that Posit formats are less affected by faults than Floating Point formats by several orders of magnitude.

Published by Springer Nature Switzerland AG 2024
I. (Abe) M. Elfadel and L. Albasha (Eds.): VLSI-SoC 2023, IFIP AICT 680, pp. 149–176, 2024.
https://doi.org/10.1007/978-3-031-70947-0_8

1 Introduction

Currently, hardware accelerators are essential units providing the high computational power demanded by a broad number of modern systems ranging from mobile to High-Performance Computing (HPC) applications [1]. Modern applications based on Machine Learning algorithms rely on linear algebra operations, particularly *General Matrix Multiplication* (GEMM, or MxM). In fact, algorithms for MxM are intrinsically parallel. They can be optimized by resorting to specialized hardware topologies, such as *Systolic Arrays* (SAs) [2], *Dot Product Units* (DPUs) [3] and *in-memory computing* [1]. These topologies are typically incorporated as main engines in application-specific devices like *Tensor Processing Units* (TPUs) in the Artificial Intelligence (AI) domain. Unlike TPUs, Graphic Processing Units (GPUs) evolved as one of the most popular and flexible accelerators in the market, and current generations incorporate compacted in-chip hardware accelerators for MxM (*Matrix Cores Units*, *Tensor Core Units* or TCUs) to provide mixed-precision computations.

The computational flexibility of TCUs makes them suitable for applications beyond the AI, such as scientific computing, cryptography [4], image and video processing [5] [6], virtual reality [7], Internet of Things (IoT) and Internet of Multimedia Things (IoMT) [8], wireless communication [9], and multidimensional data processing [10–16]. In safety-critical domains (e.g., autonomous driving, robotics, space, and healthcare systems), TCUs are widely deployed in GPU-based devices. In this regard, reliability concerns play a fundamental role in conducting advanced and autonomous tasks [17]. Nevertheless, for safety-critical systems, reliability represents a paramount aspect that has to be accomplished by satisfying strict safety standards (e.g., ISO26262 in the automotive domain [18]). Hence, the TCUs inside GPUs must fulfill those reliability criteria as well.

Unfortunately, the astonishing performance of in-chip TCU accelerators in GPUs is sometimes balanced by reliability concerns associated with the vulnerabilities of modern semiconductor technologies that make them prone to faults [19,20]. The permanent faults model describes defects happening due to different situations, such as *1)* test-escaped manufacturing flaws, *2)* infant mortality phenomena, and *3)* abrupt damage to the device during in-field operations caused by process variation, premature aging, harsh environment, or high operating temperatures [19]. Furthermore, during the in-field operation of a GPU, permanent faults in TCUs can be eventually activated, and their effects propagate silently to the outputs, leading to catastrophic consequences that endanger the reliability and overall safety of a running application. In this regard, evaluating the impact of permanent faults in TCUs is imperative to identify critical hardware vulnerabilities that allow the devising of innovative hardening strategies during the design phase of the accelerator.

Similarly, the increasing problem of *Silent Data Errors* [21,22] (SDEs) that are caused by hardware defects demands the development of new techniques for detecting and correcting them [23], while preserving application integrity. In fact, the complexity involved in modern safety-critical applications (i.e., data-intensity applications and transistor-dense devices) represents a challenge to address the detection and correction of SDEs [24,25]. The current software-based strategies for reliability assessment resort to low-level micro-architecture and architectural/functional evaluations. Despite the high accuracy provided by micro-architectural evaluations, these approaches involve unfeasible simulation times, which makes them almost impossible to apply to the assessment of large and dense applications, such as those involved in Machine Learning domains. On the other hand, architectural approaches arise as acceptable candidates to perform preliminary reliability characterizations on hardware accelerators since they provide an affordable balance between accuracy and computational effort but supply minimal information regarding the fine-grain characterization of a component or system. Finally, other strategies based on the clever combination of several abstraction levels (e.g., micro-architecture and architectural) arise as a suitable alternative to combine the high accuracy of low-level evaluations with the flexibility and speed of architectural ones [26].

In the literature, most of the efforts to evaluate the reliability of GEMM accelerators are concentrated on assessing the effect of transient faults on different SA topologies [27–29]. Authors in [30] analyzed the impact of soft errors in machine learning accelerators (e.g., NVDLA). Their results show that most of the fault effects might produce slight variations during the training/inference stages of Convolutional Neuronal Networks, or CNNs (i.e., up to 90.3% of all effects do not significantly affect the expected result). However, their evaluations were limited to soft error effects on CNN workloads. The authors in [31] evaluated the impacts of radiation in TCUs and mixed-precision formats on the overall reliability of MxM operations. The reported experiments indicate that TCU-based workloads have higher failure rates than workloads avoiding them. Other works studied the impact of permanent faults in SAs in the context of Deep Neural Network (DNN) workloads. Still, these works did not consider the architectural features of TCUs or their internal structures [32–36]. In addition, all works focused on the evaluation of mature number formats, such as Floating Point (FP).

Recently, new arithmetic formats have been proposed, particularly suited to neural network processing (e.g., *Posit*). In this regard, most of the studies are focused on the evaluation and comparison of the encoding benefits of each number format, as well as the area and power costs of their implementations [37–42]. In particular, several works have carried out experiments (in software) to address the implicit resiliency associated with the encoding representation of real numbers (e.g., in FP and Posit) for CNN workloads and HPC datasets [43–46]. Their results suggest that Posit formats are more error-resilient than FP ones. Unfortunately, all previous works in the literature mainly used fault models based on corrupting software-accessible data values (e.g., bit-flips), so neglecting the impact of faults inside the structures of hardware accelerator cores, such as TCUs, which could lead to inaccurate assessments.

In some preliminary works [47,48], we made a first attempt to characterize permanent faults and their impact effects on TCU structures for two real number formats (*Posit* and *Floating Point*). For this purpose, we developed

PyOpenTCU, an open-source functional model of TCUs inside GPUs, which follows the architectural behavior of TCU cores. Moreover, PyOpenTCU integrates a custom reliability evaluation framework, which allows the evaluation of hardware defects located in the internal hardware structures of TCUs (i.e., DPUs). Our preliminary results suggest that TCUs implementing the Posit format are more resilient to the error impact of permanent faults by up to three orders of magnitude for 16 bits and by up to twenty orders of magnitude in the 32-bit case. However, due to the high density of components inside TCU cores, a detailed reliability assessment of the internal structures of TCU cores (i.e., Dot-Product units or 'DPUs') and their error propagation effects were not analyzed nor considered in those preliminary works.

The current work goes beyond the architectural reliability evaluation of TCUs. It performs an in-depth characterization and assessment of hardware faults in TCUs, working both at the detailed micro-architecture and the functional level for two real number formats, *Floating Point* (FP) and *Posit*. This work introduces a hierarchical strategy to evaluate the resilience of large hardware accelerators (e.g., TCUs) by characterizing low-level fault impacts in their internal structures (i.e., DPUs). Then, the effects are propagated and evaluated at the application level using higher-level functional approaches.

Our proposed hierarchical evaluation considers two stages: *1)* low-level micro-architecture characterization of permanent faults in the internal structures of TCUs (i.e., DPUs), and *2)* functional (but still structural) reliability assessment of representative machine learning workloads. First, the low-level micro-architecture assessment resorts to two representative descriptions of DPUs, Posit (*Percival* [49]) and FP (*FloPoCo* [50]), and an exhaustive reliability evaluation targeting all fault locations inside the gate-level description of each DPU core. Subsequently, the approach uses the findings provided by the fine-grain characterization and propagates their error impacts across the complete workload (e.g., GEMM) by exploiting the advantages of PyOpenTCU. The whole evaluation required a total of 46 Fault Injection campaigns (6 at the low level and 40 at the structural level), injecting around 200,000 faults per campaign and requiring around 216 h.

The major contributions of this work are as follows:

- We adapted a hierarchical multi-level methodology to evaluate TCUs by combining the fine-grain micro-architectural assessment of DPUs with the fast evaluations of structural/functional characterization of TCUs in GPUs. Our approach uses the most representative error effects findings (from the fine-grain evaluation of DPUs) to propagate their effects on the structures of TCUs executing representative CNN workloads.
- We report the results and analyses of extensive micro-architectural and structural reliability assessments of permanent faults in DPUs and TCUs for two number formats (FP and Posit). The gathered results have also been validated, and they have been compared with those from detailed experiments performed on low-level models.

- We show the advantages of the hierarchical methodology in execution performance and accuracy to perform fault characterization of hardware accelerators, such as TCUs in GPUs.

The rest of the paper is organized as follows. Section 2 provides the necessary background regarding GPUs, TCUs, floating point data representations, and reliability evaluation techniques. Section 3 describes the evaluation methodology. Section 4 introduces the framework and experimental setup. Section 5 presents experimental results. Finally, Sect. 6 concludes the paper by drawing some conclusions.

2 Background

2.1 Organization of Graphics Processing Units (GPUs)

Modern generations of GPUs are massive general-purpose hardware accelerators that provide high operative throughput by resorting to a set of homogeneous clusters of parallel cores (a.k.a. *Streaming Multiprocessors*, or SMs). In fact, the SM is the primary execution unit in a GPU and comprises up to four sub-cores to handle the simultaneous execution of several threads (e.g., 32 threads or one *warp*). In detail, each SM resorts to a set of scalar processing cores and in-chip accelerators, such as *Integer Units* (INTs), *Floating Point Units* (FPUs), *Special Function Units* (SFUs), and *Tensor Core Units* (TCUs). This variety of resources, in combination with register file banks, memories, and clever scheduling policies, allows the processing of several parallel applications executing large amounts of data with minimal latency effects. Typically, one SM comprises 32/64 INTs and FPUs, 4 SFUs, and 2 TCUs. In particular, the special operation of TCUs involves special and clever management of the running threads and the memory resources in an SM, which is also extended into the GPU's ISA capabilities to operate TCU cores. The following subsection details and highlights the main operative features of TCUs as in-chip accelerators of GPUs.

2.2 Organization and Operation of TCU Cores

In modern GPU architectures, the TCUs (*Matrix Core engines* [51,52], or *Xe Matrix Extensions engines*, or 'XMX' [53]) are sophisticated in-chip accelerators devoted to increase the performance of machine learning algorithms [3,54]. In NVIDIA GPUs, a TCU core mainly comprises two-dimensional arrays of DPU cores, e.g., 4×4 array, which computes 16 *Multiply-and-Add* (MaA) operations per instruction cycle. Each TCU operates on matrix segments (e.g., 4×4-size A, B, and C inputs) and performs MxM operations (see the scheme in Fig. 1).

Due to the large amount of data to be processed in modern parallel applications, including those in the machine learning domain (e.g., operands or *input matrix tiles*), modern GPU architectures implement clever schemes to hide the latency effects when submitting and processing operation on the TCU cores. In particular, TCUs are intended to reuse the available hardware structures

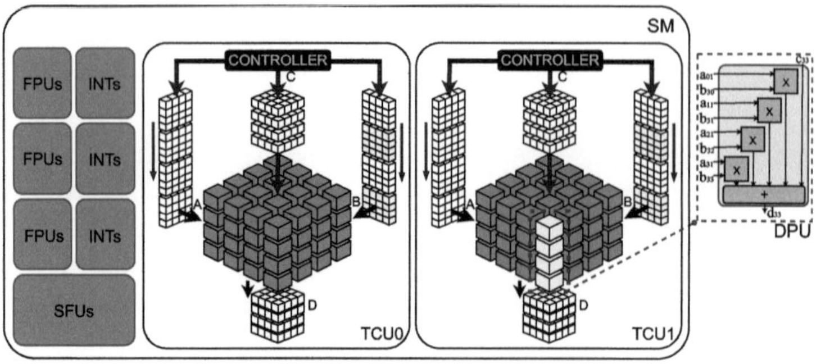

Fig. 1. A general scheme of 2 TCUs inside an SM core for NVIDIA GPU architectures. Each TCU comprises 16 DPU cores (adapted from [3,47,54]).

(i.e., DPUs) several times during the processing of large input workloads (e.g., 120×120-size matrices), so MxM operations reuse several times the TCUs and updated/accumulates intermediate and final results. In fact, the GPU architecture is adapted to efficiently manage and exploit the operation of TCU cores by resorting to three mechanisms: *1)* smart scheduling, *2)* effective operand organization, and *3)* multi-size and multi-precision support.

First, the scheduling of parallel operations on the TCUs is adapted to use all available threads per warp and execute operations efficiently. For this purpose, its micro-architecture programming model uses *Thread groups* (set of 4 threads) to effectively provide operands (e.g., 4 operands per thread) and execute operations on TCUs per clock cycle. The same scheduling organization of the TCUs shares operands among thread groups to reduce the latency effects. The scheduling of *Thread groups* into TCUs hides latency impacts of the loading and storing procedures (e.g., in Fig. 1, TCU0 processes *Thread groups* 0, 1, 4, and 5, while TCU1 operates the 2, 3, 6, and 7 *Thread groups*) [3].

Similarly, the second effective mechanism to reduce latency on the operations executed on TCUs is the use of special registers (a.k.a. buffers, *immediate registers*, *register file cache*, or *near-registers*) [55] to exploit the temporal locality (e.g., consecutive registers to store input operands, intermediate and final results during the TCU's execution) and reduce the memory bottlenecks when addressing TCU operands from the main memory. In detail, the programming model (i.e., machine instructions) and the scheduling of the TCUs inside the GPUs cleverly handle the interconnections between the near-registers and the general register files of the GPU to avoid latency effects.

Regarding the multi-size and multi-precision support, the TCUs are flexible to allow several configurations (e.g., number format and precision), which, in combination with the programming model, provide the scalability to process large-size fragments of matrices (e.g., 16×16) in TCUs. In fact, NVIDIA has introduced assembly instructions (i.e., *HMMA*) to process large matrix dimensions (e.g., 16×16) in TCU cores as a sequence of instructions operating 4×4 array segments (as depicted in the example of Fig. 2). Each HMMA instruction has four operands, and each one uses a pair of registers. Consecutive instructions typically produce partial, accumulative, and final results. The partial and accumulated results are stored in the register file (or in buffers) for subsequent reuse with other input segments.

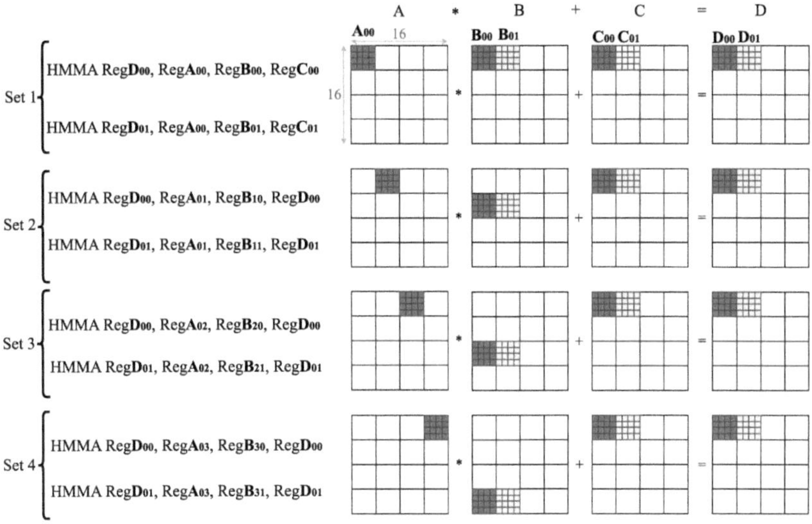

Fig. 2. A general scheme of instructions and input segments (i.e., A, B, and C input matrices) used by the *Thread group* 0 to calculate two output segments in the 16×16 mode. The HMMA instructions are grouped in sets to process 4×4 input segments and handle the intermediate results. The result of segment D is a combination of the outputs of four sets. The register banks (or buffers) serve as temporal accumulators for partial results (adapted from [3]).

2.3 Formats for Real Numbers

Floating Point (FP) Format: This format encodes a real number into a binary representation code defined by the IEE-754 standard [56]. This standard defines and describes the format using k bits (i.e., 1-bit sign, w-bit exponent, and t-bit fraction). Mathematically, a real value can be described in FP format using Eq. 1, where $bias$ is a constant offset used to normalize the exponent.

$$value = (-1)^{sign} * 2^{exp-bias} * (1 + \sum_{i=1}^{fn-1} b_{fn-1-i} * 2^{-i}) \tag{1}$$

Posit Format: This format provides higher accuracy and dynamic range, emerging as an alternative and drop-in replacement for the IEEE-754 format for machine learning applications. The *Posit* representation encodes any real number into a binary representation using N bits distributed in four fields (i.e., 1-bit sign, r-bit regime, e-bit exponent, and f-bit fraction). This binary encoding describes mathematically any real number according to Eq. 2.

$$value = (-1)^{sign} * useed^k * 2^{exp} * (1 + \sum_{i=1}^{fn-1} b_{fn-1-i} * 2^{-i}) \tag{2}$$

where $useed^k$ is a scale factor ($useed = 2^{2^{es}}$), and es is the exponent size. The parameter k is determined by *run length* of 0 or 1 bits in the string of regime bits. The $useed^k$ value is used to compute the min_{pos} and max_{pos} values. Those values determine the Posit dynamic range, maintaining it perfectly balanced around 1.0, and every *power of 2* has an exact reciprocal. Additionally, the posit format does not include redundancy representations or overflow/underflow cases during operations [57].

Several studies [58] have demonstrated that most of the common values employed in CNN domains are mainly composed of small magnitudes. In this regard, the Posit format outperforms the FP one on accuracy [49,50,59,60]. Thus, Posit arises as an attractive option for deep learning applications.

2.4 Approaches for Fault Characterization

Most traditional methods for reliability characterization of digital circuits (e.g., processor-based systems and hardware accelerators) resort to *Fault Injection* (FI) techniques that evaluate the impact of faults arising on the structures of a targeted design. In-depth, FI techniques can be classified into four main groups: *1) Hardware-based, 2) Emulation-based, 3) Software-implemented*, and *4) Simulation-based* FIs.

In detail, in *Hardware-based techniques*, the evaluation is based on physical distortions affecting a real device. In-depth, the device is exposed to external effects, such as modifying parameters (e.g., voltage, temperature, among others) or direct interaction with radiation. In fact, this technique might resort to beam experiments, which allow the evaluation of transient faults on parallel applications [61]. Nevertheless, these characterizations are effective in evaluating complete applications but can hardly provide fine-grain fault characterizations on the underlying hardware. Thus, in large hardware accelerators (e.g., TCUs), this reliability assessment strategy can not identify the vulnerable structure with the highest accuracy. Other strategies, such as *Emulation-based FIs*, exploit prototyping platforms (e.g., FPGAs) to speed up evaluations. In this context, the assessment demands custom FI frameworks [62] and design models. Unfortunately, their use directly depends on the availability of hardware models suitable for synthesis.

Regarding evaluations based on *Software-implemented FI*, it mainly changes the code of the applications in order to represent the hardware defect, which mimics the impact error of hardware defects at the instruction level (i.e., source code mutations representing faults). In fact, this kind of assessment allows the characterization of applications. However, this evaluation is mainly restricted to a few locations and structures inside resources visible for a user (i.e., register-files or memory locations) [63]. Finally, the *Simulation-based FI* is one of the most versatile and accurate approaches. In detail, this method extends the information of available abstractions (i.e., RT-, Gate-, or high-level) of a design. Despite fine-grain (low-level) assessments offering an accurate evaluation, they demand a high computational effort and extensive simulation times, which make unfeasible their usage for massive hardware accelerators, like GPUs or TCUs [64]. On the other hand, functional/structural approaches are simplified versions of a design that provide flexibility and allow the analysis of different parameters and architectural configurations with an affordable balance between accuracy and simulation time.

In the current scenario, the assessments of large hardware accelerators, such as GPUs, demand clever solutions that address the most critical issues in traditional FI techniques, e.g., simulation time and accuracy. In this context, solutions based on cross-layer approaches (combining low-level and structural evaluations) might offer smart techniques for assessing huge accelerators.

3 A Mixed-Level Method to Evaluate the Influence of Number Formats in the Reliability Assessment of TCUs

Our approach combines the structural, functional, and behavioral operation of TCUs with the fine-grain features of their internal structures (i.e., DPUs) to evaluate and characterize the impact of two number formats (*Posit* and *FP*) in the presence of permanent (i.e., stuck-at) faults. To handle the hierarchical complexity of large hardware accelerators, such as TCUs, our strategy first characterizes the effects of hardware faults at the fine-grain level by resorting to fault evaluation on the low-level micro-architecture descriptions of the DPU cores, which are the main components inside TCUs. Then, we determine error impacts from the micro-architecture evaluations and identify their principal propagation features. These results are later used to feed the evaluation of the structural interaction of the TCUs with the GPU units, as depicted in Fig. 3.

For this purpose, we perform a functional characterization of fault effects on TCUs when executing typical workloads. In detail, typical workloads of machine learning domains are based on matrices (e.g., *matrix's fragments* or *tiles*) with a random distribution of low magnitude values, which are in concordance with other works in the field [65].

In-depth, the low-level micro-architecture fault characterization resorts to RT- and gate-level descriptions of the DPU cores for both formats (*FP* and *Posit*), while the functional TCU fault evaluation uses an architectural TCU model. In particular, our approach comprises two steps: *1)* micro-architectural assessment of DPUs, and *2)* functional evaluation of TCUs. The following subsections provide a deep description of each step.

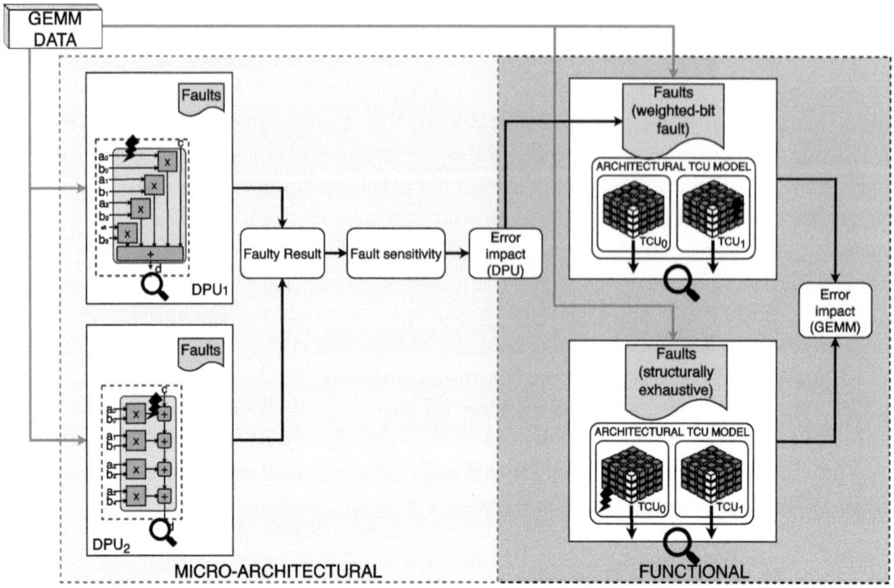

Fig. 3. A general scheme of the proposed methodology for fault characterization of TCUs in GPUs.

3.1 Micro-architectural Reliability Assessment of DPUs

In this step, we focus on the fine-grain evaluation of the effects of permanent (i.e., *stuck-at*) faults affecting the internal structures of DPUs inside TCUs. In this evaluation, we determine the main features of the fault activation and propagation effects across structures of the DPUs during the fine-grain execution of CNN operations (e.g., *Multiply-and-Add*).

For the micro-architecture assessment, we resort to exhaustive FI campaigns targeting all fault locations inside the gate-level description of a DPU per number format (*FP* and *Posit*). It is worth noting that our evaluation injects one permanent (i.e., stuck-at) fault in the hardware per simulation.

After the FI campaign experiments, our approach analyzes the experimental FI results to provide clean reports for analysis purposes (i.e., the obtained logic fault simulations are translated into equivalent DPU errors). In particular, a detailed list correlates all input operands from the input stimuli (i.e., *matrix tiles*) and the observed discrepancies between the fault-free scenario and the faulty ones that support the identification of the impact assessment on the DPU cores for both number formats (FP and Posit).

Since our evaluation targets structures of the TCUs, we classify the hardware fault effects at the output of the DPU for both formats as: *1) Silent Data Corruptions* or SDCs, which represent mismatches between the golden and faulty scenarios on the output, and *2) Masked*, when a hardware fault does not produce any visible effects on the output results. Moreover, we determine the fault sensitivity of each bit in the DPU's output result when affected by internal hardware faults, e.g., analyzing the probability density, which is a statistical representation of the probability of one particular bit being influenced by an internal hardware fault. Then, we also characterize figures associating the number of corrupted bits when faults arise inside the DPUs.

Both error impact features (fault sensitivity of the bit-field and the number of corrupted bits) on the DPUs are then used to propagate fault effects during the GEMM operation by the TCUs.

3.2 Functional Reliability Assessment of TCUs

In this step, our assessment focuses on the evaluation of the complete GEMM execution of the TCU core and its interaction with other structures in the GPU. In detail, we evaluate the impact of permanent hardware faults in the internal structures of TCUs (i.e., DPUs) and also their propagation effects on typical machine learning operations (e.g., GEMM) on large data structures. It is worth noting that the complete assessment of large GEMM operations requires high computational effort. Thus, we exploit a structural/functional model to evaluate the complete GEMM execution under affordable simulation times. In detail, our structural strategy resorts to FI campaigns based on two main stages: *1)* weighted-bit fault injections and *2)* structurally exhaustive approaches.

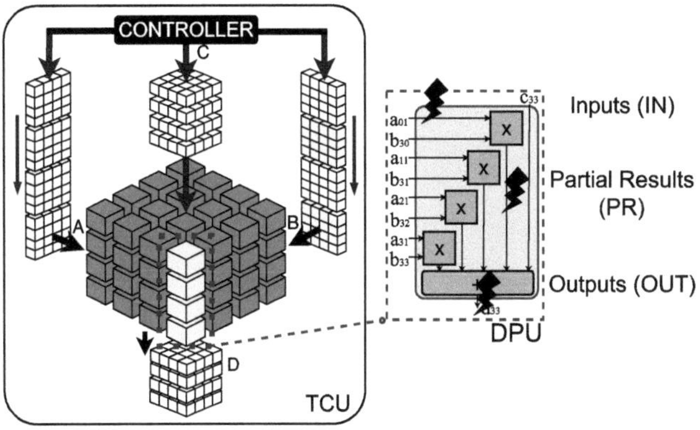

Fig. 4. A general scheme of the fault locations inside one TCU core (adapted from [3,47,54]). In the illustration, the fault locations are represented by black rays.

In the *weighted-bit fault injection*, we use the fine-grain characterization of DPUs and its findings to propagate the most common errors observed during the evaluation of the DPUs. In particular, this approach takes into account the bit sensitivity and the most common amount of corrupted bits to place one error on one DPU output core per simulation. Then, the GEMM operation is executed on the faulty TCU model. Thus, the cores propagate the error effect across the complete application, and we are able to observe the impact of hardware faults on the final output result (i.e., *final output matrix*).

The *structurally exhaustive approach* performs an FI evaluation by considering all possible fault locations in the structure of the TCUs to represent a faulty hardware effect. In detail, we target three critical locations for the evaluation of the TCU structures: *input* (IN), *output* (OUT), and *Partial Results* (PR) of each DPU (see Fig. 4). The faults affecting the *IN* signals represent faulty interconnections in the data path, which are in charge of loading the data from the near-registers or the register file of the GPU. Meanwhile, a fault arising in the *PR* structure mimics an internal defect on one of the hardware multipliers in the DPUs and its error propagation. Finally, faults placed on the *OUT* signals model a hardware fault in any component in the adder.

The functional reliability assessment of the TCUs under both approaches (*weighted-bit fault injection* and *structurally exhaustive*) considers the accumulative and hardware reuse features in TCUs. Thus, the analysis and evaluation of the whole structural assessment are performed at the end of the process (i.e., *final output matrix*) by following an analysis composed of three main steps: *1)* general classification of results, *2)* quantitative evaluation of the individual results, and *3)* spatial assessment of the observed errors.

First, during the *general classification step*, we classify the effect of each fault according to the impact produced by grouping the results in three severity levels:

- *Masked* when the fault does not affect the outputs,
- *Silent Data Corruption* (SDC) that causes a corrupted output result and
- *Detected Unrecoverable Error* (DUE) when the hardware fault causes a special number encoding that can crash the application or handle an exception. It means that the encoding can represent either a number that exceeds the range representable (i.e., $\pm inf$) or undefined/invalid results (i.e., *Not a Number*, or NaN), such as the square root of a negative number.

Afterward, we perform a *quantitative evaluation.* This analysis compares each element of the fault-free matrix with the faulty one and performs a deep evaluation to determine the impact of hardware faults at the application level. In detail, it uses the *relative error* as an evaluation metric to determine the error magnitude of failures impacts observed as errors/discrepancies on the GEMM results. In addition, we perform a *spatial assessment* to identify spatial corruption patterns in the GEMM results by considering the propagation effects of faults in TCUs in one or multiple elements of the outputs. In this regard, the proposed evaluation is based on the identification of regions on the output matrix having the highest probability of being affected.

Finally, our method compares the results gathered by the weighted-bit fault and structurally exhaustive evaluations to determine the main discrepancies (e.g., issues with accuracy) between both approaches, as well as mechanisms to evaluate the accuracy of the mixed methods (fine-grain and functional approaches). The comparison between the mixed and the structurally exhaustive methods allows us to understand the main benefits of considering fine-grain characterization in the reliability analysis of hardware accelerators, such as TCUs.

4 Experimental Setup

This section provides a detailed description of the experimental setup to characterize the effect of permanent faults in the DPUs and TCUs. Our setup is composed of two frameworks for the evaluation of *1)* micro-architectural and *2)* functional features in TCUs.

4.1 Low-Level Micro-architectural Framework

We use two commercial-grade simulators (i.e., *ModelSim* by *Siemens EDA* and *Z01X* by *Synopsis*) to perform the fault evaluation of two low-level micro-architectural models (one per number format, i.e., *FP* and *Posit*). In addition, one general controller module (in *Python*) handles the execution of the FI campaigns. First, we use the logic simulator (*ModelSim*) to calculate the fault-free execution of the CNN operations on the hardware of a DPU. In this step, we store all input operations and golden output results that serve as references for the next steps. Then, the functional fault simulator (*ZO1X*) is configured to employ the golden reference results when performing exhaustive fault simulation campaigns on each DPU core. It is worth noting that individual DNN operations in the DPU (e.g., 4×4x1 Dot-Product operations) are exhaustively evaluated for all possible fault locations in the hardware core. Moreover, our evaluation injects one permanent (e.g., stuck-at) fault in the hardware per simulation. Furthermore, the general controller module employs smart multi-threading schemes that in combination with the implicit parallel execution of *Z01X* aim at reducing the simulation times of the FI campaigns.

For our fault characterization, we use two representative low-level micro-architecture descriptions (VHDL) of DPU cores for the Posit (*Percival* [66]) and FP (*FloPoCo* [67]) formats. The synthesis of both cores resorts to *Design Compiler* (by *Synopsis*) and the FreePDK 15nm technology library [68]. Moreover, we use random input matrices following the random distribution in the range of ± 1.0 since CNNs commonly use weights and intermediate feature maps in the neighborhoods of ± 1.0 [58]). It must be noted that for our experiments, we employ the same random tiles encoded in their respective number format.

4.2 Functional Framework

We developed and extended the features of an architectural TCU model (*PyOpenTCU* [47,48]) that describes the instruction-accurate operation of TCU cores inside modern NVIDIA architectures. Moreover, the scheduling and the parallel thread operation are described as part of the model execution. Similarly, the near-registers and register files in one GPU's SM are described. Due to its optimized description. i.e., mainly focused on TCUs operations, *PyOpenTCU* allows the evaluation of large GEMM operations on TCUs under affordable simulation times.

The TCU model includes a FI framework designed to analyze the impact of permanent (i.e., stuck-at) and transient (e.g., bit-flips) faults located on the internal structures of the TCUs (e.g., *IN*, *PR*, and *OUT* signals of each DPU). For the purpose of this work, we focused only on the evaluation of the effects of permanent stuck-at faults in the TCUs.

The FI framework in *PyOpenTCU* supports the execution of four main steps: *performing the ideal* (golden or fault-free) application, *generating the fault list*, *injecting the faults* (based on the pin-level fault injection strategy [69]), and *classifying the results* (i.e., comparing each result obtained for the faulty model with the fault-free result). The first step (*performing the ideal application*) computes the fault-free MxM results employing the TCUs. Then, the input and output matrices are stored for analysis purposes. After this, the framework produces the fault list (*generating the fault list*) to be executed during the Fault Simulation (FSim). Each fault includes the target information (i.e., the faulty internal structure of the DPU), the target bit affected by the fault, and the type of stuck-at-fault applied (0 or 1).

Two FI campaigns (*weighted-bit fault injection* and *structurally exhaustive*) are performed on the TCU model configured for both number formats. The weighted-bit FI campaign takes into account the fine-grain characterization of the DPUs and places faults according to the fault sensitivity of each bit obtained for the low-level micro-architecture evaluation. In contrast, the structurally exhaustive FI campaigns target the complete fault list, which considers all the possible targets to mimic the hardware defects in the TCUs. During the *fault injection* step, the framework reads each fault and configures *PyOpenTCU* to mimic the faulty behavior. Each fault is placed inside the TCUs through the saboteurs technique [70]. This configuration allows error propagation at the MxM level. Afterward, the MxM is executed, and the output result is collected for analysis. Then, the fault injection step is performed using a new fault, and the process restarts. Due to the intrinsic accumulative nature of the TCUs, the *classification* step is performed only at the final output matrix. Finally, the framework computes and stores the discrepancies between the faulty results and the golden reference.

5 Experimental Results

We target the reliability assessment of TCUs through the combination of two evaluation approaches: *1)* the low-level micro-architectural and *2)* the functional one. First, our fine-grain characterization of TCUs resorts to exhaustive FI campaigns on the DPUs, which allows us to determine the impact of all possible stuck-at faults arising on the sub-units and their structures of DPU cores under two number formats, i.e., FP (*FloPoCo*) and Posit (*Percival*). In detail, the fine-grain reliability assessment of both DPUs (FP and Posit) comprises a total of six exhaustive FI campaigns. Each FI campaign resorts to one workload (e.g., 4,096 MxM operations following the typical distribution of CNN operations) as input stimuli and targets the evaluation of a total of 48,414 and 49,392 permanent faults in the FP and Posit cores, respectively.

Regarding the functional evaluation of the TCU, we address the fault characterization by resorting to one architectural TCU model (*PyOpenTCU*) to mimic the faulty behavior of permanent faults on the structures of the TCUs and propagate their impacts across complete workloads (e.g., GEMM). In our experiments, *PyOpenTCU* uses a typical configuration on modern NVIDIA architectures (e.g., Volta), with one SM comprising 2 TCUs, and each TCU core is built with 16 DPUs executing a total of 8 thread groups per warp. It is worth noting that we employ two TCU configurations, one per number format (FP and Posit) with 32 bits-width. Thus, a total of 114,668 permanent faults can be evaluated per TCU version by considering all possible stuck-at faults in the DPUs (comprising 9 INs, 4 PRs, and 1 OUT target fault places per DPU).

Since our approach combines low-level micro-architecture evaluations with the functional ones on the TCUs, the experimental results of the micro-architecture evaluation of the DPU are used to determine the bit sensitivity of their underlying structures (i.e., activation and propagation effects on the DPU outputs). Then, we used the bit sensitivity analysis to conduct the weighted-bit FI campaigns at the functional level on the *PyOpenTCU* model. At this level, the functional characterization of the TCUs resorts to 20 statistical FI campaigns (10 per number format), and each statistical FI campaign is composed of 2,048 faults, which represents 25% of all possible *OUT* targets in TCUs. It is worth noting that each simulation analyzes the error impact of one single hardware fault placed on the internal structures of one TCU core. Moreover, as input stimuli for each FI campaign, we used ten matrices with typical values in CNN domains, which are composed of values with a distribution around the neighborhood ± 1.0.

All the experiments (low-level micro-architecture and functional) required an overall 216 h and were performed on two server machines with 12 Intel Xeon CPUs at 2.5 GHz and 256 GB of RAM. The next subsections analyze the micro-architectural and functional evaluations of the TCUs. For performance and accuracy comparison purposes, we performed a structurally exhaustive evaluation (targeting all possible faults) of both TCUs (FP and Posit) using the same input stimuli.

5.1 Low-Level Micro-architectural Assessment of DPU Cores

Firstly, we study the fine-grain impact of permanent faults on the main structures of DPUs and how these propagate effects on their outputs. Since TCUs are homogeneous two-dimensional arrays of DPUs (e.g., 4×4), our evaluation focuses on one DPU to determine the impact of hardware faults and their propagation effects across the complete operation of GEMM.

Figure 5 depicts the fault rate per each core and shows that both cores (FP and Posit) are highly sensitive to propagate and corrupt DPU operations (SDCs) in the presence of hardware faults. Faults in the Posit and FP DPU cores corrupt 72.98% and 87.42% of all DPU operations ($4 \times 4 \times 1$ multiply-and-add), respectively. Thus, our experimental results indicate that a faulty Posit DPU core is less likely to propagate effects by up to 14.44% in comparison with the FP one.

Then, we analyze the bit sensitivity of each output bit on the DPU results. The sensitivity represents the number of corrupting effects on each bit part of

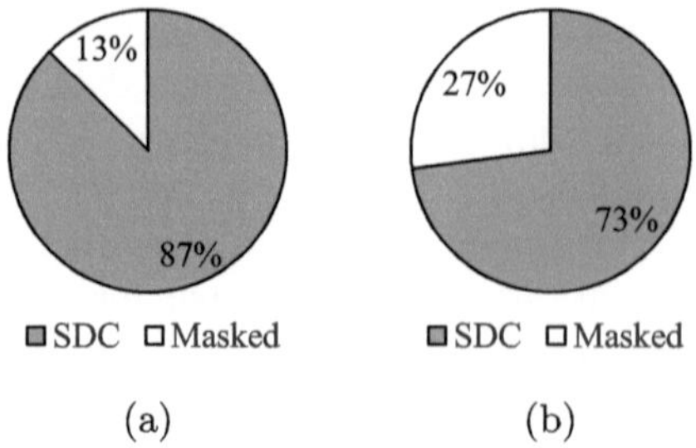

Fig. 5. Fault rate for the micro-architecture evaluation of the DPU cores in the FP (a) and Posit (b) formats.

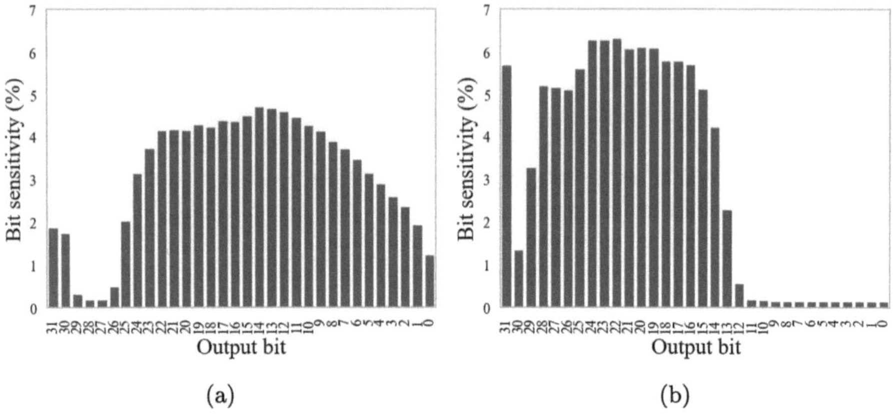

Fig. 6. Normalized output bit sensitivity of DPU cores for the FP (a) and Posit (b) formats.

the output result. Figure 6 depicts the normalized bit sensitivity for each bit-field in the output results for the FP (a) and Posit (b) cores. A first look shows that the most critical bit fields affected by hardware faults in the FP DPUs are the mantissa (bits 22-0) and exponent (bits 30-23), while for the Posit DPUs, the most critical bit fields are the regime, exponent, and the most significant bits of fraction (bits 23-12), respectively.

A detailed analysis of the FP core shows that the bit sensitivity is widely distributed across the whole number encoding. In detail, the mantissa field is associated with huge bit sensitivity. Our experiments demonstrate that around 93% of all hardware faults impacted the mantissa (bits 22-0) and the lower part of the exponent (bits 25-23) fields. On the other hand, faults in the internal structures of the FP DPU core only influence the high part of the exponent (bits 30-26) and the sign fields up to 5% and 2%, respectively. In fact, the selected range as input stimuli (values around the neighborhood of ± 1.0) produces few error corruption effects on the high part of the exponent. Moreover, the DPU operation and its accumulation scheme might mask some of the effects of corruption.

Moving to the Posit DPU core, the results show that most corruption effects are concentrated in the regime, exponent, and the most significant bits of the fractions fields (bits 23-12). In-depth, the bit sensitivity reveals that the fraction field is highly vulnerable with up to 63% of corruption effects. The results also demonstrate that the least significant bits of the fraction field (bits 11-0) have a bit sensitivity lower than 1%. This behavior seems to be related to the codification of the Posit format. A detailed analysis shows that permanent faults affecting the least significant bits of a Posit number are associated with small-magnitude errors, which are mainly masked during the addition process inside the DPU. Thus, corruption in the least significant bits of a result can hardly produce large changes in its expected value.

In contrast, for the regime and exponent fields, their fault propagation sensitivity decreases up to 19% and 12%, respectively, with respect to the fraction field. Interestingly, the results show that the sign bit is affected by permanent faults up to 6%. A detailed look shows that this low vulnerability is related to the input workload. In machine learning domains, the operations are mainly based on workloads with low-magnitude values. Thus, hardware faults affecting the most significant bits of a Posit number might not be activated, and the probability of propagating their error effect is small.

Subsequently, we focus our evaluation on the total number of bits in the DPU results affected by a single hardware fault. In this context, the results for both DPU (FP and Posit) cores seem to indicate an equivalent trend, with mostly one particular bit corrupted by a permanent fault arising in the structures of DPUs, as shown in Fig. 7. In fact, the results show that around 46% and 33% of all observed errors corrupt one bit in FP and Posit DPUs, respectively. The results also indicate that each hardware fault is highly likely to impact two or three different bits. In detail, hardware faults arising in the FP core might affect two or three bits up to 18% and 8%, respectively.

Moreover, Posit DPU shows a similar behavior. In this context, the impact of a single permanent fault might be related to one or two bit-flips up to 14% and 8%. Complementary analysis based on multi-bit injections might be required to effectively model the effects of hardware faults in the internal DPU structures. However, the analysis of that kind of injection is out of the current work scope.

In our evaluation, the low-level micro-architectural assessment provides the most critical figures associated with the error propagation of hardware faults in the DPU cores for both formats. In principle, individual permanent faults inside DPUs are mainly linked to one bit-flip on the DPU outputs (46% and 33% for FP and Posit cores, respectively). Moreover, the experimental results demonstrate that the mantissa is the most vulnerable field in FP format for the analyzed workloads (93% of observed effects), while corruptions on the sign and exponent fields represent up to 7%, only.

Regarding Posit DPU cores, the fraction part of the Posit format is the most impacted field by hardware faults (63%), with its bit sensitivity concentrated

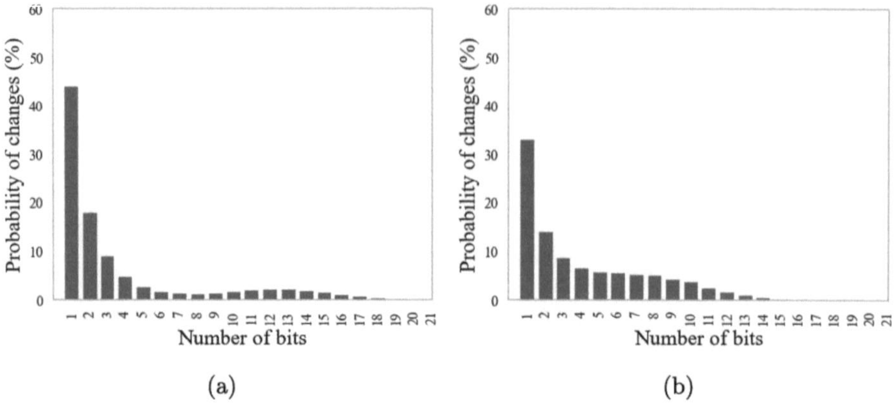

Fig. 7. Normalized number of bits affected by a permanent fault arising in the structures of DPU cores for the FP (a) and Posit (b) formats.

in the most significant bits. Meanwhile, the regime and exponent fields show low sensitivity (19% and 13%, respectively) to propagate individual permanent hardware faults on the DPU results.

5.2 Hierarchical Functional Evaluation of TCU Cores

The hierarchical functional evaluation and assessment of the TCU cores for both formats consider the main features and figures established during the fine-grain evaluation of the DPU cores. In particular, we employ the bit sensitivity and corruption occurrence (e.g., the number of bits affected by the output of a DPU operation) to define the fault sites and targets for the FI campaigns using the architectural model of TCUs. During our experiments, each campaign considers the impact of one hardware fault placed in one TCU core (*TCU0*). According to our approach, the main target for fault injection is the output structures of the DPUs. Interestingly, the architectural model provides additional features on the TCUs, such as the accumulation impacts of TCU reuse and the interaction with other infrastructures in GPUs, such as the scheduling.

The functional TCU assessment for both formats (FP and Posit) is performed in three main steps: *1)* general classification of each observer error according to its severity level, *2)* an analysis of the error at the application level, and *3)* a spatial evaluation.

According to the experimental results, TCUs are highly sensitive to the propagation effect of hardware faults. Figure 8 depicts the fault rate for both TCUs (i.e., *Posit* and *FP*). In general terms, hardware faults propagating during the execution of the TCUs impact the final output matrix in 96% of the cases. Moreover, the results confirm that Posit cores are less likely to propagate the fault effect by up to 4.8% compared to FP ones. Our results demonstrate a strong relation between the number format of the TCU cores and the impact of hardware faults in the generation of DUEs. We find that faulty TCU Posit cores do not produce exceptions (DUEs). Meanwhile, FP TCUs crashed the workload in 1.2% of the evaluated cases.

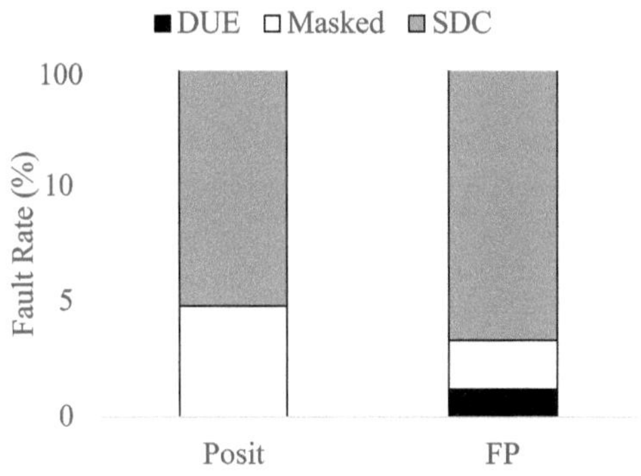

Fig. 8. Fault rate of TCU cores.

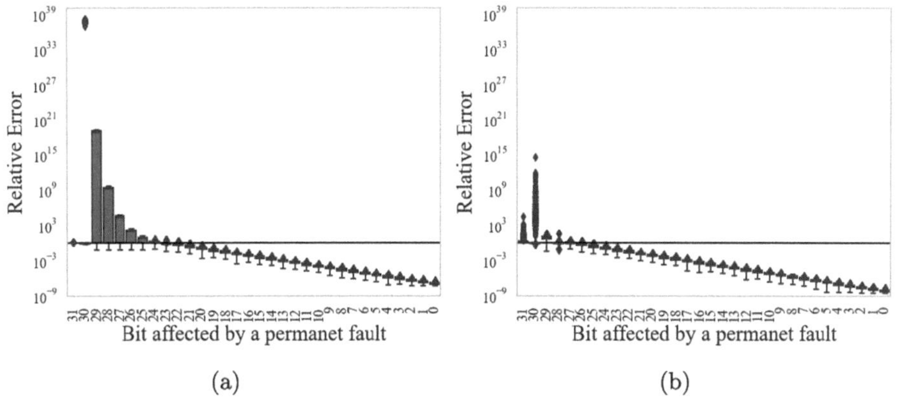

Fig. 9. Relative error of TCU cores for the FP (a) and Posit (b) formats. The black line represents the relative error magnitude of 1.0.

Subsequently, we study the error impact at the application level (e.g., GEMM) by calculating the *relative error*, which allows us to quantify the impact of a single hardware fault. The results show that TCU cores are highly affected by permanent faults, independently of the number format. Moreover, the error magnitude is linked to the number format, and the most significant affected bit by the hardware fault. This trend is shown in Fig. 9, where we report the relative error per bit affected by one hardware fault on the TCU output for the FP (a) and Posit (b) formats. For a simple identification of errors with a small error magnitude, in the figure, we introduce a black line, which indicates the errors of magnitude equal to 1.0. The results show that the exponent (FP) and the regime (Posit) are the most critical fields and reach large-magnitude errors of up to 10^{38} and 10^{14} in FP and Posit, respectively. Curiously, the results also demonstrate that one hardware fault has less than a 10% probability of impacting those fields. On the other hand, the results indicate that the mantissa (FP) and the fraction and exponent (Posit) fields are more prone to propagate the error. Despite this fact, the error magnitude associated with them is less than 1.0, which is controlled chiefly or neglected in machine learning domains such as CNN [30, 71, 72].

It is worth noting that the accumulative scheme of TCUs and their hardware reuse might impact the error propagation of hardware faults. In fact, the results show that small errors tend not to strongly impact the expected results, and some effects may even be completely masked during the complete GEMM execution. On the other hand, error impacts in the most significant bits, independently of the number format, might accumulate their impact, and the final effect might be uncontrollable and, in some cases, crash the application.

Finally, we analyze the spatial distribution of errors on the TCU outputs (i.e., matrix outputs) and their impacts. Since each TCU inside an SM computes, in parallel, different segments of the output result matrix. The segment's distribution depends on the scheduling policies (in the GPU) and the tiling schemes used to split them (i.e., the SM reuses each TCU to compute different segments) [73] [3]. In our experiments, we observed that several output corruption patterns arise in specific sectors of the output matrix when faults affect a DPU. Thus, the distribution of corrupted elements has a strong relationship with the fault location in the TCU and its execution policy, regardless of the number format.

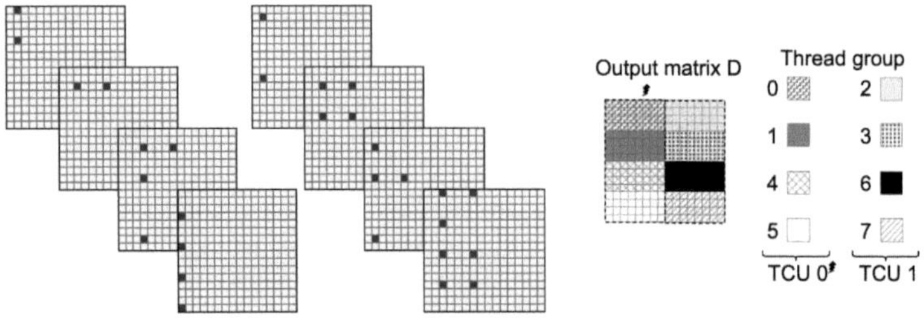

Fig. 10. Spatial distribution of the corruptions in the output matrix D from a faulty DPU inside TCU0 (*left*) and distribution of the *Thread groups* in an SM with two TCUs for the 16×16 configuration mode (*right*). Since our injection targeted TCU0, the corrupted elements (from 1 up to 8) per output matrix only appear from the operations processed in TCU0.

Figure 10 (*left*) shows that the most commonly observed corruption patterns in the output matrix (shown in the illustration as *Output matrix D*) impact from 0 to 8 elements. Interestingly, the location of the corrupted values is related to the workload being mapped into the DPUs inside the TCU. Thus, a faulty DPU can corrupt up to 8 equally distributed values in the output. In addition, the *Thread group* distribution influences the areas of the result that can be affected by faulty TCUs (*right*). The illustrated corruption patterns are produced by faults in TCU0. Nevertheless, the number of locations corrupted can change depending on the type of tile input.

Interestingly, the scheduling policy in the SMs for the TCUs and the internal mapping of DPUs seem to play important roles in terms of faults' impact on the output results. The identification of the spatial error distribution serves as a starting point for the high-level evaluation of applications using TCU cores and the definition of the error model for TCUs.

Summarizing this section, the structural and statistical assessment identifies the most critical errors in TCUs stemming from hardware faults. Then, the error impact is mostly linked to the number format. In fact, permanent faults arising in TCUs produce error magnitude up to 10^{14} and 10^{38} in Posit and FP formats, respectively. However, the mantissa (FP) and fraction and exponent (Posit) demonstrate that they are more prone to propagating the impact of hardware faults. In addition, the scheduling policies and the internal mapping schemes exhibit a key role in terms of the error distribution in the final output matrix.

5.3 Validation of the Proposed Reliability Assessments

In order to determine the main discrepancies and also identify the main benefits of mixed approaches in the reliability analysis of hardware accelerators, we perform a structurally exhaustive fault characterization. This fault characterization is based on an exhaustive evaluation (i.e., all possible fault sites) at the architecture level of both TCUs by resorting to the PyOpenTCU model. The exhaustive evaluation of TCUs shares the same features as our proposed method, e.g., the number of fault injection campaigns and workloads as input stimuli (*input matrices*) and all the experiments required around 297 h.

Clearly, both techniques demonstrate that TCUs are highly sensitive to permanent faults, as shown in Fig. 11. In fact, the fault rate demonstrates small discrepancies between the weighted-bit and structurally exhaustive approaches (only 2%). Curiously, in our experiments, DUE cases are presented only in FP format. This behavior is linked to the number format encoding of each TCU. In fact, Posit formats have unique encoding for $\pm inf$ and *NaN* numbers, so reducing the probability of gathering one corrupted number with those values to almost zero.

Furthermore, TCUs and their accumulative scheme can increment the impact of one single fault, and its accumulative effect is demonstrated in the exhaustive approaches for both formats. In fact, when the reliability evaluation targets internal faults (e.g., *PR* structures in the exhaustive evaluation of the TCUs) in combination with the TCU operation (e.g., accumulation and thread scheduling), the obtained DUE cases increase by up to 3% in comparison to the weighted-bit ones. The behavior observed by the experimental results seems to be associated

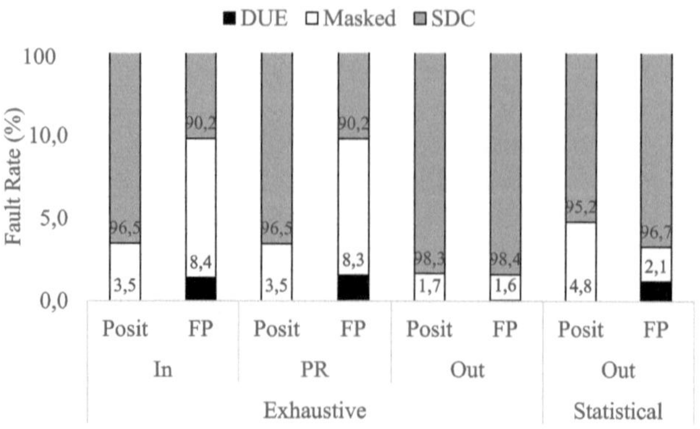

Fig. 11. Comparison between the fault rate of TCUs on both formats by employing the proposed method (weighted-bit approach) and structurally exhaustive FI techniques.

with the reuse of a faulty hardware unit. This indicates that a complete functional operation should be included in the TCU characterization. Our low-level micro-architecture characterization did not consider the accumulative impact of one fault. It focused on the propagation effects as corruptions on the DPU outputs, which provide accurate results at the unit level but might neglect additional operative features of the unit, such as the accumulation. Our results indicate that hardware accelerators operating as the combination of several steps of hardware and software, such as TCUs, require mixed methods that consider the functional operation of the unit in combination with fine-grain execution of the hardware to provide accurate reliability assessments effectively.

Then, we evaluate the impact of errors on the output of parallel workloads. Figure 12 depicts the cumulative distribution of relative errors for the structurally exhaustive (*gray*) and weighted-bit (*black*) evaluations. We report the results for faulty TCUs operating in FP (a) and Posit (b) formats.

A first look at the relative error results indicates that both approaches (*weighted-bit fault injection* and *structurally exhaustive*) provide the same shape of error distributions, which suggests that hardware faults on TCUs similarly propagate their effects, according to each specific number format. In detail, around 80% (weighted-bit fault injection) and 95% (structurally exhaustive) of all observed errors are associated with magnitudes less than 1.0. Interestingly, when the error magnitude is less than 1.0, the cumulative distribution shows a strong discrepancy between the exhaustive and weighted-bit evaluations for both TCUs (FP and Posit). In fact, exhaustive approaches have up to 10% more amount of errors with a magnitude less than 1.0, which are mostly negligible in CNN applications. Curiously, some features presented in the exhaustive assessment might not be represented by the weighted-bit evaluation. This tendency is clearly seen in the Posit format, where our approach is not able to display the worst error magnitude (i.e., error magnitudes of 10^{18}). This trend seems to

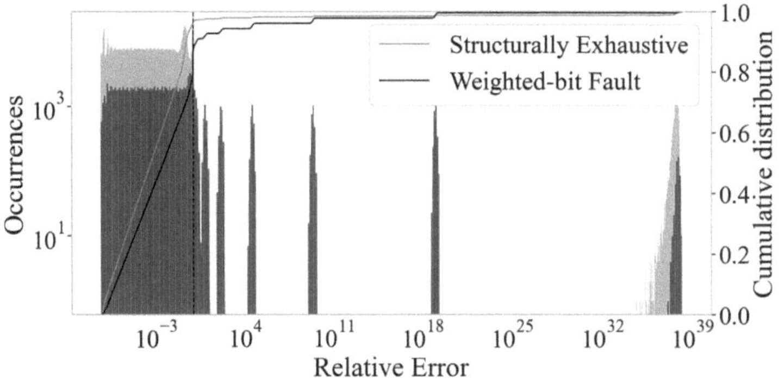

(a)

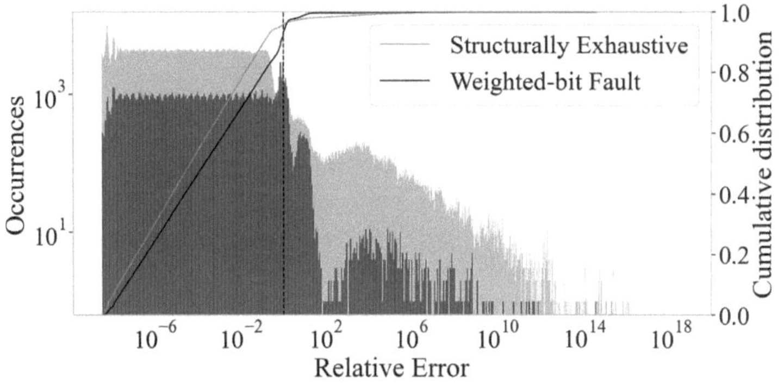

(b)

Fig. 12. Occurrences of relative errors (*left*) and cumulative distribution of errors (*right*) for the *FP* (a) and *Posit* (b) TCUs. The vertical dot-line represents an error magnitude of 1.0.

be associated with critical cases gathered by the accumulative scheme in TCUs, which was not included as part of our fine-grain characterization.

The results also demonstrate that large error magnitudes are produced by hardware faults in the exponent (FP) and regime (Posit) fields. In detail, the distribution in FP TCU cores is mainly concentrated across 10^1, 10^2, 10^4, 10^{11}, 10^{18}, and 10^{38}. On the other side, the error distribution is widely distributed between 10^0 and 10^{18} for Posit TCU one, which are mostly a product of bit-flips in the regime and exponent fields.

Our analysis shows the link between number formats and their impact on the reliability of machine learning accelerators, such as TCUs. Interestingly, our results demonstrate that permanent faults have less impact on Posit cores than FP ones. Moreover, our findings contribute to the design and exploration of reliable hardware accelerators, taking into account the number format as a critical parameter. In addition, our results demonstrate that reliability evaluations based on the combination of fine-grain low-level micro-architecture evaluations with structural ones might represent the error impact of hardware defects in a similar proportion to those using exclusively architectural evaluations combined with instruction-accurate and functional features of the hardware accelerator.

6 Conclusions

This work introduces a mixed strategy for analyzing the reliability of large hardware accelerators (e.g., TCUs) for machine learning domains. This strategy takes into account the advantages of fine-grain structural and high-level functional assessments to evaluate large applications.

The experimental results show that the exponent and the regime fields are the most critical fields with respect to permanent faults. In fact, a single fault affecting the exponent and regime fields might produce error magnitudes up to 10^{18} and 10^{38}. However, one hardware fault might influence them in up to 12% and 5% of the cases in Posit and FP cores, respectively.

The experimental results prove that clever strategies, like the proposed one, might support the assessment of large hardware accelerators (e.g., TCUs) with affordable simulation times. In fact, the results show that the findings gathered by exhaustive and mixed approaches are equivalents from the error impact point of view. The results also demonstrate that the fault rate only shows small discrepancies (only 2%) between the exhaustive and the proposed assessments.

In future works, we plan to extend the findings of the current work to devise clever error models in order to assess huge applications like deep CNNs.

Acknowledgements. This work has been supported by the National Resilience and Recovery Plan (PNRR) through the National Center for HPC, Big Data, and Quantum Computing.

References

1. Peccerillo, B., et al.: A survey on hardware accelerators: taxonomy, trends, challenges, and perspectives. J. Syst. Architect. **129**, 102561 (2022)
2. Jouppi, N.P., et al.: In-datacenter performance analysis of a tensor processing unit. SIGARCH Comput. Archit. News **45**(2), 1–12 (2017)
3. Raihan, M., et al.: Modeling deep learning accelerator enabled GPUs. In: IEEE International Symposium on Performance Analysis of Systems and Software (ISPASS), pp. 79–92 (2019)
4. Lee, W.-K., et al.: Tensorcrypto: high throughput acceleration of lattice-based cryptography using tensor core on GPU. IEEE Access **10**, 20 616-20 632 (2022)
5. Groth, S., et al.: Efficient application of tensor core units for convolving images. Association for Computing Machinery (2021)
6. Dally, W.J., et al.: Evolution of the graphics processing unit (GPU). IEEE Micro **41**(6), 42–51 (2021)
7. Oakden, T., et al.: Graphics processing in virtual production. In: 2022 14th International Conference on Computer and Automation Engineering (ICCAE), pp. 61–64 (2022)

8. Gati, N.J., Yang, L.T., Feng, J., Mo, Y., Alazab, M.: Differentially private tensor train deep computation for internet of multimedia things. ACM Trans. Multimed. Comput. Commun. Appl. **16**(3s), 1–20 (2020). https://dl.acm.org/doi/10.1145/3421276
9. Fu, C., Yang, Z., Liu, X.-Y., Yang, J., Walid, A., Yang, L.T.: Secure tensor decomposition for heterogeneous multimedia data in cloud computing. IEEE Trans. Comput. Soc. Syst. **7**(1), 247–260 (2020). https://ieeexplore.ieee.org/document/8960318/
10. Wang, H., Yang, W., Hu, R., Ouyang, R., Li, K., Li, K.: A novel parallel algorithm for sparse tensor matrix chain multiplication via TCU-acceleration. IEEE Trans. Parallel Distrib. Syst. **34**(8), 2419–2432 (2023). https://ieeexplore.ieee.org/document/10159508/
11. Chen, H., Ahmad, F., Vorobyov, S., Porikli, F.: Tensor decompositions in wireless communications and MIMO radar. IEEE J. Sel. Top. Signal Process. **15**(3), 438–453 (2021). https://ieeexplore.ieee.org/document/9362250/
12. Xu, H., Jiang, G., Yu, M., Zhu, Z., Bai, Y., Song, Y., Sun, H.: Tensor product and tensor-singular value decomposition based multi-exposure fusion of images. IEEE Trans. Multimed. **24**, 3738–3753 (2022). https://ieeexplore.ieee.org/document/9522049/
13. Sofuoglu, S.E., Aviyente, S.: Graph regularized tensor train decomposition. In: ICASSP 2020 - 2020 IEEE International Conference on Acoustics, Speech and Signal Processing (ICASSP), pp. 3912–3916. IEEE, Barcelona (2020). https://ieeexplore.ieee.org/document/9054032/
14. Zeng, H., Xue, J., Luong, H.Q., Philips, W.: Multimodal core tensor factorization and its applications to low-rank tensor completion. IEEE Trans. Multimed. **25**, 7010–7024 (2023). https://ieeexplore.ieee.org/document/9927348/
15. Chen, L., Liu, Y., Zhu, C.: Robust tensor principal component analysis in all modes. In: 2018 IEEE International Conference on Multimedia and Expo (ICME), San Diego, CA, pp. 1–6. IEEE (2018). https://ieeexplore.ieee.org/document/8486550/
16. Chang, S.Y., Wu, H.-C., Yan, K., Chen, X., Wu, Y.: Novel personalized multimedia recommendation systems using tensor singular-value-decomposition. In: 2023 IEEE International Symposium on Broadband Multimedia Systems and Broadcasting (BMSB), Beijing, China, pp. 1–7. IEEE (2023). https://ieeexplore.ieee.org/document/10211188/
17. Lee, A.: Train spotting: Startup gets on track with AI and nvidia Jetson to ensure safety, cost savings for railways (2022). https://resources.nvidia.com/en-us-jetson-success/rail-vision-startup-uses?lx=XRDs_y
18. Mariani, R.: Driving toward a safer future: NVIDIA achieves safety milestones with drive hyperion autonomous vehicle platform (2023). https://blogs.nvidia.com/blog/2023/04/20/nvidia-drive-safety-milestones/
19. IEEE. The international roadmap for devices and systems: 2022. In: Institute of Electrical and Electronics Engineers (IEEE) (2022)
20. Strojwas, A.J., et al.: Yield and reliability challenges at 7nm and below. In: 2019 Electron Devices Technology and Manufacturing Conference (EDTM), pp. 179–181 (2019)
21. Hochschild, P.H., et al.: Cores that don't count. In: Proceedings of the Workshop on Hot Topics in Operating Systems, HotOS 2021, New York, NY, USA, pp. 9–16. Association for Computing Machinery (2021). https://doi.org/10.1145/3458336.3465297
22. Dixit, H.D., et al.: Silent data corruptions at scale. CoRR, vol. abs/2102.11245 (2021). https://arxiv.org/abs/2102.11245

23. Constantinides, K., Mutlu, O., Austin, T., Bertacco, V.: Software-based online detection of hardware defects mechanisms, architectural support, and evaluation. In: 40th Annual IEEE/ACM International Symposium on Microarchitecture (MICRO 2007), pp. 97–108 (2007)
24. Gizopoulos, D., Papadimitriou, G., Chatzopoulos, O.: Estimating the failures and silent errors rates of CPUs across ISAS and microarchitectures. In: 2023 IEEE International Test Conference (ITC), pp. 377–382 (2023)
25. Papadimitriou, G., Gizopoulos, D.: Silent data corruptions: microarchitectural perspectives. IEEE Trans. Comput. **72**(11), 3072–3085 (2023)
26. Zeng, Y., Huang, B.-Y., Zhang, H., Gupta, A., Malik, S.: Generating architecture-level abstractions from RTL designs for processors and accelerators part I: determining architectural state variables. In: 2021 IEEE/ACM International Conference in Computer Aided Design (ICCAD), 1–9 (2021)
27. Libano, F., et al.: On the reliability of Xilinx's deep processing unit and systolic arrays for matrix multiplication. In: 2020 20th European Conference on Radiation and its Effects on Components and Systems (RADECS), pp. 1–5 (2020)
28. Omland, P., et al.: HPC hardware design reliability benchmarking with HDFIT. IEEE Trans. Parallel Distrib. Syst. **34**(3), 995–1006 (2023)
29. Rech, R.L., Rech, P.: Reliability of Google's tensor processing units for embedded applications. In: 2022 Design, Automation & Test in Europe Conference & Exhibition (DATE), pp. 376–381 (2022)
30. He, Y., et al.: Understanding and mitigating hardware failures in deep learning training systems. In: Proceedings of the 50th Annual International Symposium on Computer Architecture, ISCA 2023. Association for Computing Machinery, New York (2023https://doi.org/10.1145/3579371.3589105
31. Basso, P.M., et al.: Impact of tensor cores and mixed precision on the reliability of matrix multiplication in GPUs. IEEE Trans. Nucl. Sci. **67**(7), 1560–1565 (2020)
32. Kundu, S., et al.: Special session: Reliability analysis for AI/ml hardware. In: 2021 IEEE 39th VLSI Test Symposium (VTS), pp. 1–10 (2021)
33. Ozen, E., Orailoglu, A.: Architecting decentralization and customizability in DNN accelerators for hardware defect adaptation. IEEE Trans. Comput. Aided Des. Integr. Circuits Syst. **41**(11), 3934–3945 (2022)
34. Chaudhuri, A., et al.: Special session: fault criticality assessment in AI accelerators. In: 2022 IEEE 40th VLSI Test Symposium (VTS), pp. 1–4 (2022)
35. Agarwal, U.K., Chan, A., Asgari, A., Pattabiraman, K.: Towards reliability assessment of systolic arrays against stuck-at faults. In: 2023 53rd Annual IEEE/IFIP International Conference on Dependable Systems and Networks - Supplemental Volume (DSN-S), pp. 230–236 (2023)
36. Tan, J., et al.: Saca-FI: a microarchitecture-level fault injection framework for reliability analysis of systolic array based CNN accelerator. Future Gener. Comput. Syst. **147**, 251–264 (2023). https://www.sciencedirect.com/science/article/pii/S0167739X2300184X
37. Elliott, J., et al.: Quantifying the impact of single bit flips on floating point arithmetic. North Carolina State University. Department of Computer Science, Technical report (2013)
38. Fu, H., et al.: Comparing floating-point and logarithmic number representations for reconfigurable acceleration. In: IEEE International Conference on Field Programmable Technology, pp. 337–340 (2006)
39. Haselman, M., et al.: A comparison of floating point and logarithmic number systems for FPGAs. In: 13th Annual IEEE Symposium on Field-Programmable Custom Computing Machines (FCCM 2005), pp. 181–190 (2005)

40. Chugh, M., Parhami, B.: Logarithmic arithmetic as an alternative to floating-point: a review. In: 2013 Asilomar Conference on Signals, Systems and Computers, pp. 1139–1143 (2013)
41. Barrois, B., Sentieys, O.: Customizing fixed-point and floating-point arithmetic—a case study in k-means clustering. In: IEEE International Workshop on Signal Processing Systems (SiPS), pp. 1–6 (2017)
42. Gohil, V., et al.: Fixed-posit: a floating-point representation for error-resilient applications. IEEE Trans. Circuits Syst. II Express Briefs **68**(10), 3341–3345 (2021)
43. Schlueter, B., et al.: Evaluating the resiliency of posits for scientific computing. In: Proceedings of the SC 2023 Workshops of the International Conference on High Performance Computing, Network, Storage, and Analysis, pp. 477–487 (2023)
44. Gavarini, G., et al.: On the resilience of representative and novel data formats in CNNs. In: IEEE International Symposium on Defect and Fault Tolerance in VLSI and Nanotechnology Systems (DFT), pp. 1–6 (2023)
45. Fatemi Langroudi, S.H., Pandit, T., Kudithipudi, D.: Deep learning inference on embedded devices: fixed-point vs posit. In: 1st Workshop on Energy Efficient Machine Learning and Cognitive Computing for Embedded Applications (EMC2), pp. 19–23 (2018)
46. Alouani, I., et al.: An investigation on inherent robustness of posit data representation. In: 34th International Conference on VLSI Design and 20th International Conference on Embedded Systems (VLSID), pp. 276–281 (2021)
47. Limas Sierra, R., et al.: Analyzing the impact of different real number formats on the structural reliability of TCUs in GPUs. In: 2023 IFIP/IEEE 31st International Conference on Very Large Scale Integration (VLSI-SoC), pp. 1–6 (2023)
48. Limas Sierra, R., Guerrero-Balaguera, J.-D., Condia, J.E.R., Sonza Reorda, M.: Exploring hardware fault impacts on different real number representations of the structural resilience of TCUs in GPUs. Electronics **13**(3) (2024). https://www.mdpi.com/2079-9292/13/3/578
49. Mallasén, D., Barrio, A.A.D., Prieto-Matias, M.: Big-percival: exploring the native use of 64-bit posit arithmetic in scientific computing (2023)
50. Murillo, R., Del Barrio, A.A., Botella, G.: Customized posit adders and multipliers using the flopoco core generator. In: 2020 IEEE International Symposium on Circuits and Systems (ISCAS), pp. 1–5 (2020)
51. Advanced Micro Devices, I.: Introducing AMD CDNA architecture the all-new AMD GPU architecture for the modern era of HPC & AI (2020)
52. Smith, A., James, N., AMD instinct MI200 series accelerator and node architectures. In: 2022 IEEE Hot Chips 34 Symposium (HCS), pp. 1–23. IEEE Computer Society (2022)
53. Jiang, H.: Intel's ponte vecchio GPU: architecture, systems & software. In: 2022 IEEE Hot Chips 34 Symposium (HCS), pp. 1–29. IEEE Computer Society (2022)
54. Boswell, B.R., et al.: Generalized acceleration of matrix multiply accumulate operations. U.S. Patent and Trademark Office, US Patent 10,338,919 (2019)
55. Gebhart, M., et al.: Energy-efficient mechanisms for managing thread context in throughput processors. In: 38th Annual International Symposium on Computer Architecture (ISCA), pp. 235–246 (2011)
56. IEEE standard for floating-point arithmetic. IEEE Std 754-2019 (Revision of IEEE 754-2008), pp. 1–84 (2019)
57. Gustafson, J.L., Yonemoto, I.T.: Beating floating point at its own game: posit arithmetic. Supercomput. Front. Innov.: Int. J. **4**(2), 71–86 (2017)

58. Blundell, C., Cornebise, J., Kavukcuoglu, K., Wierstra, D.: Weight uncertainty in neural network. In: Bach, F., Blei, D. (eds.) Proceedings of the 32nd International Conference on Machine Learning. Proceedings of Machine Learning Research, Lille, France, 07–09 Jul 2015, , vol. 37, pp. 1613–1622. PMLR (2015). https://proceedings.mlr.press/v37/blundell15.html
59. Lindstrom, P., et al.: Universal coding of the reals: alternatives to IEEE floating point. In: Proceedings of the Conference for Next Generation Arithmetic, CoNGA 2018. Association for Computing Machinery, New York (2018). https://doi.org/10.1145/3190339.3190344
60. Mishra, S.M., et al.: Comparison of floating-point representations for the efficient implementation of machine learning algorithms. In: 2022 32nd International Conference Radioelektronika (RADIOELEKTRONIKA), pp. 1–6 (2022)
61. Ito, K., et al.: Analyzing due errors on GPUs with neutron irradiation test and fault injection to control flow. IEEE Trans. Nucl. Sci. **68**(8), 1668–1674 (2021)
62. Benevenuti, F., et al.: Investigating the reliability impacts of neutron-induced soft errors in aerial image classification CNNs implemented in a softcore SRAM-based FPGA GPU. Microelectron. Reliab. **138**, 114738 (2022). 33rd European Symposium on Reliability of Electron Devices, Failure Physics and Analysis
63. Tsai, T., et al.: NVBitFI: dynamic fault injection for GPUs. In: 2021 51st Annual IEEE/IFIP International Conference on Dependable Systems and Networks (DSN), pp. 284–291 (2021)
64. Condia, J.E.R., et al.: A multi-level approach to evaluate the impact of GPU permanent faults on CNN's reliability. In: 2022 IEEE International Test Conference (ITC), pp. 278–287 (2022)
65. Previlon, F.G., et al.: A comprehensive evaluation of the effects of input data on the resilience of GPU applications. In: 2019 IEEE International Symposium on Defect and Fault Tolerance in VLSI and Nanotechnology Systems (DFT) (2019)
66. Mallasen, D., et al.: Percival: open-source posit RISC-V core with quire capability. IEEE Trans. Emerg. Top. Comput. **10**(03), 1241–1252 (2022)
67. de Dinechin, F., et al.: Designing custom arithmetic data paths with FloPoCo. IEEE Design Test Comput. **28**(4), 18–27 (2011)
68. Martins, M., et al.: Open cell library in 15nm freePDK technology. In: Proceedings of the 2015 Symposium on International Symposium on Physical Design. Proceedings of the International Symposium on Physical Design (ISPD 2015), pp. 171–178 (2015)
69. Gil, P., et al.: Pin-level hardware fault injection techniques. In: Fault Injection Techniques and Tools for Embedded Systems reliability Evaluation, pp. 63–79 (2003). 978-0-306-48711-8
70. Jenn, E., Arlat, J., Rimén, M., Ohlsson, J., Karlsson, J.: Fault injection into VHDL models: the MEFISTO tool. In: Randell, B., Laprie, J.C., Kopetz, H., Littlewood, B. (eds.) Predictably Dependable Computing Systems. ESPRIT Basic Research Series, pp. 329–346. Springer, Heidelberg (1995). https://doi.org/10.1007/978-3-642-79789-7_19
71. Češka, M., Matyáš, J., Mrazek, V., Vojnar, T.: Designing approximate arithmetic circuits with combined error constraints (2022)
72. Jiang, H., Santiago, F.J.H., Mo, H., Liu, L., Han, J.: Approximate arithmetic circuits: a survey, characterization, and recent applications. Proc. IEEE **108**(12), 2108–2135 (2020)
73. Huang, J., Yu, C.D., van de Geijn, R.A.: Implementing Strassen's algorithm with cutlass on NVIDIA Volta GPUs (2018)

Advanced Quality Assurance Platform for Robust Process Design Kits

Anton Datsuk(✉), Philip Ostrovskyy, Frank Vater, and Christian Wieden

IHP - Leibniz-Institut für Innovative Mikroelektronik, Im Technologiepark 25, 15236 Frankfurt (Oder), Germany
datsuk@ihp-microelectronics.com

Abstract. Process design kits (PDKs) and their robustness verification are pivotal to a semiconductor foundry's growth and customer retention. This paper presents an extended version of our automated PDK quality assurance (QA) platform, initially introduced to maintain production-quality PDKs deployable at any time. The platform utilizes continuous integration and continuous delivery tools to detect and resolve problems early, significantly reducing the time required for pre-release PDK verification. We have embedded this QA platform into the PDK verification flow for 0.13 µm and 0.25 µm SiGe BiCMOS technologies, ensuring reliable on-demand PDK releases. Additionally, we extend our discussion to include the results viewer application that enhances identification and organization of the issues across various PDKs, further improving verification efficiency. This paper also introduces a new analysis of the trend in PDK issues reported by customers, illustrating the platform's effectiveness in quality assurance and optimization of the PDK development process for semiconductor technologies. The enhanced features and insights detailed in this paper reinforce our approach and highlight significant improvements in interoperable PDK verification, utilizing previously released PDKs as benchmarks.

Keywords: process design kit · quality assurance · continuous integration · continuous delivery · interoperable PDK

1 Introduction

A PDK development includes many steps such as coding, building, releasing, configuring, setting up runtime environment, testing, troubleshooting, and final deployment. A typical PDK represents a set of files for certain EDA (Electronic Design Automation) tools to provide an interface between a semiconductor technology supplied by foundry and an integrated circuit (IC) designer [1]. The complexity of a PDK is increasingly growing due to constant scale down of the technology nodes. Moreover, extending the technology by adding new modules, e.g. Through-Silicon Via (TSV) process module, MEMS devices or Silicon Photonic (SiP) elements and so on adds additional degree of complexity. Due to increased complexity of PDK and its modularity, the probability of error to

I. (Abe) M. Elfadel and L. Albasha (Eds.): VLSI-SoC 2023, IFIP AICT 680, pp. 177–195, 2024.
https://doi.org/10.1007/978-3-031-70947-0_9

creep into the final PDK increases. Such instances may incur severe penalties. In worst cases, this may lead to malfunctioning of ICs causing severe financial damage to both the foundry and its customer. Thus, the PDK development must involve a set of verification steps to ensure a quality PDK release and stable lifecycle delivery. The common practice is to perform quality assurance (QA) tests when the PDK team completed the development. Detecting an error at this stage requires longer time to trace its source, especially in case of a complex problem. QA steps are usually not fully automated and may potentially lead to errors due to manual verification. To overcome the aforementioned complications, any PDK modification injected in version control repository of PDK should be subjected to verification. Such a technique renders a robust source code of a PDK and consequently a deployment ready PDK on demand. On account of high PDK complexity, a group of programmers are typically deployed for PDK development. Therefore, any changes introduced by a group member must be checked to localize the error at an early stage. It will also be beneficial to initiate the verification process automatically after any committed change. Upon completion, a detailed report must be distributed across the developers. A fully automated verification enables effective man power utilization in that the focus is on development rather than resolving mistakes prior to PDK release. This holds even greater significance for a semiconductor foundry that offers a variety of running technology nodes which may requirement occasional maintenance.

In view of the aforementioned challenges, we present an extended version of PDK QA platform [2]. It is dedicated to further enhancing our discussion on the automation and debugging processes for maintaining high-quality PDK releases on a daily basis. The remainder of this paper is organized as follows. Section 2 presents the constituents of the QA platform architecture and the QA work flow. Section 3 introduces an application case, which demonstrates the QA platform deployment for 0.13 µm and 0.25 µm PDK verification. Additionally, verification of PDK modules and digital libraries are discussed. Section 4 describes an application case of utilizing the QA platform for an interoperable PDK verification. It focuses on development details of the most important verification steps required before deployment to circuit designer. Section 5 introduces a new analysis on the QA tool's effectiveness in identifying and organizing issues within PDKs, iPDKs, and DDKs, along with a description of the results viewer application developed to facilitate this process. Section 6 presents a study on the quality assurance efficiency, demonstrating a trend in the number of PDK issues reported over time and discussing strategies for their resolution. Finally, Sect. 7 presents our conclusions, summarizing the impact and advancements made through the extended capabilities of the QA platform.

2 QA Platform Architecture

The proposed methodology of PDK QA is based on continuous integration (CI) and continuous delivery (CD) approaches [3]. PDK developers constantly address technology optimization, bug fixes and enhancement implementation for every new release. CI assumes frequent integration of the PDK source code by PDK developers via version control system. CD allows organizing the delivery process in a way that PDK can be released to production at any time. The PDK verification flow ensures that each change is free of errors and does not block the development of other PDK members.

A verification core engine of the QA platform is running on a CI/CD pipeline server. The CI/CD server [4] provides a realtime code tracking functionality for faster problem detection and has a close integration with different version control systems. It allows extracting of only that specific PDK data, which were changed instead of populating a complete suite. Figure 1 depicts the complete PDK QA platform based on the CI/CD server. After submitting the changes to the version control system, the CI/CD server automatically detects the changes done by PDK developers and checks these modifications by executing a verification flow. The core engine starts quick tests. In case of error-free completion, a full test is automatically scheduled for an overnight execution. To avoid collisions between PDK developers, the first submitted change is verified immediately. The next submissions are put into a queue until the first process is idle. If a later submission in the chain has more changes and covers the changes of an earlier submission then the earlier submission is replaced by the later one.

In case of a failure at any verification step, the process is aborted and a corresponding error message is logged into a report. Then, the notifications with the test status are sent to the users according to the user's configured notification rules. The error is to be investigated and fixed by PDK developers. In case of a more complicated problem, which requires more time to get it solved, the developer has to roll back the changes. The target is to maintain an error free PDK data base at all times. Upon successful verification run, the project leader receives a message from the CI/CD server that a PDK has been verified and it is ready for an official release.

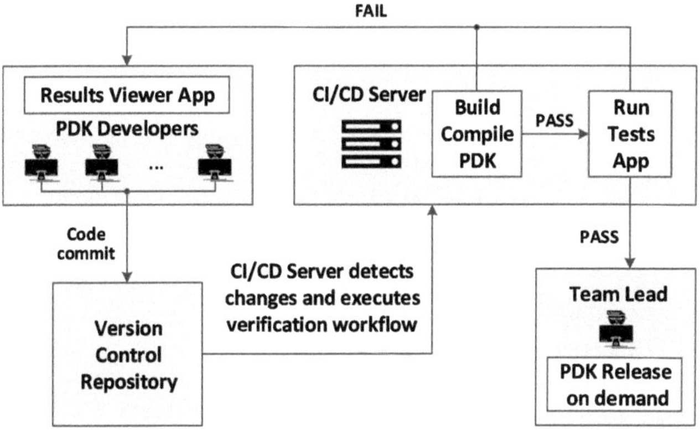

Fig. 1. Proposed PDK QA platform based on CI/CD pipeline.

The CI/CD flow was extended by developing a crossplatform engine. The engine consists of a set of custom scripts that can be executed from command line with the basic Perl distribution installed. These scripts are configured via run parameter files for required PDK which contain a set of variables to control the run of verification flow. These files follow LISP syntax, as this language is machine-independent and can be easily extended for specific implementation. The engine was developed to support the overall PDK QA workflow shown in Fig. 2. The flow is invoked under a CI/CD test user on a separate server to avoid collisions with environment of PDK developers.

Fig. 2. PDK QA workflow run on the CI/CD server.

The verification flow can also be executed in a smart mode for automatic selection of the checks to cover the submitted changes. The checks are picked out by CI/CD engine based on the map-file which defines the correspondence between directories and checks. The approach helps to decrease overall run time and can be used for quick verification of changes performed by PDK developer. However, the default mode is a full-check verification run to avoid accidental and data dependent errors.

PDK Populating. This check utilizes version control systems to ensure that the latest changes are to be verified. Any PDK change committed to the version control is automatically detected by the CI/CD server. For the very first test-run, the server downloads a complete PDK, while for the next runs only submitted changes are applied to the project. This helps to significantly reduce the run-time of the PDK QA workflow.

Run Environment Verification. The test is executed to validate compatibility of the installed EDA tools and their versions required for a certain PDK. At this stage, the run-specific environment variables required for the verification flow are checked. This procedure tests that the populated PDK data as source code, technology library data, documentation meets the company-accepted hierarchy template structure and every file is located at an appropriate place. The IHP company template defines the directory structure and the file naming convention.

PDK Build. This is a process to assemble source code, display files, parametrized cells (PCell), simulation model files, physical verification and parasitic extraction rule decks, etc. into one folder. During the building procedure, the different technology modules can be included into PDK on demand, e.g. LDMOS devices, TSV, SiP, etc.

The routine utilizes the GNU Make [5] tool that parses a make-file that is to be supplied for each PDK. A make-file contains a set of instructions that controls the PDK build. The instructions for building of PDKs are defined for specific technology process. The Make tool iteratively processes the instructions to build targets (context files, physical verification rule decks, PCells etc.) for PDK. The PDK and module parameters are defined in key-files that are a set of parameters to control the build of a required module or PDK. A module can be optionally applied to the building process of basic PDK. The modules are independent units and must be applied to the basic PDK during the building stage. The Make tool is capable of automatically detecting the PDK files that were updated for release. Moreover, the tool evaluates the proper order for updating PDK sources and accomplishes the same. In case a PDK release is newer than all of its dependencies, the regeneration of PDK is omitted and a PDK compiling step is executed.

PDK Compilation. At this step, the PDK source code is compiled into the binary files. This procedure is required to protect sensitive technology data as compiled files are hard to decode. On the other hand, the compiled files significantly speed-up the PDK loading time. During the compilation phase, all PCells and their properties are configured. Any syntax errors are reported by the compiler and saved to the report file.

PDK Pre-release. This procedure removes the source code and internal data from the PDK and copies the required data to the release folder, which is then ready for delivery. It assigns suitable data permissions and performs integrity verification of the released data. When subsequent verification steps report no errors, these PDK data are compressed and can be released by team lead for deployment to IC designers

PDK Verification. The aim of the PDK QA is to have stable design kits for product development. At this stage, the verification flow runs a set of tests targeted to validate the basic functionality of the released PDK. The detailed discussion of the PDK verification tests in contest of considered technology nodes is presented in Sect. 3.1.

Digital Design Kit Verification. After having a basic PDK approved, the correctness of the digital design kit (DDK) libraries must be evaluated. This test can be considered as a higher level PDK verification since it is performed on PDK elements combined in a variety of circuits. The DDK verification approach is demonstrated in Sect. 3.2 in detail.

Regression Tests. Regression tests are required to perform continuous retesting of PDK and DDK design modification to ensure that the expected problem is addressed and that either the PDK or the DDK corrections/enhancements do not introduce new errors. These tests can isolate the errors which could be overlooked by a designer and a PDK developer, and provide the appropriate diagnostics of the issues. DDK regression testing meets this goal by running a variety of test cases each time a change is injected in either PDK or DDK database.

Reporting and Notification. The verification engine searches for test reports in the run directory according to the specified path or path patterns. The matching files are combined into the final summary report, which is then uploaded to the server. Through the server, it is made available for download via web user interface.

The CI/CD engine sends the status report per email to the PDK developers about all of failed builds in the specified projects. If a certain developer is assigned to specific project, the failed test notification is sent only to that developer. In case the run-time significantly exceeds the average run-time for the project the workflow is considered to be hanging and all the PDK members receive an appropriate notification.

3 Application Case I: Cadence Virtuoso PDK

The QA platform presented in the previous section is implemented for Cadence Virtuoso PDK verification in two technology nodes: 0.13 μm and 0.25 μm SiGe BiCMOS. For the given technology nodes, four basic PDKs with a fixed set of primitives including SiGe HBT and CMOS transistors, diodes, passive components, ESD devices were developed. Depending on the technology node, one or more specific modules can be added to a basic PDK. An overview of basic PDKs and available modules is shown in Fig. 3.

Each module reflects IC manufacturing steps and/or a corresponding set of technological structures. For instance, one of the basic PDKs in 0.25 μm technology node has an additional silicon photonic module option. For the fabrication of low-loss photonic components local silicon-on-insulator (SOI) areas must be considered beside bulk BiCMOS substrate areas. The Silicon Photonics module offers a set of passive photonic components: couplers, splitters and waveguides. Additionally, modules such as waveguide-coupled Ge photodiode and phaseshifters are also available. Thus, this module contains the complete information about required technological layers, PCells, DRC/LVS rules etc. related to silicon photonics components.

As some modules are still under development, the QA platform scalability was addressed to easily extend basic PDKs by additional modules. The QA platform was implemented in a way that it senses whether any changes injected in any module. The modified module is applied to basic PDK and the verification tests are executed. The same is valid for the combined PDK. Any change of a basic PDK can potentially affect a PDK module. In this case the verification is executed for the PDK and all applicable module combinations. This guarantees having PDK and its modules to be ready for use at any time.

The following subsections focus on implementation details of the main verification steps within the QA platform in the context of specific technology nodes.

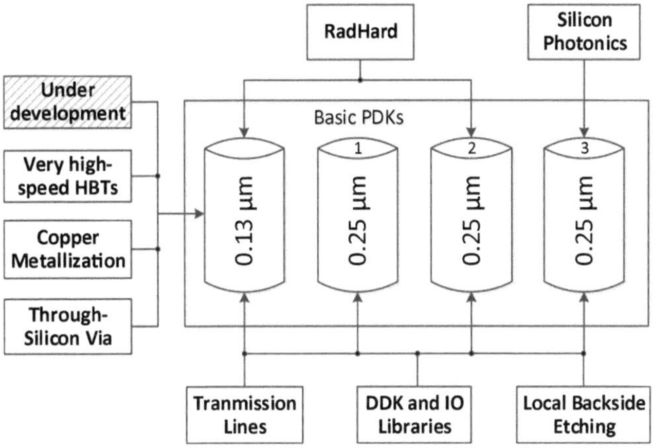

Fig. 3. Basic PDK databases and available modules.

3.1 PDK Verification

A variety of developed QA tests were combined into a complete automated flow to perform a comprehensive PDK verification. Figure 4 presents a simplified structure of the verification flow that is used by the QA platform, shown in Fig. 1. The flow invokes an iterative process of PDK verification which is split into three main categories: general, front-end and back-end checks. Each category consists of a variety of tests that are executed by the core engine. In the event of a test failure, the problem is to be investigated and assigned to an appropriate PDK developer. If the cause of the failure is a PDK bug, the problem is assigned to a PDK developer. It is also possible that the test is not valid any more, for instance, due to technology changes, and then the problem is assigned to a QA engineer, who should update the test. The tests are created with Cadence SKILL language. The source code is structured the way that new tests can be easily added.

The checks are executed in a batch mode using interprocess communication (IPC) functionality of SKILL. The approach allows to execute any verification step as a child process accessed by IPC and process control functionality of the running task. Communication with the task can be carried out in either synchronous or asynchronous mode. The approach helps to distribute the tasks over available processors and decrease overall verification run-time.

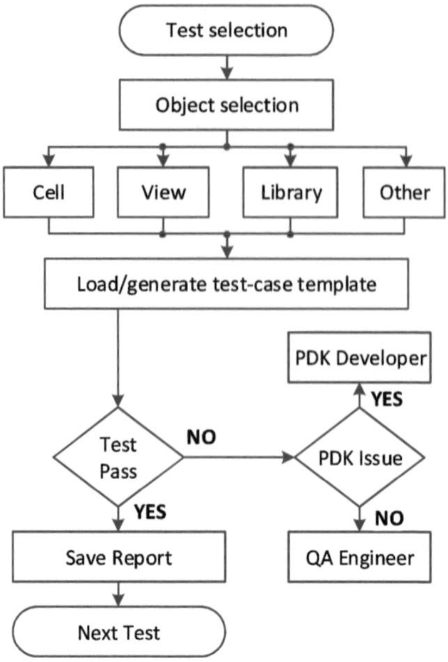

Fig. 4. PDK verification flow.

The general category verifies integrity of released data and PDK structure to satisfy requirements of the predefined naming and data convention. Since a PDK is deployed for different EDA vendors, the compatibility between the technology file, callback functions, simulation models and physical verification rules are checked during this process.

Front-end QA tests are dedicated to check proper functionality of the PDK primitive devices (e.g. resistors, capacitors, transistors etc.) when instantiated in schematic editor, as well as correct netlisting and linking to simulation models. The device models themselves are verified for the supported simulators. The simulations are executed on a variety of tests that have preliminary calculated simulation results. These results are proved by QA engineer and they are considered as a reference. The test verifies that there is no deviation within a certain tolerance between the new simulation results and the reference. Thus, model degradation is avoided.

Back-end QA tests verify the functionality of PCells and non-parametrized cells representing physical view of the PDK components, it's extraction, physical verification and other aspects related to preparation of an IC design for manufacturing. The verification process involves design rules check (DRC), layout versus schematic comparison (LVS), exclusive OR layout comparison, parasitic extraction, slits and filler generation tests. These tests are executed for each EDA vendor supported by PDK.

3.2 Digital Design Kit Verification

The quality of DDK libraries depends on the integrity of PDK. Despite the fact that the PDK verification flow helps to detect major issues, it is not sufficient to guarantee the robustness of DDK libraries, due to their complexity. Thus, the DDK requires its own verification flow, that covers the integrity and basic functionality (general checks), synthesis and regression aspects.

An overview of the DDK verification flow is presented in Fig. 5. The general checks validate library consistency and the functional characteristics of the standard cells. These checks are well known and their description is omitted in this paper. In addition to these checks, a synthesis test is required to validate the correctness of LEF (Library Exchange Format) views, liberty and Verilog models. The digital library contains two kind of information in LEF format: technology information that defines DRC rules and process parameters and layout information (macro LEF) that defines geometry of standard cells at the metallization level. The Liberty model includes information for timing, static leakage and dynamic power values for each standard cell. The Cadence Innovus Implementation System was used for a simplified digital backend flow. In addition, the verification flow includes a design import step for checking the syntax quality of library models. An imported design was specially developed to ease the flow automation and to detect potential library bugs during the digital design steps such as floorplan creation, placement, routing and timing optimization of the design. Even if the syntax of library models is correct, the model parameters might be implemented with mistakes. Therefore, the verification core engine also checks the content quality of digital libraries.

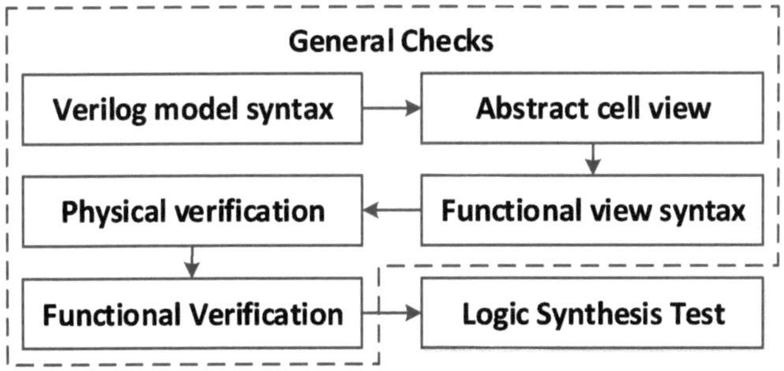

Fig. 5. DDK verification checks.

3.3 Regression Tests

Regression testing is a verification technique that involves continuously re-testing the PDK throughout modification and implementation to ensure that new fixes and enhancements do not destroy the PDK consistency. In case the end user reports a new error which is not covered either by the PDK verification flow or by any of regression tests, a new test must be developed and added to the regression suite. In the developed PDK QA platform, regression tests cover digital, mixed-signal and customer designs.

These tests address a variety of bugs found by end users in different parts of the PDK/DDK, e.g. during digital and analog simulations, physical verification, parasitic extraction, postlayout simulation, characterization and logic synthesis. The regression suite can always be extended by adding new test cases when a new error is found. This prevents further occurrences of the problem future releases. In addition, some reference designs that are sensitive to PDK and DDK changes are also included in the regression suite to guarantee their stability for every release.

For the validation of the digital library in the considered SiGe BiCMOS technologies, a special IC was developed and fabricated. The IC uses the delay chain principle described in [6] to perform timing validation of the digital library cells. Figure 6 shows a simplified block diagram of the digital library validation IC. The demultiplexer distributes the input signal to chains consisting of the same type cells (e.g. flip-flops, inverters, NAND-gates etc.) connected in series. The input and the output of each chain is applied to an XOR element which shows the difference between a reference signal and a signal, passed through the chain of cells. The timing information can be obtained by calculating the duration of the XOR's output signal. The outputs of all XOR gates are combined by a multiplexer to the output of the IC. The design data of the digital library validation IC were used as a reference design in the regression tests for the PDK and DDK verification.

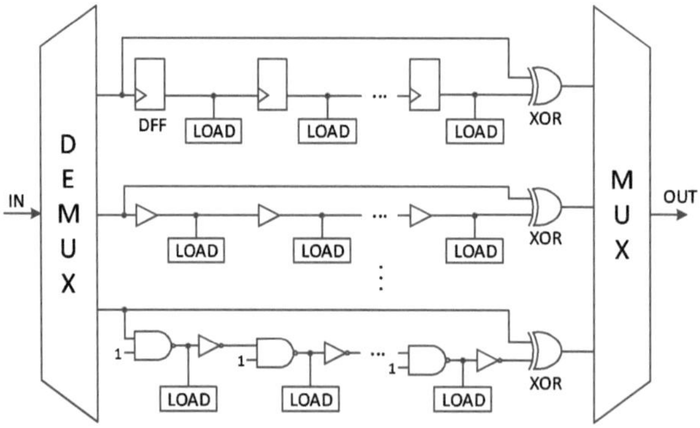

Fig. 6. Block diagram of the digital library validation IC.

For another combined real-world PDK and DDK verification test, a mixed-signal silicon proven IC would be a proper choice. As a reference design for this purpose, a fractional-N frequency synthesizer was used [7]. Figure 7 depicts the architecture of the fractional-N frequency synthesizer. It suits very well for such

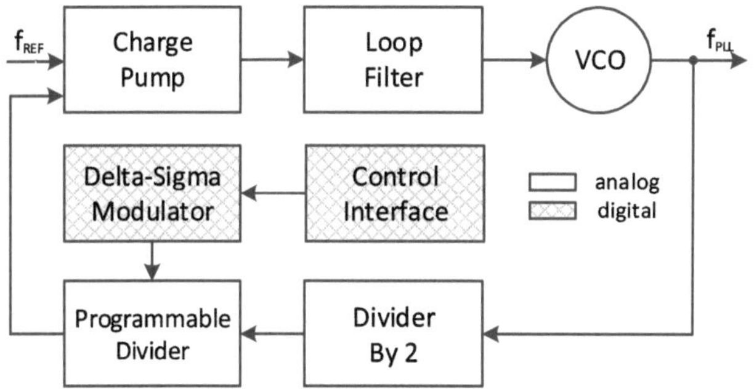

Fig. 7. Fractional-N frequency synthesizer used for the mixed-signal regression test.

a verification case, since it contains a variety of the basic PDK and DDK components representing high frequency and analog blocks such as voltage-controlled oscillator, high frequency dividers, charge pump; as well as digital circuits: delta-sigma modulator, digital control interface.

4 Application Case II: Interoperable PDK QA

Development of mm-wave ICs in the semiconductor technologies considered in this work requires utilization of Keysight ADS. It has to have a dedicated PDK format which implies that the ADS PDK has to be developed afresh. A basic PDK consists of a large amount of data, which includes model cards for circuit simulations, schematic symbols, cells' library, physical verification and parasitic extraction rule decks. To reduce the effort for developing all these components from the beginning, we used the interoperable PDK (iPDK) functionality implemented in Keysight ADS. It enables working with a shared OpenAccess database, component description files, data display files and technology layers that are the parts of the Cadence Virtuoso PDK [9]. In addition, iPDK supports PCell callbacks developed in LISP language for parameter calculations. Almost all of these data can be reused directly from the reference Cadence Virtuoso PDK which would already be verified by the PDK QA platform. However, layout PCells that implement geometry drawing can be reused only upon incorporating suitable modifications, as the scripting languages for both EDA tools are different. Therefore, a sk2ael program was developed to perform conversion between PCells written in Cadence SKILL to the ones in Keysight AEL. Despite the fact that most of the PDK data can be reused from the reference Cadence Virtuoso PDK, verification tests are still required to ensure correct functionality of the iPDK in ADS environment. For this purpose, the verification engine on the CI/CD server was extended to support the ADS iPDK verification and we obtain a fully automated PDK QA platform, which is capable of delivering highly robust ADS iPDKs for the considered technology nodes. A released Cadence Virtuoso PDK was used as a reference and the verification engine performs custom developed ADS interoperability tests as shown in Fig. 8. The verification flow of the ADS iPDK consists of the following steps.

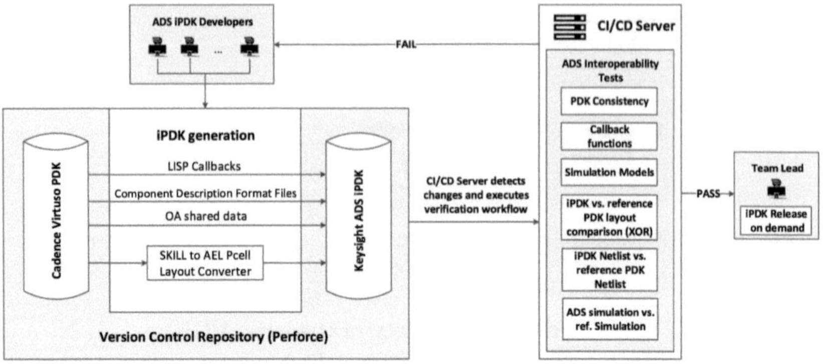

Fig. 8. PDK QA platform application to verify a Keysight ADS interoperable PDK.

4.1 PDK Consistency

This check ensures that the iPDK files are consistent with the reference PDK. During the verification process the data are checked to meet requirements of the company naming and data convention. This step verifies material parameters, corresponding layers and their thicknesses in stack-up files for electro-magnetic and thermal simulations. The check is implemented in C++ language to reduce verification run-time.

4.2 Callback Functions

Verification of the callback functions is realized in AEL language. At this step, the iPDK PCells are instantiated in both schematic and layout views to verify the correctness of PCell evaluation. A variation check of the device can be enabled on demand to verify all possible parameter combinations. This check is time consuming and is switched on only for the final PDK verification.

4.3 Simulation Models

The ADS iPDK reuses exactly the same device model cards of the reference PDK. The device models are described in the Cadence Spectre format. The check verifies that these models are parsed correctly by Keysight ADS simulator.

4.4 ADS iPDK vs. Reference PDK Layout Comparison (XOR)

The test ensures that the layers are correctly imported from OpenAcess data base into GDSII file and vice versa. The test also ensures that the PCells have the same layers and geometry for both PDKs: the reference and the ADS iPDK. The same PCells' layouts are instantiated in Cadence Virtuoso environment and in the Keysight ADS. The XOR operation performed on both layouts shows either they are identical or not. The check is applied for both GDSII and OpenAccess layout formats. The test utilizes two independent physical verification tools namely Cadence Assura and Mentor Calibre.

4.5 iPDK Netlist vs. Reference Netlist Comparison

A custom verification netlist-versus-netlist program was developed to check whether the ADS simulation netlist matches the reference one. The program verifies that the instances have the same number of terminals, model names and parameter values.

4.6 ADS Simulation vs. Reference Simulation

A variety of circuit test cases in netlist format are used to ensure that the simulation results between Spectre and ADS simulators are the same within allowed tolerance. The tolerance can be specified globally or for an individual signal. The global tolerance values apply to all signals in a simulation run.

5 Debugging Methodology

The verification process for PDKs, iPDKs, and DDKs involves many of steps, which require an effective tool for the prompt identification and classification of PDK bugs. A results viewer application was developed to accumulate QA test data within a singular, coherent, and user-centric interface. The results viewer application shown in Fig. 9 presents a graphical user interface (GUI) for the examination and verification of IHP PDKs. The interface is divided into distinct panels for efficient navigation and review. On the left-hand side, one can observe a panel listing various technologies, denoting different semiconductor fabrication processes under verification. The panel on the right-side serves as a comprehensive report area detailing the verification steps: ranging from the main report logs to release, build, and the QA log. The QA log is a dedicated section within the interface designed to display various verification report files, which users can access from the main report log window.

The results viewer application's interface allows an immediate identification of pass/fail conditions across various PDK technologies. It allows user to have a convenient view insight of the QA log data for technologies under verification. The application automatically documents failures reported by QA engine and creates a tracking report that is useful for reference and compliance purposes.

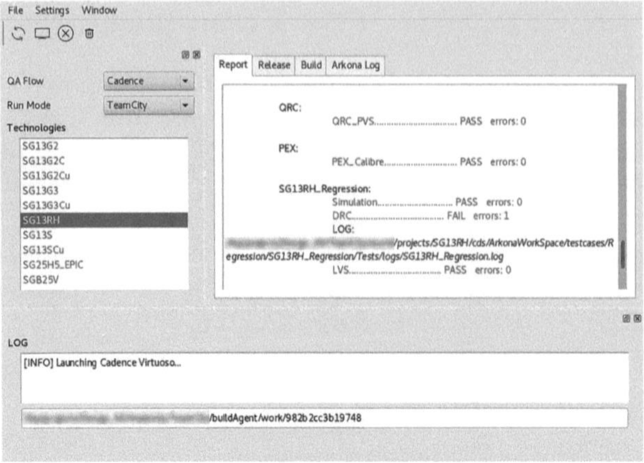

Fig. 9. Results viewer user interface for examination and verification of the QA flow output.

Additionally, the log area at the bottom of the interface reflects error messages indicating the failure to locate certain QA report and compilation files, suggesting either a misconfiguration or absence of the files in the specified directories.

The results viewer application incorporates an integration feature with the CI/CD engine, providing PDK developers the functionality to restart verification flow on-demand and to keep them informed through a real-time feedback loop on build status and progress. For initiation of the CI/CD quality assurance flow, the REST API was utilized alongside command-line utilities like curl [8] to trigger the run process effectively. This extended functionality can be pivotal in automating complex workflows, such as automatically reverting changes in the version control system for a specific user when QA verification run detects a bug in PDK. Such automation not only heightens efficiency of communication with CI/CD server but also reinforces consistency and quality in the development process. The results viewer application is equipped with robust security features, including user access control mechanisms, which are designed to guarantee that build initiation, log access, and configuration modifications are exclusively performed by authorized PDK engineers. This aspect is rather critical for technologies with restricted access, such as those designed for radiation-hardened applications, where stringent control over operational permissions is required. The viewer is engineered to support scalability, adeptly maintaining its effectiveness and responsiveness across a big range of PDK technologies and various technology options, even as the scale of verification processes expands.

Each build on the CI/CD Server uses a hash directory name, ensuring distinct identification for every verification run. This approach is critical in environments where multiple technologies are being verified simultaneously or where verification needs to be tracked over time [10]. When verifying multiple technologies, it becomes challenging to distinguish the correct directory name associated with the run. The results viewer application assists in navigating to the work directory related to the QA run. This functionality is beneficial for PDK developers, allowing them to compare the data populated by the CI/CD engine with the version control database. This approach also enables developers to manually reproduce build, compile, and release steps, which is essential for replicating and troubleshooting errors. Additionally, the results viewer application serves as a tool in the QA postprocess to allow developers to not only invoke EDA software linked to a QA run but also to load the requisite tools specified for a specific technology process. This capability is important for the rapid reproduction of PDK bugs that may arise during the CI/CD verification flow.

The results viewer application is also designed to enable has an option to the execution of the verification routines using local datasets, which is essential required to for ensuring the accuracy and integrity of data prior to its commitment to a version control system. Upon request, the results viewer application is capable of performing a complete verification flow utilizing local PDK data. This is particularly important when modifications are technology-specific. The engine is able to identify the changes and can to initiate only the required checks only. For instance, in case of modifications related solely to a DRC rule deck, the platform intelligently omits unnecessary verification steps such as simulation or parametric cell checks, thus effectively speeding-up the preverification process.

Furthermore, the viewer commits the local report file to the version control system. This step helps tracing the contributions of individual PDK developers. It becomes crucial when the changes are submitted concurrently by multiple users, ensuring a clear attribution of responsibility for any run failures encountered.

Figure 10 illustrates a run test application that has been developed to assist developers in selecting, configuring, and monitoring verification tests via a unified GUI. This interface is programmed for seamless integration with industry-standard EDA tools, including Cadence Virtuoso and Keysight ADS. Furthermore, the platform enables users to accurately reproduce errors identified in the

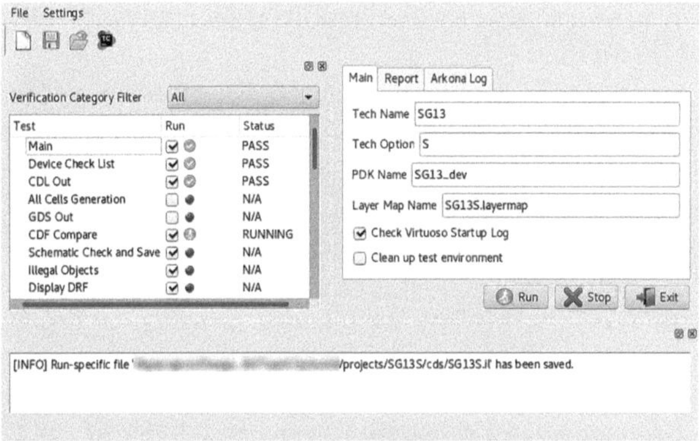

Fig. 10. Run Tests Application GUI for configuring and run the verification tests.

CI/CD verification flow and facilitates the loading of specific run-control data used in CI/CD for PDK verification. This run-control data consists of verification steps and the input parameters required for quality assurance checks. When executed from the results viewer application, the interface is automatically loaded within the requisite EDA environment.

6 QA Flow Performance Metrics

A bug tracking system was used to monitor all kind of PDK issues reported by customers. Submitted bugs are divided into different categories such as PDK bugs, enhancements, documentation and configuration issues, which helps to prioritise bug fixes and assign them to PDK developers. For the QA flow performance demonstration, we consider only confirmed PDK bugs reported by users, while issues related to documentation, PDK reconfiguration and enhancements were excluded from the analysis.

To gain insight into the progression of PDK bugs over a certain time period, which spans from one tape-out to the next has been analyzed. A typical time frame between tape-outs at IHP is six months. This analysis affects various technology processes, specifically selecting those that are fully qualified. Technologies under development were excluded from the overview, as bugs reported in these cases mostly belong to the technology process itself, rather than the quality of the PDKs. For example, model cards require continuous tuning during the technology qualification process, resulting in a higher number of reported PDK bugs.

For the development of the Keysight ADS PDK, interoperable functionalities were employed to share most of the data from the Cadence Virtuoso PDK. This approach resulted in resolving of numerous bugs during the development phase of the Cadence PDK. The remaining bugs in the Keysight ADS PDK were primarily associated with enhancing the interoperability between Virtuoso and ADS. The target was to achieve consistent results across circuit simulation, parametric cell, and layout processes. For the purpose of effective tracking and addressing these issues, all 0.13 µm technologies were combined to aggregate all reported bugs related to the ADS PDK.

For each reported bug, a specific test case was developed and integrated into the regression suite. The approach allows to avoid replication of the same problem in future releases. Additionally, if a bug is related to the performance of the PDK, a specialized performance regression test was included. This step is important to ensure that there is no degradation in processing time in next PDK versions. Furthermore, each test case undergoes a code coverage verification step to eliminate redundancy in the regression suite, ensuring that each test is unique and necessary.

The data, depicted in a Fig. 11, shows a general trend of declining bugs, indicating improvements in PDK quality over time. Most of the 0.13 µm PDKs demonstrate a reduction in bugs already after the second tape-out, suggesting effective bug resolution QA flow.

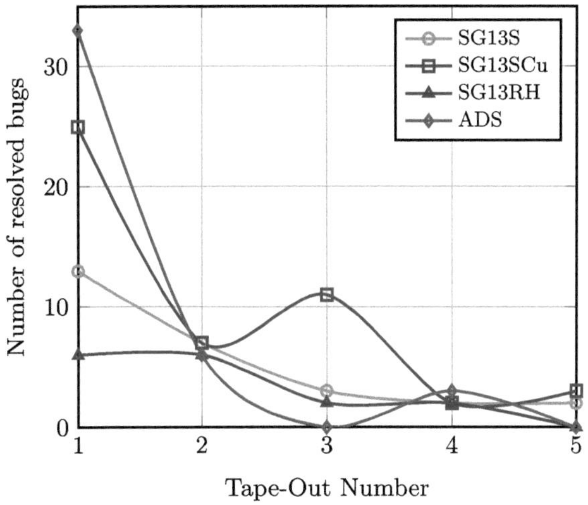

Fig. 11. Number of detected and resolved bugs related to a certain tape-out.

Figure 12 illustrates the QA flow run-time for different PDKs. The run-time is greatly affected by the size of the PDK, with larger PDKs necessitating more time to synchronize changes with version control systems prior to verification. Other contributing factors include the number of parametric cells requiring verification and extension of regression tests. The BiCMOS 0.25 µm technology, which has been supported by IHP for over twenty years, accumulated a significant number of regression test cases, that results in the longer run-time compared to the recent 0.13 µm technologies. Figure 12 shows that the SG25H5-EPIC process has the longest run-time of 45 min, indicating its comprehensive testing flow. On the other hand, the QA flow on the SG13S PDK presents a run-time of

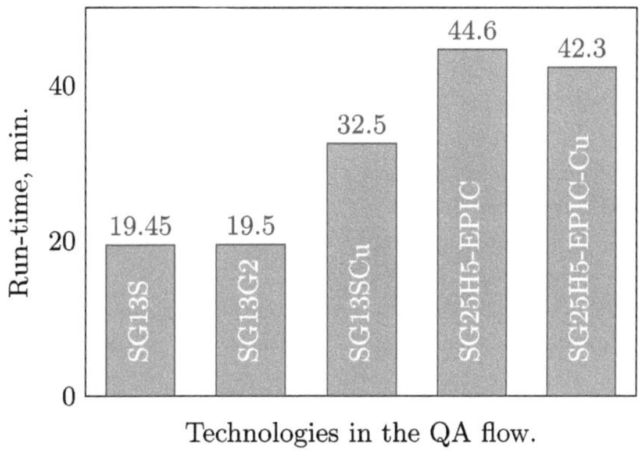

Fig. 12. QA flow run-time comparison for different technologies.

25 min, reflecting its more recent development and consequently fewer regression tests and verification data.

7 Conclusion

The presented PDK QA platform is based on continuous integration and continuous deployment techniques that ensure the PDK database remains free of errors, thereby reducing the effort required for the final verification process. This methodology was successfully applied to the commercially available 0.13 µm and 0.25 µm SiGe BiCMOS technologies and submodules to perform releases of reliable PDKs and DDK libraries. Additionally, the CI/CD approach was extended for the verification of ADS interoperable PDKs. The proposed debugging methodology offers significant benefits in terms of rapid bug detection and resolution within the PDK development cycle. This efficiency is further enhanced by the ability to reproduce errors within the CI/CD verification flow, allowing for a more immediate and accurate troubleshooting process. The integration of the graphical platform with standard EDA tools facilitates the debugging process, enabling developers to visualize and understand complex issues in a more intuitive manner. The platform demonstrates scalability and adaptability to a variety of technology nodes and manufacturing processes, demonstrating its versatility and applicability across different foundry environments. This flexibility ensures that the flow is not restricted to a specific technology node and can be utilized by other manufacturing foundries to keep their PDKs constantly in a healthy state and ready for deployment at any moment.

References

1. Li, Y., Li, M., Wong, W.: A complete process design kit verification flow and platform for 28 nm technology and beyond. In: 2012 IEEE 11th Conference on Solid-State and Integrated Circuit Technology, pp. 1–4 (2012)
2. Datsuk, A., Ostrovskyy, P., Vater, F., Wieden, C.: Towards robust process design kits with a scalable devops quality assurance platform. In: 2023 IFIP/IEEE 31st International Conference on Very Large Scale Integration - System on a Chip, pp. 1–6 (2023)
3. Soni, M.: End to end automation on cloud with build pipeline: the case for devops in insurance industry, continuous integration, continuous testing, and continuous delivery. In: 2015 IEEE International Conference on Cloud Computing in Emerging Markets, pp. 85–89 (2015)
4. JetBrains. TeamCity. https://www.jetbrains.com/teamcity/
5. Martin, D.H., Cordy, J.R., Adams, B., Antoniol, G.: Make it simple - an empirical analysis of GNU make feature use in open source projects. In: 2015 IEEE 23rd International Conference on Program Comprehension, pp. 207–217 (2015)
6. De Carvalho, M., Altieri, M., Puricelli, L., Butzen, P., Ribas, R.P., Fabris, E.: On-silicon validation of a benchmark generation methodology for effectively evaluating combinational cell library design. In: 2016 IEEE 17th Latin-American Test Symposium, pp. 135–140 (2016)

7. Ergintav, A., Herzel, F., Fischer, G., Kissinger, D.: A study of phase noise and frequency error of a fractional-N PLL in the course of FMCW chirp generation. IEEE Trans. Circuits Syst. I Regul. Pap. **66**(5), 1670–1680 (2019)
8. Hostetter, M., Kranz, D.A., Seed, C., Terman, C., Ward, S.: Curl: a gentle slope language for the web. World Wide Web J. **2**(2), 121–134 (1997)
9. Silicon RFIC interoperability w/Virtuoso element. https://www.keysight.com/de/de/product/W2319EP/silicon-rfic-interoperability-virtuoso-element.html
10. JetBrains. Custom checkout directory. https://www.jetbrains.com/help/teamcity/build-checkout-directory.html

FPGA-Implementation Techniques to Efficiently Test Application Readiness of Mixed-Signal Products

Gabriel Rutsch, Konrad Maier(✉), and Wolfgang Ecker(✉)

Infineon Technologies AG, Neubiberg, Germany
{gabriel.rutsch,konrad.maier,wolfgang.ecker}@infineon.com

Abstract. We present FPGA-implementation techniques to efficiently validate application readiness of a product for analog/mixed-signal (AMS) applications that lead to a reduction of overall runtime by two orders of magnitude on the example of a power conversion application compared to state-of-the-art simulation based approaches. Further, we use this example to analyze area utilization, timing impact and scalability at increased application complexity. The open source synthesizable model generator for mixed-signal blocks **msdsl** is extended to support reconfigurable variables within a model description. Further, the control API of the open source FPGA prototyping automation **anasymod** is enhanced to allow updating these variable values on FPGA at runtime. The end-result is a unique framework for application scenario driven product validation that to our knowledge for the first time allows reconfiguration of analog dynamics on FPGA at runtime and leverages benchmark AMS system simulation throughput on FPGA to enables fast system property sweeping at different modeling abstractions.

1 Introduction

Applications in the automotive, industrial and consumer sector rapidly become more heterogeneous, connected and therefore more complex as the wish to continuously improve products drives the need to collect and process more and more information from the environment and neighboring applications [1,2]. One of the instruments to assure fast time-to-market at this increased level of product complexity is to early on validate a product in context of its application before committing to a hardware tapeout. A common approach to test for this application readiness is to simulate application scenarios with different system properties including PVT variations of the chip, the application circuit, sensors or actuators, and environment conditions, e.g. driver weight or ground moisture.

FPGA-based AMS simulation has shown outstanding simulation throughput for a variety of different AMS applications [3–6] and could be well suited for these kinds of simulations. Even more important though is total validation runtime including: model generation, bitstream re-/generation and programming, test execution and result data extraction and editing. Current strategies

Published by Springer Nature Switzerland AG 2024
I. (Abe) M. Elfadel and L. Albasha (Eds.): VLSI-SoC 2023, IFIP AICT 680, pp. 197–216, 2024.
https://doi.org/10.1007/978-3-031-70947-0_10

to map analog behavior on FPGA focus on minimizing hardware resource utilization through pre-computation of analog dynamics [5,7,18–20]. Consequently, every model behavior adjustment results in a change of the FPGA design and requires time consuming bitstream regeneration. This significantly increases total validation runtime. To circumvent bitstream regeneration, we present FPGA-implementation techniques to recompute and update analog dynamics at runtime. Varying system properties are described as dependent variables (DVs) or independent variables (IVs) within an analog model that can be used in conjunction with almost all modeling features of **msdsl** [8], including assignments, functions, a system-of-equations (SoE) and netlists [7]. On FPGA, these variables are either represented as writable registers or lookup tables for which values can be recomputed and updated using **anasymod** [9] instrumentation.

After an overview on related work, we present developed model of computation (MoC), domain specific language (DSL) and generator and control API extensions. Further, we discuss usage, benefits and limitations using a power application.

2 Related Work

Several AMS system analysis techniques are in use today and can be grouped into the following categories: reachability analysis, theorem proving and simulation based methods. The former two are not a good fit to study application readiness of a product as theorem proving lacks the required feature of time domain analysis and reachability analysis may suffer from state space explosion or even undecidability [10]. This leaves simulation-based methods, despite potentially very long runtimes, as the best choice. To reduce total runtime, two main research directions are pursued: boost AMS system simulation throughput, which is where FPGA-based methods excel [3–6], and reduce the total number of simulation runs while maintaining similar coverage. For the latter numerical approaches, such as Monte Carlo or DoE, linearization or ranged-based techniques are used [10,11]. Most of these techniques can be applied to simulation environments, such as **anasymod** and **msdsl**, that support a description of analog behavior by sets of differential equations, e.g. a SPICE netlist and a time aware MoC [10,12]. In this case both research directions complement each other.

Further, AMS system analysis can be conducted using and FPGA in conjuction with an field-programmable analog array (FPAA) [22]. An FPAA works similar to an FPGA as a bitstream is used to route and configure analog blocks and modules to emulate the desired analog behavior. While yielding very high execution throughput, FPAAs are no general purpose solution, as they are tuned for specific voltage and power conditions of a targeted application and primarily used for computing and signal processing applications only [21].

Using an FPGA may be the best choice for analyzing AMS systems as it yields benchmark simulation throughput and the usage is not limited to a subset of applications. However, there is major drawback as FPGA based AMS simulation approaches rely on computing analog behavior at compile time and time consuming bitstream regeneration is needed for every changing system property that affects analog behavior. In previous work this drawback was partially addressed by custom reconfiguration solutions, such as a model of a sinewave generator with reconfigurable amplitude, phase and frequency [13], a stimulus generator unit with a reconfigurable PWL function [14] or a reconfigurable set of test vectors as part of a test bench to stimulate a device under test (DUT) [3]. These solutions can only be used for DUT stimulation and not for analog dynamics such as filter, switching or amplifier characteristics. The growing need for a holistic approach to efficiently analyze AMS applications under varying system properties encouraged us to develop comprehensive techniques that for the first time also cover analog dynamics, which is subject of this paper.

3 Reconfigurable Model Variables

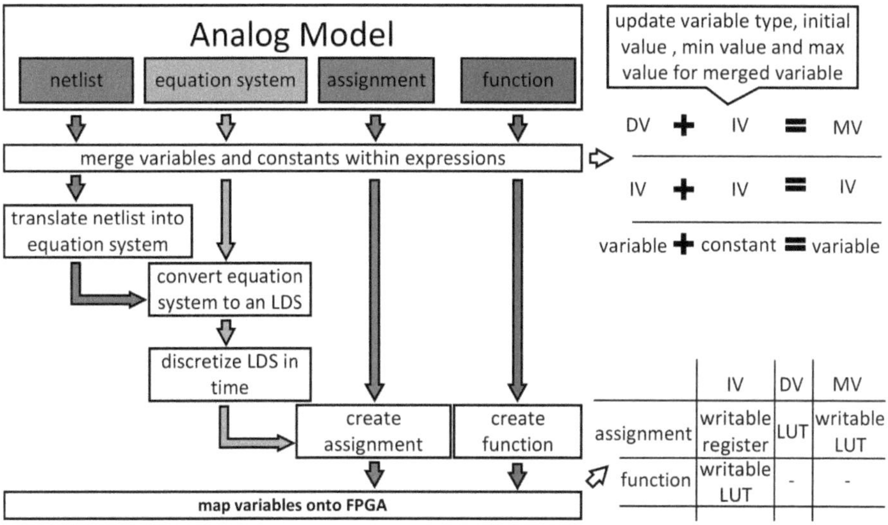

Fig. 1. Re-programmable **variables** are used for reconfiguration. These variables are merged, categorized into DVs, IVs and MVs, and mapped onto FPGA fabric.

For application scenario simulation on FPGA with varying system properties most time is spent during bitstream regeneration. Partial synthesis and reconfiguration are both well suited to circumvent this step. We opted for the latter and introduced a new variable type: reconfigureable variables. This makes FPGA resource allocation for analog behavior independent of optimization steps during bitstream generation and therefore easier. Like other numerical quantities, these variables can be used in conjunction with most **msdsl** description features, including assignments, functions, SoEs or netlists. Especially when diverging from the well established principle of pre-computing analog dynamics offline [7], it is important to assure that FPGA resource utilization and timing impact are kept in check. To optimize mapping strategies accordingly, we introduced two sub-types of variables: **dependent variables** that depend on a control signal and **independent variables**. Each sub-type is designed to represent different kinds of system properties as detailed in subsections below. To cover the case, where both an IV and a DV are used in one expression, a third mixed variable (MV) sub-type is used, that does require its own mapping strategy. An overview on how variables are mapped onto FPGA fabric is given in Fig. 1.

First, to assure variables can be freely combined with one another within expressions a variable merge step is needed, according to the pattern shown at the top right of Fig. 1, when parsing a model description. For every variable merge a new variable is created and init, min and max values are computed. Second, to support several model abstractions, translation steps that we highlight on the example of a RC low-pass filter as in [7] are needed. The underlying principles can also be applied to more complex systems with multiple variables, as shown later in the results section. The dynamics of the RC filter are described as:

$$C \cdot \frac{dy}{dt} = \frac{x - y}{R} \tag{1}$$

where input voltage is x, output voltage is y, capacitance is C and resistance is R. Assuming x is constant over an interval $[t, t + \Delta t]$ the solution is given by:

$$y(t + \Delta t) = \alpha \cdot y(t) + (1 - \alpha) \cdot x(t) \tag{2}$$

where $\alpha = e^{-\Delta t/(RC)}$.

While Eq. 2 can directly be used as **msdsl** assignment expression, the same behavior may also be described via a SoE or a netlist, which are the preferred formats for non-trivial circuits, see Listing 1.

```
# create a dependent variable
func = lambda v: 1e-9 + v * 0.8e-9 + v**2 * 0.2e-9
C = m.add_variable(name='c', min_ctrl=0, max_ctrl=10,
  ctrl_signal=y, expr=func)
# create an independent variable
R = m.add_variable(name='r', init_val=1e3,
  min_val=100, max_val=1e3)
R, C, dt = 950, 1e-9, 50e-9
# a) define dynamics via assignment
set_next_cycle(
    y, y * exp(-dt / (R * C)) +
     (x*(1 - exp(-dt / (R * C)))
)
# b) define dynamics as system of equations
add_eqn_sys([Deriv(y) == (x - y)/(R*C)])
# c) define dynamics via netlist
capacitor('net_y', gnd, C, voltage_range=RangeOf(y))
resistor('net_x', 'net_y', R)
voltage('net_x', gnd, x)
```

Code Listing 1. Different RC filter descriptions using **msdsl**. The same descriptions can be used for static (yellow) or variable (orange) values.

The former is a very compact representation and the latter is a well established format within the analog circuit design community. In both cases no additional effort is required to map these representations onto FPGA, as the translation to the assignment representation is automated using **msdsl**. In doing so, **msdsl** converts the description to the standard form of a linear dynamic system (LDS):

$$\dot{x} = Ax + Bu \tag{3}$$

$$y = Cx + Du \tag{4}$$

where x is a vector of state variables, u are the system inputs, and y is a vector of outputs. As in the case of Eq. 2, the system is discretized in time assuming inputs are constant during the interval $[t, t + \Delta t]$. The states update solution is:

$$x(t + \Delta t) = \tilde{A} \cdot x(t) + \tilde{B} \cdot u(t) \tag{5}$$

where, if A is invertible:

$$\tilde{A} = e^{\Delta t \cdot A} \tag{6}$$

$$\tilde{B} = A^{-1} \cdot (\tilde{A} - I) \cdot B \tag{7}$$

The discretized solution is used to generate the assignment [7].

Let's assume the value of the capacitance in Eq. 1 needs change. In that case, we need to know which model coefficients, in our case α $(= 0.9)$ and $1 - \alpha$ $(= 0.1)$, need to be updated, in order to reflect this change in behavior. Consequently, variable impact must be traceable throughout the model generation process outlined above. All three descriptions lead to the same solution and RTL code as shown for $\alpha = 0.9$ in Listing 2 (a).

```
module RC #(
   `DECL_REAL(x),
   `DECL_REAL(y)
) (
   ‘INPUT_REAL(var_ctrld_coeff_0),
   ‘INPUT_REAL(var_ctrld_coeff_1),
   `INPUT_REAL(x),
   `OUTPUT_REAL(y)
);
   ‘MAKE_REAL(tmp_c_2, ‘RANGE_PARAM_REAL(y));
   ‘MUL_REAL(tmp_c_2, var_ctrld_coeff_0, tmp0);
   ‘MUL_REAL(x, var_ctrld_coeff_1, tmp1);
   ‘MUL_CONST_REAL(0.9, y, tmp0);
   ‘MUL_CONST_REAL(0.1, x, tmp1);
   `ADD_REAL_GENERIC(tmp0, tmp1, tmp2, 33);
   ‘DFF_INTO_REAL(tmp2, y, ‘RST, ‘CLK, 1’b1, 0);
   ‘DFF_INTO_REAL(tmp2, tmp_c_2, ‘RST, ‘CLK, 1’b1, 0);
   ‘ASSIGN_REAL(tmp_c_2, y);
endmodule
```

Code Listing 2. RTL code of an RC filter generated by **msdsl** for a static version shown in yellow and a reconfigurable version shown in orange (b)

3.1 Independent Variables

IVs are well suited to represent static system properties, e.g. a capacitance, a IO delay or OpAmp gain as their value does not change during a simulation, but it may change between simulation runs. In consequence, re-computation of analog dynamics can be conducted offline, which does not affect simulation throughput. When used in an assignment, a SoE or a netlist, an IV influences coefficient values of the generated model. In conjunction with a function, however, it affects all values of the lookup tables used to map the function on FPGA as described in [7]. Thus, whenever the IV changes, coefficient or lookup table values are recomputed offline and updated on the FPGA using instrumentation of **anasymod**. While the update functionality for a coefficient is implemented by instantiating a writable register on FPGA, lookup tables require an additional serializer unit with a serial communication interface to the host PC as detailed later.

3.2 Dependent Variables

In contrast to an IV, a DV does change its value during simulation. Its value is controlled by a changing quantity that must be defined as a signal, such as the input voltage to an application circuit or the simulated time step. Hence, DVs can be used, for instance, to make a model variable timestep aware or to model an oscillator with a voltage dependent frequency. Similar to IVs being used within a function, model coefficients affected by DVs are represented on FPGA using writable lookup tables. These lookup table values are computed initially during model generation and whenever the behavior of an influencing variable changes. For the filter example, values of C for all possible values of V_{in} at a given precision are stored in a lookup table for α and another lookup table for $1 - \alpha$. Assuming that a DV has an impact on a large amount of behavior within a model, such as a non-linear inductance of a transformer with several secondary windings, FPGA resource utilization may increase significantly as the number of affected coefficients and therefore lookup tables rapidly increases. This is due to the complexity of the behavior to be represented in general and not due to enabling reconfiguration. The only additional overhead for the latter is the sequencer and additional routing. Further, using DVs makes modeling nonlinear dynamic behavior a lot easier in general, besides enabling reconfigurability. Taking the previous RC filter with a non-linear capacitance described as: $C = 0.2e - 9 \cdot V_{in}^2 + 0.8e - 9 \cdot V_{in} + 1e - 9$ as an example, $\alpha = e^{-\Delta t/(RC)}$ would need to be computed by hand and expressions mapped onto LUTs using **msdsl** functions. Our extensions automate this process.

4 Framework Modifications

The leveraged framework translates analog values that are represented as floating-point data types within model descriptions into a synthesizable format. In doing so, these floating-point data types are translated to fixed-point data types and mapped onto a bitarray. In order to assure that all possible analog signal values can be properly represented via this bitarray, additional information, such as the maximum value range, is needed. Compared to most CPU based simulation environments, analog dynamics are not computed at runtime, but already during model compilation. Pre-computed coefficients that represent analog dynamics are stored as constant fixed-point values, which makes value range computation trivial. Changing system properties however may lead to a change of analog dynamics and therefore these coefficient values. To assure system property reconfigurability, coefficient values cannot be treated as constants any longer and coefficient value ranges need to be computed based on the specified ranges of related reconfigurable system properties. In consequence, it must be possible to holistically trace analog signal value propagation throughout model generation. This is especially challenging while working with SoE or netlist based descriptions of analog behavior. Netlist descriptions make use of primitive blocks, such as resistors, inductors and capacitors. Using domain specific laws, namely KVL and KCL for electrical systems, the corresponding SoE can be derived. A SoE, either derived from a netlist or provided within the model description, is translated into a set of assignments. This process includes non-trivial steps, such as solving the SoE and a discretization in time of this solution, which further complicates tracing ranges of coefficient that describe analog dynamics. In the remainder of this section, we outline extensions to address this issue and provide an easy to use modeling frontend using the previous filter as an example.

4.1 Model Computation Adaptations

Figure 2 shows the main computational steps for model generation. First, the netlist or SoE description of an analog model is converted to an LDS representation. As the LDS describes a continuous time system, it must be discretized in time next to allow pre-computation of dynamics. Further, to implement computed analog dynamics a fixed-point format, ranges of corresponding coefficients must be calculated at compile time as well. In doing so, we first solve the SoE symbolically. Next, we substitute range interval of affecting reconfigurable variables into this symbolic solution to compute these coefficient ranges. In addition, we use this symbolic solution to calculate initial coefficient values and store these values within the FPGA bitstream. Finally, the solutions are used to generate assignments. To show qualitatively how much time each of these steps takes, we have used an nth-order RC filter, where the number of states is equal to n, see Fig. 3b. The time needed for the each computational step is measured for different values of n. According to these measurements, shown in Fig. 3b, the total model generation time for higher numbers of n is mainly dominated by the matrix exponential calculation used to discretize the A matrix and described by Eq. 6. Accordingly, this step is mainly considered in the following, where we focus on computational efficiency improvements.

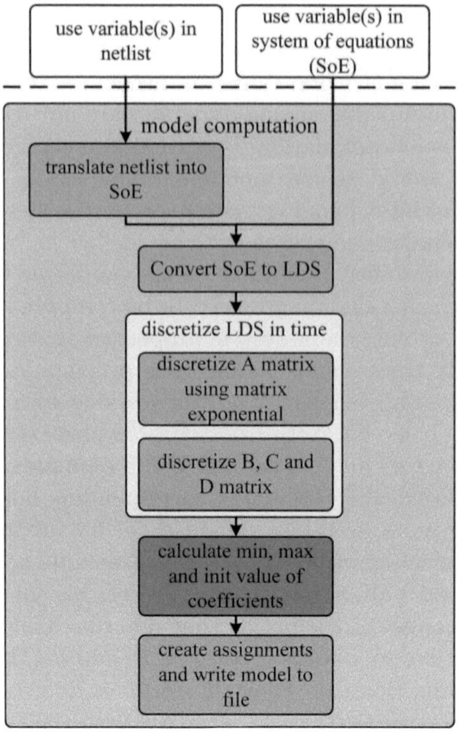

Fig. 2. Main computational steps for model generation. Compute times for each step are shown and colour-coded in Fig. 3a for a nth-order RC filter.

The first approach we employed to calculate the matrix exponential was based on the Jordan canonical form (JCF) [26], which is reliant on matrix decomposition. While it is in general considered to be one of the most computationally efficient methods [25], our main motivation to make use of it was a readily available and easy to use implementation within sympy version 1.9 [15]. Unfortunately, this implementation turned out to be very slow as it is a pure Python-based implementation and for symbolic computation eigenvalues had to be computed explicitly, which is necessary to represent a matrix in it's JCF and inefficient. Based on actual matrix element values, eigenvalue expressions already for a matrix of rank three can become very complex, as finding the roots of the determinant requires using Cardano's formula. To address this explosion in result matrix element expression complexity, we employed another approach to calculate the matrix exponential via Inverse LaPlace Transform (ILPT) and partial fraction expansion [25]. This allowed us to represent result matrix element expressions in a more compact way using a sympy class object called RootSum, which represents the sum of all roots of a univariate polynomial, instead of terms of radical or RootOf [27]. In conclusion, we could observe a reduction in matrix exponential computation time of two to three orders of magnitude using the ILPT instead of the JCF based implementation. This is mainly due to the reduction of result expression complexity and further analyzed further down in the result section.

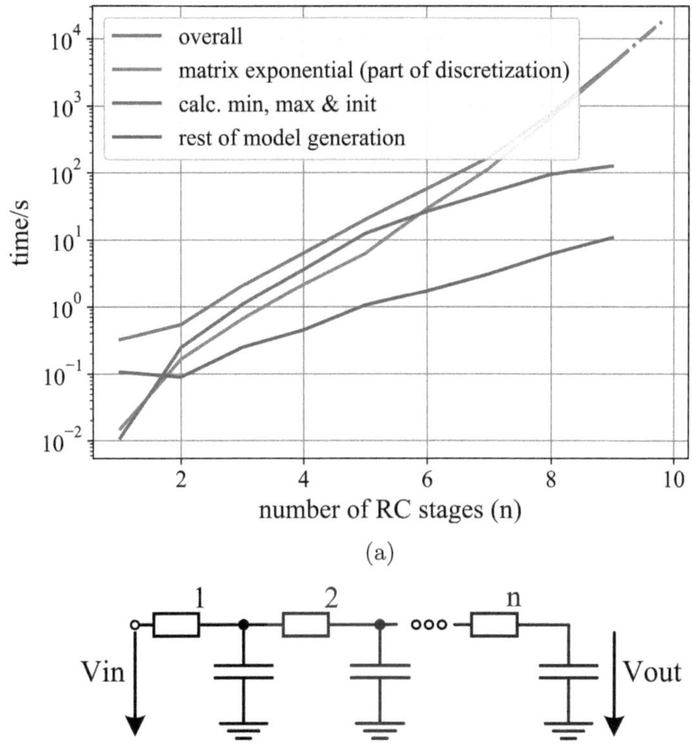

Fig. 3. (a) Breakdown of the time required to generate an n-th order RC filter shown in (b) using the ILPT method for matrix exponential

4.2 DSL Extensions

To make a numerical quantity of a **msdsl** model reconfigurable, it can be replaced by a *Variable* object. This works for all modeling features of **msdsl** except for transfer functions. Listing 1 (orange) shows how the *add_variable* function can be used to make the resistance and capacitance of the RC filter reconfigurable. A variable C that is dependent on the output voltage y according to a lambda function represents the capacitance and a variable R represents the resistance. For IVs, such as R, an initial value (*init_val*) is required for initial coefficient value computation. As behavior is expressed using fixed-point arithmetic, coefficient ranges must be calculated based on either the minimum and maximum value of an IV or the control signal's minimum and maximum value of a DV. Finally, accuracy of DVs can be adapted by changing the number of sample values and interpolation method when mapping the expression onto lookup tables.

4.3 Model Generator Extensions

We focused on two aspects while extending **msdsl** to assure ease-of-use. First, it should be easy to switch between reconfigurable and static models, i.e. model instances shall stay the same. Therefore, additional reconfiguration IOs are connected to **anasymod** instrumentation via out-of-module references and a wrapper is created to hide these IOs. The wrapper consists of a core module instantiation that includes the behavior of the **msdsl** model and an instantiation of a reconfiguration module to compute and update coefficients. Second, both model types shall be generated from the same model description to keep one code base. To maximize code reuse, a reconfigurable variable must be usable like any other numerical quantity supported in **msdsl**, which in turn requires traceability of a reconfigurable variable's impact throughout model generation. For most modeling features it is sufficient to create a new variable during a variable merge step and store how it was created as its root. Only when used in conjunction with modeling features that introduce abstraction, such as an equation system or a netlist where translation to an LDS and time discretization is needed, variables are replaced by sympy [15] symbols and arithmetic operations are conducted symbolically. Finally, coefficients in the resulting matrix that contain sympy symbols are converted back to variables, keeping previous variable traces intact. Besides the RTL code of the reconfigurable RC filter example, see Listing 2 (b),a reconfiguration file is created containing information to recompute register and lookup table values, generate **anasymod** instrumentation and connect it to model instances.

4.4 Control API Extensions

The **anasymod** control API was extended to enable recomputation and update of model coefficients. First, the **anasymod** config file parser now also queries for a *reconfig.yaml* file. This allows adding control signals for every instantiation of a reconfigurable model, as well as one shared serializer instance to update lookup table values if needed. These control signals are correctly connected with model instances using the hierarchical paths provided via the **anasymod** modelconfig file *modelcfg.yaml* for each instance. An overview of the resulting FPGA design architecture is shown in Fig. 4.

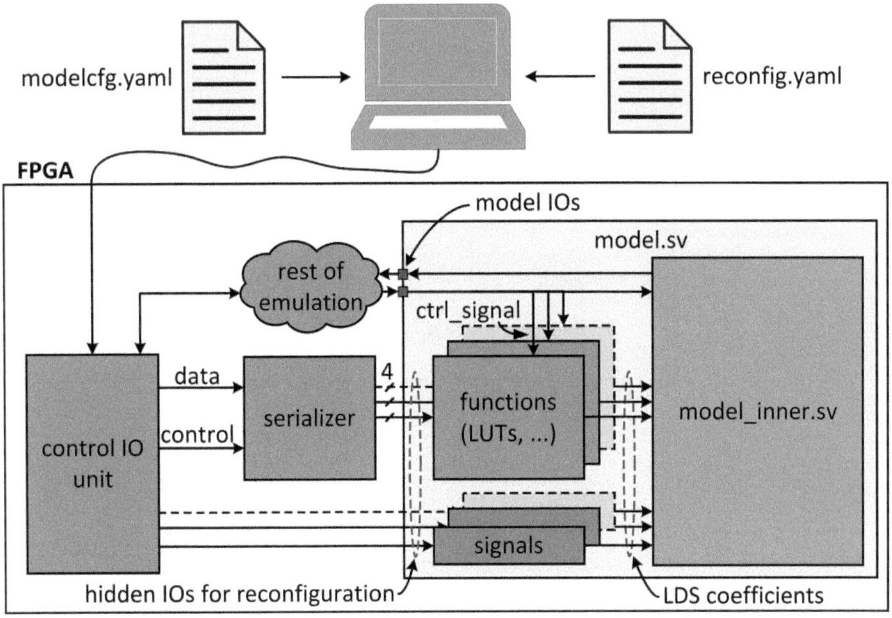

Fig. 4. Structure of an FPGA emulation using reconfigurable models

Further, we added a function called *re_configure()*, which takes the model type, derivative, instance name, name of the changing variable and the new value as input. Using information from the *reconfig.yaml* file, this function identifies and recomputes coefficients that are affected by the given variable, and updates corresponding registers and lookup tables on FPGA. Listing 3 shows how to set a new resistive value.

```
ctrl = ana.launch(debug=True) # launch FPGA simulation
ctrl.set_reset(1) # reset FPGA simulation
ctrl.re_configure(model='RC', derivative='RC1',
                  instance='rc1', r=500)
ctrl.set_reset(0) # start FPGA simulation
```

Code Listing 3. Reconfiguration of the Filter model in Listing 1

5 Results

We employed our framework extensions to analyze a power conversion application with a varying load. The chosen topology depicted in Fig. 5 is a buck converter used for DC-to-DC conversion. To analyze power conversion under different load conditions, we added variables for the load resistance and capacitance to the buck converter model that are reconfigured using the *re_configure* function. Alternatively, by adding variables for the snubber circuit, it would be possible to analyze related manufacturing deviations.

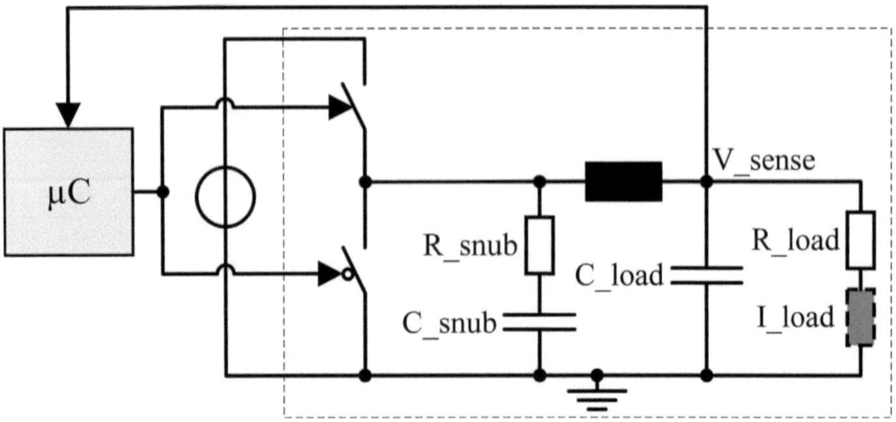

Fig. 5. Schematic of a buck converter topology

Three aspects were considered while evaluating the proposed approach: overall execution speed, impact on timing and FPGA resource utilization. All experiments were conducted on a windows 10 workstation with 32 GB RAM and an i7-12800H CPU with 14 physical cores using Vivado 2020.1.

5.1 Execution Speed

Execution speed of an experiment to assess a product's application readiness is dependent on several aspects, such as the efficiency of the computationally expensive steps during model creation, the amount, type and system impact of employed reconfigurable variables and overall system complexity. To better understand these dependencies, we consider these aspects separately in the following and conclude with a comparison of the proposed techniques with state-of-the-art methods on the example of a complete DC-DC power conversion application.

Comparison of Matrix Exponential Computation Implementations. As shown in the previous section, the increase in model generation time at increasing model complexity is mainly due to the symbolic computation of the matrix exponential. In practise, already at the complexity level of the three state buck converter circuit, we had to replace sympy's default *exp()* function with an approach to compute the matrix exponential using the inverse laplace transform and partial fraction expansion [17], as the matrix exponential could not be computed over night. To quantify why the default JCP method is significantly slower, we show the number of operations in the symbolic solution of the a_{11} coefficient of the discretized A matrix in Table 1 for a two-stage RC filter. In the case of the JCF method, the result expression is more than twice as long as in the case of the INFT method. It also contains six complex square root operations, whereas the INTF solution has only one rootsum and one lambda function operation. As more states are introduced into the model, this complexity difference explodes.

Not only are these expressions used to compute initial coefficient or LUT values, but also corresponding range information for fixed-point representation and updated values after a system property change. This is why the impact of expression complexity of model compilation time is significant and therefore the JCF method significantly slower compared to INFT.

Table 1. Expression complexity for matrix exponential computation approaches

	JCF	INFT
additions	9.50	3.50
substractions	3.50	2.75
multiplications	14.00	9.75
divisions	6.00	1.0
exponentiations	8.00	3.25
square roots	6.00	0.00
lambda functions	0.00	1.00
rootsum operators	0.00	1.00

Addition and Variation of Reconfigurable Variables. In addition to the matrix exponential computation method itself, the choice of reconfigurable variables also affects model creation time. To highlight this dependency, we conducted a set of experiments, where derivates of the buck converter model were compared with one another. We added an IV to make the resistive load of the first derivate reconfigurable, another IV to make the capacitive load of the second derivate reconfigurable and finally two IVs to the third derivate to make both resistive and capacitive load reconfigurable. Results are summarized in Table 2.

Table 2. Model computation time for different IV setups

	reconfig. R	reconfig. C	reconfig. R+C
total preparation time	450.21 s	463.43 s	464.09 s
translate to LDS	0.13 s	0.13	0.12 s
LDS discretization	3.82 s	5.10 s	5.27 s
calc. min, max, init vals	8.82 s	18.34 s	18.74 s
rest of model generation	0.08 s	0.11 s	0.12 s
bitstream generation	403.50 s	405.78 s	406.60 s
bitstream programming	33.86 s	33.97 s	34.24 s
total time per iteration	4.89 s	9.41 s	9.61 s
calc. of new coefficients	4.71 s	9.20 s	9.39 s
update coeffs on FPGA	0.18 s	0.21 s	0.22 s

To better highlight computational effort during model generation, we split this task into several steps: translation to an LDS, LDS discretization, calculation of min, max and init values for coefficients and remaining steps. Further, we listed the time needed to compute new coefficient values and update these on FPGA using the bitwise firmware-in-the-middle approach described in [16]. While most steps are nearly unaffected by the choice of IVs, we see a change for LDS discretization and coefficient min/max/init value calculation. To better understand where this dependency comes from, we took a closer look at the expressions of the elements of the discretized LDS matrices and, similar to the previous experiments, could again see a correlation between the complexity of these expressions and the increase in computate time for the aforementioned steps. To illustrate this correlation, we chose one element of a LDS matrix where the expression complexity between these model derivatives was larger and split the expression into individual operations, see Table 3. In conclusion we could observe a difference of up to 90 percent in total model compute and 97 percent in reconfiguration time between the best and worst configuration.

Table 3. Expression complexity for different IV setups

	reconfig. R	reconfig. C	reconfig. R+C
additions	12	29	31
substractions	11	20	16
multiplications	27	71	68
exponentiations	14	34	31
lambda functions	1	1	1
rootsum operators	1	1	1

Changing Accuracy for Dependent Variables. Including DVs in a model description does yield significantly higher model computation and host-to-FPGA communication effort compared to IVs. To better illustrate these implications another set of experiments, including three configurations with a nonlinear capacitive load modeled as a DV, was conducted and results are depicted in Table 4. The first two experiments differ in numel i.e. number of LUT elements and order of the polynomial approximation. It can be seen that computation times scale linearly with numel and order. The most time is spent during coefficient recomputation, which is mainly due to result expression complexity again. As an improvement, we performed another step during model creation, which we call simplify equations. As seen in the third configuration, simplify equations takes a long time, but does reduce coefficient recomputation time resulting in a shorter overall runtime already after eight iterations. Compared to the use of IVs, host-to-FPGA communication and especially model computation effort is still significantly higher, but does scale linear with the number of LUT elements and order. As LUT element computations are independent from one another though, further considerable improvements are possible via parallelization.

Table 4. Model generation time with DV approximations at varying accuracy

numel/order	512/0	64/1	64/1 simp. eqns.
translate to LDS	0.16 s	0.17 s	0.16 s
LDS discretization	5.40 s	5.31 s	5.49 s
calc. min, max, init vals	14.84 s	7.91 s	16.97 s
simplify eqns	–	–	1047.39 s
calc. zero order LUTs	1539.11 s	197.28 s	63.27 s
rest of model generation	32.42 s	25.93 s	53.96 s
total model gen. time	1591.92 s	236.60 s	1187.24 s
calc. of new coefficients	–	198.86 s	67.28 s
update coeffs on FPGA	–	4.26 s	3.25 s
time per simulation run	–	203.12 s	70.53 s

Increasing System Complexity. To better understand how reconfiguration techniques scales with respect to application circuit complexity, we prepared further experiments, shown in Table 5. The buck converter circuit was extended by an additional inductive load to add a fourth state with either reconfigurable resistive or capacitive load. As an example for a five state circuit with three active elements, the core partition of a flyback circuit described in [16] was taken. While the extended buck circuits already show a significant increase in model creation time, the flyback core partition circuit, where a matrix of rank five needs to be solved for 2^3 different system states, really shows where this approach starts to become inefficient. To reduce circuit complexity, i.e. total number of states and state variables, state constraining to eliminate unnecessary or unreachable states or circuit partitioning methods could be employed. The latter was applied to the flyback circuit itself already as it consists of source, core, load and auxiliary winding partitions to keep model creation time in check.

Table 5. Model generation time of more complex models

	4 state buck reconfig. R	4 state buck reconfig. C	flyback core 1 reconfig. var.
translate to LDS	0.15 s	0.19 s	3.96 s
LDS discretization	12.38 s	148.65 s	740.72 s
calc. min, max, init vals	25.35 s	65.29 s	620.94 s
rest of model generation	1.46 s	1.19 s	42.88 s
total model gen. time	39.34 s	215.32 s	1408.48 s

Comparison of Simulation Approaches. To evaluate the practical usefulness of FPGA-based application scenario simulation for application readiness checking using proposed reconfiguration techniques, we mapped the complete DC-to-DC power conversion application onto FPGA. This includes the previous buck converter application circuit model and a tiny SoC using a RiscV core of the size of an ARM M0 core. Analog-to-digital conversion and vice versa that occurs in the chip's analog front end was abstracted to simple conversion functions to reduce preparation effort. Using this example application, we compared three simulation approaches: CPU simulation via RTL simulator, FPGA simulation without reconfigurable variables and FPGA simulation using two IVs for resistive and capacitive load. Results on simulation preparation times, time per iteration and overall validation runtime on the example of 500 iterations can be seen in Table 6. Preparation time comprises all steps necessary until the actual simulation can start. This effort has to be considered for each iteration of an FPGA simulation without reconfiguration as the bitstream and model both need to be updated. For the other two approaches however, this effort only needs to be spent once, as both yield reconfiguration capabilities. Consequently, we can not only observe the expected major difference in total time per iteration between CPU and FPGA simulation, due to the boost in simulation throughput of three to four orders of magnitude when using an FPGA [3,7,16], but also an even bigger difference between the two FPGA-based approaches. While preparation effort is higher for both FPGA-based approaches, they already outperform CPU simulation after one iteration.

Table 6. Comparison of different simulation approaches

	CPU sim. Vivado xsim	FPGA w/o rcfg. Pynq Z1	FPGA R+C rcfg. Pynq Z1
total preparation time	39.24 s	563.68 s	591.09 s
translate to LDS	0.004	0.004 s	0.12 s
LDS discretization	0.001	0.001	5.27 s
calc. min, max, init vals	–	–	18.74 s
rest of model generation	0.009	0.009 s	0.12 s
bitstream generation	–	530.20 s	532.60 s
bitstream programming	–	33.47 s	34.24 s
source code compilation	39.23 s	–	–
total time per iteration	1.12 h	9.40 min	9.85 s
calc. of new coefficients	–	–	9.39 s
update coeffs on FPGA	–	–	0.22 s
simulation time	1.12 h	0.24 s	0.24 s
update & program bitstream	–	563.68 s	–
runtime for 500 iterations	23.26 d	3.26 d	1.53 h

For application readiness checking the number of simulation runs range from 500 Monte Carlo runs [11] up to 10000 runs for design-in validation of an automotive magnetic sensor application [13] and simulated time per simulation run ranges from several tens of milliseconds [13] up to several seconds [14]. We consider regulation bringup scenarios for this power conversion application that do require simulation of roughly 300 ms and 500 iterations with changing resistive and capacitive load. For this validation setup the total verification runtime is reduced from 23.26 days to 3.26 days and 1.53 h on FPGA without and with reconfiguration respectively. This is a speedup of 365× compared to CPU simulation in the latter case, which is similar to results reported in [13].

5.2 Timing Impact and FPGA Resource Utilization

To assess the impact on timing and resource utilization while using reconfigurable variables within a model, we again took the buck converter example circuit from above and compared four different configurations: no reconfigurable variable, reconfigurable resistive load, reconfiguration for both resistive and capacitive load described as independent variables and a mixture of independent and dependent variables. Experimental results are shown in Table 7 and further discussed in following subsections.

Table 7. Resource utilization and timing of different buck variants

variants	no rcfg.	R	R + C	R + dep. C
Clock	25 MHz	25 MHz	25 MHz	25 MHz
WNS	2.903 ns	2.704 ns	1.868 ns	2.401 ns
LUT	3110 (4.9%)	3881 (6.1%)	3882 (6.1%)	6075 (9.6%)
FF	4384 (3.5%)	7250 (5.7%)	7250 (5.7%)	4935 (3.9%)
BRAM	53 (39.3%)	53 (39.3%)	53 (39.3%)	95 (70.4%)
DSP	12 (5.0%)	24 (10.0%)	24 (10.0%)	67 (27.9%)

Timing Impact. As shown in Table 7 and calculated using the Worst Negative Slack (WNS), the simulation throughput only decreases by 0.50 % when a reconfigurable variable is added to the model. Adding another dependent or independent variable does not lead to a significant change either, as we could observe a maximum timing degeneration of only 2.72 %. To understand why this is the case, we need to consider how variables are mapped onto FPGA. Variables influence the coefficients of the LDS matrices, which are usually implemented as constants on FPGA and multiplied by current state and input values of the system to calculate the new state and output values. This combinatorical path is typically the critical path of an FPGA design using synthesizable models of analog behavior. If coefficients are influenced by a change of an IV, their values, which are stored in a register on FPGA, are updated by the control IO unit and can be assumed to be constant during simulation. In the case of DVs, coefficients are calculated by approximating their value using linear interpolation.

This interpolation is already conducted a timestep before the coefficient values is used, is therefore not part of the critical path and barely contributes to overall timing.

FPGA Resource Utilization. Table 7 also shows resource utilization of different buck converter configurations. The addition of IVs, see columns two and three, is negligible on larger FPGA boards from resource utilization perspective. Furthermore, the utilization is independent of the number of IVs used. This is true as long as the same amount of coefficients is affected by reconfigurable variables, which is the case in our example and for all connected netlists, as in thsi case all coefficients are affected by each variable. The resource utilization for DVs depend mainly on how accurately their nonlinear curve is approximated. In this experiment, we were quite conservative and opted for a high degree of accuracy, which is why a lot of resources were needed. However, the utilization can be significantly reduced by reducing the accuracy or using LUT optimization techniques.

6 Outlook

Despite the achieved compute efficiency, there is still a need for further improvement as the complexity of circuits for which the current implementation of our proposed techniques can be employed is quite low. Fortunately, there is still room for improvement. An obvious improvement would be switching from a Python based to a C/C++ based implementation of the symbolic solver, such as **symengine** [23], which when combined with sympy reportedly does provide a speedup over plain sympy of 60× [24]. Unfortunately, the current release of symengine does not support matrix exponential computation, which is why we could not use **symengine** within our implementation. Another area of improvement could be to employ a matrix exponential computation approach where compute speed dues not vary based on matrix element values, such as an ordinary differential equation solver or series based method. This does make compute time more predictable and independent of the amount of reconfigurable variables that are employed within a model [25]. Following the notion of result expression complexity reduction, further computational efficiency improvements may be possible by switching from a method where the SoE is solved symbolically to a method where the SoE is solved numerically. This does allow representing result elements of the matrices as plain real values, but would require re-computation of changing dynamics before coefficient reprogramming for every system property reconfiguration. Finally, additional runtime reduction may be achieved by improving FPGA instrumentation for control and communication, as the firmware-in-the-middle approach for instance does not yield throughput that can be expected from a pure hardware solution, or model reduction methods, such as state-space constraining or mechanisms to actively control trade-off between computational complexity and model accuracy.

7 Conclusion

Complexity of modern application solutions steadily increases, which as a consequence strengthens the need to assure early and continuous application readiness. State-of-the-art-methods are either limited in features or very time consuming. To overcome this impediment, we showed FPGA-implementation techniques that allow fast simulation of application scenarios with changing system properties on FPGA. This novel approach leverages an existing AMS FPGA prototyping framework to assure low overhead and a high degree of applicability. Using tightly integrated extensions to reconfigure analog dynamics at runtime, validation time is reduced to 1.5 h from 23 days using state-of-the-art CPU based simulation for the presented power conversion example. To extend applicability of the presented techniques further, we plan to speedup model generation by improving efficiency LDS discretization computation and reduction of overall model complexity of a given application circuit through state-space constraining.

Acknowledgment. The authors would like to thank the Federal Ministry of Education and Research (Germany) via the KI4BoardNet program for supporting this work.

References

1. Gao, P., et al.: Automotive revolution - perspective towards 2030. https://www.mckinsey.com/industries/automotive-and-assembly/our-insights/disruptive-trends-that-will-transform-the-auto-industry
2. Stanley, B.: Digital disruption and the future of the automotive industry. https://www.ibm.com/multimedia/portal/H752407R29967B14/IBMCAI-Digital-disruption-in-automotive.pdf
3. Stanley, D., et al.: Fast validation of mixed-signal SoCs. IEEE Open J. Solid-State Circuits Soc. **1**, 184–195 (2021)
4. Herbst, S., et al.: Fast FPGA emulation of analog dynamics in digitally-driven systems. In: Proceedings of the International Conference on Computer-Aided Design, ICCAD 2018. Association for Computing Machinery, New York (2018)
5. Nothaft, F., et al.: Pragma-based floating-to-fixed point conversion for the emulation of analog behavioral models. In: Proceedings of the 2014 IEEE/ACM International Conference on Computer-Aided Design, ICCAD 2014, pp. 633–640. IEEE Press (2014)
6. Bhattacharya, R., et al.: FPGA based chip emulation system for test development of analog and mixed signal circuits: a case study of DC-DC buck converter. Measurement **45**(8), 1997–2020 (2021)
7. Herbst, S., et al.: An open-source framework for FPGA emulation of analog/mixed-signal integrated circuit designs. IEEE Trans. Comput. Aided Des. Integr. Circuits Syst. **41**(7), 2223–2236 (2022)
8. Herbst, S.: msdsl (2021). https://git.io/msdsl
9. Rutsch, G.: anasymod (2021). https://git.io/anasymod
10. Kaergel, M., et al.: Simulation based verification with range based signal representations for mixed-signal systems. In: 2014 27th Symposium on Integrated Circuits and Systems Design (SBCCI) (2014)

11. Rafaila, M., Decker, C., Grimm, C., Pelz, G.: Design of experiments for effective pre-silicon verification of automotive electronics. In: Borrione, D. (ed.) Advances in Design Methods from Modeling Languages for Embedded Systems and SoC's. LNEE, vol. 63, pp. 141–158. Springer, Dordrecht (2010). https://doi.org/10.1007/978-90-481-9304-2_9
12. Schupfer, F., Kärgel, M., Grimm, C., Olbrich, M., Barke, E.: Towards abstract analysis techniques for range based system simulations. In: Kaźmierski, T., Morawiec, A. (eds.) System Specification and Design Languages. LNEE, vol. 106, pp. 105–121. Springer, New York (2012). https://doi.org/10.1007/978-1-4614-1427-8_7
13. Rutsch, G., et al.: Boosting mixed-signal design productivity with FPGA-based methods throughout the chip design process. In: Design and Verification Conference in Europe (2020)
14. Rutsch, G., et al.: A framework that enables systematic analysis of mixed-signal applications on FPGA. In: 2022 IEEE International Workshop on Rapid System Prototyping (RSP) (2023)
15. SymPy Development Team. sympy (2022). https://www.sympy.org/en/index.html
16. Herbst, S., et al.: Open-source framework for FPGA emulation of analog/mixed-signal integrated circuit designs. IEEE Trans. Comput.-Aided Des. Integr. Circuits Syst. **41**(7), 2223–2236 (2021)
17. oscarbenjamin, Matrix exponential using RootSum #21585 (2023). https://github.com/sympy/sympy/issues/21585
18. Tertel, P., et al.: Real-time emulation of block-based analog circuits on an FPGA. In: 14th SMACD (2017)
19. AMD Xilinx, System Generator for DSP User Guide. https://www.xilinx.com/support/documents/sw_manuals/xilinx14_7/sysgen_user.pdf
20. Donchin, D.: AMS emulation comes to the rescue with rapid, pre-silicon DDR verification. https://www.synopsys.com/content/dam/synopsys/verification/white-papers/a-g-ams-emulation-ddr-verification-wp.pdf
21. Hasler, J.: Large-scale field-programmable analog arrays. Proc. IEEE **108**(8), 1283–1302 (2020)
22. Bouzid, A., et al.: High resolution large scale ADC. Case study of an N bit per volt ADC implemented using FPAA and FPGA applied for precision altimetery. In: 21th ICCC (2020)
23. Ĉertík, O.: symengine (2023). https://github.com/symengine/symengine
24. Entought: SymEngine A Fast Symbolic Manipulation Library [Video]. YouTube (2016). https://www.youtube.com/watch?v=03rBe2RdMt4
25. Moler, C., et al.: Nineteen dubious ways to compute the exponential of a matrix, twenty-five years later. Soc. Ind. Appl. Math. **45**(1), 3–49 (2003)
26. Jordan, D., et al.: An efficient algorithm for calculation of the Luenberger canonical form. IEEE Trans. Autom. Control **18**(3), 292–295 (1973)
27. Benjamin, O.: Matrix exponential using RootSum #21585 (2021). https://github.com/sympy/sympy/issues/21585

Radiation Tolerant 14T SRAM Cell for Avionics Applications

Sagheer Ahmed, Jayesh Ambulkar, Debabrata Mondal, and Ambika Prasad Shah(✉)

IC-ResQ Lab, Department of Electrical Engineering, Indian Institute of Technology Jammu, Jammu 181221, J&K, India
ambika.shah@iitjammu.ac.in

Abstract. The impact of high-energy particles in space like cosmic rays and alpha particles flips the stored data in an SRAM cell. This chapter proposes a highly reliable soft error immune with enhanced critical charge 14T (SIC14T) SRAM cell that is radiation-hardened by design and has an increased critical charge that can withstand both single-event upsets (SEU) and single-event multi-node upsets (SEMNU). We compare the performance of the proposed cell with that of other considered SRAM cells, such as the SRRD12T, RSP14T, SEA14T, and 6T SRAM cell which were simulated in 45-nm CMOS technology in Cadence Virtuoso with a supply voltage of 1 V and 27 °C operating temperature. Both SEU and SEMNU caused at the storage node of SIC14T are successfully recovered. The proposed SRAM cell has 1.02×, 0.6×, 0.72×, and 4.64× better write stability, read access time, leakage power, and critical charge than the SRRD12T with 1.68× area overhead. We also investigated the effect of supply voltage and temperature variations on SRAM stability. For the process variations analysis, we performed 2000 Monte Carlo simulations for the leakage power dissipation for all the considered circuits.

Keywords: RHBD · SRAM · SEU · SEMNU · soft-error · Static noise margin

1 Introduction

As technology trends advance, technology nodes are getting smaller and require lower supply voltage which leads to reduced power dissipation [2]. The high-performance integrated circuits used in avionics applications need memory particularly SRAM for data storage and computation. The static noise margin (SNM) of the SRAM is decreased with technology advancement and reduced supply voltage [8,10]. Because of the lower node voltage and lower SNM, SRAM is susceptible to high-energy particles. The harsh environment of space includes temperature variations, radiation dose variations, and consistency. When these high-energy particles strike an integrated circuit at its sensitive node, it generates electron-hole pairs that move over the silicon bulk. This procedure could

Published by Springer Nature Switzerland AG 2024
I. (Abe) M. Elfadel and L. Albasha (Eds.): VLSI-SoC 2023, IFIP AICT 680, pp. 217–236, 2024.
https://doi.org/10.1007/978-3-031-70947-0_11

change the data stored at the sensitive nodes, and the original data might get altered. This phenomenon is known as single event transients (SETs) [2]. These errors are also known as soft errors because these errors are temporary and stay for some time, and after recovery, these errors are automatically removed [7].

When high-energy particle strike the sensitive node of the device, the electron-hole pairs are separated by the electric field [2]. The reverse-biased drain diffusion region (sensitive area) is where the particle-induced charge travels and the additional charge is successfully collected at the drain. Due to this, a short voltage pulse is created by the accumulated charge. The recorded information in the memory may be changed if the voltage pulse's amplitude is greater than the switching threshold of a logic circuit. This could result in a single event upset (SEU). However, until the subsequent write operation occurs, this data with error continue to exist there [2,5]. The other phenomenon that exists is Single Event Multi Node Upset (SEMNU). In this, multiple nodes flip their logic due to the same cause of high-charge particles. The aerospace environment also consists of highly energetic particles which induce single event transient (SET) and ultimately cause single event upsets (SEU) or soft errors in the memory cell.

Two methods have been suggested in the literature to deal with the impact of soft error (SE) in memory. In the first method, SRAM cells are independent of the transistor's size and the node capacitance of the SRAM cell. This technology-free method fails when there is additional circuitry present. The second method involves increasing the node capacitance in order to create an SEU-tolerable circuit. The critical charge (Q_{crit}) is the minimum charge needed to be collected at a sensitive node that has the potential to change the cell's data storage. However, these methods worsen stability or require more energy. Consequently, There is still a need for an extremely reliable, energy-efficient, and radiation-hardened-by-design (RHBD) SRAM cell [2,9].

Cross-coupled inverters and positive feedback are used in conventional 6T SRAM. If the SEU attacks one of the storage node, the other one will automatically get affected. The probability of soft error in the 6T SRAM cell is very high. So we need to design a robust radiation-hardening SRAM cell [1]. Soumitra Pal *et al.* in [2] proposed SRRD12T SRAM cell as shown in Fig. 1(a), which consumes less power during hold operation and has a greater write capability and higher read stability but suffers from longer read delay and has less critical charge compared to modern radiation-hardened SRAM cells. Soumitra Pal *et al.* in [3] proposed SEA14T SRAM cell, which has a higher critical charge (Q_{crit}) but has a higher read delay, write delay, and high hold power. C. Peng *et al.* in [1] proposed the RSP14T SRAM cell as shown in Fig. 1(b). As compared to contemporary radiation-hardened SRAM cells, the RSP14T SRAM cell has higher read and write stability but has poor critical charge (Q_{crit}) and high leakage power consumption.

This paper proposes a design that effectively mitigates Single Event Upset (SEU) issues while maintaining the stability criterion intact. Here, our proposed circuit exhibits less read access time t_{rat}, leakage power, and critical charge than the above-discussed RSP14T, SEA14T, and SRRD12T SRAM cell.

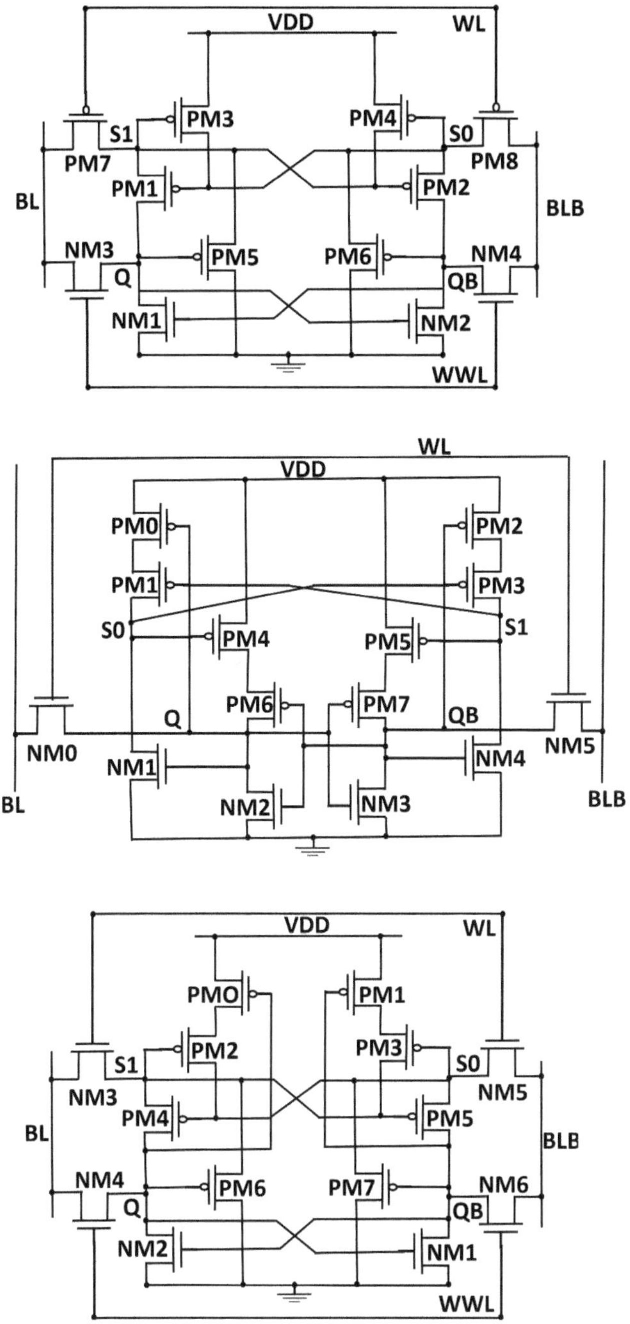

Fig. 1. Schematic of (a) SRRD12T SRAM cell (b) RSP14T SRAM cell (C) Proposed SIC14T SRAM Cell.

The paper is structured as follows: The architecture and operation of the proposed 14T memory cell are discussed in Sect. 2. The simulation results and analysis are discussed in Sect. 3, and the conclusion in Sect. 4.

2 Proposed 14T SRAM Cell

The proposed soft-error immune with enhanced critical charge 14T (SIC14T) SRAM cell is shown in Fig. 1(c). The proposed SRAM cell consists of 14 transistors, with being PMOS transistors (PM0∼ PM7) and the other being NMOS transistors (NM1∼ NM6). The access transistors are NMOS (NM3∼ NM6) with word lines (WL and WWL), these word lines are connected with their gates.

The proposed SIC14T SRAM cell is inspired by the RSP14T [1] and SRRD12T [2], where the two upper PMOS access transistors P7 and P8 in SRRD12T [2] are replaced by NMOS transistors NM3 and NM5 in the proposed 14T circuit to improve read access time. The two PMOS transistors PM0 and PM1 in the proposed cell have been added and are inspired by RSP14T [1] to increase the critical charge (Q_{crit}). In summary, the proposed circuit may offer less read access time and increased critical charge.

2.1 Working Principle

In the proposed circuit, the storage nodes are Q and QB where as the internal nodes are S0 and S1. To understand the working of the proposed 14T SRAM cell, initially, we consider the logic states of nodes Q, QB, S0, and S1 to be '1', '0', '0', and '1', respectively. During the hold mode, all of the access transistors are maintained OFF. The only transistors that remain ON are PM0, PM3, PM4, PM6, and MN2. As a result, SIC14T keeps its original stored data.

Before the read operation starts, bit lines are precharged to VDD and WL is charged to VDD. In order to disable access transistors NM4 and NM6, WWL is kept low, ensuring read operation without any error. BLB, therefore, discharges through NM5 and PM7, and BL remains at VDD because PM6 is turned OFF. When the sense amplifier reads the recorded data at a 50 mV voltage difference between BL and BLB, the read process is complete. It is important to note that throughout the read operation, the storage nodes Q-QB are not accessed. The write operation in the SRAM cell is to update the stored data, WL/WWL is charged to VDD, and BL/BLB is updated to GND/VDD. For the successful read operation, if BLB is at VDD and BL is at GND, nodes QB and S0 charge through NM6 and NM5. As the gates of PM7, NM2, PM1, PM3, and PM4 rise, it becomes easier for the associated access transistor to pull down the nodes Q and S1 to GND.

2.2 SEU Recovery Analysis

In this section, a brief explanation of the proposed circuit's sensitive nodes (S0, S1, Q, and QB) under SEU/SEMNU is provided. To begin with, in order to understand how our proposed 14T SRAM cell functions, we assume that the logic states of the storage nodes Q, QB, S0, and S1 are '1', '0', '0', and '1', respectively.

- **SEU at Q**: NM1 and PM6 are momentarily turned ON and OFF, respectively, when an SEU affects the '1' storing storage node Q and causes it to change to '0'. PM3 is made stronger than PM6 so that S1 maintains its logic state even after PM6 is turned ON. PM2 and PM5 are thus still OFF, keeping the values of S0 and QB constant. As a result, PM3 and PM5 continue to be ON but NM2 is still OFF. Thus, Q returns to its original condition.
- **SEU at QB**: When '0' storing storage node QB is hit by an SEU and transits to '1', PM7 is turned OFF, and NM2 is turned ON. Node Q stays at '1' even though NM2 is turned ON because PMOS is pulling the node up relatively more strongly (both PM4 and PM3 are made larger). Q, therefore turns OFF PM6. S1 thereby keeps PM2 and PM5 OFF while also maintaining their current condition. In addition, node QB returns to its original state because Q keeps NM1 ON.
- **SEU at S0**: In the presence of an SEU, S0 changes from '0' to '1'. Transistors PM3 and PM4 are consequently switched off. Both nodes S1 and Q reach a high impedance condition and keep their initial values as NM2 is still in its hold mode and PM3 is disabled. QB keeps its original storage state of '0' as a result. Q, QB, and S1 all continue to be in their respective states, hence S0 returns to its initial condition.
- **SEU at S1**: S1 becomes '0' when it is affected by an SEU, changing from '1'. Transistors PM2 and PM5 are consequently turned ON. Nodes S0 and QB enter a high impedance condition and maintain their initial values since PM2 is switched ON and NM1 is also kept ON (due to its hold mode). Q, therefore, remains in the '1' storage state. S1 returns to its initial state because Q, QB, and S0 all maintain their states.
- **SEMNU at Q-QB**: When SEMNU concurrently affects both storage nodes Q and QB change from '0' to '1' and Q transits from '1' to '0'. As a result, node Q switches PM6 ON while turning NM1 OFF. QB simultaneously switches NM2 and PM7 ON and OFF. PM2/PM5 is always OFF because S1 keeps its initial logic value even while PM0 and PM6 are switched ON. This means that S0 maintains its initial condition and transitions to a high-impedance state. Therefore, S0's maintenance of the comparatively stronger PM4 and PM3 causes node Q to get back to '1'. NM1 is then turned ON by Q, bringing QB back down to '0'. Thus, nodes Q and QB return to their previous states.
- **SEMNU at S0-S1**: When SEMNU affects both storage nodes S1 and S0 at once, S0 switches from '0' to '1' and S1 switches from '1' to '0'. As a result, node S1 activates PM2 and PM5. S0 simultaneously turns PM3 and PM4 OFF. PM0 and PM6 are always turned OFF because Q maintains its initial logic value, despite PM0 and PM6 being switched OFF. It is also acknowledged that QB maintains its initial condition while transitioning to a high-impedance state. As a result, the QB-maintained, significantly stronger

PM7 and PM1 lift node S1 back to '1'. S1 then causes PM5 to become OFF, bringing S0 back to '0' in the process. As a result, nodes S1 and S0 are restored to their previous states.

3 Simulation Results and Discussions

We evaluate the performance parameters of the proposed SRAM cell against those of other considered SRAM cells already in use, such as 6T, SRRD12T [2], RSP14T [1], and SEA14T [3]. All the SRAM memory cell designs and simulations have been implemented in Cadence Virtuoso using industry-standard 45nm CMOS technology with a supply voltage of 1.0 V and 27 °C operating temperature unless specified. Further, we also analyzed the effect of PVT variations on all the considered SRAM cells.

3.1 Stability Analysis

In this section, we have discussed the stability of all the considered SRAM cells. We have evaluated the hold, read and write stabilities of the proposed SRAM cell along with the other considered SRAM cells. SNM is the lowest noise voltage necessary at each storage cell node to flip the cell's logic. Cell ratio (CR) and pull-up ratio (PUR) decide the stability of SRAM cells. Cell ratio is defined as the ratio of pull-down transistor to access transistor, and is used in read stability. The pull-up ratio is defined as the ratio of the pull-up transistor to the access transistor and is used in write stability. If the cell ratio is increased, then the robustness will be better so that the static noise margin and speed both increase [3]. Figure 2 shows the Hold Static Noise Margin (HSNM), Read Static Noise Margin (RSNM), and Write Static Noise Margin (WSNM) of the proposed SRAM cell. The results show that the SNMs for the proposed SRAM cell are 381 mV, 376 mV, and 586 mV for the hold, read, and write operations, respectively, at a supply voltage of 1.0 V and 27 °C operating temperature.

For a better comparison, we also compared the HSNM, RSNM, and WSNM of various SRAM cells at different supply voltages, as shown in Fig. 3. Results demonstrate that the SNMs increase with supply voltage for all the considered SRAM cells. Results indicate that the proposed cell offers superior performance as compared to other considered cells. The WSNM of the proposed cell at 1 V supply voltage is 1.02×, 1.16×, 1.397×, and 1.14× higher as compared to the SRRD12T [2], RSP14T [1], SEA14T [3], and 6T SRAM cells, respectively. Similarly, the HSNM of the proposed cell is increased by 1.04×, and 1.19× as compared to SRRD12T [2], and SEA14T [3] respectively and reduced hold stability as compared to 6T and RSP14T [1] SRAM cells.

SRAM cells are also vulnerable to read upset. During a read operation, if the voltage increases at the storage node(s) with logic '0', it could alter the information that is stored initially. The noise tolerance of the cell exhibits an inverse relation with the supply voltage. As a result, there is a higher chance that the cell will change the data it has stored. From Fig. 3(b) it can be observed

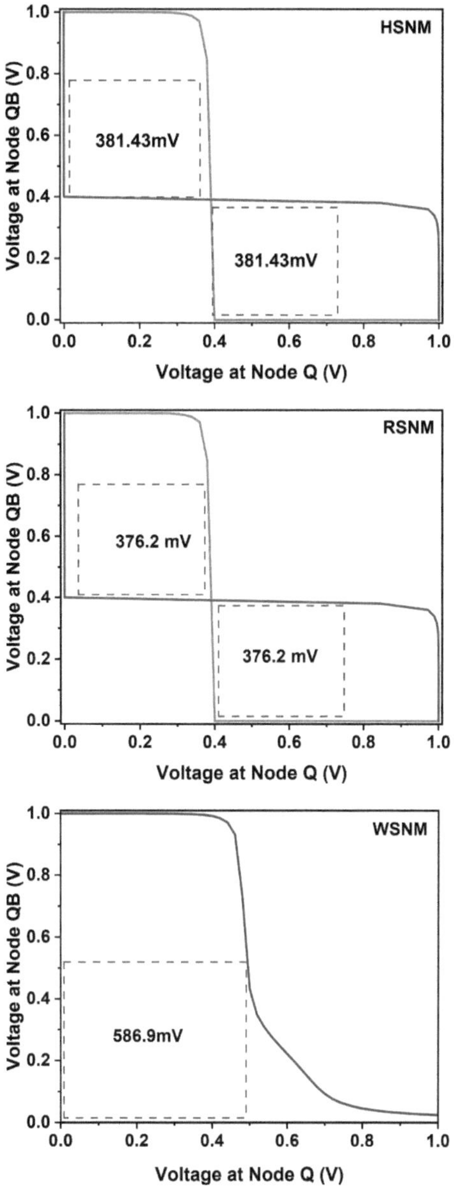

Fig. 2. SNM curves for (a) HSNM, (b) RSNM, and (c) WSNM at the supply voltage of 1 V for the proposed SIC14T SRAM cell.

that the proposed cell and SRRD12T display a significant RSNM compared to other cells because these are read-decoupled. The storage nodes of SRRD12T and the proposed cell SIC14T are not accessible by the bit lines and are read upset-free. The read operation exclusively involves accessing the internal nodes

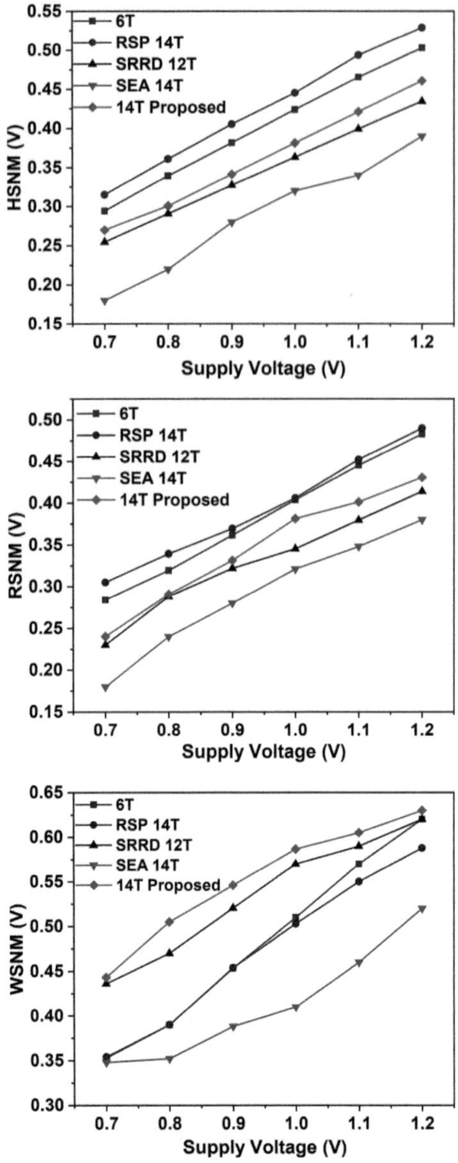

Fig. 3. (a) HSNM and (b) RSNM (c) WSNM variation with different supply voltages and comparison between proposed 14T and other SRAM cells.

within the Proposed cell and SRRD12T. Among these internal nodes, only the '0' storing internal node (S0) is vulnerable to read noise. Even if the voltage at S0 rises to a level that can flip its logic state, data stored at the storage node pair, Q-QB, is unaffected. Read upset is a phenomenon where the unnecessary voltage develops at the storing node and flips the data due to this, read stability decreases [2].

The RSNM of the proposed cell is increased by 1.07×, and 1.23× as compared to SRRD12T [2], and SEA14T [3] respectively and reduced read stability as compared to 6T and RSP14T [1] SRAM cells. The reason for the improvement of SNM in the proposed cell is the strength of access transistors increases, which increases the robustness and better reading capability.

Also, We compared the HSNM, RSNM, and WSNM of various SRAM cells at different temperature variations and at a supply voltage of 1.0 V. The SNM are inversely proportional to the temperature, it means that when the temperature increases the SNM decreases. The reasons for the decrease in SNM are as follows:

- **Leakage Currents:** Increase in temperatures leads to higher leakage currents. This leakage can degrade the stored value (voltage level) in a memory cell, thereby reducing the noise margins.
- **Data Retention:** For HSNM, the ability of the SRAM cell to retain data without a refresh is affected by temperature. The stability of the '1' or '0' state in an SRAM cell is reduced as temperature rises, making it more susceptible to noise and thus reducing the hold noise margin.
- **Degraded Write Margin:** During a write operation, the bit lines and word lines are used to force the SRAM cell to change state. Higher temperatures can affect the timing and signal levels, making it harder to overcome the feedback stability of the cell and properly change its state, thus reducing the write noise margin.

The WSNM of the proposed cell at 27 °C temperature is 1.03×, 1.17×, 1.39×, and 1.13× higher as compared to the SRRD12T [2], RSP14T [1], SEA14T [3], and 6T SRAM cells, respectively. The HSNM of the proposed cell is increased by 1.05×, and 1.18× as compared to SRRD12T [2], and SEA14T [3] respectively and reduced hold stability as compared to 6T and RSP14T [1] SRAM cells. Similarly, the RSNM of the proposed cell is increased by 1.07×, and 1.23× as compared to SRRD12T [2], and SEA14T [3] respectively and reduced read stability as compared to 6T and RSP14T [1] SRAM cells.

Figure 4 shows the effect of temperature variations on the stability of all the considered SRAM cells. Results show that the HSNM, RSNM, and WSNM of all the considered SRAM cells reduce with the temperature.

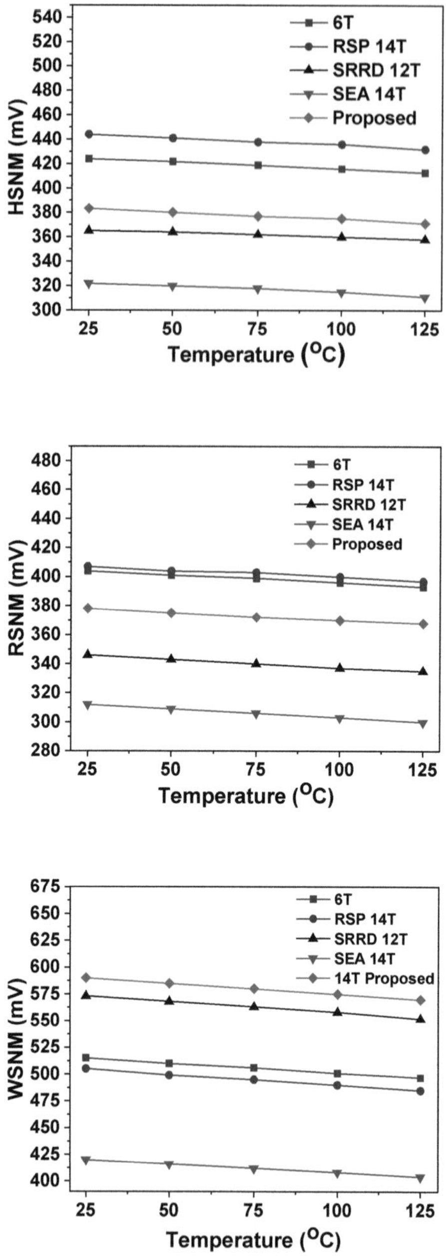

Fig. 4. (a) HSNM and (b) RSNM (c) WSNM with temperature variations and comparison between proposed 14T and other SRAM cells.

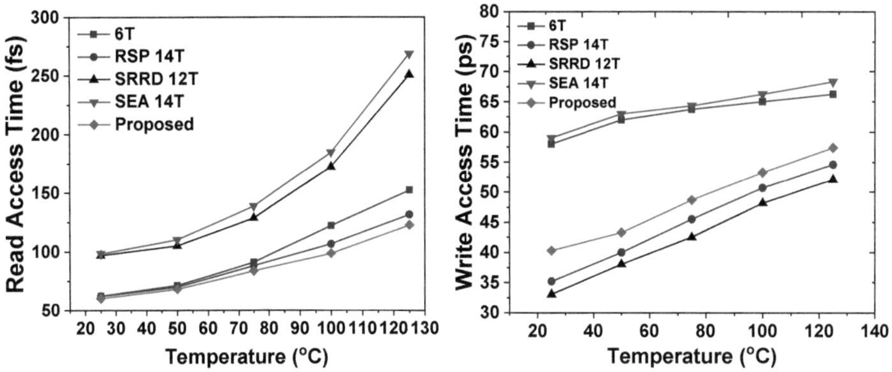

Fig. 5. (a) Read access time (b) Write access time variation with temperature variations for all considered SRAM cells.

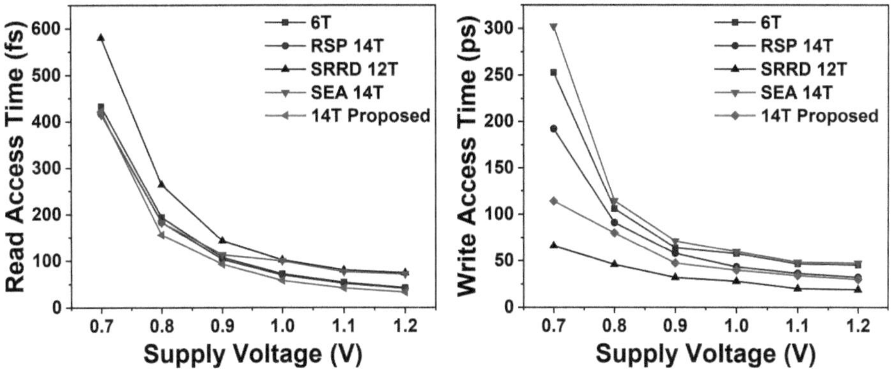

Fig. 6. (a) Read access time (b) Write access time variation with supply voltage for all considered SRAM cells.

3.2 Delay Analysis

The time taken by the bit line capacitor to discharge by 50 mV is known as read delay or read access time (t_{rat}) [6]. Similarly, the amount of time needed to successfully write data into a memory cell is known as the write delay (t_{wat}) [4]. We measured the read and write access times for each SRAM cell at different supply voltages, as shown in Fig. 5. Results show that the read access time (t_{rat}) of the proposed 14T SRAM cell at standard voltage 1 V is 0.60×, 0.95×, 0.60×, and 0.95× of SRRDD12T [2], RSP14T [1], SEA14T [3], and 6T SRAM cells, respectively. Also, the write access time (t_{wat}) of the proposed 14T SRAM cell at standard voltage 1 V is 1×, 0.67×, 1.17×, and 0.68× of RSP14T [1], SEA14T, SRRD12T [2], and 6T SRAM cells, respectively.

Also, we measured the read and write access times for each SRAM cell at different temperature variations, as shown in Fig. 6. Results show that the read access time (t_{rat}) of the proposed 14T SRAM cell at standard temperature 27 °C is 0.66×, 0.96×, 0.61×, and 0.96× of SRRDD12T [2], RSP14T [1], SEA14T [3], and 6T SRAM cells, respectively. The read access time is proportional to the temperature. Also, the write access time (t_{wat}) of the proposed 14T SRAM cell at standard temperature 27 °C is 1.14×, 0.68×, 1.21×, and 0.69× of RSP14T [1], SEA14T [3], SRRD12T [2], and 6T SRAM cells, respectively. Results demonstrate that the proposed cell outperforms as compared to the other considered SRAM cells. The write access time is proportional to the temperature. As temperature increases, various physical and electrical properties of the semiconductor materials change, which can lead to increased write access times and read access time to maintain reliable operation.

- As the temperature rises, the mobility of the charge carriers (electrons and holes) decreases. The reduction in the mobility decreases the transistor's strength of changing and holding the state.
- As the temperature increases the leakage current also increases, it will lead to oppose in the changing states during write operation.
- With increase in temperature the threshold voltage decreases due to which leakage current and power also increase, Collaboratively increase write access time.
- As the temperature increases, signals are more degraded as they transmit through the circuitry due to increased resistance and capacitance effects. It can lead to longer propagation delays, requiring additional time for the read circuitry to accurately interpret and process the signals, thereby increasing the read access time.

Read access time (t_{rat}) depends on multiple factors such as the read current, stacking, and bit-cell ratio [3]. The proposed circuit consists of all NMOS access transistors whereas SRRD12T consists of 2 upper PMOS access transistors, which are weak low, due to which SRRD12T takes more time to read the data from the storage node. Whereas RSP14T and SEA14T have less cell ratio than the proposed SRAM cell. The write access time (t_{wat}) depends on the feedback path and the type of transistor used in access transistors like PMOS/NMOS [3]. Four access transistors provide better writability than two access transistors because four access transistors connected to their internal nodes and storage nodes increase the strength and make the transition faster than two access transistors. Hence SRRD12T and the proposed cell have less write access time (t_{wat}) than the other considered SRAM cells.

3.3 Leakage Power Consumption Analysis

During the hold mode, SRAM cells retain the stored data. Consequently, a significant portion of the overall power used by an SRAM cell is lost while the SRAM is in hold mode [2]. For the leakage power (P_l) analysis, we calculated the leakage power of all the considered SRAM cells, as shown in Table 1. The leakage power for the proposed SRAM cell is 0.73×, 0.21×, 0.09×, and 0.696× than the SRRD12T [2], RSP14T [1], SEA14T [3], and 6T SRAM cells, respectively. In the Proposed SIC14T cell, the stacking effect has increased by adding

Table 1. Performance parameters and comparison of different SRAM cells at 1.0 V supply voltage and 27 °C operating temperature

SRAM Cell	HSNM (mV)	RSNM (mV)	WSNM (mV)	Read Delay t_{rat}(fs)	Write Delay t_{wat}(ps)	Leakage Power (pW)	Critical Charge (fC)	$Area_N$	Relative FOM
6T	423	403	510	63	60	41.36	10.26	**1.00**	0.12
RSP14T [1]	**441**	**406**	503	63	36	141.8	44.94	1.81	0.08
SRRD12T [2]	363	345	571	100	**35**	39.53	32.65	1.63	0.25
SEA14T [3]	320	310	418	100	60	329.0	75.00	1.94	0.02
Proposed 14T	381	376	**586**	**60**	41	**28.82**	**151.7**	2.74	**1.00**

two extra PMOS transistors PM0 and PM1 in the pull-up region as compared to SRRD12T. By increasing the stacking effect, the leakage power (P_l) has been reduced.

There are many factors on which leakage power depends, the leakage power of SRAM cell increases with increase in voltage supply and temperature variations. The causes of leakage power are as follows:

- **Subthreshold Leakage Current** The current flows from the transistor when it is in off state. It increases exponentially when voltage between gate and sources increases. When we increases the supply voltage the leakage current increases because gate source voltage depends on the supply voltage.
- **Gate oxide leakage** Gate oxide leakage occurs due to electron tunneling through the thin gate oxide layer of MOSFET transistors. This leakage current is controlled by the electric field across the gate oxide, which increases with higher applied voltages. Increases voltage supply increase the gate oxide leakage, contributes to high leakage power.
- **Reverse Bias Leakage** reverse bias leakage occurs when the drain-source voltage of a transistor is reversed, leading to leakage current flow through the transistor's drain and source regions. This leakage mechanism becomes more prominent at higher voltages.

We calculated the leakage power of all the considered SRAM cells at different supply voltages and operating temperatures as shown in Fig. 7(a) and (b). Results show that the rate of change in leakage power with supply voltage variations for the proposed SRAM cell is minimum as compared to the other considered SRAM cells. This indicates that the proposed cell is robust against the supply voltage variations. Figure 7(b) shows that the rate of change in leakage power with temperature variations for the proposed SRAM cell is minimum as compared to the other considered SRAM cells. This indicates that the proposed cell is robust against temperature variations.

Further, for the effect of process variations on leakage power, we performed the 2000 Monte Carlo simulations for the proposed 14T SRAM and other considered SRAM cells, as shown in Fig. 7(c). Results indicate that the proposed 14T SRAM cell is less affected by process variation than the other considered SRAM cells. The Proposed cell has the least standard deviation when compared to the

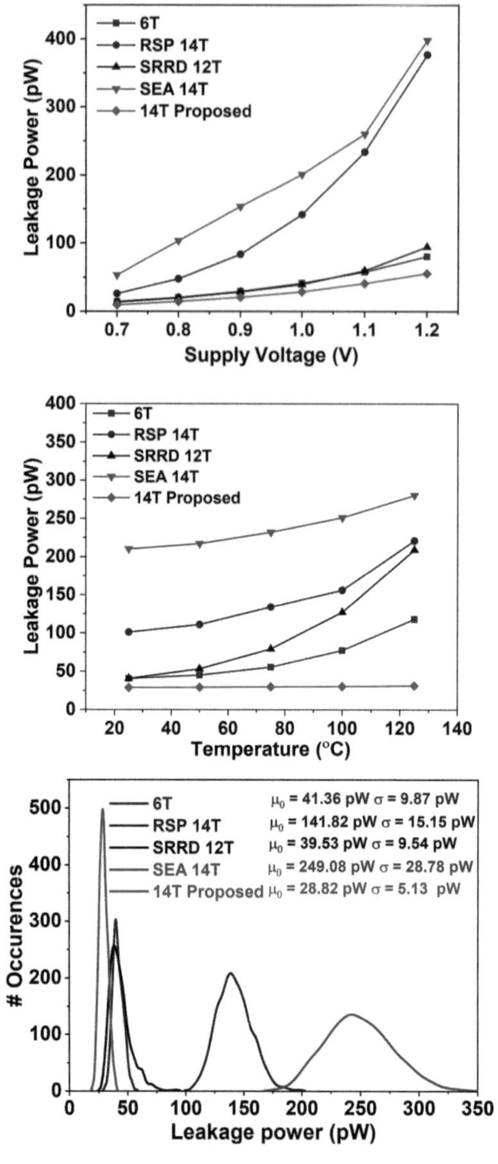

Fig. 7. Effect of PVT variations on leakage power of different SRAM cells at TT process corner (a) Supply voltage variations (b) Temperature variations (c) 2000 Monte Carlo simulations for process variations.

SRRD12T [2], RSP14T [1], SEA14T [3], and 6T SRAM cells. The standard deviation for the proposed SRAM cell is 1.85×, 2.95×, 7.43× and 1.92× less than the SRRD12T [2], RSP14T [1], SEA14T [3], and 6T SRAM cells, respectively. This indicates that the proposed 14T SRAM cell is robust against leakage power process variations and suitable for reliable operation.

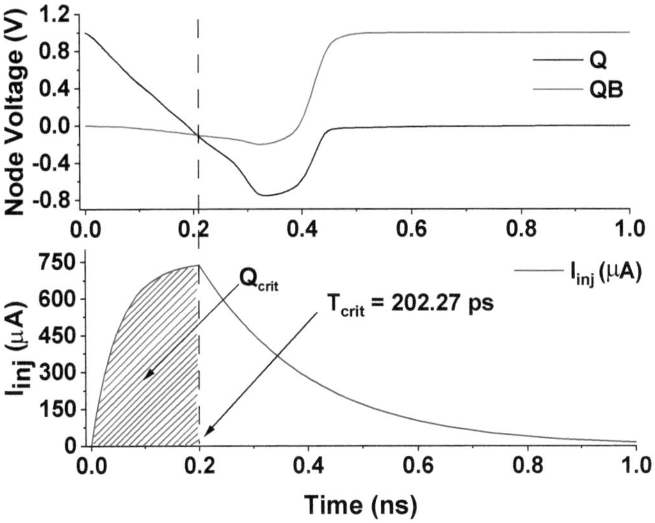

Fig. 8. Critical charge calculation of proposed SIC14T SRAM cell.

3.4 Critical Charge Analysis

The critical charge (Q_{crit}) refers to the minimum amount of charge required to accumulate at a sensitive node with the capacity to flip the data stored in the SRAM cell. [5]. A double exponential current waveform [6] is used to model the current transient pulse formed by SEU, which is given as:

$$I_{inj}(t) = \frac{Q_c}{\tau_\alpha - \tau_\beta}\left(e^{\frac{-t}{\tau_\alpha}} - e^{\frac{-t}{\tau_\beta}}\right) \tag{1}$$

where Q_c accounts for the entire amount of positive or negative charge that a radiation particle impact has left at the sensitive node, and τ_α (50ps) and τ_β (200ps) are the collection time constants of the p-n junction and the time constant of ion-track formation, respectively [6]. In order to determine Q_{crit}, I_{inj} of different amplitudes has been applied on one of the sensitive nodes and then noted down the minimum value of Io and critical time (t_{crit}) when the stored data are flipped. The t_{crit} is the time when Q and QB intersect with each other and flip their logic. The area under the curve of I_{inj} and t_{crit} gives Q_{crit} as shown in Fig. 8. The Q_{crit} is calculated at all of the sensitive nodes in order to estimate the soft-error tolerance of a cell and the minimal magnitude is then determined. The minimum one is considered the effective Q_{crit} of the considered SRAM cells [2].

The proposed SRAM cell comparison with existing SRAM in terms of Q_{crit} is given in Table 1. Results show that the proposed SIC14T SRAM cell is better than other conventional SRAM cells. The Q_{crit} of the proposed SRAM cell is 3.37×, 4.64×, 2.02×, and 14.7× higher than the RSP14T, SRRD12T, SEA14T, and 6T SRAM cells, respectively. The addition of two PMOS transistors in the proposed

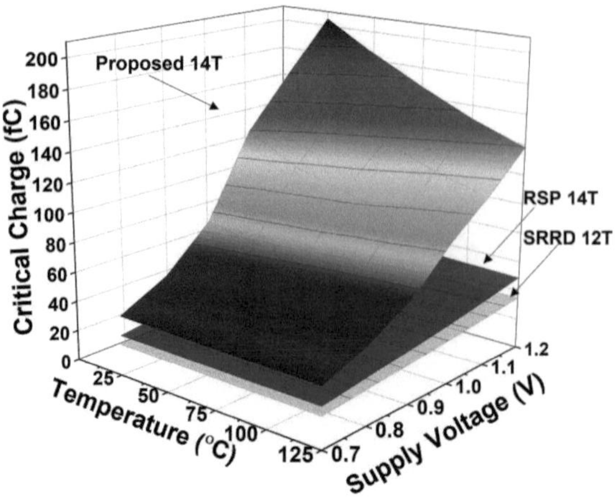

Fig. 9. Critical charge of the different SRAM cells with different supply voltages and operating temperatures.

cell increases the node capacitance as compared to SRRD12T. Hence the proposed cell becomes more resilient against radiation. When an SRAM cell becomes more resilient due to high critical charge, it results in improved data stability, reduced vulnerability to noise, and increased tolerance to process variations. These benefits contribute to the overall reliability and performance of the SRAM cell. Further, we calculated the critical charge of RSP14T, SRRD12T, and the proposed cell with varying supply voltage and operating temperature as shown in Fig. 9. Results show that the critical charge increases with the increase in supply voltage while decreasing with the temperature. Results also demonstrate that the critical charge of the proposed cell is higher as compared to other considered SRAM cells at all the operating conditions. This indicates that the proposed cell is robust and can be used in a radiation environment without data flip.

Logic flipping and overlap voltage are the threshold voltage at which the logic changes its state. Peak current is the maximum current a transistor can draw through the circuit. Logic flipping margins and overlap voltages are critical parameters because they reflect the reliability of logic circuits in the presence of radiation. Higher flipping margins and overlap voltages generally indicate greater enough to tackle radiation-induced errors.

To determine the tolerance of SRAM against high-energy radiations, the relationship between overlap voltage w.r.t. peak current I_{peak} is measured. The relationship between the overlap voltage w.r.t peak current (I_{peak}) is shown in the Fig. 10. The proposed SRAM cell comparison with existing SRAM in terms of I_{peak}. Results show that the proposed SIC14T SRAM cell is better than other conventional SRAM cells. The I_{peak} of the proposed SRAM cell is 1.62×, 1.85×, 1.30×, and 5.22× higher than the RSP14T, SRRD12T, SEA14T, and 6T SRAM cells, respectively. The comparison of I_{peak} and Q_{crit} of different SRAM cell are shown in the Fig. 11 where the Q_{crit} of the proposed SRAM cell is 3.37×, 4.64×,

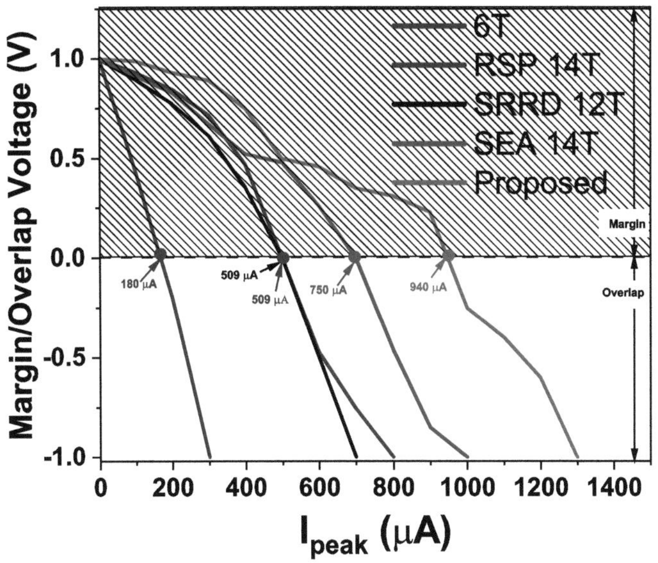

Fig. 10. Logic flipping margin/overlap Voltage with Peak Current for radiation hardening analysis.

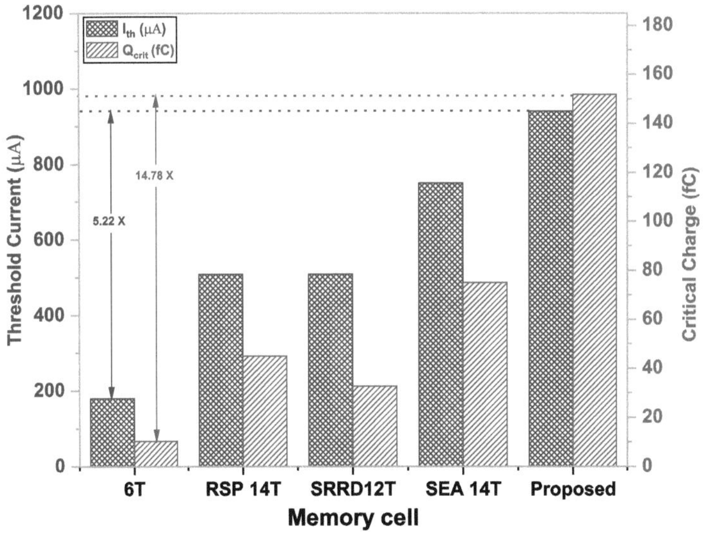

Fig. 11. Peak current and Critical charge analysis.

2.02×, and 14.7× higher than the RSP14T, SRRD12T, SEA14T, and 6T SRAM cells, respectively. The addition of two PMOS transistors in the proposed cell increases the node capacitance as compared to SRRD12T. Hence the proposed cell becomes more resilient against radiation.

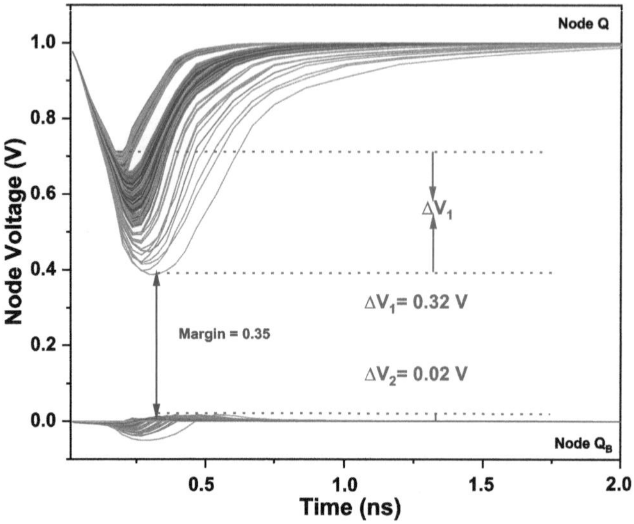

Fig. 12. 2000 Monte Carlo Simulations samples for SEU tolerant storage nodes of Proposed 14T SRAM cell.

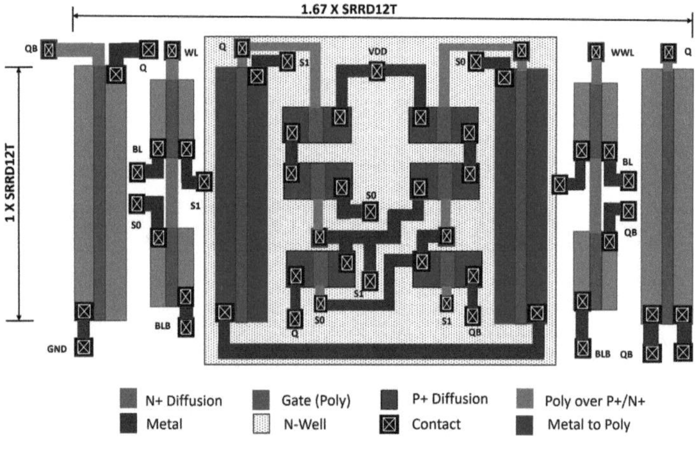

Fig. 13. Layout of the proposed SIC14T SRAM cell.

We have done the SEU analysis of the proposed circuit SIC14T on giving radiation charge at which 6T SRAM cell gets flipped and performed 2000 Monte Carlo simulations. The result shown in Fig. 12 shows that there is a margin of 0.35 V between both the nodes Q and QB which shows that the circuit is immune, it also shows that the circuit can handle higher level radiation. This indicates that the proposed SRAM cell is best suited for high energy radiation environment.

3.5 Area and Figure of Merit

The SRAM cell layout configuration of the proposed cell is shown in Fig. 13. To understand area requirements with performance, we normalize the area of all the considered cells with respect to 6T SRAM as listed in Table 1. The Proposed SIC14T cell require 1.67×, 1.51×, 1.41×, and 2.74× more area as compared to the SRRD12T [2], RSP14T [1], SEA14T [3], and 6T SRAM cells, respectively. The area of the proposed SRAM cell is more because it consists of 14 transistors, where 8 are PMOS transistors, and 6 are NMOS transistors. We have managed all the PMOS transistors in such a way that all are together to put the N-well layer on the PMOS transistors.

SRAM cell usage in a space environment highly depends on Q_{crit}, but while improving one parameter, other parameters deteriorate. To determine the overall performance of the proposed cell, a Figure of Merit (FOM) is defined and it depends on various parameters like Q_{crit}, HSNM, RSNM, WSNM, t_{rat}, t_{wat}, Area, and Leakage Power (P_l). The FOM is given as:

$$FOM = \frac{HSNM \times RSNM \times WSNM \times Q_{crit}}{t_{rat} \times t_{wat} \times Area \times P_1} \quad (2)$$

We calculated the relative FOM of all the considered SRAM cells and normalized them with respect to the proposed cell as listed in Table 1. Results show that the relative FOM of the 6T, RSP14T, SRRD12T, and SEA14T is only 12%, 8%, 25%, and 2% of the proposed SRAM cell. This indicates that the proposed SRAM cell is best suited for low-power, high-performance, and radiation-hardened applications.

4 Conclusion

This paper proposed a highly reliable soft-error immune with enhanced critical charge 14T (SIC14T) SRAM cell for avionics applications. The proposed cell is completely tolerable to SEU occurring at any of its sensitive nodes. Furthermore, SEMNUs that have occurred at its internal node pair are completely recovered by the proposed SIC14T SRAM cell. SIC14T consumes the least leakage power, lower read access time, better writability, and highest critical charge as compared to other SRAM cells. It also demonstrates the highest relative FOM making it overall better than other SRAM cells indicating a better choice for avionics applications.

Acknowledgments. This research work received funding from the FIST scheme of DST with grant no. SR/FST/ET-II/2021/814.

References

1. Peng, C., et al.: Radiation-hardened 14T SRAM bitcell with speed and power optimized for space application. IEEE Trans. Very Large Scale Integr. (VLSI) Syst. **27**, 407–415 (2018)

2. Pal, S., Sri, D.D., Ki, W.-H., Islam, A.: Soft-error resilient read decoupled SRAM with multi-node upset recovery for space applications. IEEE Trans. Electron Devices **68**, 2246–2254 (2021)
3. Pal, S., Mohapatra, S., Ki, W.-H., Islam, A.S.: Design of soft-error-aware SRAM with multi-node upset recovery for aerospace applications. IEEE Trans. Circuits Syst. I: Regular Pap. **68**, 2470–2480 (2021)
4. Ch, N.R., Gupta, B., Kaushal, G.: Single-event multiple effect tolerant RHBD14T SRAM cell design for space applications. IEEE Trans. Device Mater. Reliab. **21**, 48–56 (2021)
5. Shah, A.P., Vishvakarma, S.K., Hübner, M.: Michael Soft error hardened asymmetric 10T SRAM cell for aerospace applications. J. Electron. Test. **36**, 255–269 (2020)
6. Bharti, P.K., Mekie, J.: GBRHQ-14T: gate-boosted radiation hardened quadruple SRAM design. In: 2022 IEEE International Conference on Emerging Electronics (ICEE), pp. 1–5 (2023)
7. Shah, Kumar, M.P., Lorenzo, R.: A 1.2 V, radiation hardened 14T SRAM memory cell for aerospace applications. In: 2022 IEEE Silchar Subsection Conference (SILCON), pp. 1–7 (2023)
8. Pal, S., Bose, S., Ki, W.-H., Islam, A.: Half-select-free low-power dynamic loop-cutting write assist SRAM cell for space applications. IEEE Trans. Electron Devices **67**, 80–89 (2019)
9. Guo, J., Xiao, L., Mao, Z.: Novel low-power and highly reliable radiation hardened memory cell for 65 nm CMOS technology. IEEE Trans. Circuits Syst. I: Regular Pap. **61**, 1994–2001 (2014)
10. Kotni, J.P., Pandey, M., Prasad, S., Islam, A.: Radiation-hardened low read delay 12T-SRAM cell for space applications. In: 2021 Devices for Integrated Circuit (DevIC), pp. 512–516 (2021)

3.125GS/s, 4.9 ENOB, 109 fJ/Conversion Time-Domain ADC for Backplane Interconnect

Solomon Micheal Serunjogi[1(✉)] and Mihai Sanduleanu[2]

[1] New York University of Abu Dhabi, Saadiyat Island, UAE
sms10215@nyu.edu
[2] Khalifa University of Science and Technology, Abu Dhabi, UAE
mihai.sanduleanu@ku.ac.ae

Abstract. This paper presents a flash Time Domain ADC with T/H amplifier, Voltage Controlled Delay Line and Time to Digital Converter. The design is operating at 3.125 GS/s with 4.9 ENOB and a Walden figure of merit of 109 fJ/Conversion. Automatic calibration means are provided as well. For measurements purposes, an integrated memory is provided. It consumes 16.2 mW from a 1 V supply. It was realized in the 45 nm PDSOI from Global Foundries.

Keywords: Sampler · Track and Hold · Time-Domain ADC · Backplane interconnect · Gigabit Radio · mm-Waves

1 Introduction

The progression of Time Domain ADCs, marked by improvements in sampling rates, energy efficiency, and integration capabilities, highlights the progress of the research community, paving the way for their widespread adoption in future digital systems. Further more, new research areas in mm-wave wireless communications on 5G at 28 GHz, cognitive radios, 60 GHz (802.15.3.c, ECMA-387, WiHD standards), and mobile/cable television require a broadband ADC converter with bandwidths in excess of 850 MHz and moderate accuracy (7–10bits) for digitizing the IF signal and/or direct sampling at RF. Other applications are backplane interconnect with digital equalization that require a 4–5 bit A/D converters, emerging technologies, particularly in high-speed communications and IoT devices and LIDAR. The new applications require high linearity at high sample rates ($fs > 2Gs/s$) with large bandwidth and low power consumption [1–4]. Time Domain ADC systems serve as alternatives to Voltage Domain ADCs, primarily due to the low voltage requirements of contemporary technologies, often below 1 V. This lower voltage threshold exacerbates the issue of offset voltages in ADC design, where even a 9-bit converter's least significant bit (LSB) nears 1.95 mV, close to the offset and noise levels. Time Domain ADCs, utilizing Time to Digital Converters (TDC), offer a solution by quantizing time intervals

Published by Springer Nature Switzerland AG 2024
I. (Abe) M. Elfadel and L. Albasha (Eds.): VLSI-SoC 2023, IFIP AICT 680, pp. 237–248, 2024.
https://doi.org/10.1007/978-3-031-70947-0_12

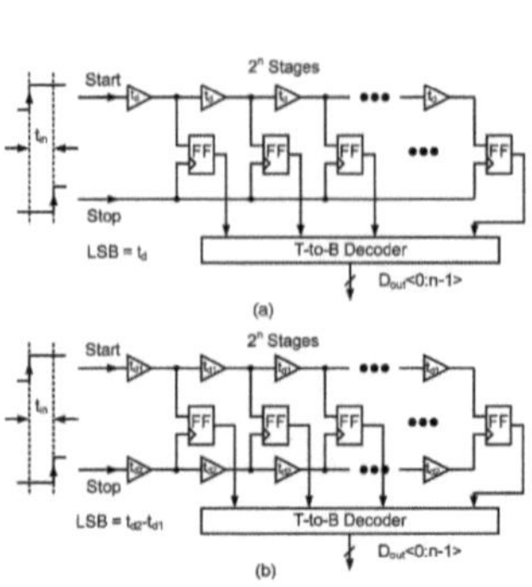

Fig. 1. (a) Delay line ADC, (b) Vernier TDC

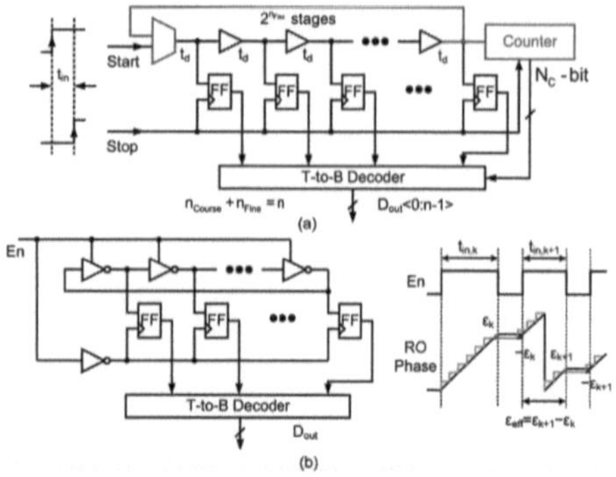

Fig. 2. (*a*) Ring based TDC (b) gated RO TDC with noise shaping

instead of voltages, providing superior time resolution. This approach is particularly advantageous when the input signal is capped at 1 V, aligning with the reduced supply voltages in modern circuits. The paper highlights a novel Time Domain ADC that incorporates a Voltage Controlled Delay Line (VCDL) for enhanced linearity and introduces an innovative TDC structure, noted for its area efficiency and rapid processing capabilities.

1.1 Overview of Time Domain ADCs

In the realm of Time Domain ADCs, Flash TDCs, recognized for their delay-line architecture, face scalability issues due to the increased need for inverters and comparators as resolution grows. To address these limitations, two innovative approaches are introduced. Notably, the Vernier TDC method, which leverages a pair of delay lines with varying stage delays, significantly improves the precision of timing difference measurements. This advancement in accuracy, facilitated by the careful calibration between the two lines (see Fig. 2), marks a pivotal step in overcoming the inherent constraints of gate delay resolutions.

By using the dual delay lines with variable stage delays, the Vernier and Pulse Shrinking (PS) TDC methods facilitate the attainment of smaller LSB sizes, albeit at a cost of greater power and spatial requirements Fig. 1. The PS TDC method [5,6], in particular, achieves this by exploiting the delay variations between buffer transitions. However, these techniques encounter challenges, including poor matching that renders conventional averaging methods ineffective, resulting in significant DNL/INL issues [7,8], and reduced conversion speeds, which limit their application in high-speed environments. Furthermore, their increased power demands, especially in less demanding operations, present obstacles to efficiency and performance in sophisticated circuit designs.

Streamlining TDC designs using ring oscillators simplifies signal folding within the time domain. This method, by integrating RO in precise TDC config-

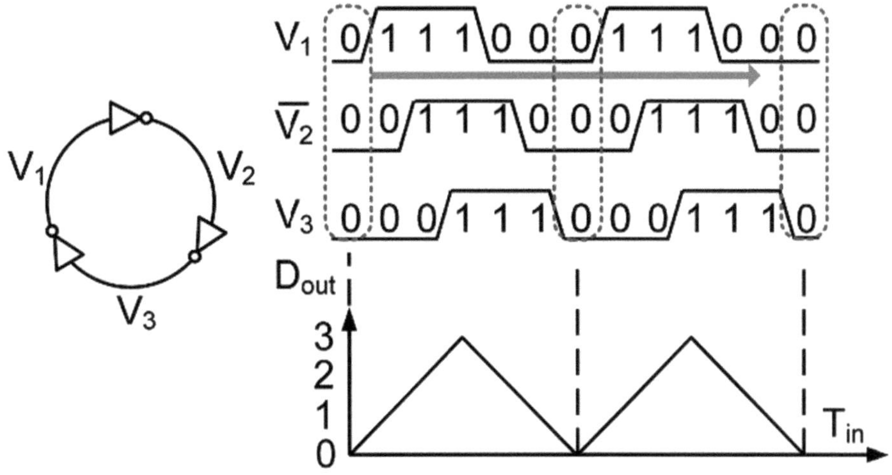

Fig. 3. Differential T/H amplifier with charge compensation

urations alongside counting mechanisms or separate coarse TDCs, creates a foldable TDC model that matches Flash TDCs in speed but with fewer delay stages and DFFs Fig. 1. RO edge transitions enhance phase interpolation, improving LSB precision and matching. Gated-RO (GRO) TDCs introduce noise shaping and energy efficiency, achieving higher SNR through oversampling [9]. However, GRO TDCs face leakage issues due to reliance on internal node capacitance, a problem addressed by Switched RO (SRO) TDCs [7,10] (Fig. 3).

Similar to Flash ADCs, Flash TDCs and RO-based TDCs exhibit a direct exponential relationship between their resolution and conversion speed, presenting a challenge for achieving high resolution quickly. Addressing this, advanced two-step or pipelined TDC designs with time amplification and multiple stages have been developed, capable of reaching resolutions over 9 bits at speeds in the hundreds of megahertz. The incorporation of a time amplifier (TA) is crucial in these designs, although the complexity of implementing a Multiplying Digital-to-Time Converter (MDTC) introduces difficulties, such as the need for extensive dummy delay stages or conversion back to the voltage domain, to store time residue effectively.

The SAR TDC eliminates the need for time amplification, allowing for finer LSB precision [11,12]. However, managing residue signals in the time domain poses a challenge. A method involves adding dummy delay stages next to the main path, using multiplexers to select edges for residue signals, leading to significant dynamic power consumption [11]. An alternative involves incorporating SAR logic into a Gated Ring Oscillator (GRO) with correlated double sampling, offering a different approach to address these challenges.

Utilizing a three-stage Ring Oscillator (RO) as exemplified, this approach captures periodic waveforms across nodes V1, V2, and V3, forming a thermometer-like digital sequence that iterates through six states each RO period. This technique, benefiting from noise shaping through oversampling, boasts the dual advantages of compactness and swift operation [13]. Unlike traditional methods that rely on power-intensive dummy stages for storing time residue, this strategy accumulates the residue signal incrementally, ensuring each transition in the thermometer sequence accurately reflects the quantizer's LSB magnitude, thereby enhancing time-domain folding's efficiency.

Hence, the RO achieves a streamlined approach to signal folding and quantization within the time domain. With an N-stage RO, the system can cycle through 2N states. This method offers two key benefits over voltage domain folding. Firstly, while voltage domain operations often suffer from non-linearity, necessitating parallel folding techniques [61] that introduce significant complexity, time-domain folding via RO maintains inherent linearity due to the cyclical phase changes without edge effects. Secondly, time-domain folding can theoretically achieve unlimited folding factors given sufficient conversion time, unlike voltage domain methods constrained by the number of available folding amplifiers.

In conclusion, the exploration of Time Domain ADCs, particularly Flash TDCs, RO-based TDCs, and Vernier and Pulse Shrinking TDCs, highlights the key tradeoff metrics such as resolution, speed, and power efficiency essential in many ADC architectures. These advancements set the stage for delving into Voltage-Controlled Oscillator (VCO) based Delay Line TDCs, promising further optimizations in the domain of high-speed and high-resolution analog-to-digital conversion, which will be the key theme of our next discussion.

1.2 Voltage Controlled Delay Line Based T/H

The Time Domain A/D converter system is shown in Fig. 4. This type of ADC relies on a Time to Digital Converter (TDC) to generate a digital output. Instead

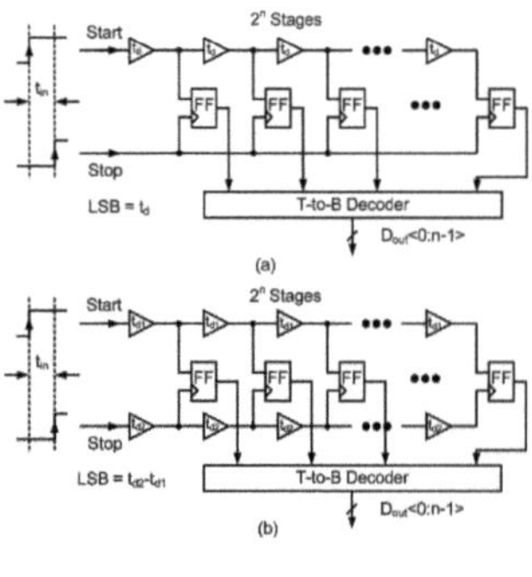

Fig. 4. Voltage to time converter preceding TDC in a TAD

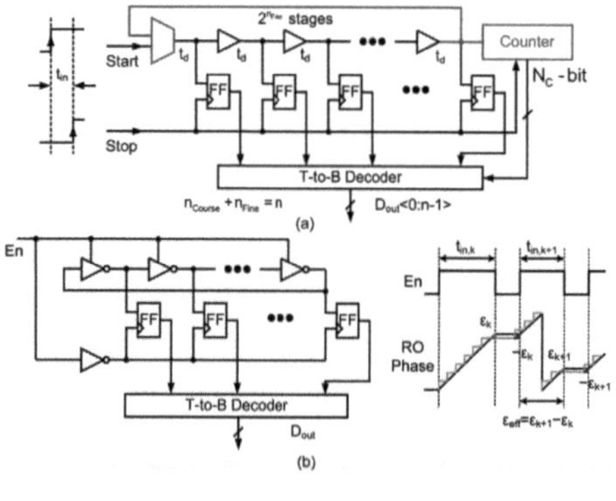

Fig. 5. Differential T/H amplifier with charge compensation

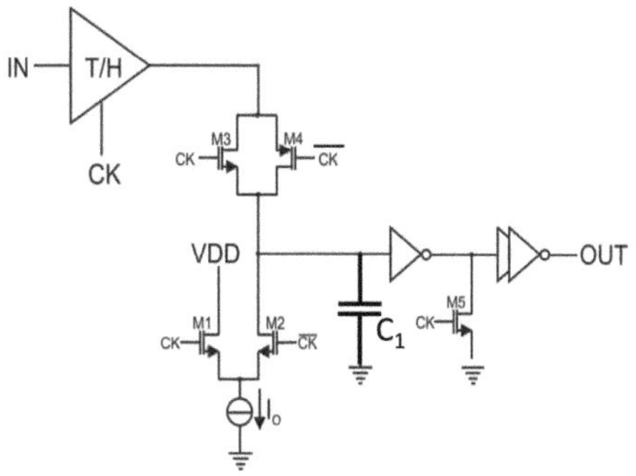

Fig. 6. Differential T/H amplifier with charge compensation

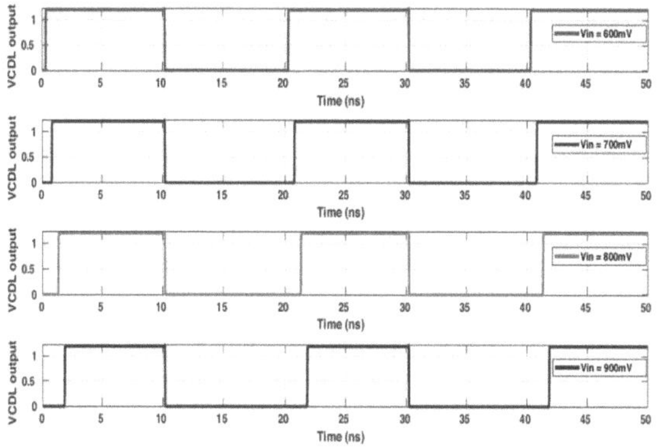

Fig. 7. The output of the VCDL for different input voltages

of quantizing a voltage this ADC quantizes a time interval. The differential T/H amplifier is shown in Fig. 5.

Transistors M2, M3, M2′ and M3′ are half width transistors and used to compensate for CK injection in the switch M1 and M1′. The transistors M4 and M4′ are compensating input/output feedthrough. The T/H amplifier cannot directly drive a Time to Digital Converter (TDC). Before the Time to Digital Converter (TDC) we need a voltage to time converter that can be realized as a voltage-controlled delay line as in Fig. 6.

The capacitor C1 is charged from the input voltage and discharged from a constant current source. When clock CK is high, the switch M3 is on and the input voltage from the T/H is charged on the capacitor C1. When CK is high, the switch M5 is ON and the output of the inverter is forced to 0, M1 is ON and the current Io is directed to the supply VDD. This leads to undetermined signal components in the voltage over the hold capacitor.

When CK is low, the switches M3, M4 are off and the switch M2 is ON and the current Io discharges the capacitor C1. When the voltage on the capacitor reaches VDD/2, the inverter will switch from 0 to 1. As the switch M5 is OFF, the

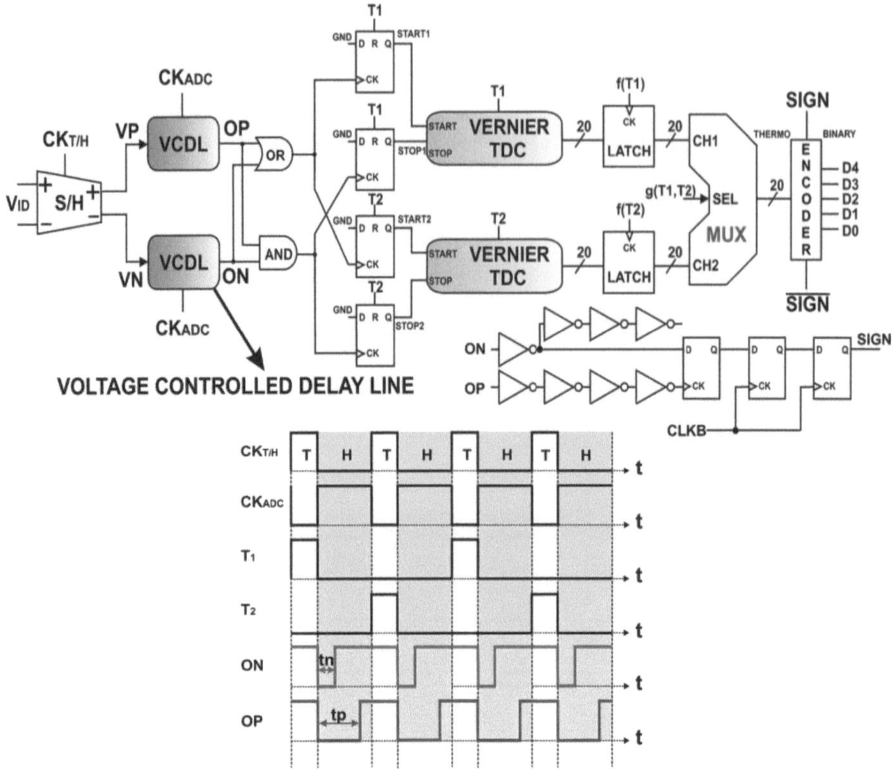

Fig. 8. TDC architecture

output of the inverter will generate a pulse with the length proportional to the input voltage Vin from the T/H output. This pulse is applied to a chain of buffers that goes to the TDC input. The simulated output of the Voltage Controlled Delay Line. (VCDL) is presented in Fig. 7. Four different input voltages of 600 mV, 700 mV, 800 mV and 900 mV respectively are applied to the input of the VCDL. The pulse width depends linearly on the input voltage. We get a pulse width modulator. The linearity of the VCDL is very important for the linearity of the TADC. For 8–9 bit accuracy, the linearity of the VCDL should be better than the 8–9 bit linearity of the TADC system. In the remainder of the paper we are introducing the Time Domain ADC Architecture and measured results.

2 3.125GS/S 4.9 ENOB TIME-DOMAIN ADC

TDC is based on voltage-controlled delay lines (VCDL) and Vernier TDC with sign and magnitude. The block diagram is shown in Fig. 8 The input is applied to a linear T/H amplifier (see Fig. 5). The two differential signals from S/H, VP and VN, are applied to two voltage-controlled delay lines (VCDL) (see Fig. 8).

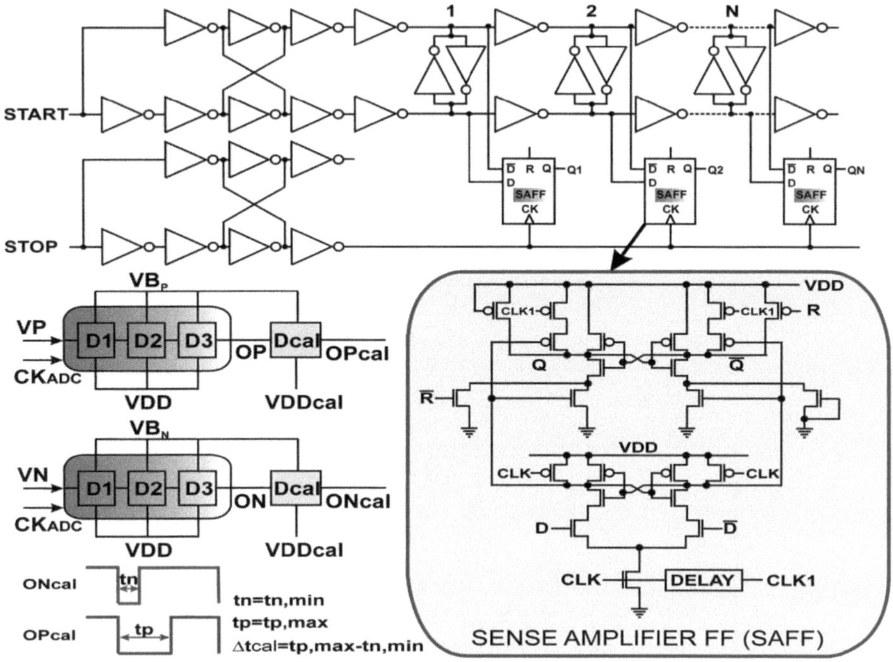

Fig. 9. Vernier TDC, sense amplifier flip-flop and calibration principle

The main idea behind conversion is inserting a known clock edge to the delay line (in this case CKADC) and generating OP and ON transitions with delays proportional to VP and VN voltages respectively. Comparing the arrival time of OP and ON signals we generate a sign bit. To resolve the other 4 bits, the Vernier TDC measures the time difference between OP and ON transitions. The START signal of the TDC is the one that is generated faster at the output of VCDL and the STOP signal is the slower one which corresponds to the larger input. START signal can be the OR function of OP and ON and STOP signal can be the AND function of OP and ON. In order to have the delay range as wide as possible, we delay the clock in the VCDLs through some buffers to pre-charge the stages sequentially and give more time to the slower signal before it gets destroyed in pre-charging process. In the worst case, the STOP signal can be very short and cannot be properly sampled by a flip-flop at the output of the TDC. The purpose of the two flip-flops at the output of OR and AND gates is to sample the START/STOP edges. In order to relax timing issues we use two TDCs that toggle between the sampling flip-flops and keep their outputs for one more cycle. This comes at the expense of two clock period latency to have the output ready. The outputs of the two TDCs are latched and MUX-ed to the encoder. The SIGN bit decides if a particular output has to be inverted or not in order to get a sign and magnitude binary output. The TDC is shown in Fig. 9.

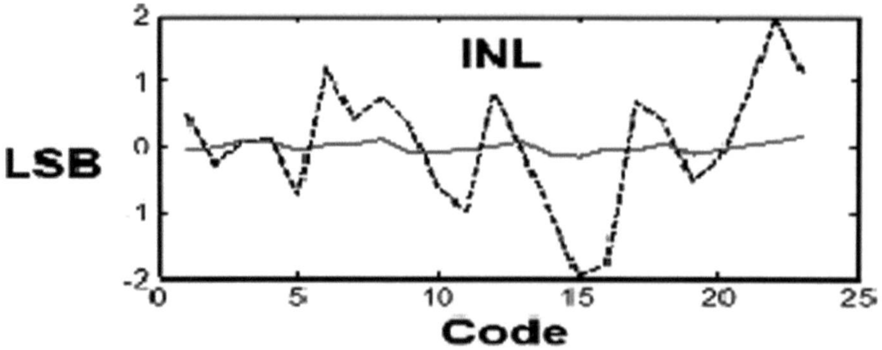

Fig. 10. Measured INL of the TADC

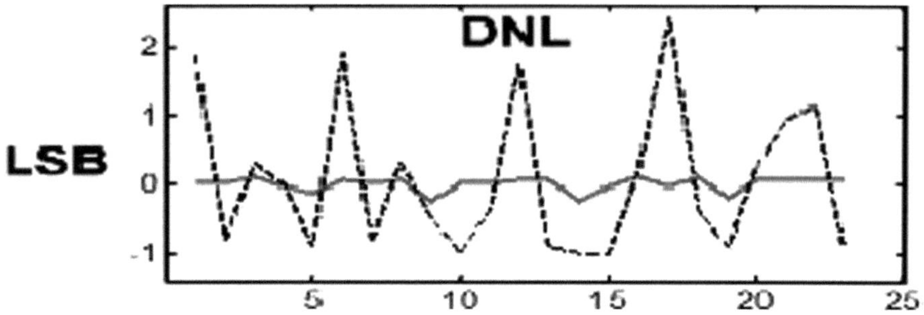

Fig. 11. Measured DNL of the TADC before (black) and after calibration (red) (Color figure online)

The faster signal, START, is inverted through an edge aligner and the two polarities go through a chain of inverters.

The inverter delay defines the resolution of TDC. The START signal and its opposite polarity travel through the inverters and the slower signal STOP samples the delayed signals. To keep the delay between START and STOP the same the STOP signal goes through the same edge aligner.

Back-to-back inverters are used for de-skewing the outputs of inverters in the delay line. They add extra delay to inverter delays but they control the falling and rising edge skew in case of process matching. The delay line inverters are tuned through the supply voltage. The sense-amplifier flip-flops Fig. 9 are based on SR flip-flops clocked with the delayed version of the main clock to reduce the meta-stability window. For calibration, the VCDLs have an extra delay cell Dcal with their own supply. The input of the S/H has maximum differential imbalance and the outputs of the extra delay cells experience a short ONcal pulse (tn = tn, min) and a long OPcal pulse (tp = tp, max). The phase of a known clock signal (fCLK = 2xfs) is adjusted to align its rising edge on the ONcal edge. We change then VBP of the VCDL to align the OPcal transition on the second clock rising edge. With differential delay calibrated we change the TDC supply to get code

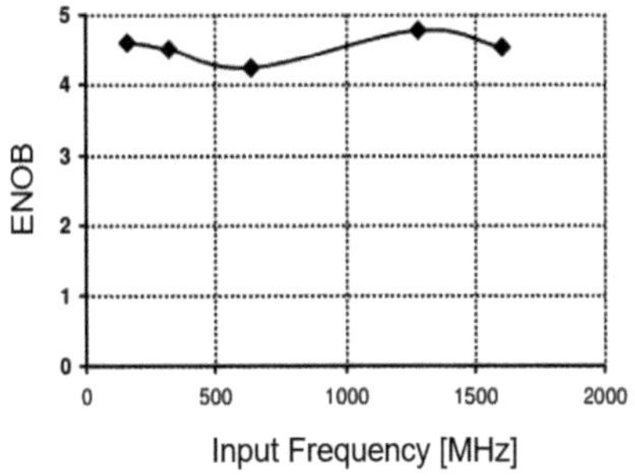

Fig. 12. ENOB variation with frequency

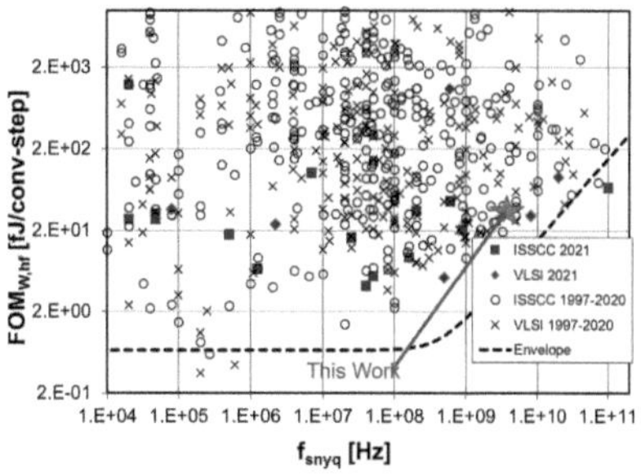

Fig. 13. Benchmarking based on Walden FOM from [15]

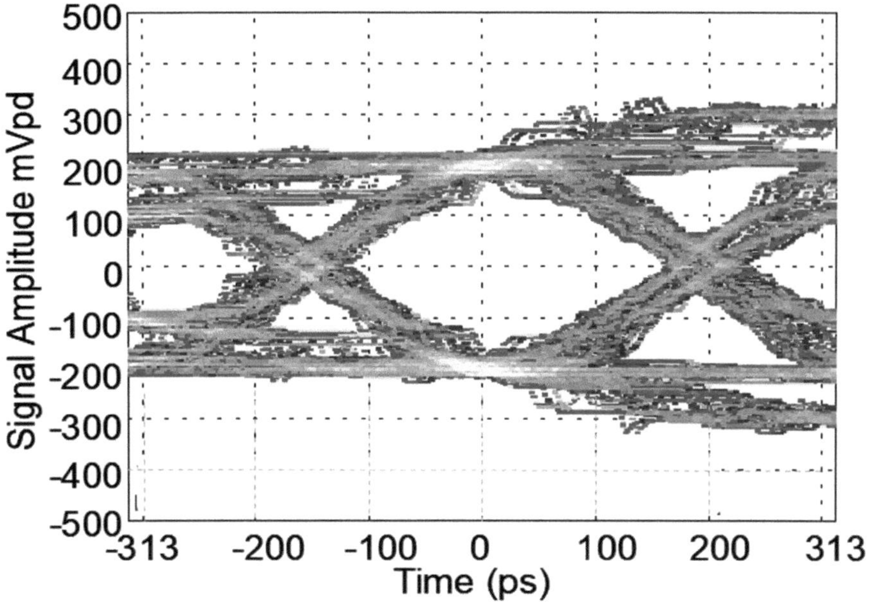

Fig. 14. Measured eye diagram for a 3.2Gs/s data

"15" at the encoder output. The TDC described above, along with a serial interface to support control functions, were implemented in a GF 45 nm SOI CMOS process. Figures 10 and 11 shows the measured DNL and INL before and after calibration and Fig. 12 show the ENOB of about 4.5 across the frequency of interest.

The Walden FOM [14] for the TADC is 109 fJ/conversion Fig. 13. For linearity measurements, we apply two input tones at 320 MHz and 400 MHz. For an input power of −16.98 dBm, the measured IIP3 is $\text{IIP3} = -16.98 + 28/2 = -2.9\,\text{dBm}$. The output spectrum is shown in Fig. 15 and the measured eye dia-

Table 1. Performance Summary and Comparison with the State of the Art

Parameter	This work	[15]	[2]	[6]	[5]	[9]
Year	2023	VLSI 2013	JSSC 2010	VLSI 2012	JSSC 2011	VLSI 2015
Process Technology	45 nm PD-SOI	32 nm SOI	40 nm CMOS	40 nm CMOS	65 nm CMOS	65 nm CMOS
Architecture	Time Domain	Flash	Pipelined	Flash	Flash/Interleaved	Interleaved
Sample Frequency	3.2 GS/s	5 GS/s	2.2 GS/s	3 GS/s	16 GS/s	25 GS/s
ENOB	4.9	6	6	6	4.9	4.62
DNL	0.1 LSB	0.52 LSB	0.8 LSB	N/A	<0.5 LSB	0.35 LSB
INL	0.1 LSB	0.37 LSB	0.8 LSB	0.35 LSB	<0.5 LSB	0.39 LSB
Power Consumption	16.2 mW	8.5 mW	2.6 mW	11 mW	435 mW	88 mW
Chip Area	0.049 mm^2	0.03 mm^2	0.03 mm^2	0.021 mm^2	1.42 mm^2	0.24 mm^2
FOM	109 fJ/Conversion	59.4 fJ/Conversion	40 fJ/Conversion	109 fJ/Conversion	91 fJ/Conversion	143 fJ/Conversion

gram of an equalized lossy backplane interconnect (with FFE and DFE 5) is shown in Fig. 14. To put things in perspective, Table 1 presents a benchmark with other comparable A/D converters from literature.

The A/D converter from [2] has a FOM of 59.4 fJ/Conversion. Our design has a better DNL and INL after calibration. The A/D converter from [2] has a FOM of 40 fJ/Conversion but the DNL and INL are 0.8 LSB. The A/D from [9] has a FOM of 109 fJ/Conversion but no DNL is reported. The reference [6] reports a FOM of 910 fJ/ Conversion. The A/D from [9] reports a FOM of 143 fJ/Conversion.

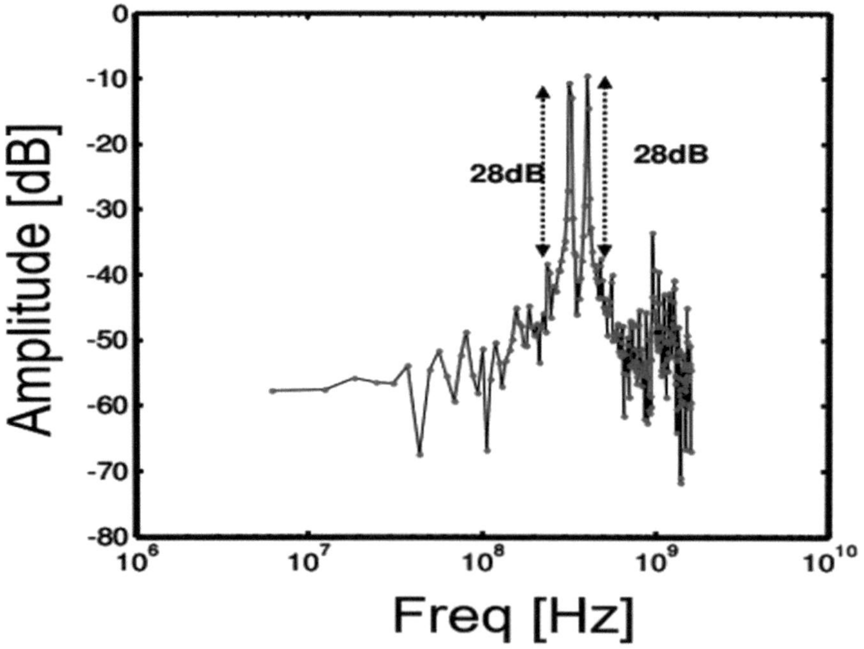

Fig. 15. Signal Amplitude

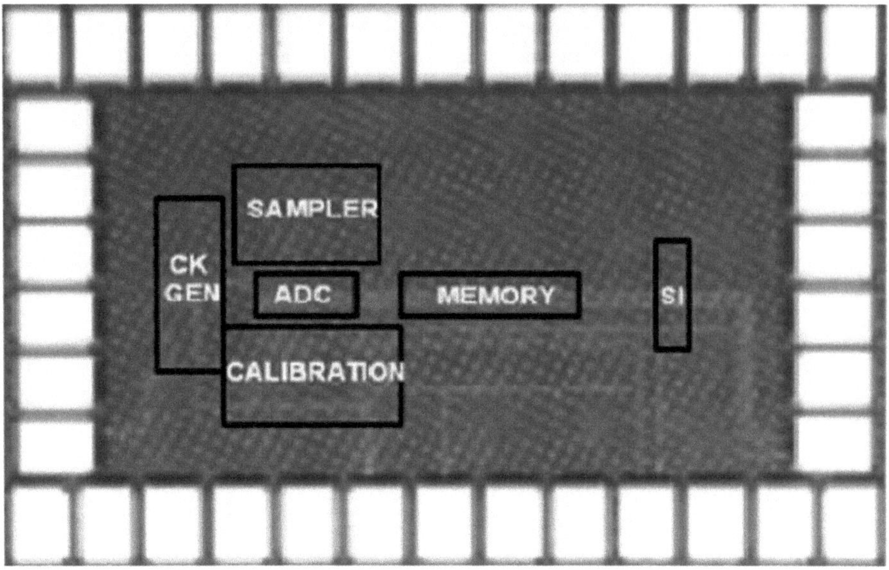

Fig. 16. Chip Micrograph

Our design compares well with other designs from literature and has a better FOM than other designs for the same sample rate and ENOB. Signal amplitude of the data at 3.2G is shown in Fig. 15 and the chip photomicrograph is presented in Fig. 16.

References

1. Yu, J., Dai, F.F., Jaeger, R.C.: A 12-bit Vernier ring time-to-digital converter in 0.13 µm CMOS technology. IEEE J. Solid-State Circuits **45**(4), 830–842 (2010)
2. Chen, V.H.C., Pileggi, L.: An 8.5 mW 5GS/s 6b flash ADC with dynamic offset calibration in 32 nm CMOS SOI. In: Symposium on VLSI Circuits, pp. C264–C265. IEEE (2013)
3. Serunjogi, S., Sanduleanu, M.: 3.125 GS/s, 4.9 ENOB, 109 fJ/conversion time-domain ADC for backplane interconnect. In: 2023 IFIP/IEEE 31st International Conference on Very Large Scale Integration (VLSI-SoC), pp. 1–4. IEEE (2023)
4. Serunjogi, S., Ademola, M., Cracan, D., Sanduleanu, M.: 2.5 GS/s, 8–9 ENOB, 8–12.7 fJ, conversion differential T, H amplifier for gigabit radio. In: IEEE International Symposium on Circuits and Systems (ISCAS), pp. 1–5. IEEE (2019)
5. Shu, Y.S.: A 6b 3GS/s 11 mW fully dynamic flash ADC in 40 nm CMOS with reduced number of comparators. In: Symposium on VLSI Circuits (VLSIC), pp. 26–27. IEEE (2012)
6. Huang, C.C., Wang, C.Y., Wu, J.T.: A CMOS 6-bit 16-GS/s time-interleaved ADC using digital background calibration techniques. IEEE J. Solid-State Circuits **46**(4), 848–858 (2011)

7. Straayer, M., et al.: 27.5 A 4GS/s time-interleaved RF ADC in 65 nm CMOS with 4GHz input bandwidth. In: IEEE International Solid-State Circuits Conference (ISSCC), pp. 464–465. IEEE (2016)
8. Yueksel, H., et al.: A 3.6 pJ/b 56Gb/s 4-PAM receiver with 6-Bit TI-SAR ADC and quarter-rate speculative 2-tap DFE in 32 nm CMOS. In: ESSCIRC Conference 2015-41st European Solid-State Circuits Conference (ESSCIRC), pp. 148–151. IEEE (2015)
9. Cai, S., Tabasy, E.Z., Shafik, A., Kiran, S., Hoyos, S., Palermo, S.: A 25GS/s 6b TI binary search ADC with soft-decision selection in 65 nm CMOS. In: Symposium on VLSI Circuits (VLSI Circuits), pp. C158–C159. IEEE (2015)
10. Chen, M.S.W., Su, D., Mehta, S.: A calibration-free 800 MHz fractional-N digital PLL with embedded TDC. IEEE J. Solid-State Circuits **45**(12), 2819–2827 (2010)
11. Chung, H., Ishikuro, H., Kuroda, T.: A 10-bit 80-MS/s decision-select successive approximation TDC in 65-nm CMOS. IEEE J. Solid-State Circuits **47**(5), 1232–1241 (2012)
12. El-Halwagy, W., Mousavi, P., Hossain, M.: A 79 dB SNDR, 10 MHz BW, 675 MS/s open-loop time-based ADC employing a 1.15 ps SAR-TDC. In: IEEE Asian Solid-State Circuits Conference (A-SSCC), pp. 321–324. IEEE (2016)
13. Bult, K., Buchwald, A.: Embedded 240-MW 10-B 50-MS/S CMOS ADC in 1-MM** 2. Comput. Standards Interfaces **2**(21), 104–105 (1999)
14. Murmann, B.: ADC performance survey 1997–2010 (2010). http://www.stanford.edu/murmann/adcsurvey.html
15. Orser, H., Gopinath, A.: A 20 GS/s 1.2 V 0.13 μm CMOS switched cascode track-and-hold amplifier. IEEE Trans. Circuits Syst. II: Express Briefs **57**(7), 512–516 (2010)

Security and Privacy

Enhancing HW-SW Confidentiality Verification for Embedded Processors with SoftFlow's Advanced Memory Range Feature

Lennart M. Reimann[1(✉)], Jonathan Wiesner[1], Karol Jaszczyk[1], Chiara Ghinami[1], Dominik Germek[2], Farhad Merchant[3], and Rainer Leupers[1]

[1] RWTH Aachen University, Aachen, Germany
{lennart.reimann,wiesner,karol,ghinami,leupers}@ice.rwth-aachen.de
[2] Corporate Research, Robert Bosch GmbH, Hildesheim, Germany
dominik.germek@de.bosch.com
[3] Newcastle University, Newcastle upon Tyne, UK
farhad.merchant@newcastle.ac.uk

Abstract. In contemporary electronic design automation (EDA), security often takes a backseat, leaving critical vulnerabilities unaddressed. This deficiency leads to the inadvertent oversight of vulnerabilities throughout the software-hardware design process. Specifically, vulnerabilities that allow leakage of sensitive data might stay unnoticed by standard testing, as the leakage itself might not result in evident functional changes. Consequently, there arises a crucial need for EDA tools that comprehensively address the confidentiality of sensitive data during the design phase. Presently, prevailing implementations tend to focus exclusively on hardware aspects or impose limitations on the expressive capacity of the security properties that require validation. Consequently, more proficient tools are required to assist in the software and hardware design. To tackle this challenge, we introduce an improved version of *SoftFlow*, an advanced analysis framework that utilizes model checking to identify software exploits in hardware leakage paths across various memory hierarchies. Based on our analysis, the leakage paths can be retained if proven not to be exploited by software. This proves beneficial in scenarios where removal would significantly impact the design's performance or functionality, or when eliminating the path is not feasible due to the chip's already completed manufacturing. A notable advancement over the original SoftFlow lies in the methodology introduced in this work, enabling the placement of sensitive information in any memory region—a capability previously constrained in SoftFlow. Furthermore, SoftFlow is now compatible with any open-source RISC-V compiler. For demonstration, we identify vulnerabilities in OpenSSL cryptographic C programs using SoftFlow, and redesign them to prevent cryptographic key leakage across RISC-V architectures.

Keywords: confidentiality · property checking · information flow analysis · risc-v

Published by Springer Nature Switzerland AG 2024
I. (Abe) M. Elfadel and L. Albasha (Eds.): VLSI-SoC 2023, IFIP AICT 680, pp. 251–272, 2024.
https://doi.org/10.1007/978-3-031-70947-0_13

1 Introduction

Malicious modifications or unintended insecure software and hardware implementations must be detected at early design stages to avoid expensive post-silicon patches. Therefore, electronic design automation (EDA) tools must consider not only performance, power, and area objectives, but also the security implications of hardware and software. Commercial approaches to running secure kernels on secured hardware have already been developed, whereby leakage paths are not considered [34]. Moreover, the academic community continues to introduce security-aware EDA tools [16].

Information flow analysis (IFA) gains approval when analyzing software or hardware for the leakage of secret data [3]. A leakage path is a signal route that carries data from a sensitive source to untrusted components (see Fig. 1). However, existing static IFA tools do not consider the software running on a processor when analyzing the information flow, thus giving *oversensitive* results. Leakage paths that might not be exploited by software are presented as dangerous. Although it is desirable to remove all leakage paths to untrusted components in hardware, it might not always be possible to do so. Sometimes the vulnerabilities are only detected after the manufacturing process, such as Spectre [18] and Meltdown [21]. Moreover, removing all leakage paths might result in the loss of functionality or performance.

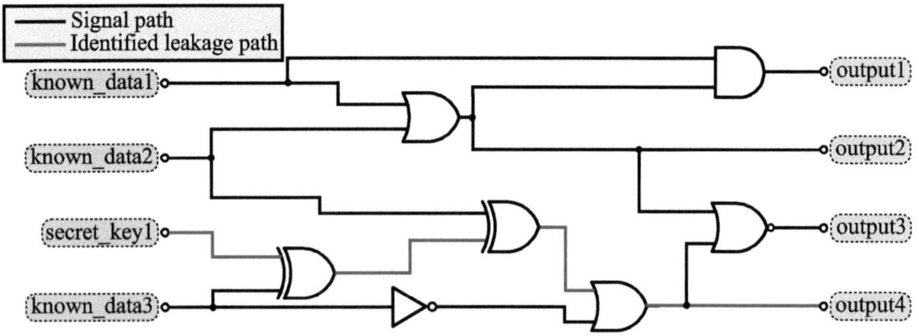

Fig. 1. A leakage path in a digital circuit, leaking a secret bit through an observable output. The grey inputs and outputs are observable by an adversary.

Fundamentally, there are two distinct flavors of information flow analysis: dynamic and static IFA. A dynamic analysis tracks the information flow within hardware for a given software running a set of test cases [31]. As only the program flow for the test cases is considered, vulnerabilities might be overlooked. Thus, static approaches that consider software *independent* of test cases yield more reliable verification results. Most state-of-the-art tools for a hardware-software co-analysis require manual translation of either software or hardware descriptions or limit the expressiveness of security properties [9,11]. Thus, a new EDA tool is required to overcome these constraints. To address this challenge, we present *SoftFlow*, a framework that allows a *hardware-software co-verification* to analyze whether determined leakage paths are activated for a given software and arbitrary input data. SoftFlow allows the designer to adapt the program and avoid leakage, or deploy software patches for manufactured chips. However, the initial implementation of SoftFlow (see [30]) was limited when it came to memory hierarchies it could evaluate. Only architectures with a dedicated memory holding the sensitive data could be analyzed. To overcome this shortcoming in [30], we developed a novel memory range feature that allows the identification of leakages for any memory hierarchy. Additionally, the novel memory range feature in SoftFlow removed the limitation of exclusively using ASIP Designer-generated processors and compilers. Previously, this restriction was due to the custom key memory requiring specific instructions integrated into the compiler. However, with the introduction of this feature, SoftFlow became compatible with other open-source compilers like Clang and GCC, expanding its versatility for hardware-software security analysis across various platforms and architectures. The contributions of this book chapter are:

1. An automated tool to convert leakage paths of a hardware description into provable hardware properties.
2. A complete framework that guarantees that determined leakage paths in hardware are not exploited by a given software.
3. Liberating SoftFlow from previous constraints, we now extend its support beyond memory hierarchies limited to a single dedicated memory for secret data.
4. An analysis of the state-of-the-art OpenSSL cryptographic algorithms to demonstrate the usability of the tool for a RISC-V architecture.
5. To provide additional insights, we incorporate a second open-source RISC-V architecture into the evaluation, demonstrating the versatility of SoftFlow.

The rest of this book chapter is organized as follows. Related work is given in Sect. 2. Section 3 provides background on the threat model, detection of leakage paths in hardware, and the property specification language used in this work. SoftFlow's functionality is elaborated in Sect. 4 and evaluated in Sect. 5. The results are discussed in Sect. 6. Finally, Sect. 7 concludes the book chapter.

2 Related Work

2.1 Security Enforcement by Property Checking

The necessity for suitable formal models to reliably verify security properties is discussed extensively in literature [12]. Several authors utilize the automatic generation of security properties to enforce information flow rules and formally prove that only desired information flow between system components is permitted [13,20]. Abstract property definitions are converted to formal rules that can be processed by model checkers to verify security features. In [19], security property definitions are used to determine if a processor architecture description represents different security modes, such as a supervisor or user mode, as desired by the designer. Properties state in which mode certain actions are permissible to be formally proven for the given hardware.

Furthermore, property checking serves as a tool to identify Trojans within hardware designs [33]. The authors of [33] assume that a Trojan remains concealed within the architecture, only activated under specific conditions or states. Typically, the Trojan resides within a conditional branch, such as an if-clause. Employing property checking techniques, the input patterns necessary to activate the potential Trojan can be identified. Subsequently, the Trojan is triggered to elaborate if any harmful actions are triggered.

Overall, the existing works *do not consider* the software running on the systems. This results in oversensitive conclusions, as secure software might protect hardware from triggering a design mistake or malicious modifications.

2.2 Software Confidentiality Verification

In addition to the tools that solely consider the hardware during the verification of security properties, a few proposals only analyze the security of the software [2,17]. Here, formal methods are used to determine the information flow within a given program to avoid a flow of data from privileged users to adversaries. However, the information flow that occurs within the hardware is not examined in the analysis as it is not modeled in software. Only the simultaneous verification of *both hardware and software* allows the user to be certain about the security features of the designed system.

2.3 Hardware-Software Co-verification

As the complete system behavior can only be modeled when considering hardware and software together, a co-verification is used frequently to enforce security properties for a given design [22]. Many tools also use code coverage plugins [4] to determine input patterns that activate code snippets that have not been activated yet during the security analysis. However, co-verification is a challenging task, as hardware and software are described in different domains. Typically, one description is either converted into the other domain, or both descriptions are converted to allow the verification of both implementations [14,23]. These methods mainly depend on model checkers that formally verify the defined properties. In [11], a manual translation of the hardware description, program, and properties into the language Gallina [35] is conducted to allow a co-verification. However, a manual translation is error-prone and could introduce vulnerabilities into the description. A model checker, similar to the one used in this work, is used in [9,24]. Additionally, [9] describes the usage of the Property Specification Language (PSL) to describe the properties that have to be proven formally, as it is done in this work. However, both proposals limit their use in the variability of the observed software and the expressiveness of the security property. Certain methodologies employ supplementary hardware to monitor information flow within a processor executing a program at runtime [5,7]. A secondary processor intervenes in program flow upon detecting specific information flow occurrences. However, if a program is predetermined during design, the inclusion of additional hardware security modules and information flow monitoring can be avoided beforehand by doing a full security analysis in advance.

With the introduction of SoftFlow, we overcome the mentioned limitations and establish a novel framework that allows an automated generation of security properties. Therefore, we enable a static security analysis of both hardware and software to *facilitate the design of secure software for insecure hardware for any memory hierarchy.*

3 Preliminaries

3.1 Threat Model

The threat model is based on the following assumptions:

- The vulnerability that exposes the secret is already present at the RTL-design stage of embedded processors.
- The adversary tries to gain information about secret signals, such as cryptographic keys.
- The complete hardware design is known to the attacker.
- The adversary can observe primary inputs and outputs of the design.
- The software cannot be replaced by the attacker.
- Arbitrary input data can be used.

3.2 Information Flow Analysis

IFA allows the static or dynamic analysis of programs and hardware descriptions to elaborate on whether unintended information flow can occur. Security labels are used to flag components as part of certain *security classes* [25]. Thus, an analysis determines whether sensitive information can be leaked to untrusted areas of the hardware. For the example in Fig. 1, it is analyzed whether the secret bit can be leaked to the observable output for all possible known input bit sequences.

State-of-the-art tools can conduct a static analysis of the Verilog hardware description to determine unwanted data leakages. QFlow [27–29] and QIF-Verilog [10] use quantitative information flow [1] to classify data leakages as negligible or a threat. A *scopechain* is provided that allows identifying the path within the hardware description. SoftFlow utilizes QFlow to gather the most suspicious leakage path in a system.

3.3 Property Specification Language (PSL)

PSL [8,15] is compatible with Verilog hardware descriptions and allows the modeling of the temporal behavior of digital architectures. A simple example is a condition for a multiplexer: ($control\_signal == 0x20$). The Boolean expression

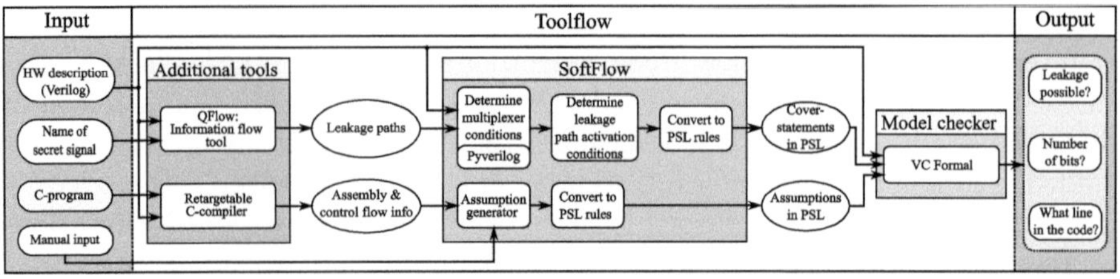

Fig. 2. Block diagram illustrating *SoftFlow's* tool flow.

enables the model checker to determine when information is forwarded. Moreover, Sequential Extended Regular Expressions (SERE) can model the temporal dependencies. *CONCAT*, *FUSE*, and *REPETITION_INF* of the SERE repertoire are used in this work, as explained in Table 1. The operators can be combined into sequences, allowing the modeling of a leakage path. The verification layer uses commands like `cover` and `assume`. `assume` indicates that the included property is expected to hold, thus restricting the state-space of the evaluated architecture for the desired property verification. However, the user must verify the assumptions to avoid introducing insecurities into the process. `cover`-statements can be used to determine whether a property is true for at least one state in the state-space using a model checker. If the property is proven to be uncoverable, the leakage cannot occur for the assumptions. SoftFlow automatically generates the assumptions and properties (see Fig. 2).

4 SoftFlow

For the identification of the leakage paths, SoftFlow [30] uses QFlow, due to its capability to analyze the information flow bitwise [28]. QFlow extracts the leakage paths from the sensitive source to the possibly harmful target. The security properties are generated by SoftFlow (see Fig. 2), as explained below. Additionally, model-checking requires information about the software to constrain the model, reducing the number of false positives. Below, we clarify how the PSL rules are generated, verified and evaluated for multiple programs.

Table 1. Sequential Extended Regular Expression (SERE) operators [6] used in this work.

Name	PSL Usage	Verilog Example	Interpretation
CONCAT	A;B	$(cntrl\_sig1 == 0x20); (cntrl\_sig2 == 0x11)$	Two cycles exist, so that first condition A is true, followed by the cycle in which B is true
FUSE	A:B	$(cntrl\_sig1 == 0x20) : (cntrl\_sig2 == 0x11)$	A cycle exists in that both Boolean expressions A and B are true
REPETITION_INF	A[*]	$(cntrl\_sig1 == 0x20)[*]$	The Boolean expression is true in every cycle

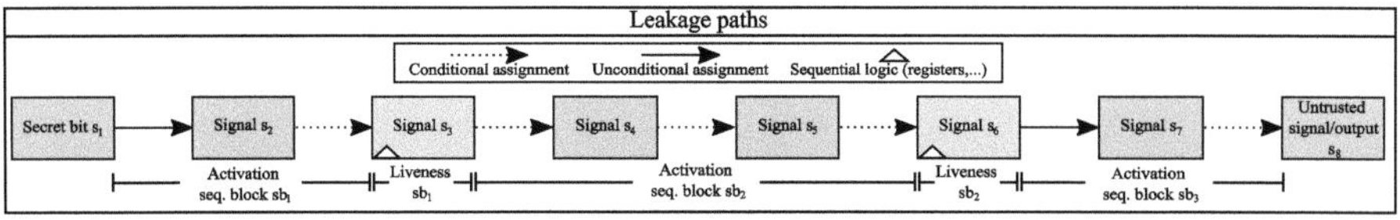

Fig. 3. Separating the leakage paths into blocks to allow a suitable environment for property generation. The arrows illustrate signal assignments in which dotted arrows describe conditional assignments.

4.1 Property Generation

This subsection describes a tool that processes the leakage paths, given by a static quantitative IFA, and the hardware description to generate properties using PSL.

Combinational: First, a combinational circuit is considered. In this case, a leakage path can consist of combinational operations and signal assignments (see Fig. 1). These assignment types can be divided into two classes: conditional and unconditional. Unconditional assignments happen independently of any control signals, while conditional assignments depend on a multiplexer's control signal. When checking whether a leak can occur, one needs to analyze whether all conditional assignments are active *at the same time.* Hereafter, *active-function A* describes whether an information flow between two signals is active.

Sequential Blocks: Due to the timing dependency, additional system behavior needs to be considered for sequential circuits. Figure 3 illustrates a single leakage path. The path leads from a trusted signal, storing a secret bit, to an untrusted signal. Due to the timing behavior of sequential logic within this path, each leakage path needs to be separated into multiple blocks. Assignments between non-sequential signals of the same block must occur in a single cycle. But the data can live for several cycles in sequential signals, such as registers, before moving on. Separating the leakage paths into blocks that always end with a sequential signal allows for a differentiation of this behavior. The separation into the sequential blocks (*sb*) is depicted in Fig. 3. Additionally, one must consider that the secret data is not overwritten within the sequential logic before forwarding it to the next *sb*.

Only conditional assignments influence the property generation. For the first sequential block in Fig. 3, only the second assignment holds a condition. Hence, the *block active-function* BA for this sequential block sb_1 is true if the conditions for the assignment are true in a single cycle.

Leakage Path Activation:
First, the sequential logic within the leakage path is identified. This is done to form the sequential blocks. The secret datum can only pass a single sequential block in each cycle. For leakage to occur, the second sequential block needs to

be activated after the previous one (see Fig. 3). Additionally, the two blocks do not have to be activated in consecutive cycles as long as the information in the previous sequential logic stays alive and is not overwritten until it passes the next sequential block, which is described with the *alive-function* L. Each sequential block results in a BA and L function, except for the last one. The datum in the last signal does not have to live longer than a cycle for it to be leaked, as the last signal represents the untrusted component. In the example (see Fig. 3), two alive-functions and three block active-functions are required to describe the activation of the path.

Active and Alive-Function Collection:
First of all, the Verilog description is parsed to form a tree structure that can be iterated over. Afterward, the algorithm iterates over the leakage paths to determine the individual activation conditions. The conditions for a single signal assignment are connected via an OR-operator as only a single true activation condition can lead to leakage. The resulting set of active-functions are temporally stored in a file to be processed to PSL. The alive-function L is determined similarly to the active-function. The alive-function returns 'true' if the current value in a sequential logic is not overwritten for a fixed amount of cycles. An empty signal assignment describes a value that is not overwritten. The activation condition from the empty node to the destination node is calculated and stored as the alive function.

Specifying SoftFlow's PSL Sequences:
The collected active-functions and alive functions need to be translated to PSL to enable model-checking. For the example in Fig. 3, the PSL sequence is shown in Eq. 1, with AS and LS describing the activation and liveness sequences.

$$\begin{aligned}
&\underbrace{\underbrace{\textbf{active}(s_2,\, s_3)}_{AS} \;;\; \underbrace{\textbf{alive}(s_3)[*]}_{LS}}_{sb_1} \;; \\
&\underbrace{\underbrace{\textbf{active}(s_3,\, s_4) : \textbf{active}(s_4,\, s_5) : \textbf{active}(s_5,\, s_6)}_{AS} \;;\; \underbrace{\textbf{alive}(s_6)[*]}_{LS}}_{sb_2} \;; \\
&\underbrace{\underbrace{\textbf{active}(s_7,\, s_8)}_{AS}}_{sb_3}
\end{aligned} \tag{1}$$

The sequence is extended with the `cover` command, forming the *cover rules*. If the model checker can cover this path, the leakage can occur for the given assumptions. The individual Boolean activation conditions are connected using the $FUSE$ operator (see Table 1), as the conditions must be true in the same cycle. After the activation conditions are converted, the liveness condition for

```
...
#define PUTU32(p,v) ((p)[0] = (u8)((v) >> 24), (p)[1] = (u8)((
    v) >> 16), (p)[2] = (u8)((v) >>  8), (p)[3] = (u8)(v))

int8_t cam_key_conf[16] =
    {0,-5,16,3,22,-101,0,3,-37,-9,110,1,72,3,-44,15};

/* S-box data */
#define SBOX1_1110 Camellia_SBOX[0]
#define SBOX4_4404 Camellia_SBOX[1]
...
```

Listing 1.1. The sensitive Camellia encryption key is identified in the source code by appending a "_conf" suffix to the corresponding variable.

the sequential logic is required. The returned liveness condition is converted to a PSL expression using the *REPETITION_INF* operator (see Table 1). The activation conditions and the alive-functions are combined into the full sequence for a single *sb* using *CONCAT* (see Table 1). *Uncoverable properties state that the leakage path cannot be taken.*

Incorporating the Memory Range Feature:
In the previous iteration, SoftFlow necessitated a processor equipped with a specialized "key memory" designated for storing confidential information. This design was premised on the belief that any activation of the signal path between the designated memory and an untrusted target would lead to an exposure of sensitive data. The dedicated memory is hardwired to the processor using fixed registers for the address and data. For this purpose, Synopsys ASIP Designer [32] was needed to allow the customization of the processor's memory structure. Furthermore, ASIP Designer enables an automatic retargeting of the compiler. This limitation disallowed the evaluation of any open-source processor without such a dedicated "key memory".

In order to obviate the need for such a dedicated key memory, SoftFlow was extended to allow differentiating between public and secret memory ranges. The revised approach permits the inclusion of secrets within any range of a conventional data memory. The underlying assumption now states that the data memory itself serves as the potential source of sensitive data using the identified leakage paths. In the C code describing the user's software, the confidential data ranges are discerned by variables suffixed with "_conf", as illustrated in Listing 1.1.

The incorporation of the "_conf" suffix enables SoftFlow to identify the variables within the memory map of the compiled program, an optional file produced by the compiler. SoftFlow parses this memory map, discerning the address range dedicated to storing sensitive data. Furthermore, users have the flexibility to designate untrusted or public memory ranges as inputs. In the absence of specified untrusted ranges, any memory ranges not designated for storing sensitive data are automatically labeled as untrusted. For the example of cryptographic algorithms, the variables holding the cryptographic keys are labeled using the suffix.

The identified memory ranges play a pivotal role in generating supplementary properties for the leakage paths, thereby overcoming the limitations of the initial SoftFlow version that mandated a dedicated memory for storing secrets. Two additional properties are generated and appended to the PSL sequence for every leakage path.

For leaking data, first, the secret datum needs to be loaded from the data memory. The generated property comprises two signals: the address bus and the Boolean signal indicating the load request.

$$conf\_load = (\text{address bus in conf. range}) \;\&\; (\text{load request}) \tag{2}$$

Sensitive loads are identified when the address bus holds a value within the confidential address range and the load request signal is True simultaneously. Additionally, at the end of the leakage paths identified with QFlow, data leakage occurs if the secret datum is written to an untrusted memory range. As mentioned before, untrusted memory ranges are either given by the user or identified automatically by labeling all memory ranges not holding the confidential variable as untrustworthy.

$$public\_store = (\text{address bus not in conf. range}) \;\&\; (\text{store request}) \tag{3}$$

As shown in Eq. 3, an untrustworthy store is a store request outside of the confidential range.

After the two properties are generated, they need to be combined with the PSL sequence (Eq. 1) generated by SoftFlow. The property describing the trustworthy load is prepended, while the property for the untrustworthy store is appended, as illustrated in Eq. 4.

$$conf\_load(\text{data bus}); path\_active(s1; s8) : public\_store(\text{data bus}) \tag{4}$$

The $path\_active(s1; s8)$ term represents the PSL sequence for the signal path generated beforehand and illustrated in Eq. 1.

The entire process of incorporating the novel memory range feature to overcome SoftFlow's limitation is depicted in Algorithm 1.

For all leakage paths identified by QFlow a PSL sequence was generated (*PslList*). The memory ranges (*ConfMemRanges*) are used to generate the Load and Store Properties, which are added to every generated PSL sequence (*pslSeq*) in the list. Both properties are either prepended or appended using the *CONCAT* operator presented in Tab. 1. Once all PSL sequences have been adapted they allow an identification of leakages beyond processors limited in their memory hierarchy.

Algorithm 1: Adding the memory range properties to the PSL sequences of each leakage path identified by QFlow.

Input: list of PSL rules **PslList**, confidential memory ranges **ConfMemRanges**

Output: PSL sequences including the confidential memory accesses **PslMemList**

```
begin
    PslMemList ← empty list
    for pslSeq in PslList do
        newMemRangeProp ← empty property
        confLoadProp ← generateLoadProperty(ConfMemRanges)
        newMemRangeProp ← combine(confLoadProp, pslSeq)
        confStoreProp ← generateStoreProperty(ConfMemRanges)
        newMemRangeProp ← combine(newMemRangeProp,
        confStoreProp)
        append newMemRangeProp to PslMemList
    end
    return PslMemList
end
```

Supported Compilers:
Initially, SoftFlow solely supported the ASIP designer compiler, a necessity due to the custom key memory requiring specialized instructions that must be integrated into the compiler. However, with the removal of this memory limitation, the tool now accommodates other open-source compilers like Clang and GCC. It is crucial to note that these new compilers generate output files in different formats, necessitating adaptations to SoftFlow. For instance, while the AD compiler produces relative jump addresses, GCC generates absolute ones, highlighting the need for exemplary adjustments to ensure compatibility.

4.2 Property Verification

By employing model-checking, one can establish a level of *certainty* regarding the reliability of the verification results. The individual cover rules allow an independent evaluation for every leakage path, enabling the model checker to work in parallel for these properties. The program memory address is used to identify the instruction and the related C code line.

SoftFlow's generated PSL properties do not consider the compiled program for the analyzed processor. As we would like to elaborate on the security of a given C program and an insecure hardware implementation, the hardware model for the model-checking needs to be constrained before running the verification. This is done to reduce the false positives, which describe a leakage of secret data for programs that would not be implemented. Those constraints are implemented using `assume`. Since the model permits the data memory to contain any information, it is necessary to contemplate all conceivable routes within a pro-

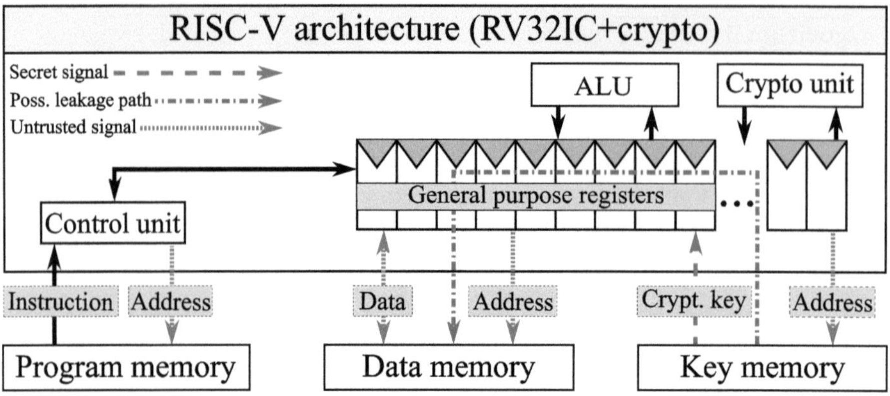

Fig. 4. Abstract block diagram of the customized RISC-V architecture implementing a dedicated memory for holding the secrets and a cryptographic computation unit.

gram. Conditional branches depend mostly on data in the data memory. Thus, all possible conditional jumps need to be considered. The user can choose from the following derived assumptions (Ⓐ to Ⓕ) to restrict the program flow.

Ⓐ *No Illegal Instructions:* A assumption is made which claims that the read port of the program memory can never hold the value of prohibited instructions.

Ⓑ *Only Used Instructions:* The formal model can be further constrained by analyzing the compiled machine-code statically. An assumption can be generated that further constrains the model by stating that only instructions present in this compiled program can be read from the program memory. The order is not yet considered.

Ⓒ *Replacing the Program Memory:* To avoid modeling an entire program memory, a lookup table is used instead, which also enables consideration of the order of instructions. Furthermore, since return addresses of function calls are stored on the stack, it is possible for a return to transpire to any point within the program.

Ⓓ *Only Legal Return Addresses:* The remaining three assumptions are generated using compiler information. The assumption is used to remove undefined return addresses, which results in arbitrary program flows for the verification.

Ⓔ *Only Correct Hardware Jumps:* Compiler information is processed to allow only valid start and return addresses for hardware loops during the evaluation.

Ⓕ *Call-Return Matching:* When a function is invoked from several locations, it is essential to account for both return addresses. Confirming a legitimate correlation between a call and its corresponding return is only achievable during runtime. Nonetheless, if an authentic hardware call-stack is utilized to store the return addresses, it can already be taken into consideration during the verification process.

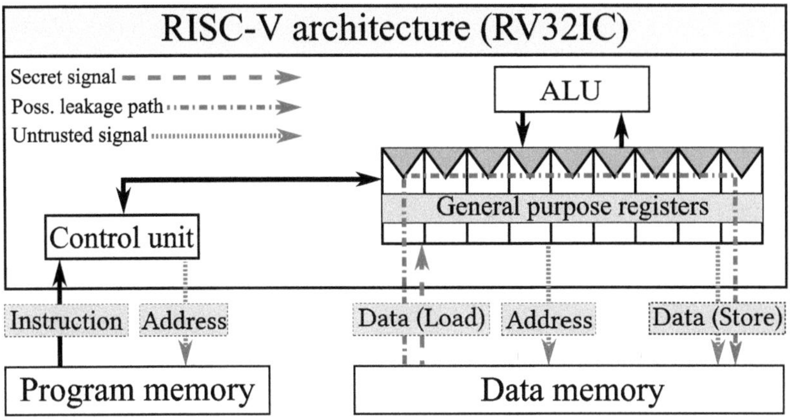

Fig. 5. Abstract block diagram of a RISC-V 32-bit processor using a program memory and a data memory holding sensitive and public data.

5 Evaluation

The evaluation is conducted for two RISC-V Verilog descriptions and two compilers. The first processor incorporates a cryptographic computation unit and a dedicated "key memory". ASIP Designer is used to generate a compiler and a Verilog description. The processor uses the RV32IC instruction set and the block diagram illustrating the architecture is shown in Fig. 4. The data input from the key memory is labeled *sensitive* in order for QFlow to yield the most suspicious leakage paths from the signal to all output ports of the design, including the memories' data and address ports.

Additionally, a second RISC-V processor is analyzed that is implemented similarly to the open-source processors (see Fig. 5). No cryptographic customization and no "key memory" are implemented. Here the leakage paths identified by QFlow lead from the load ports of the data memory, through the general-purpose registers to the store ports of the same memory. Now, SoftFlow's novel memory range feature can be used to identify between leakages of sensitive data to public memory ranges and a write-back of the sensitive data to a trusted range.

The analysis is performed for several cryptographic algorithms from OpenSSL [26]: ChaCha20, AES-256, Camelia, Aria, and SHA-256. SoftFlow is evaluated for different assumptions to elaborate on their efficiency and security.

5.1 Verification Cases

The used assumptions are listed behind each mode.

<u>NONE:</u> No assumptions are added to the model checker. The verification tool works solely with the properties generated from our property generator for the leakage paths.

LEGAL Ⓐ: The loading port of the program memory is restricted, disallowing all illegal instructions to be read.

USED Ⓐ & Ⓑ: The data port of the program memory is restricted using an `assume` statement that allows only instructions present in a compiled machine-code to be read.

JUMPS Ⓐ to Ⓔ: In this mode, only valid return addresses can be used for a return command and hardware loops, allowing a more realistic program flow.

STACK Ⓐ to Ⓕ: A hardware stack allowing the return-call matching is added as supplemental Verilog code.

FULL: First, the assumptions for USED are utilized. If the property for this path cannot be proven to be uncoverable, all verification cases are tried until the model checker is successful. Considering the valid states S of a processor model, the valid states for STACK are present in USED, resulting in:

$$S_{\text{STACK}} \subseteq S_{\text{JUMPS}} \subseteq S_{\text{USED}} \subseteq S_{\text{LEGAL}} \subseteq S_{\text{NONE}}$$

The inclusiveness of the more restrictive verification cases further reduces the state space that has to be analyzed. The non-activation of leakage paths can already be proven for some of the given paths with an extensive set of valid processor states. However, more restrictions commonly lead to higher runtimes.

5.2 Results: Initial Configuration

First, an evaluation is conducted for the processor implementing a "key memory" (see Fig. 4). The memory range feature is elaborated on the unmodified RISC-V architecture (see Fig. 5) in a later section.

Coverages:
The verification modes are applied to the five cryptographic algorithms for the RISC-V.

Without Software: The assumptions of the modes NONE and LEGAL are applied to the verification model. These two modes are independent of the actual software running. QFlow yields **3776** leakage paths that need to be elaborated for the given architecture. Leakage paths are **uncoverable** if the leakage cannot occur for the given assumptions. The paths that can be activated are labeled **covered**. Both, the LEGAL and NONE modes yield **857** uncoverable paths, which indicates that the processor only accepts legal instructions and that the 857 paths are false positives from QFlow. *With SoftFlow, the false positives are removed entirely!*

With OpenSSL Cryptographic Algorithms: Next, the capabilities of SoftFlow are elaborated for the different OpenSSL algorithms for the remaining verification modes. An example of how the applications are modified for the architecture is shown in Fig. 6b. The key can be accessed with a pointer to the key memory KM.

```
.
ldk  x7,  1(x6!)
addi x10, x13, 40
sw   x13, 0(x2)
li   x6,  1
sw   x7,  4(x13!)
mv   x14, x7
ldk  x7,  1(x6!)
sw   x7,  4(x13!)
mv   x15, x7
ldk  x7,  1(x6!)
sw   x7,  4(x13!)
sw   x7,  4(x2)
```

(a) Assembly program

```
int chess_storage(KM:0) km[4];
int Camellia_Ekeygen(int keyBitLength
    ,
                     KEY_TABLE_TYPE k)
{
    register u32 s0, s1, s2, s3;

    k[0] = s0 = km[0];
    k[1] = s1 = km[1];
    k[2] = s2 = km[2];
    k[3] = s3 = km[3];
    .
    s0 ^= k[0], s1 ^= k[1],\
```

(b) C program

Fig. 6. A naive implementation of Camellia: The dashed line symbolizes the reported instructions activating the leakage path. The corresponding C-code is marked with an arrow.

Table 2 illustrates the results of the elaboration for the modes STACK, JUMPS, and USED. As one can see, the number of uncoverable paths increases for all applications when more restrictive assumptions are used.

Table 2. Summarized metrics for the five applications grouped by verification case.

	Application	Aria	ChaCha20	Camellia	AES	SHA
	Instr. count	2112	1347	1973	1409	649
	Call depth	4	4	4	6	5
USED	Covered	65	74	58	58	48
	Uncoverable	3711	3702	3718	3718	3728
JUMPS	Covered	32	32	32	32	32
	Uncoverable	3744	3744	3744	3744	3744
STACK	Covered	32	32	32	32	32
	Uncoverable	3744	3744	3744	3744	3744

No difference in the results between the modes STACK and JUMPS can be observed.

The call tree depths are limited for all five applications, which is required if the STACK mode is used. Otherwise, the hardware stack would have to be of unlimited size. Thirty-two leakage paths are still covered for the design and applications. The cause for this leakage detection can be seen in Fig. 6 for the application Camellia.

The remaining exemplary elaborations are only presented for Camellia. Final results are presented for all applications. The assembly code in Fig. 6a shows that the compiler loads the key values from the dedicated key memory (*ldk*, load key) and stores them in the untrusted data memory (*sw*, store word) for the array *k*. The programmer can avoid the usage of the leakage path by modifying the C program. Listing 1.2 shows the replacement of the variable *k* with the pointer *km*, so that the values are not automatically stored in the untrusted data memory. Additionally, the pointer is marked as *volatile* (Listing 1.3), instructing the compiler not to optimize any data movements for KM's data. Table 3 depicts the outcomes of SoftFlow subsequent to this modification. The leakage paths are not activated anymore except for the Aria application.

For Aria, the compiler places the key in a register that is directly connected to the address port of the key memory, which is marked as untrusted. Forcing the compiler to pick a different register can also avoid this leakage. However, the limited intrusion into the compiler does not allow this change. The final evaluation shows an example of finding software Trojans inside the program. In the four applications that achieved 100% avoidance of leakage, a software Trojan is implemented. An example Trojan for the Camellia application can be seen in Listing 1.4. For a particular input value stored in the data memory, the keys are written to the untrusted memory.

```
    s0 ^= km[0], s1 ^= km[1],\
    s2 ^= km[2], s3 ^= km[3];
```

Listing 1.2. Replacing k with km in the application camellia

```
volatile int chess_storage(KM:0) km[4];
```

Listing 1.3. Declaring km as **volatile**

```
if (input[0] == 0x4d2)
{
  u32* leakage = (u32*) malloc(sizeof(u32)*8);
  for (int j=0; j<8; j++) leakage[j] = km[j];
}
```

Listing 1.4. The malicious lines implementing a simple Trojan in the application Camellia.

The results for the evaluations of the FULL mode illustrate *that all Trojans that use the leakage paths are detected despite their difference in the trigger*, as shown in Table 4. The value of the trigger does not play a role in the detection, as the data coming from the untrusted data memory is assumed to be of any possible value.

Runtime. For the unmodified applications (e.g., Fig. 6b) that still carry 32 covered paths, the verification is conducted by using the available verification

Table 3. Metrics of the modified applications.

	Application	Aria	ChaCha20	Camellia	AES	SHA
FULL	covered	473	0	0	0	0
	uncoverable	3303	3776	3776	3776	3776
	time	16016	16780	3213	1337	4432

Table 4. Verification of the modified applications with embedded Trojans.

	Application	ChaCha20	Camellia	AES	SHA
FULL	covered	32	32	32	32
	uncoverable	3744	3744	3744	3744
	time	26045	2127	1386	1321
	trigger (hex)	12345678	4d2	fedcba	12ef34dc

modes. LEGAL is not presented here, as it yielded the same verification results as NONE. As shown in Fig. 7, the lowest runtimes are given by the verification modes that restrict the hardware model the least. However, some leakage paths could not be marked as **uncoverable** for the less restrictive assumptions (see Table 2).

The runtime increases drastically for all applications at JUMPS. Moreover, as expected, the lowest runtime can be achieved using the verification mode FULL. The overall runtime is optimized, while yielding a precise result for all applications. As the verification of the properties for every leakage path can be parallelized, depending on the available resources of the designer, the runtimes can be drastically reduced. Figure 8 illustrates how successful the different verification modes are in their task. It can be observed that most leakage paths can be flagged as uncoverable by assuming that only the instructions given in a program will be used.

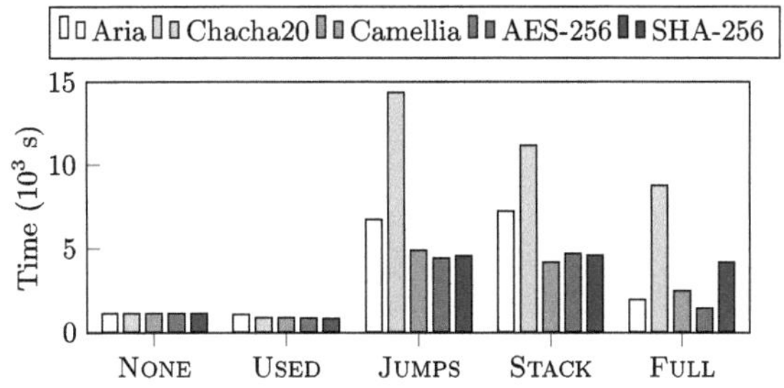

Fig. 7. The summarized runtime of the verification procedure for the different verification modes and applications.

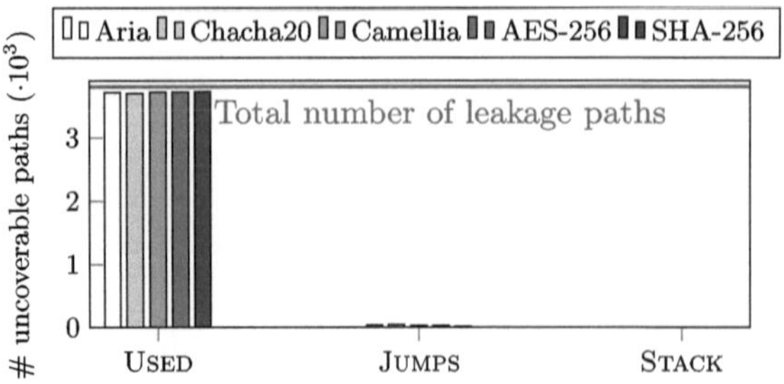

Fig. 8. A histogram showing what modes are mostly successful when verifying the model for different applications.

The higher number of cases verified using USED explains the reduced runtime of the FULL-mode in Fig. 7.

5.3 Results: Memory Range Feature

Below, we present a comprehensive evaluation of the memory range feature for the second RISC-V (see Fig. 5), using the Camellia application as a benchmark.

Leakage Path Generation: In our analysis, the load port is designated as "secret" for QFlow as illustrated in Fig. 5. The identified leakage path traverses through register x7, extending from the load port to the store port:

$$\text{Data Load Port} \longrightarrow \text{Register x7} \longrightarrow \text{Data Store Port}$$

Notably, our methodology only identifies the most probable path, hence solely recognizing paths through register x7. Consequently, any potential data leakage through other registers remains undetected by this analysis.

Memory Range Analysis of Camellia: The memory range feature is evaluated using the Camellia application. In the previous evaluation the C code snippet causing a leakage was identified and is shown in Fig. 9b. Sensitive data from the variable km, which is placed in the confidential memory region is moved to the variable k in the public memory space. The resulting assembly code is presented in Fig. 9a.

However, the verification tool determined the leakage property to be uncoverable across the full spectrum of assumptions. To comprehend why the verification tool fails to identify any cover for the given scenario, an examination of the data path in the assembly code is critical. Firstly, each leakage includes loading from the confidential range utilizing Register x15. This configuration hinders the detection of any leakage based on the path through x7, identified by QFlow. Additionally, the data is not retained in the register until it is stored in memory, further restricting leakage detection, as only leakage from the same

```
li x15, 43584
lb x15, 0 (x15)
mv x14, x15
mv x5, x14
lw x15, −124(x8)
addi x15, x15, 4
sw x14, 0 (x15)
```

(a) Assembly program

```
...
...
k[0] = s0 = km[0];
k[1] = s1 = km[1];
k[2] = s2 = km[2];
k[3] = s3 = km[3];
...
```

(b) C program

```
li x15, 43584
lb x7, 0 (x15)
mv x14, x7
mv x10, x14
lw x15, −124(x8)
addi x15, x15, 4
sw x7, 0 ( x15 )
```

(c) Mod. assembly program

Fig. 9. A snippet of the Camellia application, the generated assembly, and a manually modified assembly for the proof-of-concept of the memory range feature.

register as used for the load can be detected within the given path. The standard executable from the compiler is not enough to confirm the effectiveness of the new solution, as SoftFlow cannot detect actual present data leakage due to the insufficient paths provided by QFlow. To validate the functionality of the developed solution, manual modifications were made to the application as outlined in Fig. 9c.

The modified application discussed herein is not integrated into the automated solution. Its sole purpose is to manually initiate the leakage condition through Register x7. As previously mentioned, this methodology can only detect a single leakage path. In Fig. 5, this path is highlighted in blue, traversing from the data input through register x7 to the primary output. However, other potential paths, depicted in black, which involve other registers and computing units, remain undetectable. The detected paths are illustrated in Fig. 5. Modifying the application proved the functionality of the new memory range feature. For the FULL verification mode it is possible to identify the leakages caused by the application for any variable labeled with the "_conf" suffix in any memory hierarchy. However, the fixed leakage path required manual modifications of the path. This limitation is further discussed below.

6 Limitations

Overall, the tool can identify vulnerabilities and assist the designer in writing software that allows safe use of insecure hardware. However, some limitations must be considered.

Leakage paths can be triggered with instructions like load and store operations, as shown in Fig. 6. The data is leaked without any change. This results in a varied attack scenario from the one used by QFlow. Additionally, the evaluation is only conducted on 3776 existing leakage paths, as QFlow only outputs the most suspicious ones. Although the elaboration of the paths was successful, all leakage paths must be considered. It might not be possible for some applications and hardware combinations to avoid leakage. This could be due to unconditional leakages or leakages caused by instruction patterns required for the application. The Stack verification mode did not bring any advantage in the evaluation. It might be the case that some applications are easier to verify using this mode. The new memory range feature in SoftFlow improves versatility but presents some drawbacks. It may overlook data leakage paths involving movement between general-purpose registers before the data is leaked, limiting its effectiveness in identifying such vulnerabilities. However, it is evident that this limitation arises from QFlow, which only provides the most probable leakage paths and does not account for movement between registers.

7 Conclusion

We presented SoftFlow, an EDA tool that utilizes formal verification to conclusively indicate whether leakage paths in hardware are activated for a given software. Therefore, SoftFlow facilitates both a security-driven system design from the ground up and post-fabrication security patches. The usability of the proposed framework was demonstrated by analyzing OpenSSL cryptographic algorithms for a RISC-V architecture. The evaluation proves that secure software disabled all 3776 leakage paths. In addition, the consideration of both software and hardware mitigated all false positives of QFlow. With SoftFlow, we enable a security-aware software-hardware co-verification process that takes into account the intricate interplay of dedicated hardware and software. Furthermore, the integration of the new memory range feature represents a significant advancement in SoftFlow's capabilities. By enabling flexible placement of sensitive information across diverse memory regions, this feature enhances the tool's adaptability and effectiveness in identifying and mitigating potential security vulnerabilities. However, additional modifications are planned for the future to allow the identification of leakages caused by a movement of sensitive data between the general purpose registers. Additionally, we plan to investigate security-aware compilers that facilitate the complete removal of vulnerabilities if allowed by both hardware and software.

References

1. Alvim, M.S., Chatzikokolakis, K., McIver, A., Morgan, C., Palamidessi, C., Smith, G.S.: The science of quantitative information flow. In: Information Security and Cryptography, Springer (2020). https://www.springer.com/gp/book/9783319961293
2. Anjaria, K., Mishra, A.: Information leakage minimization using a negative information flow based confidentiality policy. In: 2017 International Conference on Emerging Trends Innovation in ICT (ICEI), pp. 21–26 (2017)
3. Ardeshiricham, A., Hu, W., Marxen, J., Kastner, R.: Register transfer level information flow tracking for provably secure hardware design. In: Design, Automation & Test in Europe Conference & Exhibition (DATE), pp. 1691–1696 (2017)
4. Bosbach, N., et al.: NQC^2: A non-intrusive QEMU code coverage plugin. In: Rapid Simulation and Performance Evaluation for Design (RAPIDO 2024) (2024)

5. Chen, K., Deng, Q., Hou, Y., Jin, Y., Guo, X.: Hardware and software co-verification from security perspective. In: 2019 20th International Workshop on Microprocessor/SoC Test, Security and Verification (MTV), pp. 50–55 (2019)
6. Cimatti, A., Mover, S., Roveri, M., Tonetta, S.: From sequential extended regular expressions to NFA with symbolic labels. In: Implementation and Application of Automata. Springer, Heidelberg (2011)
7. Delshadtehrani, L., Canakci, S., Zhou, B., Eldridge, S., Joshi, A., Egele, M.: PHMon: a programmable hardware monitor and its security use cases. In: 29th USENIX Security Symposium (USENIX Security 2020), pp. 807–824. USENIX Association (2020). https://www.usenix.org/conference/usenixsecurity20/presentation/delshadtehrani
8. Eisner, C., Fisman, D.: A Practical Introduction to PSL Introduction. Integrated Circuits and Systems. Springer, Boston (2006)
9. Grosse, D., Kühne, U., Drechsler, R.: HW/SW co-verification of embedded systems using bounded model checking. In: Proceedings of the 16th ACM Great Lakes Symposium on VLSI, GLSVLSI 2006, pp. 43–48. Association for Computing Machinery, New York (2006). https://doi.org/10.1145/1127908.1127920
10. Guo, X., Dutta, R.G., He, J., Tehranipoor, M.M., Jin, Y.: QIF-verilog: quantitative information-flow based hardware description languages for pre-silicon security assessment. In: 2019 IEEE International Symposium on Hardware Oriented Security and Trust (HOST), pp. 91–100 (2019)
11. Guo, X., Dutta, R.G., Mishra, P., Jin, Y.: Scalable SoC trust verification using integrated theorem proving and model checking. In: 2016 IEEE International Symposium on Hardware Oriented Security and Trust (HOST), pp. 124–129 (2016)
12. Hu, W., Althoff, A., Ardeshiricham, A., Kastner, R.: Towards property driven hardware security. In: 2016 17th International Workshop on Microprocessor and SOC Test and Verification (MTV), pp. 51–56 (2016)
13. Hu, W., Ardeshiricham, A., Gobulukoglu, M.S., Wang, X., Kastner, R.: Property specific information flow analysis for hardware security verification. In: Proceedings of the International Conference on Computer-Aided Design, ICCAD 2018. Association for Computing Machinery, New York (2018). https://doi.org/10.1145/3240765.3240839
14. Huang, B.Y., Ray, S., Gupta, A., Fung, J.M., Malik, S.: Formal security verification of concurrent firmware in SoCs using instruction-level abstraction for hardware. In: 2018 55th ACM/ESDA/IEEE Design Automation Conference (DAC), pp. 1–6 (2018)
15. IEEE: IEEE Standard for Property Specification Language (PSL). IEEE Std 1850-2010 (Revision of IEEE Std 1850-2005) (2010)
16. IEEE Council on Electronic Design Automation: CADForAssurance (2020). https://cadforassurance.org/
17. Katkalov, K., Stenzel, K., Borek, M., Reif, W.: Model-driven development of information flow-secure systems with IFlow. In: 2013 International Conference on Social Computing, pp. 51–56 (2013)
18. Kocher, P., et al.: Spectre attacks: exploiting speculative execution. In: 2019 IEEE Symposium on Security and Privacy (SP), pp. 1–19 (2019)
19. Kumar, B., Jaiswal, A.K., Vineesh, V.S., Shinde, R.: Analyzing hardware security properties of processors through model checking. In: 2020 33rd International Conference on VLSI Design and 2020 19th International Conference on Embedded Systems (VLSID), pp. 107–112 (2020)

20. Li, D., Shen, W., Wang, Z.: A noval method of security verification for JTAG protection function. In: 2019 IEEE 19th International Conference on Software Quality, Reliability and Security Companion (QRS-C), pp. 487–492 (2019)
21. Lipp, M., et al.: Meltdown. Workingpaper, Cornell University Library (2018)
22. Lugou, F., Apvrille, L., Francillon, A.: Toward a methodology for unified verification of hardware/software co-designs. J. Cryptogr. Eng. 1–12 (2016)
23. Mukherjee, R., Joshi, S., O'Leary, J., Kroening, D., Melham, T.: Hardware/software co-verification using path-based symbolic execution. CoRR abs/2001.01324 (2020). http://arxiv.org/abs/2001.01324
24. Nguyen, M.D., Wedler, M., Stoffel, D., Kunz, W.: Formal hardware/software co-verification by interval property checking with abstraction. In: 2011 48th ACM/EDAC/IEEE Design Automation Conference (DAC), pp. 510–515 (2011)
25. Oberg, J., Hu, W., Irturk, A., Tiwari, M., Sherwood, T., Kastner, R.: Theoretical analysis of gate level information flow tracking. In: Design Automation Conference, pp. 244–247 (2010)
26. Open SSL Project: OpenSSL (1998). https://github.com/openssl/openssl
27. Reimann, L.M., Erdönmez, S., Sisejkovic, D., Leupers, R.: Quantitative information flow for hardware: advancing the attack landscape. In: 2023 IEEE 14th Latin America Symposium on Circuits and System (LASCAS) (2023)
28. Reimann, L.M., Hanel, L., Sisejkovic, D., Merchant, F., Leupers, R.: QFlow: quantitative information flow for security-aware hardware design in Verilog. In: 2021 IEEE 39th International Conference on Computer Design (ICCD), pp. 603–607 (2021)
29. Reimann, L.M., et al.: Qtflow: quantitative timing-sensitive information flow for security-aware hardware design on RTL. In: 2024 IEEE International Symposium on VLSI Design, Automation and Test (VLSI-DAT), Hsinchu, Taiwan (2024)
30. Reimann, L.M., Wiesner, J., Sisejkovic, D., Merchant, F., Leupers, R.: SoftFlow: automated hw-SW confidentiality verification for embedded processors. In: 2023 IFIP/IEEE 31st International Conference on Very Large Scale Integration (VLSI-SoC), pp. 1–6 (2023)
31. Ruwase, O., et al.: Parallelizing dynamic information flow tracking. In: Proceedings of the Twentieth Annual Symposium on Parallelism in Algorithms and Architectures, pp. 35–45 (2008)
32. Synopsys Inc.: ASIP Designer (2021). https://www.synopsys.com/dw/ipdir.php?ds=asip-designer
33. Veeranna, N., Schafer, B.C.: Hardware trojan detection in behavioral intellectual properties (IP's) using property checking techniques. IEEE Trans. Emerg. Top. Comput. **5**(4), 576–585 (2017)
34. Šišejković, D., Merchant, F., Reimann, L.M., Leupers, R., Giacometti, M., Kegreiß, S.: A secure hardware-software solution based on RISC-V, logic locking and microkernel. In: Proceedings of the 23th International Workshop on Software and Compilers for Embedded Systems, SCOPES 2020, pp. 62–65. Association for Computing Machinery, New York (2020). https://doi.org/10.1145/3378678.3391886
35. Yale: Gallina Specification Language. http://flint.cs.yale.edu/cs428/coq/doc/Reference-Manual003.html

Confidential Inference in Decision Trees

Rupesh Raj Karn[1], Mizan Gebremichael[1], Kashif Nawaz[2], and Ibrahim M. Elfadel[1](✉)

[1] Center for Secure Cyber Physical Systems, Khalifa University, Abu Dhabi, UAE
ibrahim.elfadel@ku.ac.ae

[2] Cryptography Research Center, Technology Innovation Institute Abu Dhabi, Abu Dhabi, UAE

Abstract. In confidential computing, arithmetic algorithms operate on encrypted inputs to produce encrypted outputs. Specifically, in confidential inference, Alice has the parameters of the machine-learning model but does not want to reveal them to Bob, who has the data. Bob wants to use Alice's model for inference, but does not want to reveal his data. Alice and Bob agree to use confidential computing to run the inference engine without revealing either the model or the data. However, they find that fully homomorphic and order-preserving encryptions are very time-consuming and very challenging to accelerate on hardware. When the machine learning model is a decision tree, these encryptions can be made computationally efficient and can even be readily accelerated on hardware. In this paper, we reveal how Alice and Bob run the inference engine of a decision tree in full confidence and show FPGA implementations of additively homomorphic, order-preserving, and post-quantum order-preserving encryption on constrained hardware platforms. We further evaluate the resources needed to implement the ciphertext decision tree and compare them with those of a plaintext decision tree. Confidential inference tests are run on the encrypted FPGA design using the MNIST data set.

Keywords: Order-Preserving Encryption · Homomorphic Encryption · FPGA Implementation · Post-Quantum Cryptosystem · Combinational Circuit · Sequential Circuit · Finite-State Machine

1 Introduction

In many fields of research and industry, machine learning (ML) and artificial intelligence (AI) are becoming dominant problem-solving tools. For example, the medical industry provides automatic medical evaluations and risk profiles for various diseases by analyzing a user's DNA profile through AI [1]. In finance, there are automated systems and services that decide loan grants based on information provided by the user. Many of these services involve the exposure of sensitive data. Such data is extremely vulnerable to a man-in-the-middle attack, in which an unauthorized party gains access and uses the data for illicit purposes. On the

Published by Springer Nature Switzerland AG 2024
I. (Abe) M. Elfadel and L. Albasha (Eds.): VLSI-SoC 2023, IFIP AICT 680, pp. 273–297, 2024.
https://doi.org/10.1007/978-3-031-70947-0_14

service end, the AI model's intellectual property must be protected. Training an AI model takes hours or even days, and once trained, it is made available in the cloud, where users may access it via an API. An AI service provider incurs a considerable cost to cover training expenditures and charges significant usage fees to sustain the business. Providing the trained model to the public without encryption can breach the privacy of training data and make it susceptible to model inversion attacks [2]. A bank, for example, that employs a decision tree model for credit evaluation in order to provide loans to its clients may not wish to divulge any information about the model. Traversing the nodes of the decision tree would reveal the thresholds utilized over each attribute of the customer's data for loan issuance decisions. The man-in-the-middle attacker can successfully tweak her data to avoid such thresholds and win the loan decision. Furthermore, to accelerate inference processing, these models are typically run on hardware accelerators using programmable ASIC, configurable, or embedded technologies. Such technologies are nevertheless easier to attack in an edge-computing context than in a cloud-computing one. In the former case, only computationally friendly or lightweight security measures are feasible. If a confidential inference solution is to be implemented end-to-end, it is the edge computing context that should receive particular attention.

2 Chapter Contributions

In this chapter, we address the issue of confidential inference in edge computing and offer a technique for evaluating an encrypted AI model on encrypted data at the edge accelerator in a computationally efficient manner. We have used an FPGA as the accelerator platform and a decision tree as the supervised machine learning model. We consider a scenario in which an FPGA (Alice) holds an encrypted model that was previously trained on plain datasets. A client (Bob) then intends to use that model to get the inference result by supplying encrypted data. The goal of confidential inference is to obtain the inference result while retaining the privacy of both the ML model and the client data. After inference, the ML result is sent to the client only in encrypted form. In this work, we address simultaneous encryption of the ML model and user data under the resource constraints of an edge FPGA accelerator. We have used a decision tree as the supervised machine learning model and explored the use of both Fully Homomorphic Encryption (FHE) [3–5] and Order-Preserving Encryption (OPE) [6,7] as privacy-protection mechanisms. The major goal of this chapter is to highlight the hardware-friendly alterations to FHE and OPE that are enabled by restricting the simultaneous encryption solution to decision trees. We will also describe canonical architectures for their FPGA implementations using both combinational and sequential circuits. Earlier work on FPGA design of decision trees include [8], in which light-weight training for large datasets is implemented. For decision tree inference, [9] proposes an FPGA design geared for drone pilot identification. Early work on confidential decision tree inference includes [2] and [10] where cloud-based implementations are used due to encryption complexity.

Unlike [2] and [10], our work is focused on the hardware acceleration of such confidential decision inference so as to make it accessible to edge devices. In summary, our contributions are as follows:

1. We describe a modified FHE based on [11] that is entirely compatible with decision tree inference.
2. We propose an OPE mechanism for the confidential inference on a supervised decision-tree learning model.
3. We further propose a novel post-quantum, NTRU-based, OPE for the confidential inference on decision trees. We call this algorithm OP-NTRU.
4. We reduce the memory footprint of the OP-NTRU ciphertext using loss-less compression [12] and illustrate the harwdare advantage of the resulting encryption.
5. We provide a Python tool that automatically translates the plaintext and ciphertext decision tree models into Verilog HDL source code that is directly synthesizable for FPGA implementation.
6. Finally, we propose sequential and combinational circuit design architectures for the ciphertext decision tree and evaluate them on a Cyclone V FPGA board.

It should be noted that this research assumes that the decision tree is trained and validated using standard machine learning techniques. When the model is ready for deployment, the encryption methods described in this chapter are applied to secure decision tree inference for both model provider and data owner.

This chapter is a synthesis of our prior work on confidential inference in decision trees as reported in [13–15].

3 Preliminaries on Decision Trees

In this Section, we provide background information on decision tree (DT) learning models, the need for their secure representation and a hardware prototyping environment for evaluating secure DT models. For more details on decision tree models, the reader is referred to [16–18], among many others.

3.1 Decision Tree Architecture and Advantages

Among the various ML methods, DT learning is a supervised-learning method that typically produces excellent accuracy when dealing with enormous datasets [19]. In its classification version, the tree representation is used such that the leaf nodes correspond to class labels, while the classification rules are expressed on the internal nodes. At each internal node, a DT asks a binary question, and based on the yes-or-no answer, it further splits two branches out of the node. The features of the training dataset are employed in the creation of rules based on which nodes are split until a leaf node is reached. An example of a DT is shown in Fig. 1(a). DT inference entails computing a class label of a given input record using decision rules at the internal nodes and the classes assigned to the leaf nodes. The advantages of DT machine learning include:

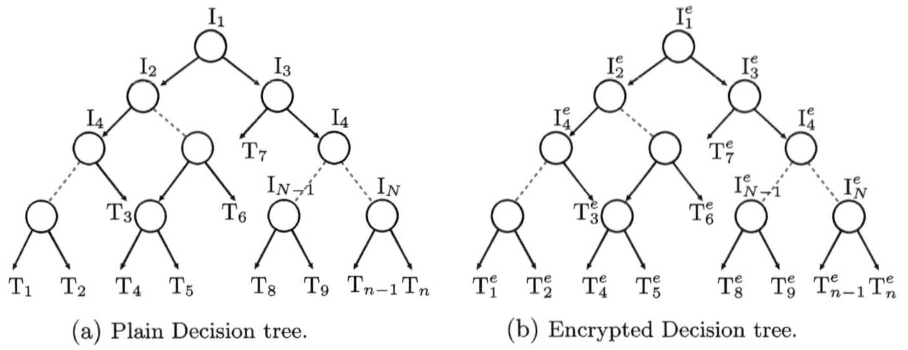

Fig. 1. Decision Tree. (a) Plaintext DT: At each node, a comparison inequality between a dataset feature $\mathbb{D}_{x_k}$ and threshold Λ_k is performed. If the inequality outcome is true, the left side of the node is evaluated otherwise the right side of the node is evaluated. (b) Ciphertext DT: The comparison in each node is performed between the encrypted data and encrypted threshold values.

1. DTs often replicate human decision-making procedures, making them simple to read, understand, and interpret.
2. The DT rules can be easily implemented in hardware using multiplexers.
3. Training a DT can be done without or with little data preparation. Other machine learning techniques may need feature extraction, data normalization, dimension reduction, and so forth.
4. A DT can handle both numerical and categorical data without the need to numerically encode the categorical data.

In general, increasing the number of nodes and branches enhances the overall accuracy of the DT model. However, DT is costly in both time and resources. As the tree size grows, so do the time and hardware resources required for inference computation. Note that the number of tree nodes grows exponentially with the number of tree levels. The amount of resources available determines the number of nodes that can be accommodated, which in turn determines the number of DT levels, the granularity of the classification, and the accuracy of the DT inference.

3.2 Decision Tree Rules

Assume the dataset $\mathbb{D} = [\mathbb{D}_x, \mathbb{D}_y]$ where $\mathbb{D}_x$ denotes the training samples and $\mathbb{D}_y$ denotes the class labels. In classification, the label of a leaf node is one of the $\mathbb{D}_y$ labels. If L is the number of features, let $\mathbb{D}_{x_i}$, $1 \le i \le L$, denote the i-th feature. The number of unique values in $\mathbb{D}_y$ represents the number of class labels, denoted ℓ. DT training is made of two basic steps: Induction and Pruning. Induction is the process of generating nodes, selecting node features, and evaluating nodal information gains to assign decision rules at each internal node and labels at each terminal node. One side effect of induction is the possible generation of duplicate nodes. Pruning is then responsible for eliminating duplicates and preventing overfitting. Assume now the trained DT model has N internal nodes: $I_1, I_2, \ldots, I_N$, and n terminal (or leaf) nodes: $T_1, T_2, \ldots, T_n$. Then the decision rule at I_k is embodied in a threshold value Λ_k. The data feature $\mathbb{D}_{x_k}$ at node I_k and the threshold Λ_k define the inequality used in the decision rule of node I_k, which is expressed as

$$\mathbb{D}_{x_k} < \Lambda_k \quad or \quad \mathbb{D}_{x_k} \geq \Lambda_k \tag{1}$$

At the end of the training, one of the class labels of the dataset $b \in [0, \ell - 1]$ is assigned to a terminal node $T_i, 1 \leq i \leq n$. A DT inference amounts to a tree traversal from the root node to one of the terminal nodes. The internal nodes visited during such traversal are the ones defined by a chain of inequalities similar to (1). The inferred label is that of the terminal node at the destination of the tree traversal.

3.3 Secure Representation of Decision Trees

The purpose of DT encryption is to convert the DT learning model into a secure representation that can be used for inference without disclosing any information about the DT model parameters. Example of such parameters are the feature and the threshold involved in a given decision rule. The secure representation must be able to receive inference data in encrypted form and deliver the correct inference result also in encrypted form.

After training, each internal node makes a "greater-than" or "less-than" comparison between the assigned threshold and the value of the data feature according to (1). To secure the DT model, the computations at the internal nodes must be encrypted, i.e., the encrypted version I_k^e of decision rules of the kth node (Eq. (1)), will be of the form:

$$\mathbf{E}(\mathbb{D}_{x_k}) < \mathbf{E}(\Lambda_k) \quad or \quad \mathbf{E}(\mathbb{D}_{x_k}) \geq \mathbf{E}(\Lambda_k) \tag{2}$$

where $\mathbf{E}$ is the encryption operation. The ciphertext representation of DT must deliver the correct inference result as a ciphertext. As a result, the leaf node labels T_k are also encrypted, i.e., $T_k^e = \mathbf{E}(T_k)$. The inferred class/label is then calculated as follows:

$$T_k = \mathbf{D}(\mathbf{E}(T_k)) \tag{3}$$

where $\mathbf{D}$ is the decryption operation. The decision tree and its encrypted form are shown in Fig. 1(a) and Fig. 1(b), respectively. In Sects. 4, 5, and 6, we will present efficient FPGA implementations of privacy-preserving DTs using, respectively, homomorphic, standard order-preserving, and post-quantum order-preserving encryption algorithms.

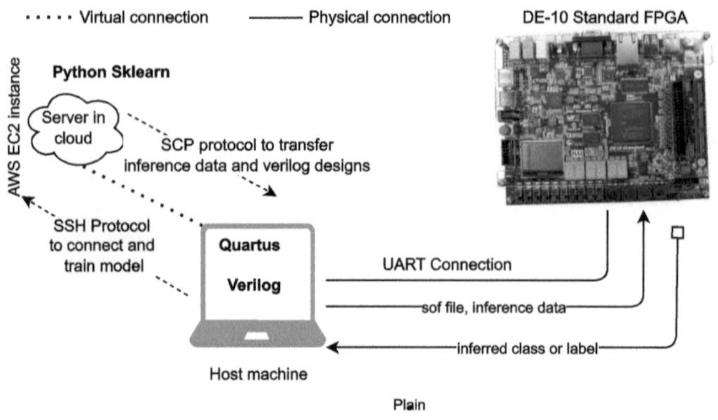

Fig. 2. Experimental testbed that simulates edge-cloud environment.

3.4 FPGA Prototyping Platform

We have developed an edge-cloud environment, shown in Fig. 2, for confidential inference, which we will demonstrate using the widely used MNIST dataset [20]. The MNIST dataset contains grayscale images of handwritten digits from 0 to 9 and has 10 features. Each feature corresponds to a pixel in a 28×28 grayscale image, resulting in a total of 784 features. For our experiments, we performed DT training and validation on a compute-intensive Amazon m5d.2xlarge EC2 virtual machine, which features 8 virtual CPUs, 32 GB memory, and 10 Gbs network bandwidth. We conducted two scenarios. In the first scenario, with *plain DT*, we used the DT model to extract decision rules, generate Verilog source code, and load the bitstream file directly onto the FPGA to enable inference on plain data. In the second scenario, with *secure DT*, we encrypted the internal nodes and end leaves of the DT model and used the encrypted model to extract decision rules, generate the Verilog source code, and run logic synthesis. The resulting bitstream file was then flashed onto the FPGA. The FPGA acts as an edge device connected to the host machine through the serial port. The host machine acts as a bridge between the cloud server and the FPGA.

4 Homomorphic Encryption of Decision Trees

FHE has been known for over 30 years [21], but it gained immense popularity when the first realistic and attainable FHE method was proposed in [11]. The major disadvantage of FHE is its computational complexity, which makes its hardware acceleration quite challenging and its support on the constrained nodes of edge devices non-realistic. Recent work on accelerating FHE on various hardware platforms is described in [22,23], and [24]. Interestingly, it turns out that in the important case of decision tree inference, the FHE of [11] can be sufficiently altered to enable confidential inference in decision trees on edge devices.

The major goal of this section is to explain such FHE alterations and illustrate their effectiveness using the MNIST dataset. We will also describe one possible FPGA implementation using purely combinational circuits.

4.1 Homomoprhic Encryption

We have used a modified version of the FHE of [11] to encrypt the DT model. The FHE of [11] is considered the foundation upon which the majority of homomorphic encryption algorithms are built. For a message bit m, FHE proceeds as follows:

(a) Select a random positive integer q as public key.
(b) Select a random positive odd integer p as private key.
(c) To strengthen the encryption, select a random integer r as a noise parameter such that $|r| < p/2$.
(d) Encrypt the message bit m as $c = pq + 2r + m$
(e) Perform homomorphic addition or multiplication as required, e.g. $C_{add} = c_1 \pm c_2$ or $C_{mul} = c_1 c_2$.
(f) Decrypt the homomorphic computations, $m_1 \pm m_2 = (C_{add}\ mod\ p)\ mod\ 2$ or $m_1 m_2 = (C_{mul}\ mod\ p)\ mod\ 2$.

In the case of a μ-bit binary message M and under the assumption that $r = 0$, each bit is encrypted independently [11]. The ciphertext of a 0 bit is $0 + pq$ and that of a 1 bit is $1 + pq$. The number of bits (or bit width b_w) required to represent the cipher of either bit 0 or 1 is

$$b_w = max(\lfloor \ln_2(pq) + 1 \rfloor, \lfloor \ln_2(1 + pq) \rfloor + 1). \tag{4}$$

The bit width of the cipher to represent μ bits of plain text is μb_w bits. To make this encryption accept any numeric value M, the following modifications to [11] are introduced:

1. In step (a), select an odd integer as a public key q.
2. In step (b), select another odd integer as a private key p such that p and q are relatively prime.
3. The private key p must be greater than the maximum value of M. For an unsigned integer with μ bits, $p > 2^{\mu} - 1$.
4. In step (c), set $r = 0$, and compute the ciphertext $c = pq + M$.
5. In step (f), decrypt as follows: $M_1 \pm M_2 = C_{add}\ mod\ p$ or $M_1 M_2 = C_{mul}\ mod\ p$.

Note that in Step 4, it is the entire μ-bit message that is encrypted rather than a single message bit as in Step (d).

Typically, p and q are chosen so that $M/pq << 1$. Using the well-known inequality that $\lfloor a+b \rfloor \leq \lfloor a \rfloor + \lfloor b \rfloor + 1$, and that $\ln_2(1+M/pq) \leq (M/pq) \ln_2 e << 1$, one can show that the number of bits required to store the ciphertext of M

is, in fact, upper bound by b_w. This represents a significant saving in storage compared to the case of independent bit encryption.

In Step 4, the value $r = 0$ is used to reduce the size of the ciphertext. To improve encryption strength, any non-zero r value randomly selected in the range $M/2 < |r| < (p - M)/2$ could be used. In such a case, the encryption and decryption equations in steps 4 and 5 should be modified to account for the non-zero r value.

4.2 Encryption of Decision Trees

Using the modified homomorphic encryption scheme of the previous subsection, the encrypted versions of the decision rules (2) are rewritten as:

$$\mathbf{E}_H(\mathbb{D}_{x_k}) - \mathbf{E}_H(\Lambda_k) < 0 \quad or \quad \mathbf{E}_H(\mathbb{D}_{x_k}) - \mathbf{E}_H(\Lambda_k) \geq 0 \tag{5}$$

where $\mathbf{E}_H$ is homomorphic encryption operator with the public key q. Note that in Eq. (5), only the additive feature of homomorphic encryption is used, i.e., $\mathbb{D}_{x_k} - \Lambda_k = \mathbf{D}_H(\mathbf{E}_H(\mathbb{D}_{x_k}) - \mathbf{E}_H(\Lambda_k))$, where $\mathbf{D}_H$ is the homomorphic decryption operator using the p private key. Along with encrypting the data features $\mathbb{D}_{x_k}$ and thresholds Λ_k, the leaf node labels are also encrypted, i.e., $T_k^e = \mathbf{E}_H(T_k)$. The inferred class label is then calculated using the private key p according to

$$T_k = \mathbf{D}_H(\mathbf{E}_H(T_k)) \tag{6}$$

4.3 Hardware Description of Decisions Trees

The flow control structure of a DT in any programming language, whether imperative such as *C/C++*, functional such as *Haskell*, or logic such as *Prolog* is that of a sequence of nested "if-then-else" statements that terminate with a clause corresponding to the class label outcome of the leaf node. In a hardware description language such as *Verilog*, the nested *if-then-else* statements are encapsulated within an *always* bock as follows:

```
always @ (*)
 if (encrypted_x[i] > encrypted_t[i])
   if (encrypted_x[k] > encrypted_t[k])
      if (encrypted_x[m] > encrypted_t[m])
           ..................
           ...............
           label <= encrypted_T1;
        else
           label <= encrypted_T2;
        ..................
    ..................
end
```

where *encrypted_x*[i] is the ith element of the one-dimensional array *encrypted_x* corresponding to the ciphertext $\mathbf{E}(\mathbb{D}_x)$, where $\mathbf{E}$ denotes any encryption method. In Verilog, the *encrypted_x* array is stored in the FPGA block RAM (BRAM) with i being the address of the i-th cell in the BRAM. Similarly *encrypted_t*[i] is the ith element of the one-dimensional matrix *encrypted_t* that corresponds to the thresholds $\mathbf{E}(\Lambda)$ to which a BRAM is allocated. The control expression inside the parentheses of *if* is evaluated. If the outcome is true, the expressions under "if" are executed. Otherwise, the procedural statements under *else* are executed. The "*" indicates that the circuit corresponding to the code within the *always* block is triggered whenever the value of *encrypted_x*[i] or *encrypted_t*[i] changes. In the high-level synthesis of the above Verilog code, a Boolean function is generated.

The FPGA synthesis tool implements such a Boolean function using Look-UP Tables (LUTs) as logic elements to optimize the FPGA area footprint.

4.4 Combinational FPGA Synthesis

The infrastructure and dataset described in Sect. 3.4 are used to demonstrate the secure representation of DT using homomorphic encryption. Once training is completed on an Amazon EC2 virtual machine (VM) [13], the plain and encrypted versions of the decision rules are converted into the *Verilog* source code. The resulting *Verilog* code is implemented on the Intel Cyclone 5 FPGA featured on the DE-10 standard SCSXFC6D6F31CN board [25].

For *Python-to-Verilog* code conversion of the plaintext and ciphertext decision rules of the DT model, a *Python* tool has been developed. This is facilitated by the fact that a DT consists of a nested sequence of *if-then-else* statements matching the inequalities in (2). We exploit this aspect of the *sklearn* DT to extract the decision rules that are then transformed into *Verilog* for FPGA implementation. The *sklearn* DT class offers an *export_text()* function for outputting the text representation of the rules. A *Python* script has been written to recursively parse every DT node and extract feature names, threshold values, inequality conditions, and child nodes. The *sklearn* functions *tree_*, $children\_left$, and $children\_right$, and the *NumPy* function $argmax$ are used to extract the decision rules. The function *NodeScan()* is recursively used to parse every node. The notation I_i denotes the i-th node (Fig. 1), Λ_j denotes the j-th threshold (Eq. (1)), and $\mathbb{D}_x$ denotes the features of the dataset. The following is a brief description of Algorithm 1:

1. The thresholds are rounded to the nearest integer to limit the bit width of the FPGA BRAM.
2. Python's assignment operator '=' is converted to a Verilog non-blocking statement '<='.
3. The feature index is used as a memory address in the FPGA BRAM.
4. The *if-then-else* statements are extracted by parsing every node as in **Function** *NodeScan()* (lines 7 to 19).
5. The generated *if-then-else* Verilog code is encapsulated within a *'always @ (*)'* block, as explained in Sect. 4.3.

Algorithm 1: Verilog source code generator for DT combinational circuit.

```
Input  : Trained decision tree model with sklearn (DT)
Output : Verilog combinational circuit source code.
from sklearn.tree import _tree;
import NumPy as np;
Function GenVerilog(DT, D_x):
    print('always @ (*)');
    tree_ = DT.tree_;
    D_x = [D_{x_i} for i in tree_.feature ];
    Function NodeScan(I_i, depth):
        indent = " " × depth;
        if tree_.feature[I_i] != _tree.TREE_UNDEFINED then
            PixelName = D_{x_i}[I_i];
            Λ_j = tree_.threshold[I_i];
            print ("{} if ({} <= {})".format(indent, PixelName, int(round(Λ_j,
            3)))) ;
            NodeScan(tree_.children_left[I_i], depth + 1);
            print (" else // if {} > {}".format(indent, PixelName, int(round(Λ_j,
            3))));
            NodeScan(tree_.children_right[I_i], depth + 1);
        end
        else
            print ("{} Label <= {};".format(indent,
            np.argmax(tree_.value[I_i][0], axis=0)));
        end
    NodeScan(0, 1);
    print('end') ;
D_x = ['pixels[{}]'.format(str(i)) for i in range(L)];
/* L = 28 × 28 = 784 for the MNIST dataset */
GenVerilog(DT, D_x);
```

Algorithm 1 is the core of a tool written in *Python* that uses *sklearn* in the background for DT learning, implements the homomorphic encryption of the DT, and generates Verilog code for FPGA implementation. The tool does not have any library dependency and can run on any version of Python.

4.5 Combinational FPGA Experiments

Two inference experiments, with *plain DT* and *secure DT*, are run using the prototyping environment shown in Fig. 2. The DT size is selected so that the FPGA implementation can be accommodated within the available FPGA resources. The number of nodes is $N = 506$, and the number of leaves is $n = 248$. This tree parameter selection has resulted in 85.52% accuracy on the validation dataset. The comparison of FPGA resources is given in Table 1. The key values $p = 20001, q = 91$ are used. Although the encrypted DT combinational architecture does not require any sequential components, the experimental testbed

Table 1. FPGA resource comparison for decision tree inference. ALMs: Adaptive logic modules, LABs: Logic array blocks, ALUTs: Combinational adaptive look-up tables, FFs: Dedicated primary registers, F_{max}: Maximum attainable clock frequency, Setup: Slack time for clock setup, Hold: Slack time for clock hold.

Attributes	Plain Decision Tree	Encrypted Decision Tree
ALMs (%)	4	38
LABs (%)	6	59
ALUTs	2592	15212
FFs (%)	3	32
$F_{max}(MHz)$	84.87	68.8
Setup (ns)	8.217	5.466
Hold (ns)	0.368	0.364

does. The sequential components of the testbed include circuits for serial transmission and for synchronizing the read-write signals of the BRAM. The FPGA clock frequency is 50 MHz. As anticipated, the encrypted DT model consumes more resources compared to the plain one. The important aspect is that the encrypted scenario uses Look-Up Tables (LUTs) and Flip-Flops (FFs), which result in increased storage requirements. This usage may lead to higher power consumption due to READ operations.

In the combinational circuit design, the critical path of the DT architecture is a path between the root node and a leaf node that traverses the largest number of internal nodes. The deeper the critical path, the smaller the setup time slack. The setup time slack determines the maximum clock frequency at which the overall FPGA implementation could run. The setup time slack values in Table 1 illustrate that the encrypted tree design is much closer to criticality than the plain one.

4.6 Potential Improvements

This section introduces an additively homomorphic encryption algorithm that is fully adapted to decision tree inference. The algorithm is based on the foundational work of [11]. In terms of FPGA implementation, the algorithm results in 7X saving on FPGA BRAM width. Furthermore, a tool for encrypting and generating the FPGA bitstream of the encrypted decision tree has been implemented and validated. The tool is written in Python and is used to translate the decision tree rules into *Verilog*. The resulting combinational circuit has been implemented on an Intel Cyclone 5 FPGA board and tested using the MNIST dataset.

To calculate the FPGA resource consumption, the user must define the hardware design and execute a logic synthesis for each of the selected DT architecture. The user must experiment with numerous alternatives to tune the design. Since each option takes several hours to compile and test, trying more than ten options is prohibitive. To overcome this constraint on design-space exploration, statistics of FPGA resource usage may be predicted using a regression model without actually running high-level synthesis. This predicted resource value helps to select the type of the FPGA board, which in turn helps predict the cost of the encrypted decision tree when implemented on FPGA. This research is in progress, and we expect to cover it in a future publication.

The gains in hardware acceleration efficiency of additively homomorphic encryption have been obtained at the expense of reduced security. This is because the noise parameter was set to zero in Step (4) of Sect. 4.4. In the next section, we will address this issue by using an alternative encryption algorithm based on order-preserving cryptography.

5 Order-Preserving Encryption of Decision Trees

5.1 Order-Preserving Encryption

Order-preserving encryption (OPE) is an encryption scheme whose encryption function preserves the numerical order of the plaintexts. It has been used mostly as a method of encrypting data in a database so that it is possible to perform range queries on the encrypted data. The OPE scheme has been known for about 20 years with [6] providing the first formal security definition of OPE and releasing realistic and executable source code [7], which allowed any inequality queries to be performed on encrypted data. For a recent survey on OPE, see [26]. Although OPE does not achieve the highest security levels, it still provides the best possible security under the order-preserving constraint. In [6], the target application was range queries in databases. In our work, the target application is secure decision tree inference.

In general, the OPE technique is not regarded as IND-CPA[1] secure since OPE is prone to leaking information about plaintext ordering [7]. As a result, its use to secure the decision tree suffers from the same weakness. On the other hand, extensive research has been conducted in OPE to limit such information leakage and safeguard the encryption mechanism [27–30]. Our use of the original OPE technique [6] for DT's is meant to illustrate the usefulness and scope of this security mechanism and demonstrate its FPGA implementation. The security level of the encrypted DT is the same as that supplied by the underlying OPE algorithm. However, it should be noted that the OPE security level is significantly higher than that provided by the modified NTRU encryption of [13].

The order-preserving function f from a domain $\mathcal{R}_p = \{0, 1, 2, ..., R_p\}$ to a domain $\mathcal{R}_c = \{1, 2, 3, ..., R_c\}$, $R_c > R_p$, can be uniquely represented by a combination of R_p out of R_c ordered elements, where R_p and R_c are the ranges of plaintexts and ciphertexts, respectively. The key of the encryption function is composed of two aspects:

[1] Indistinguishable under Chosen Plaintext Attack.

1. Probability distribution of the ciphertexts over $\mathcal{R}_c$;
2. Unique mapping $j = f(i), i \in \mathcal{R}_p,\ j \in \mathcal{R}_c$ that produces a unique combination of elements from the plaintext and ciphertext domains.

For any two pairs of plaintexts and ciphertexts (m_a, c_a) and (m_b, c_b), such that $m_b > m_a$, inequality $c_b > c_a$ must be satisfied for the encryption function f to be order preserving. The OPE in [6] is based on the relationship between the random-order preservation function and the hypergeometric probability distribution. It is a symmetric scheme consisting of three algorithms $(K_{gen}, \mathbf{E}_{\mathbb{K}}, \mathbf{D}_{\mathbb{K}})$.

1. A key generation algorithm K_{gen} that returns a secret key $\mathbb{K}$.
2. An encryption algorithm $\mathbf{E}_{\mathbb{K}}$ that takes the secret key, along with $\mathcal{R}_p$, $\mathcal{R}_c$, and a plaintext message m_i and returns a ciphertext c_i such that $\forall i \geq 1,\ m_i > m_{i-1} \implies c_i > c_{i-1}$.
3. A decryption algorithm $\mathbf{D}_{\mathbb{K}}$ that takes $\mathbb{K}, \mathcal{R}_p, \mathcal{R}_c$ and a ciphertext c_i to return the corresponding plaintext message m_i.

The user is referred to [6] for details on $(K_{gen}, \mathbf{E}_{\mathbb{K}}, \mathbf{D}_{\mathbb{K}})$.

Following Eq. (2), the encrypted versions of the decision rules are rewritten as:

$$\mathbf{E}_{\mathbb{K}}(\mathbb{D}_{x_k}) < \mathbf{E}_{\mathbb{K}}(\Lambda_k) \quad or \quad \mathbf{E}_{\mathbb{K}}(\mathbb{D}_{x_k}) \geq \mathbf{E}_{\mathbb{K}}(\Lambda_k) \tag{7}$$

with the order of the inequalities $(<, \geq)$ of $\mathbb{D}_{x_k}$ with respect to Λ_k preserved as in Eq. (1), i.e.,

$$\mathbb{D}_{x_k} - \Lambda_k = \mathbf{D}_{\mathbb{K}}(\mathbf{E}_{\mathbb{K}}(\mathbb{D}_{x_k}) - \mathbf{E}_{\mathbb{K}}(\Lambda_k))$$

Along with encrypting the data features $\mathbb{D}_{x_k}$ and thresholds Λ_k, the leaf node labels are also encrypted. The inferred class/label is then calculated using the key $\mathbb{K}$ as follows:

$$T_k = \mathbf{D}_{\mathbb{K}}(\mathbf{E}_{\mathbb{K}}(T_k)) \tag{8}$$

5.2 Sequential Circuit Architecture

In Sect. 4.4, a combinational logic implementation of an encrypted decision tree was presented and implemented. In this section, an alternative sequential logic design for an OPE-secure DT is proposed.

In a sequential circuit design, the transition graph of the finite-state machine (FSM) is identical to the DT with each DT node becoming one FSM state. The number of DT nodes is equal to the number of FSM states. Flip-flops are used to store the states and are triggered synchronously by the same clock signal. The FSM diagram of the encrypted DT is the same as the DT diagram of Fig. 1(b). In each clock cycle, one of the FSM states is evaluated by querying one inequality relation as in Eq. (7). In hardware, this query is implemented using a comparator and a multiplexer. The comparison attributes, including the dataset, the features $\mathbb{D}_{x_i}$, and the threshold values Λ_j's for every DT node are stored in a distributed block RAM (BRAM).

Inference data samples are read from BRAM and fed into the DT root node, that is, the initial FSM state. The subsequent state is evaluated in the next clock cycle based on the query result of the previous state. This process is repeated until the evaluation reaches a leaf state representing an encrypted terminal node $\mathbf{E}_{\mathbb{K}}(T_i)$. Once the leaf state is reached, the class/label of $\mathbf{E}_{\mathbb{K}}(T_i)$ is returned as the inference result. The FSM is then reset, the inference logic stopped, and the system remains on standby until a new inference is requested.

5.3 Sequential FPGA Synthesis

The infrastructure and dataset described in Sect. 3.4 are utilized again to verify the secure DT design using OPE. After completing training on an Amazon EC2 virtual machine (VM) [13], the plaintext and ciphertext versions of the decision rules are converted into *Verilog* source code. The resulting code is synthesized using Intel's *Quartus* and ported onto an Intel Cyclone 5 FPGA on the DE-10 standard SCSXFC6D6F31CN board [25].

A two-stage *Python* script has been crafted to generate a sequential *Verilog* design from the *Python* DT model code. The first stage is performed by a script based on Algorithm 1 as previously described in Sect. 4.4. Algorithm 2 uses the decision rules generated by Algorithm 1 and outputs the finite-state machine (FSM) in *Verilog*. Algorithm 2 is briefly described as follows:

1. The decision rules generated by Algorithm 1 are read in line 2 and each consecutive rule is processed as shown in line 11.
2. The state machine is developed using the *Verilog Case* statement and saved in the *fsm.v* file as in line 6.
3. Each *if* statement possesses a state in the FSM.
4. When the state contains *Label*, the state transition register is reset, and *ml_inference_completed* register is pulled high to signal the end of inference. It also indicates that the current state contains a leaf. This logic is shown in lines 15 and 22.
5. The algorithm includes the three following key functions:
   (a) *search_content_file*: It takes a string and a file name as input. It looks for that string in the given file name and returns the line number where it is found.
   (b) *write_file*: It takes a string and a file name as arguments and appends the string to the end of the file without altering the existing content.
   (c) *write_line_file*: It takes a string, a file name, and a line number as input and appends the string at the specified line number without altering the existing file content.

(6) The generated *Verilog* code of the sequential design is encapsulated within a *always @ (posedge clk)* block for synchronizing the circuit with every rising edge of the clock as given in line 6.

This *Python* tool has been packaged as a module that can be installed using *pip install package-name*.

Algorithm 2: Finite state machine generation using "case" statement for Algorithm 1.

```
Input  : Decision rules in the decision_rules.txt file generated by Algorithm 1.
Output : Verilog finite-state machine (FSM)
import itertools;
with open('decision_rules.txt', 'r') as f:
    tree_rules = f.read();
    f.close();
with open('fsm.v', 'a', encoding = 'utf-8') as f:
    f.writelines('always @ posedge(clk) begin \n case(state) \n');
    f.close();
line_num = 0, else_state = 0, else_nextif_state = 0;
curr_line, next_line = itertools.tee(tree_rules.split('\n'));
next(next_line, None);
foreach i,j in list(zip(curr_line,next_line)) do
    if 'else' in i and 'Label' in j: then
        else_state = i.strip().split(':')[0];
        line_num = search_content_file('fsm.v', ' '+str(else_state)+':if' );
        write_line_file('fsm.v', f'\n else begin {j.strip()}
        state<= 0;ml_inference_completed<= 1; end', line_num)
    else if 'else' in i and 'if' in j then
        else_state = i.strip().split(':')[0];
        else_nextif_state = j.strip().split(':')[0];
        line_num = search_content_file('fsm.v', ' '+str(else_state)+':if' );
        write_line_file('fsm.v', f'else begin state<={else_nextif_state}; end ',
        line_num)
    else if 'if' in i and 'Label' in j then
        write_file('fsm.v', f'\n {i.strip()} begin {j.strip()} state <= 0;
        ml_inference_completed <= 1; end ');
    else if 'if' in i and 'if' in j then
        write_file('fsm.v', f'\n {i.strip()} begin state <= {j.strip().split(":")[0]};
        end \n ') ;
    else
        /* 'Label' in i                                                    */
        pass;
    end
end
with open('fsm.v', 'a', encoding = 'utf-8') as f:
    f.writelines('endcase \n end');
    f.close();
```

5.4 FPGA Experiments Ith OPE-Secure Decision Trees

Two inference experiments were conducted using *plain DT* and *secure DT* in the prototyping environment shown in Fig. 2. Recall that the number of internal nodes was $N = 506$, and the number of leaves was $n = 248$. These tree parameters resulted in an inference accuracy of 85.62%. The critical path has $P = 8$ nodes. Plaintexts containing $[\mathbb{D}_{x_k}, \Lambda_k]$ have a range $R_p = 2^8 - 1$. It corresponds

Table 2. FPGA resource comparison for decision tree inference. ALMs: Adaptive logic modules, LABs: Logic array blocks, ALUTs: Combinational adaptive look-up tables, FFs: Dedicated primary registers, F_{max}: Maximum attainable clock frequency, Setup: Slack time for clock setup, Hold: Slack time for clock hold.

Attributes	Combinational [13]		Sequential	
	Plain	Enc	Plain	Enc
ALMs (%)	4	38	2	38
LABs (%)	6	59	4	60
ALUTs	2592	15212	1217	14911
FFs (%)	3	32	2	32
$F_{max}(MHz)$	84.87	68.8	122	73.83
Setup (ns)	8.217	5.466	11.803	6.456
Hold (ns)	0.368	0.364	0.355	0.365

to the pixel values of the grayscale images of the MNIST dataset from 0 to 255. Their respective ciphertexts in OPE have a range $R_c = 2^{32} - 1$. Such R_c has produced ciphertexts $[\mathbf{E}_{\mathbb{K}}(\mathbb{D}_{x_k}), \mathbf{E}_{\mathbb{K}}(\Lambda_k)]$ of 32 *bits*. The comparison of FPGA resources is given in Table 2. The FPGA clock frequency is set to $50MHz$.

The reliability of the sequential design is determined by the setup/hold time slacks, which determine proper functionality and the maximum clock frequency F_{max} at which the design operates. The utilization in Table 2 refers to the percentage of total ALM, LAB, and FF of the DE-10 standard FPGA used in the DT implementation.

As expected, the ciphertext DT needs more FPGA resources than the plaintext one. The results also show that the sequential design consumes comparable amounts of FPGA resources with that of the combinational implementation in terms of ALMs, LABS, and FFs. Because the sequential design includes state machines that are triggered by a clock cycle, the number of ALUTs is fewer than that of the combinational one. In this regard, one may claim that the sequential design is superior to the combinational design. Furthermore, as theoretically explained in [14], the value of F_{max} decreases for the ciphertext DT compared with the plaintext one. This behavior is also shown by the setup time slack. Compared to combinational design, one may also claim that the sequential design could run at higher clock frequency.

Ensemble methods such as random forests can help resolve the conflicting requirements of accuracy, throughput, and resource utilization. The focus of this work is on a single DT. The trade-offs enabled by random forests are addressed in [31].

6 Post-quantum, Order-Preserving Encryption of Decision Trees

To improve the resiliency of encrypted decision trees to post-quantum attacks, we explore, in this section, the use of the lattice-based cryptosystem, NTRU, in the context of decision tree encryption. The selection of NTRU is motivated by two main considerations:

1. It is one of the finalists in the third round of NIST's post-quantum standardization process [32] in the key-encapsulation mechanism.
2. It is supported by open-source code, including versions that enable homomorphic encryption.

One disadvantage of NTRU is the overhead of key generation, which may be mitigated in the confidential inference case by assuming that the ciphertext decision tree has been generated off-line in its entirety. Extending OPE to the lattice-based CRYSTAL-Kyber [32] algorithm will be the subject of future work.

6.1 NTRU Cryptosystem

NTRU is an open source, public-key, lattice-based cryptosystem [33]. The underlying algebraic structure of NTRU arithmetic is the modulo polynomial ring $\mathbb{R}_2[x] = \mathbb{Z}_2[x]/(x^N - 1)$ where all polynomials $a(x)$ have binary coefficients[2] and are of degree $N - 1$ or less

$$\mathbf{a}(x) = \sum_{k=0}^{N-1} \alpha_k x^k. \tag{9}$$

The polynomial $\mathbf{a}(x)$ can be identified with the vector $(\alpha_0, \alpha_1, \alpha_2, ..., \alpha_{N-1})^T \in \mathbb{Z}_2^N$. The NTRU cryptosystem is defined by three integer parameters (N, p, q), where N is the number of polynomial coefficients in $R[x]$, p a small modulus, and q a large modulus. The cryptosystem also consists of four polynomials of degrees at most $N - 1$ that are defined as follows:

1. Polynomial $f(x)$ corresponding to the private key.
2. Polynomial $g(x)$ corresponding to the public key.
3. Polynomial $m(x)$ representing the message. For example, a message $M = 13$ has a binary representation (1101) and a polynomial representation $\mathbf{m}(x) = x^3 + x^2 + 1$.
4. Polynomial $r(x)$ representing random noise to increase the entropy of the cryptosystem.

Since the introduction of the original NTRU cryptosystem in 1996 [12], several versions have been proposed with the main goal of improving NTRU performance. The particular version that we use to satisfy the order-preserving DT requirement is that of [3–5], which endows NTRU with the homomorphic property *NTRUEncrypt*.

In *NTRUEncrypt*, the cryptosystem is parameterized with four positive integers (N, p, q, d), where the integer d has been added to improve decryption performance. These integers must satisfy the following constraints:

[2] The standard description of NTRU uses the ring of integers $\mathbb{Z}$ rather than the binary field $\mathbb{Z}_2$.

1. The pair (p, q) is coprime as is the pair (N, q), i.e., $gcd(p, q) = gcd(N, q) = 1$.
2. The integer q is large enough and satisfies $q > (6d + 1)p$.
3. The integer $N > M$, where M is the largest decimal value of a message.

The parameters (N, p, q, d) are publicly known and used to generate the public and private keys of the NTRU.

Private Key: To generate the private key, a random polynomial $f(x)$ is selected so that it has inverses in both moduli $p(x)$ and $q(x)$. In other words, there exist two polynomials $f_p(x), f_q(x)$ such that

$$f_p(x)f(x) = 1 \ mod \ p(x), \quad f_q(x)f(x) = 1 \ mod \ q(x) \tag{10}$$

The NTRU generator polynomial $g(x)$ is also randomly selected with the polynomial triplet $(f(x), f_p(x), g(x))$ constituting the private key.

Public Key: The public key $h(x)$ is calculated using

$$h(x) = f_q(x)g(x) \ mod \ q(x) \tag{11}$$

The integers (N, p, q, d) are part of the public key and are publicly known.

Encryption: A random polynomial $r(x)$, known as the blinding value [4] and representing noise, is chosen to further obfuscate the message $m(x)$. This is an essential step in encryption because the unknown and arbitrary polynomial $r(x)$ conceals the polynomial $m(x)$ and makes decryption impossible without knowing the private key. The encryption equation to generate the ciphertext polynomial $C(x)$ is

$$C(x) = p(x)h(x)r(x) + [m(x) \ mod \ q(x)] \tag{12}$$

The polynomial $r(x)$ should be capped by the polynomial $T_d(x)$ [4] where $T_d(x) \in R[x]$ is defined as

$$T_d(x) = \begin{cases} \text{d coefficients equal to 1} \\ \text{all other coefficients zero.} \end{cases} \tag{13}$$

The reader is referred to [5] for the decryption equation. For the remainder of this section, we will identify a plain message m with its binary polynomial representation in $\mathbb{R}_2[x]$. Since the decimal value of m is $< N$, $m(x) = m(x) \ mod \ (x^N - 1)$ and the decimal values of the messages inherit their NTRU order from their natural decimal order. To simplify notation, the dummy variable x is removed from the polynomial expressions of the next paragraph.

Order-Preserving NTRU: To encrypt the decision tree, *NTRUEncrypt* should satisfy the relationship of Eq. (2) corresponding to Eq. (1). The decision tree requires the *order-preserving* property instead of the *additive or multiplicative* homomorphic properties, i.e., for any two messages m_i and m_j:

$$\text{if } m_i > m_j \text{ then } E(m_i) > E(m_j) \tag{14}$$

NTRU fulfills such *order-preserving* property.

For the two messages, m_i and m_j where $m_i > m_j, (m_i - m_j) > 0$, their ciphers are as per Eq. (12)

$$\begin{aligned} C_{m_i} &= phr_i + m_i \ (mod\ q) \\ C_{m_j} &= phr_j + m_j \ (mod\ q) \end{aligned} \tag{15}$$

whose difference is

$$\begin{aligned} C_{m_i} - C_{m_j} &= m_i \ (mod\ q) - m_j \ (mod\ q) + ph(r_i - r_j) \\ &= (m_i - m_j) \ (mod\ q) + ph(r_i - r_j) \end{aligned} \tag{16}$$

In the arithmetic of Z_2, we have $m_i - m_j$ are $\in \{0, 1\}$, and since q is large, $(m_i - m_j)\ (mod\ q) = (m_i - m_j)$. So

$$C_{m_i} - C_{m_j} = m_i - m_j + ph(r_i - r_j) \tag{17}$$

The above equation shows that the difference between two ciphers equals the difference between their respective plaintext values augmented with the noise difference $ph(r_j - r_i)$. From Eq. (14), $m_i - m_j > 0$. So $C_{m_i} - C_{m_j} > 0$ if $r_i > r_j$. The noise value r_i should be carefully selected so that NTRUEncrypt is order-preserving. This can be achieved by keeping track of all previously encrypted plaintexts and their ciphertexts, and by selecting the noise r_k for each new plaintext so that if $m_i > m_{i-1} > m_{i-2} > \ldots > m_1 > m_0$ then the noise values should be $r_i > r_{i-1} > r_{i-2} > \ldots > r_1 > r_0$.

6.2 Encrypted Decision Nodes

From Eq. (2), if we use the NTRUEncrypt encryption scheme explained above to secure the pre-trained DT model, the encrypted versions of decision rules are rewritten as follows:

$$\mathbf{E}_{PQ}(\mathbb{D}_{x_k}) < \mathbf{E}_{PQ}(\Lambda_k) \quad or \quad \mathbf{E}_{PQ}(\mathbb{D}_{x_k}) \geq \mathbf{E}_{PQ}(\Lambda_k) \tag{18}$$

where $\mathbf{E}_{PQ}$ is the NTRU encryption operation using the public key. In Eq. (2), the order $(<, \geq)$ of $\mathbb{D}_{x_k}$ with respect to Λ_k is preserved, just as in Eq. (1) due to the order preserving modification of NTRUEncrypt. Specifically, $\mathbb{D}_{x_k} - \Lambda_k = \mathbf{D}_{PQ}(\mathbf{E}_{PQ}(\mathbb{D}_{x_k}) - \mathbf{E}_{PQ}(\Lambda_k))$, where $\mathbf{D}_{PQ}$ denotes the NTRU decryption operator using the private key. The leaf node labels T_k are also encrypted as $\mathbf{E}_{PQ}(T_k)$, and the inferred class/label is then determined in the following manner:

$$T_k = \mathbf{D}_{PQ}(\mathbf{E}_{PQ}(T_k)) \tag{19}$$

Compact Ciphertext Using Lossless Compression: The storage of large ciphertexts for $[\mathbf{E}(\mathbb{D}_{x_k}), \mathbf{E}(\Lambda_k), \mathbf{E}(T_k)]$ of a decision tree within an on-chip memory is a hurdle for FPGA implementation. It may also prevent genuinely lightweight implementations on other hardware platforms, including microcontrollers and machine learning accelerators. Lossless compression is a type of data compression that allows the original data to be properly reconstructed from the compressed cipher with no information loss. Because most real-world data, including NTRU encryption, have statistical redundancy, lossless compression is conceivable. In the NTRU case, the cipher C_m of message m is given by Eq. (12). To maintain the OPE property, $r_{m+1} < r_m$, and the cipher C_{m+k}, for the message $m+k, 1 \leq k \leq n < q$, is given by

$$\begin{aligned} C_{m+k} &= phr_{m+k} + [(m+k) \ mod \ q] \\ &= ph(r_{m+k-1} + r_{m+k} - r_{m+k-1}) \\ &+ [(m+k-1) \ mod \ q] + [1 \ mod \ q] \\ &= ph(r_{m+k} - r_{m+k-1}) + C_{m+k-1} + 1 \end{aligned} \tag{20}$$

Identical Noise: Consider the case where the noise value r_i is the same across all the ciphers, then Eq. (20) becomes

$$C_{m+k} - C_{m+k-1} = 1, \ \ 1 \leq k \leq n < q. \tag{21}$$

which implies the following:

1. The polynomials of two adjacent ciphers differ by one.
2. The polynomials of the ciphers C_m and C_{m+n} differ by the numerical value n.
3. Since the coefficients have binary values, the polynomial coefficients of C_m and C_{m+n} differ only at $(\lfloor log_2(n) \rfloor + 1)$ positions, where $(\lfloor log_2(n) \rfloor + 1)$ is the number of bits in the binary representation of n.
4. For a polynomial of degree $N-1$, there are $N - (\lfloor log_2(n) \rfloor + 1)$ coefficients that are shared between ciphers C_m and C_{m+n}.

It follows from Statement 4 that not all the $N - (\lfloor log_2(n) \rfloor + 1)$ coefficients for the ciphers between C_{m+1} and C_{m+n} need to be stored. All the N coefficients of C_m are stored in the FPGA memory, but for all other ciphers, a compressed representation using only $(\lfloor log_2(n) \rfloor + 1)$ coefficients is sufficient to recreate their ciphertexts. The compression ratio $\mu_{m+k}, 1 \leq k \leq n$, for all ciphers, is calculated as

$$\mu_{m+k} = \frac{N - (\lfloor log_2(k) \rfloor + 1)}{N}. \tag{22}$$

Note that $\mu_m = 0$.

Reusable Noise: Consider now the case where some of the noise values are reused such that n messages share $|\mathcal{N}| < n$ noise values, where $\mathcal{N}$ is a subset of $\{1, \ldots, n\}$. In this case, the encryption strength is stronger than that given in Sect. 6.2. N polynomial coefficients are stored for each of $|\mathcal{N}|$ ciphers, with the compression ratio $\mu_{m+k} = 0, \ k \in \mathcal{N}$. The other ciphers have the compression ratio

$$\mu_{m+k} = \frac{N - (\lfloor log_2(k) \rfloor + 1)}{N}, \ \ 1 \leq k \leq n, \text{ and } \ k \notin \mathcal{N}. \tag{23}$$

Non-uniform Noise: In the case where all the noise values are different, the encryption is the strongest and no compression is possible.

6.3 OP-NTRU FPGA Implementation with Lossless Compression

As in our previous experiments, we have used the prototyping environment of Sect. 3.4 to assess the hardware utilization and performance of the secure DT based on OP-NTRU. Using the reference MNIST data for handwritten digits recognition, the training and validation processes of the DT model were executed on an Amazon EC2 VM. The *NTRUEncrypt* encryption was implemented using open source code available at [5]. Upon completion of the training, the plain and encrypted versions of the decision rules were extracted from the root node to each leaf node. Subsequently, these rules were transformed into Verilog source codes using the Python tool discussed in Sects. 4.4 and 5.3. The resulting verilog codes are then implemented on the Intel Cyclone 5 FPGA on the DE-10 standard SCSXFC6D6F31CN board. Two inference experiments were conducted, one with *plain DT* and another with *secure DT*.

Cipher Compression Evaluation: The features of the MNIST data set are grayscale image pixels with a minimum value of 0 and a maximum value of 255. The threshold Λ_k can be any number between 0 and 255. According to the handwritten digits in the MNIST dataset, the class T_k of a leaf ranges from 0 to 9. In NTRU, N must be the next prime number greater than 255 (refer to Sect. 6.1). Thus, N cannot be 256. Consequently, we set $N = 257$. Instead of MNIST, any other dataset with a maximum value of 256 could be used when $N = 257$. The C_i ciphertexts for messages $i, 0 \leq i \leq 255$ have the polynomial representation

$$C_i(x) = \sum_{j=0}^{256} \alpha_{ij} x^j$$

where $\alpha_{ij} \in \mathbb{Z}_2$ is the j-th coefficient of message i with respect to x^j. The number of bits to represent a message $i \in \{0, \ldots, 255\}$ is $\lfloor log_2 255 \rfloor + 1 = 8$ bits. As per Sect. 6.2, when the same noise value is used across all C_i's, their polynomial coefficients differ only at $\lfloor log_2 255 \rfloor + 1 = 8$ positions. In our examples, the polynomial coefficients are arranged so that these positions always correspond to the coefficients $\alpha_{ij}, j \in \{250, \ldots, 256\}$. In other words, we have: $\alpha_{ij} = \alpha_{lj}, \forall i, l \in \{0, \ldots, 255\}, \forall j \in \{0, \ldots, 249\}$.

The storage requirements are restricted to the 256 coefficients α_{0j} of ciphertext C_0 and the coefficients $\alpha_{ij}, 250 \leq j \leq 256$ for ciphertexts $C_i, 0 \leq i \leq 255$. This results in a compression ratio of $\frac{257-8}{257} \times 100\% = 96.88\%$. This is consistent with Eq. (22) and the compression scheme given in Sect. 6.2.

6.4 OP-NTRU Hardware Experiments

We have measured the inference accuracy on various decision tree architectures given in [14]. To select appropriate architectures, we have scanned the values of

Table 3. FPGA resource comparison of plain and NTRUEncrypt based encrypted decision trees. ALMs: Adaptive logic modules, LABs: Logic array blocks, ALUTs: Combinational adaptive look-up tables, FFs: Dedicated primary registers, F_{max}: Maximum attainable clock frequency, Setup: Slack time for clock setup, Hold: Slack time for clock hold.

Attributes	Plain Decision Tree	Encrypted Decision Tree
ALMs (%)	4	74
LABs (%)	6	95
ALUTs	2592	28072
FFs (%)	3	65
$F_{max}(MHz)$	84.87	61.6
Setup (ns)	8.217	3.766
Hold (ns)	0.368	0.349

the arguments *max_depth* and *max_leaf_nodes* of *sklearn's DecisionTreeClassifier* during the training phase. The selected architecture has 506 nodes and 254 leaves, resulting in 86.62% accuracy on the validation dataset. Two inference experiments, *plain DT* and *secure DT* are run as explained in Sect. 3.4. The comparison of FPGA resources is given in Table 3. The % utilization in Table 3 refers to the percentage of total ALMs, LABs, and FFs of the DE-10 standard FPGA used in the DT implementation. The key size is chosen in line with a real-world use case in which a brute-force attack is not feasible [34]. The FPGA clock frequency is $50MHz$. As anticipated, the resources utilized by the NTRU-encrypted Decision Tree (DT) model surpass those of the unencrypted counterpart. The noteworthy aspect is the utilization of Look-Up Tables (LABs) and Flip-Flops (FFs) in the encrypted scenario, contributing to the increased storage demands. This usage could potentially contribute to an increase in power consumption attributed to READ operations. The functionality and performance of the design are determined by the setup/hold time slacks. The resource utilizations for reusable noise and different noise compression, according to Sect. 6.2, and their comparisons with Table 3 will be included in a future publication.

6.5 Conclusions

In this chapter, we have explored three different algorithms for the confidential inference in decision trees and evaluated their FPGA implementations in a realistic edge-computing scenario. Both combinational and sequential circuit architectures have been designed and evaluated. The three algorithms are (1) additively homomorphic encryption, (2) standard order-preserving encryption, and (3) post-quantum order-preserving encryption using the lattice-based NTRU cryptosystems. In particular, we have applied lossless compression to the ciphertext produced by the latter algorithm to facilitate its hardware acceleration.

Confidential inference experiments have been performed in hardware using the MNIST dataset and have been shown to have favorable outcomes in accuracy and resource utilization.

Acknowledgment. This research has been conducted at Khalifa University with financial support provided by the Technology Innovation Institute (TII), Abu Dhabi, UAE, under contract TII/CRP/2036/2020. The authors are grateful to Elena Kirshanova, Nitin Satpute, and Jinson Thomas, all from TII, for enlightening discussions and helpful comments. Rupesh Raj Karn is now with New York University, Abu Dhabi, UAE.

References

1. Wu, D.J., Feng, T., Naehrig, M., Lauter, K.E.: Privately evaluating decision trees and random forests. Proc. Priv. Enhanc. Technol. **2016**(4), 335–355 (2016)
2. Tueno, A., Boev, Y., Kerschbaum, F.: Non-interactive private decision tree evaluation. In: IFIP Annual Conference on Data and Applications Security and Privacy, pp. 174–194 (2020)
3. Malekian, E., Zakerolhosseini, A.: NTRU-like public key cryptosystems beyond Dedekind domain up to alternative algebra. Trans. Comput. Sci. X 25–41 (2010)
4. Saudy, N.F., Shalash, A.F., Hassan, A.-K.S.: Security improvement for NTRU by using error analysis and detection procedures. In: The International Conference on Mathematics and Engineering Physics. International Conference on Mathematics and Engineering Physics (ICMEP-7), vol. 7, pp. 1–12 (2014)
5. Sapphirine. NTRU python library with application to encrypted domain. https://github.com/Sapphirine/ntru. Accessed 22 June 2024
6. Boldyreva, A., Chenette, N., Lee, Y., O'neill, A.: Order-preserving symmetric encryption. In: EUROCRYPT 2009, pp. 224–241 (2009)
7. Chenette, N., Lewi, K., Weis, S.A., Wu, D.J.: Practical order-revealing encryption with limited leakage. In: 23rd International Conference on Fast Software Encryption (FSE 2016), Selected Papers, pp. 474–493 (2016)
8. Lin, Z., Sinha, S., Zhang, W.: Towards efficient and scalable acceleration of online decision tree learning on FPGA. In: 27th IEEE Annual International Symposium on Field-Programmable Custom Computing Machines (FCCM 2019), pp. 172–180 (2019)
9. Alharam, A.K., Shoufan, A.: Optimized random forest classifier for drone pilot identification. In: 2020 IEEE International Symposium on Circuits and Systems (ISCAS), pp. 1–5 (2020)
10. Wu, D.J., Feng, T., Naehrig, M., Lauter, K.: Privately evaluating decision trees and random forests. Cryptology ePrint Archive (2015)
11. Gentry, C.: A fully homomorphic encryption scheme. Stanford University (2009)
12. Hoffstein, J., Lieman, D., Pipher, J., Silverman, J.H.: NTRU: a public key cryptosystem. NTRU Cryptosystems (1999)
13. Karn, R.R., Elfadel, I.M.: Confidential inference in decision trees: FPGA design and implementation. In: 30th IFIP/IEEE International Conference on Very Large Scale Integration (VLSI-SoC 2022), pp. 1–6 (2022)

14. Karn, R.R., Nawaz, K., Elfadel, I.A.M.: Securing decision tree inference using order-preserving cryptography. In: 5th IEEE International Conference on Artificial Intelligence Circuits and Systems (AICAS 2023), pp. 1–5 (2023)
15. Karn, R.R., Nawaz, K., Elfadel, I.A.M.: Post-quantum, order-preserving encryption for the confidential inference in decision trees: FPGA design and implementation. In: 2023 IFIP/IEEE 31st International Conference on Very Large-Scale Integration (VLSI-SoC), pp. 1–6 (2023)
16. Safavian, S.R., Landgrebe, D.: A survey of decision tree classifier methodology. IEEE Trans. Syst. Man Cybern. **21**(3), 660–674 (1991)
17. Song, Y.-Y., Ying, L.: Decision tree methods: applications for classification and prediction. Shanghai Arch. Psychiatry **27**(2), 130 (2015)
18. Myles, A.J., Feudale, R.N., Liu, Y., Woody, N.A., Brown, S.D.: An introduction to decision tree modeling. J. Chemomet.: J. Chemomet. Soc. **18**(6), 275–285 (2004)
19. Narayanan, R., Honbo, D., Memik, G., Choudhary, A., Zambreno, J.: An FPGA implementation of decision tree classification. In: 2007 Design, Automation & Test in Europe Conference & Exhibition, pp. 1–6 (2007)
20. LeCun, Y., Bottou, L., Bengio, Y., Haffner, P.: Gradient-based learning applied to document recognition. Proc. IEEE **86**(11), 2278–2324 (1998)
21. Acar, A., Aksu, H., Uluagac, A.S., Conti, M.: A survey on homomorphic encryption schemes: theory and implementation. ACM Comput. Surv. (CSUR) **51**(4), 1–35 (2018)
22. Gong, Y., Chang, X., Mišić, J., Mišić, V.B., Wang, J., Zhu, H.: Practical solutions in fully homomorphic encryption: a survey analyzing existing acceleration methods. Cybersecurity **7**(1), 5–27 (2024)
23. Gupta, S., Cammarota, R., Šimunić, T.: MemFHE: end-to-end computing with fully homomorphic encryption in memory. ACM Trans. Embed. Comput. Syst. **23**(2), 1–23 (2024)
24. Nabeel, M., et al.: Silicon-proven ASIC design for the polynomial operations of fully homomorphic encryption. IEEE Trans. Comput. Aided Des. Integr. Circuits Syst. **43**(6), 1924–1928 (2024)
25. DE-10 standard FPGA. http://de10-standard.terasic.com/. Accessed 16 Jan 2023
26. Agrawal, R., Kiernan, J., Srikant, R., Xu, Y.: Order preserving encryption for numeric data. In: Proceedings of the 2004 ACM SIGMOD International Conference on Management of Data, SIGMOD 2004, pp. 563–574 (2004)
27. Liu, Z., Lv, S., Li, J., Huang, Y., Guo, L., Yuan, Y., Dong, C.: EncodeORE: reducing leakage and preserving practicality in order-revealing encryption. IEEE Trans. Dependable Secure Comput. **19**(3), 1579–1591 (2022)
28. Bogatov, D., Kollios, G., Reyzin, L.: A comparative evaluation of order-revealing encryption schemes and secure range-query protocols. Proc. VLDB Endow. **12**(8), 933–947 (2019)
29. Dyer, J., Dyer, M., Djemame, K.: Order-preserving encryption using approximate common divisors. J. Inf. Secur. Appl. **49**, 102391 (2019)
30. Tueno, A., Kerschbaum, F.: Efficient secure computation of order-preserving encryption. In: Proceedings of the 15th ACM Asia Conference on Computer and Communications Security, ASIA CCS 2020, pp. 193–207 (2020)
31. Karn, R.R., Nawaz, K., Elfadel, I.M.: Order-preserving cryptography for the confidential inference in random forests: FPGA design and implementation. In: 61st Design Automation Conference (DAC 2024) (2024, to appear)
32. Alagic, G., et al.: Status report on the third round of the nist post-quantum cryptography standardization process. US Department of Commerce, National Institute of Standards and Technology (2022)

33. Nejatollahi, H., Dutt, N., Ray, S., Regazzoni, F., Banerjee, I., Cammarota, R.: Post-quantum lattice-based cryptography implementations: A survey. ACM Comput. Surv. (CSUR) **51**(6), 1–41 (2019)
34. Tahir, R., Hu, H., Gu, D., McDonald-Maier, K., Howells, G.: Resilience against brute force and rainbow table attacks using strong ICMetrics session key pairs. In: 2013 1st International Conference on Communications, Signal Processing, and their Applications (ICCSPA), pp. 1–6 (2013)

Enhancing the Security of IJTAG Network Using Inherently Secure SIB

Anjum Riaz(✉), Gaurav Kumar, Pardeep Kumar, Yamuna Prasad, and Satyadev Ahlawat

Indian Institute of Technology Jammu, Jammu, India
{anjum.riaz,gaurav.kumar,pardeep.kumar,yamuna.prasad, satyadev.ahlawat}@iitjammu.ac.in

Abstract. Modern VLSI circuits contain various embedded instruments that support non-functional features, e.g., test/debug, diagnosis, post silicon validation, in-field maintenance, etc. The IEEE Std. 1687 (IJTAG) facilitates efficient access to these on-chip instruments using a special scan cell known as Segment Insertion Bit (SIB). Concomitantly, it provides a covert channel for potential intruders to gain unauthorized access to these embedded instruments, enabling them to extract confidential data such as FPGA firmware, secret keys, etc. Therefore, it is quite imperative to restrict access to embedded instruments. Various techniques are present in the literature for enhancing the security of IJTAG network. However, securing the test infrastructure at the cost of complex hardware resources is not always a feasible solution.

In this work, a new mechanism to secure the IJTAG network, which is based on a new Inherently Secure SIB (ISSIB), is proposed. The proposed technique makes use of an LFSR that is formed using the update cell of the ISSIBs. The proposed scheme is simple to implement, highly scalable and provides high level of security against unauthorized access. In addition to that, the proposed scheme preserves the conventional IJTAG features and has negligible area overhead.

Keywords: SIB · IEEE Std. 1687 · LFSR · ISSIB

1 Introduction

The exponential growth in the number of transistors on a single chip due to advancements in VLSI technology results in enhanced performance and increased functional complexity. Concomitantly, due to continuous technological miniaturization, there is a higher probability of circuit malfunctioning. In order to prevent in-field failures, various embedded instruments that support auxiliary features such as test, diagnosis, debug, in-field monitoring, etc., are embedded on the chips. These on-chip instruments could be I/O configuration hardware, error detection sensors, MBIST/LBIST engines, etc. [7,10,13,21,23]. Since the number of on-chip instruments on an SoC may vary from a few hundred to thousands, it is essential to have a scalable and flexible mechanism for accessing these

Published by Springer Nature Switzerland AG 2024
I. (Abe) M. Elfadel and L. Albasha (Eds.): VLSI-SoC 2023, IFIP AICT 680, pp. 299–318, 2024.
https://doi.org/10.1007/978-3-031-70947-0_15

on-chip instruments with a reasonable access time [16]. Over the years, several standards such as IEEE Std. 1149.1 [12], IEEE Std. 1500 [4], and IEEE Std. 1687 [11] have been developed. The objective of developing these standards is to increase the controllability and observability of the chip's internal nodes, as well as mitigate the access time to the embedded instruments. Initially, the IEEE Std. 1149.1 (JTAG) was used to gain access to the on-chip instruments, which uses instruction-based encoding for accessing these instruments. However, with the increasing number of instruments, the instruction-based encoding becomes ineffectual. To address this limitation, the IEEE Std. 1687 (IJTAG) was developed.

The IEEE Std. 1687 facilitates reconfigurable access to on-chip instruments. It defines two languages: Instrument Connectivity Language (ICL) and Procedural Description Language (PDL), to describe the dynamic topologies and operation of instruments, respectively. These instruments are accessed via Test Access Port (TAP) controller of JTAG. Also, the dynamic reconfigurability of the IJTAG network is accomplished by using a standard cell called SIB. To establish communication with the instrument, the update cell of the SIB is clocked with a logic '1' value. Similarly, to bypass the on-chip instrument that is behind an SIB, the update cell of the corresponding SIB is clocked with a logic '0' value. In this way, SIB provides flexible mechanism to access the embedded instruments. This flexibility reduces the test sequence length for accessing the embedded instruments on an SoC.

Although the IEEE Std. 1687 eases instrument access and minimizes access time; this standard has been developed without taking security aspects into consideration. For instance, a malicious user may shift in a predefined sequence in the scan path and set the TAP controller to update state. This may open a few SIBs, and hence, the instruments behind the SIBs are added to the scan path. Consequently, once the instruments are accessible, the attacker may mount various types of existing scan-based attacks [24] to steal confidential information such as Chip ID, FPGA firmware and secret keys [15]. At first, Dworak et al. put forth the concept of Locking SIB (LSIB) to prevent on-chip instruments from being accessed by unauthorized users [8]. The LSIB can be unlocked if the user supplies the correct key in the active scan path. This ensures that only authorized users with the correct key can access the on-chip instruments. Furthermore, various advanced techniques that build over the concept of LSIB have been proposed [1,17,25]. Although these advanced LSIB structures prevent unauthorized users from accessing the IJTAG network, these techniques either do not provide sufficient security or are very complex and incur a very large area overhead. Since the modern VLSI circuits are embedded with hundreds of on-chip instruments, thus securing instruments with complex hardware resources is not always viable, especially for resource constraint systems. In this work, an Inherently Secure SIB ($ISSIB$) is proposed. The main motivation behind designing the ISSIB is to bring testing/functionality and security together in the design of SIB. The proposed ISSIB keeps the dynamic reconfigurability feature of SIB intact, concomitantly, it protects the IJTAG network from malicious users. The rest of the chapter is organized as follows: Sect. 2 provides a brief introduction to the design of SIB and the existing techniques for the security of the IJTAG network. The proposed ISSIB is discussed in detail in Sect. 3. Section 4 discusses the experimental results. Finally, Sect. 5 concludes the chapter.

2 Background

The SIB is the basic building block of IJTAG network. The schematic diagram of a standard SIB is depicted in Fig. 1. It has two cells: shift cell and update cell. SIB allows the dynamic reconfiguration of the scan network by including or excluding the instrument/scan segment in the active scan path. To accomplish this functionality, SIB is operated in two modes of operation: open mode and close mode. During open mode, a logic '1' value is clocked into the update cell of SIB via Test Data Input (TDI) port through the shift cell, when update signal is enabled ($UpDr$ = '1'), and thus the *Select** signal is asserted. The **Select* signal acts as a selection signal for multiplexer (M1), which then selects input from Test Data Output2 (From_TDO2 port in Fig. 1). It is to be noted that *Select** and **Select* are connected. The data from TDO2 is then fed to the shift cell of the SIB when shift signal is at logic '1' ($ShDr$ = '1'). In this way, the instrument/scan segment that is between TDI2 and TDO2 port is included in the active scan path. Note that the *Select** signal is also used to gate the capture ($CapDr$), shift ($ShDr$) and update ($UpDr$) signals to control the capture, shift and update operations, respectively, in the corresponding instrument. During the close mode, the update cell is clocked with the logic '0' value, and hence, *Select** signal is de-asserted. Therefore the instrument/scan segment is excluded from the active scan path. The active scan path now includes the shift cell only between TDI1 and TDO1 ports. It is noteworthy that upon initialization (reset/power-up) all the SIBs are in close mode.

To understand the IJTAG functionality, let us consider the IJTAG network as shown in Fig. 2. Since on reset/power-up, all the SIBs are closed, and hence the scan path includes the shift cell of $SIB1$, $SIB2$, $SIB3$ and $SIB4$ between the TDI and TDO port. Now, for example, to access the instrument $I3$, $SIB3$ and $SIB5$ need to be opened. First, the configuration bits "0100" (with MSB being shifted in first) are shifted into the scan path. After applying the update cycle ($UpDr = 1$), the update cell of the SIB3 is clocked with the logic '1' value. This opens SIB3, and therefore, the scan segment behind SIB3 is incorporated in the scan path. Now, the active scan path becomes $TDI \rightarrow SIB1 \rightarrow SIB2 \rightarrow SIB5 \rightarrow SIB6 \rightarrow SIB3 \rightarrow SIB4 \rightarrow TDO$. Now, to include the instrument $I3$ in the scan path, the update cell of SIB5 needs to be clocked with a logic '1' value. Hence, the configuration bits "010100" are shifted into the scan path. After applying the update cycle, SIB5 is opened, and instrument $I3$ is included in the scan path. As a result, the active scan path becomes $TDI \rightarrow SIB1 \rightarrow SIB2 \rightarrow I3 \rightarrow SIB5 \rightarrow SIB6 \rightarrow SIB3 \rightarrow SIB4 \rightarrow TDO$. In this way, SIB allows to include or exclude the instrument in the scan path in an efficient manner. However, any user (authorized or unauthorized) can shift in a walking '1' or '0' sequence, thereby gaining access to the sensitive embedded instruments.

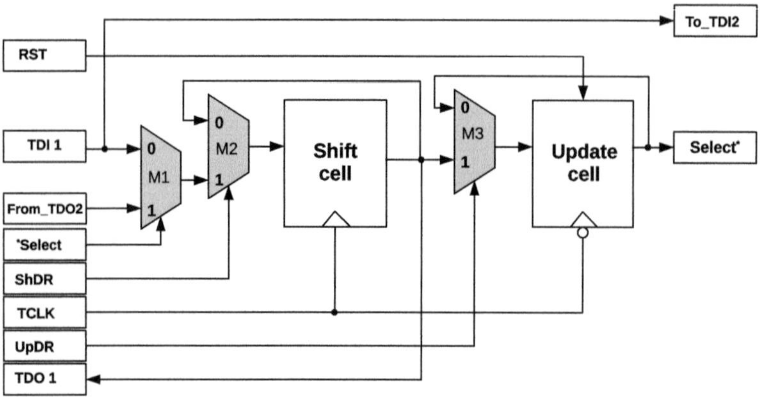

Fig. 1. Standard SIB Implementation [11]

To introduce the security in SIB, Dworak et al. proposed a Locking SIB (LSIB) [8]. In this scheme, the LSIB is unlocked only when some of the bits in the scan path are set to predefined values. This is achieved by gating the update signal of the SIB with an n-bit key. The second approach for key insertion is that the dummy flip-flops are added to the scan path for storing the key bits. Thus, only the users with information about the key can open the LSIB and hence gain access to the on-chip instruments. However, in an IJTAG network, if hundreds of instruments need to be secured, then each SIB is replaced by LSIB. If n dummy flip-flops are added into the scan path to store the n-bit key of each LSIB, then the area overhead becomes very high. Also, if these n dummy

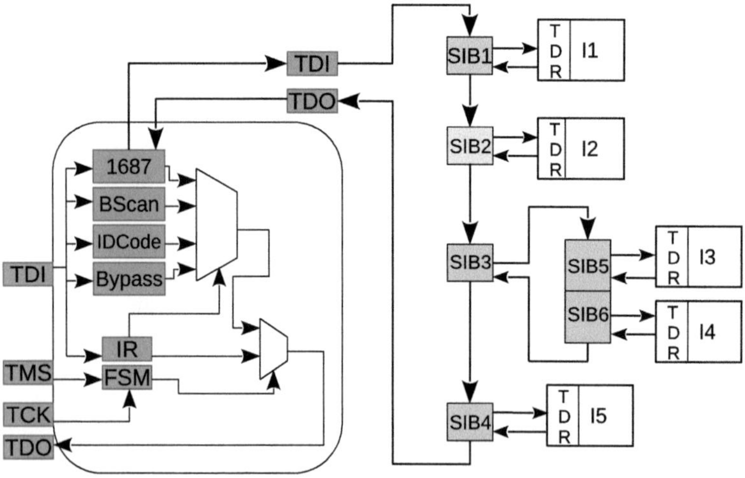

Fig. 2. A hierarchical IJTAG network

flip flops are at the top layer of IJTAG network, then it will increase the test pattern insertion time with n cycles. As a result, the timing overhead increases with the increase in the number of LSIBs and the dummy flip-flops. Despite the size of LSIB key, it is still feasible for a malevolent user to bypass its security by inserting a random pattern and applying the update state. As a result, some of the LSIBs might open, which will include the corresponding instrument/scan segment in the active scan path. Hence, the intruder can observe the change in the scan path length at TDO port, which provides feedback to the intruder that LSIB is unlocked. In order to prevent the feedback to the intruder, trap bits are introduced in the scan path. If an incorrect value is clocked into the trap bit, then the scan network is self-locked until a global reset is asserted. Furthermore, the same authors introduced honeytrap LSIBs, switching LSIBs and naturally open LSIBs that make the opening of LSIB harder using brute-force attack [25]. Although these advanced LSIB structures enhance the security mechanism, the attacker could still potentially unlock LSIB using basic enumeration with increased computational efforts [17]. The same authors in [6] have proposed a secure access protocol based on LSIB for preventing unauthorized users from accessing the on-chip instruments. At the same time, this protocol detects counterfeit/pirated boards. Although this scheme is simple and effective for enhancing board security, in a recent work, it has been shown that the secure access protocol is vulnerable to machine learning attack [15].

To elevate the security of the IJTAG network, Liu et al. devised to introduce a Security Linear Feedback Shift Register (SLFSR) into the scan path. The SLFSR is used to generate some of the key bits for LSIB, while the user externally supplies the remaining key bits. The rationale behind adding the SLFSR is to prevent the user from knowing the scan path length. In this scheme, until the user is authorized, the pseudorandom sequence produced by the SLFSR is visible at the TDO port. Hence, the user cannot deduce the scan path length from this information. However, in [14], it is shown that this scheme is vulnerable to a hybrid attack that includes power-analysis attack and known plaintext attack. As a result, the security enhancement provided by this scheme is nullified.

In another technique, Baranowski et al. in [1] have proposed a Secure SIB (SSIB) for securing the on-chip instruments. This technique makes use of an authorization controller, a True Random Number Generator (TRNG), secret memory and a hash core. It is based on a challenge-response protocol. At first, the user sends a request to the authorization controller for accessing the on-chip instruments. The authorization controller generates a challenge using a TRNG. The response to the challenge is calculated using a one-way hash function. If the response sent by the user matches the expected response, then the sensitive on-chip instruments become accessible. Otherwise, the access is denied. Although this technique provides improved security to the on-chip instruments, it is very complex. Also, securing the test infrastructure at the cost of such a large area overhead is not practically feasible in resource constraint design. In [18], the authors have proposed an Encryption SIB (eSIB) that is the extension of SSIB [1] with some additional XOR gates to include the encryption capabilities as well as user authorization. The area overhead for eSIB is almost twice as compared to the SIB. Also, this approach suffers from key alignment issues [18].

The encryption of test vector/response to prevent the attackers from eavesdropping the scan chain is explored in [13]. If a test vector is encrypted externally and decrypted on board, and if an instrument happens to be malicious, then the potentially malicious instrument may mount the data alteration/sniffing attack [3,9,20]. To prevent this, test data may be decrypted locally by the instrument. However, the area overhead of the dedicated cryptographic module will be too high. Therefore, a countermeasure is required to enhance the security of IJTAG network without impacting test time, test data volume, or incurring significant area overhead. This work proposes an Inherently Secure SIB (ISSIB) designed to thwart attacks from malicious users while preserving testability.

3 Inherently Secure SIB

This section presents a novel approach for enhancing the security of the IJTAG network against unauthorized access. In the standard SIB, update cell is initialized with zero at reset/power-up. It remains idle until the update cycle is applied after the complete configuration vector is shifted into the scan path. Initially, the scan path consists of shift cells of those SIBs which are part of the active scan path. The intruder can easily open or close an SIB and access the sensitive instruments by applying the walking logic '1' (...0001000...) or walking logic '0' patterns, respectively. To inhibit the attacker from exploiting this capability, a new Inherently Secure SIB (ISSIB) is proposed. The proposed ISSIB brings the testability/functionality and security features together by incorporating the security mechanism in the SIB itself. Additionally, the proposed Inherently Secure SIB (ISSIB) maintains the dynamic reconfigurability feature of IJTAG network with a negligible area overhead. The proposed ISSIB uses the LFSR based authorization, which is formed using the update cell of ISSIB, to secure the IJTAG network from unauthorized access.

3.1 Inherently Secure SIB Architecture

The ISSIB is formed with a minor modification in the standard SIB. The schematic of the proposed ISSIB is shown in Fig. 3. The additional components (highlighted in grey colour) in the ISSIB other than standard SIB are multiplexer $M4$, AND gates $A1$ and $A2$. Additionally, the ISSIB has two extra inputs, i.e., $Feed\_In$ and $Auth$ and one extra output $Feed\_Out$. The ISSIB operates in two modes: Standard mode and Authorization mode. The mode of operation is decided by the $Auth$ signal. When $Auth$ is deasserted (i.e., '0'), the ISSIB operates in Authorization mode. Alternatively, if $Auth$ is asserted (i.e., '1'), the ISSIB operates in Standard mode. In Standard mode, the ISSIB simply mimics the functionality of standard SIB. As $Auth$ signal is always asserted in Standard mode, the update enable ($UpDr$) and $Select^*$ signal propagates through AND gates (A1 and A2), respectively. Therefore, the user can perform update operation, and whenever logic '1' is clocked into the update cell of ISSIB, a new scan segment is included in the active scan path. On the other hand, if a logic '0' is clocked into it, then the scan segment is bypassed. Also, the multiplexer M4 always selects the output of update cell and the *Feed_In* remains disconnected. Consequently, the output of the update cell propagates to one of the inputs of M3. This is exactly the functionality of standard SIB. However, to use the ISSIB in standard mode, the user needs first to get authorized himself/herself.

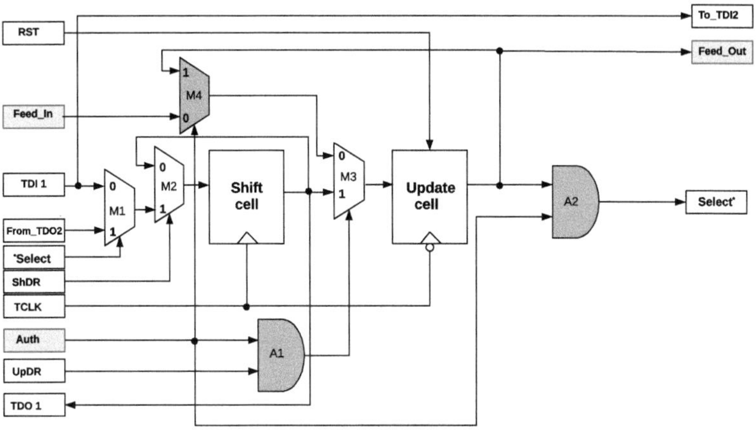

Fig. 3. Proposed Secure SIB Implementation

3.2 User Authorization Using ISSIB

Upon reset/power-up, the *Auth* signal is deasserted, and the ISSIB is initialized in Authorization mode. It remains in the Authorization mode until the user authorization is successful, i.e., *Auth* signal is asserted. The proposed ISSIB uses the LFSR based authorization, which is formed using the update cells of ISSIBs. For successful authorization, user needs to shift-in the authorization key from TDI port into the shift cell of the ISSIB. The authorization key supplied by the user should match with the key generated by the LFSR, which is formed by the update cell of ISSIBs of IJTAG network. Since, during the authorization phase, *Auth* signal is always 0 and hence *Feed_In* is always selected at M4 and the output of M4 is selected at M3. As a result, *Feed_In*, M4, M3, Update cell and *Feed_Out* signals form the feed forward path of the LFSR. The *Feed_Out* signal of an ISSIB is XORed with the *Feed_Out* signal of another ISSIB to generate the *Feed_In* signal (feedback path of LFSR). The number of XOR gates required depends on the feedback polynomial of the LFSR. It should be noted that in authorization mode, the update cell forms the LFSR and both '0' and '1' values may propagate into it. As the output of the update cell forms

*Select** signal, it may include a scan segment into the active scan path whenever a '1' value is propagated into it. Because of this, active scan path will change. In order to avoid it, the output of the update cell is gated with *Auth* signal. As a result, *Select** remains always deasserted during authorization mode. For authorization, the user shifts the key bits via TDI port into the scan path which is formed by the shift cells of ISSIBs in the initial scan path. For instance, if the initial scan path has n number of ISSIBs, it requires n number of cycles to insert the key bits into the scan path. In n cycles, the first key bit inserted by the user reaches the last ISSIB of the scan path. From $(n+1)^{th}$ cycle onwards, the key bits inserted by the user are matched against the key bits (pseudorandom sequence) generated by the L-bit LFSR, where L denotes the number of ISSIBs used to form LFSR. It should be noted that the size of LFSR is not restricted by the number of ISSIBs in the initial scan path length. The number of ISSIBs (L) used to form LFSR may vary from n (number of ISSIBs in the initial scan path of IJTAG network) to N (number of ISSIBs in the IJTAG network) depending upon the required security level. Moreover, the LFSR can be formed by the ISSIBs present at different hierarchical levels. Now, for authorization, the user key bit in the shift cell of the last ISSIB is matched against the LFSR key bit in the update cell of the last ISSIB of initial scan path. If there is a match, then a signal ($Match$) is passed to a down counter, which counts K down to 0. In order to authorize, the $Match$ signal must remain asserted continuously for K number of cycles. In case any key bit supplied by the user mismatches with the LFSR key bit, the $Match$ signal deasserts and resets the counter back to the value K. Whenever the counter value reaches zero, it asserts the *Auth* signal, which denotes successful authorization. It should be noted that the value K of the counter is decided as per the required security level, which is decided during the design phase.

3.3 Working Example of IJTAG Network with ISSIB

An example IJTAG network using the proposed ISSIB with a single LFSR is shown in Fig. 4. From TDI to TDO, it has 'N' number of ISSIBs, which form the initial scan path ($ISSIB1, ISSIB2, \ldots, ISSIBN{-}2, ISSIBN{-}1, ISSIBN$). In case of industrial SoC design, N can vary from 50 to 400 [22]. For simplicity, out of N ISSIBs, only four are used to form the LFSR (i.e. $L = 4$) for user authorization ($ISSIB1$, $ISSIB2$, $ISSIBN-1$, $ISSIBN$). The rest of the ISSIBs can be made to operate in standard mode and work as a standard SIB by assigning the specific values to *Auth* and $Feed\_In$ signals. For this, the *Auth* and $Feed\_In$ signals are tied to logic '1' and '0', respectively. Note that if the intruder randomly applies the update operation during the authorization phase, it might open some of the ISSIBs which are not part of the LFSR feed forward path. This will change the scan shift path length. However, the intruder will not be able to observe any change in the scan path length due to the gating of TDO port. It will also increase the complexity of brute-force attack because now the intruder does not know about the new length of the active scan path. Moreover, the update cycle during the authorization phase will not open ISSIBs of LFSR feed forward path because $Auth$ signal remains deasserted until the authorization is complete. It is important to emphasize that in this configuration, the LFSR, which is formed using the update cells of ISSIB, is resistant to algebraic attacks such as known plaintext attack [2]. This is because the pseudorandom patterns generated by the LFSR are not visible to the attacker due to the gating of the TDO port. If somehow the attacker gets access to the $2L$ (L being the size of the LFSR) bits of the LFSR, which is a prerequisite to mount a known plaintext attack, the attacker can retrieve the primitive polynomial of the LFSR. Therefore, to fortify our proposed scheme against known plaintext attack, particularly those leveraging insider information, an enhanced security methodology is introduced in the next subsection.

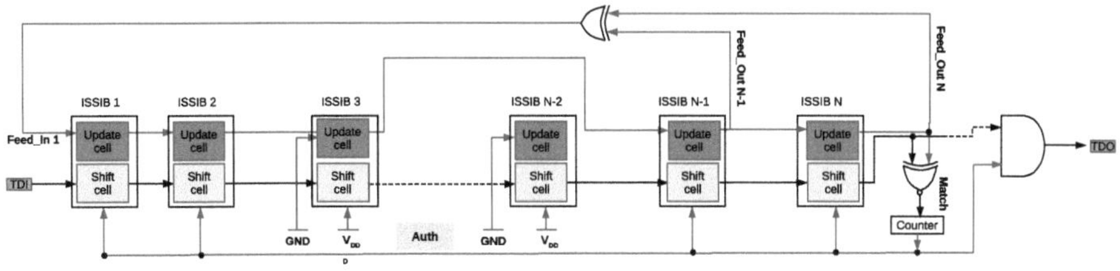

Fig. 4. Secure IJTAG Network with Proposed ISSIB

3.4 LFSR Configurations for Enhanced Security

As previously mentioned, ISSIBs are used to form a single LFSR, which is one of the possible configurations for the formation of LFSR. Instead of forming a single LFSR, the designer has the flexibility to opt for multiple LFSRs using the available ISSIBs. This approach not only enhances security by leveraging multiple LFSRs but also offers a modular and adaptable design strategy. For instance, if the number of ISSIBs in the IJTAG network is N. In such a case, the designer can create three LFSRs with lengths denoted as $N1$, $N2$ and $N3$. Now, to generate the LFSR key, the outputs of all three LFSRs are XORed together, as shown in Fig. 5. Additionally, the output of LFSR_i is XORed with the $Feedback$ signal of LFSR_{i+1} to generate the $Feed\_In$ signal of LFSR_{i+1}, as illustrated in Eq. 1.

$$Feed\_In_{i+1} = LFSR_i \oplus Feedback_{i+1} \tag{1}$$

Now, the sequence generated by each LFSR depends not only on its own state but also on the output of the previous LFSR. This interdependency of LFSRs makes it challenging for the attacker to predict the output sequence of any given LFSR even if (s)he has partial knowledge of its internal state. Furthermore, as the number of LFSRs increases, the interdependency of the LFSRs increases, which makes it resistant to the known plaintext attack even if the attacker knows the

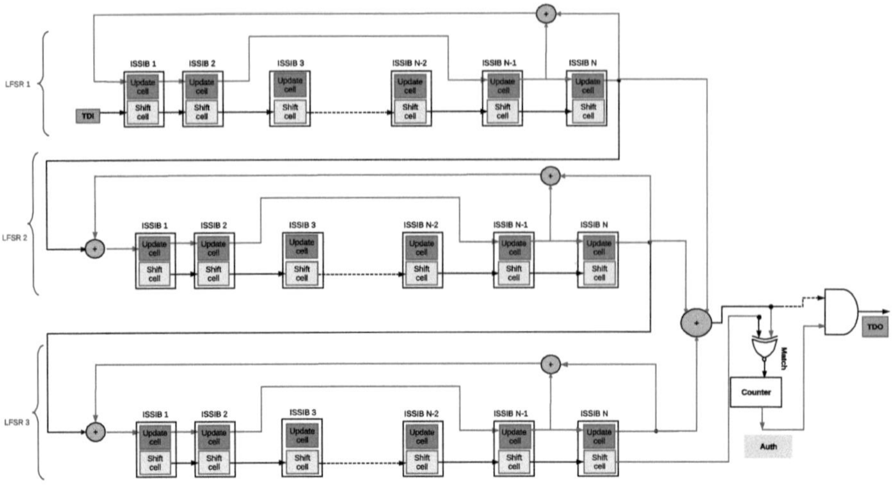

Fig. 5. Secure IJTAG Network with three LFSRs

$2L$ bits of the LFSR. Thus, the utilization of multiple LFSRs allows for increased complexity and variability in key generation, contributing to enhanced security measures within the IJTAG network.

To fortify our proposed scheme against known plaintext attacks, particularly those leveraging insider information, another secure configuration based on Non-linear LFSR (NLFSR) inspired by the Trivium cipher [5] is introduced. This approach incorporates non-linear operations into the LFSR key generation process, rendering it more resistant to attacks based on known plaintexts and insider knowledge. This non-linearity is introduced through the execution of AND operations on specific bits within the NLFSR [19]. Subsequently, these computed AND operations are used to construct the LFSR key. Consequently, it thwarts the attacker from exploiting the linear nature of the LFSR. This way, the security of the IJTAG network with the proposed scheme increases significantly.

In this configuration, rather than using all ISSIBs to form a single LFSR, the ISSIBs are now partitioned into multiple groups, each contributing to the formation of an LFSR. These LFSRs are connected in a serial fashion to form an NLFSR, as shown in Fig. 6. In this example, three LFSRs are formed from the ISSIBs. The input of each LFSR_i is computed as the XOR of the output of the LFSR_{i-1} and the *Feed_In* signal of LFSR_{i+1}. Notably, the primitive polynomials for the individual LFSRs can vary. Moreover, AND operation is executed on some specific bits of every LFSR. Now, to introduce non-linearity in the LFSR key, the output of AND gates are XORed with the output of all three LFSRs, as shown in Fig. 6. This LFSR key is compared with the user key and if they match, it implies successful authorization. It should be noted that the authorization time using brute force attack for both LFSR and NLFSR will be the same. The objective of introducing non-linearity in the multiple LFSR configuration is to make the design resistant to algebraic attacks, which may be

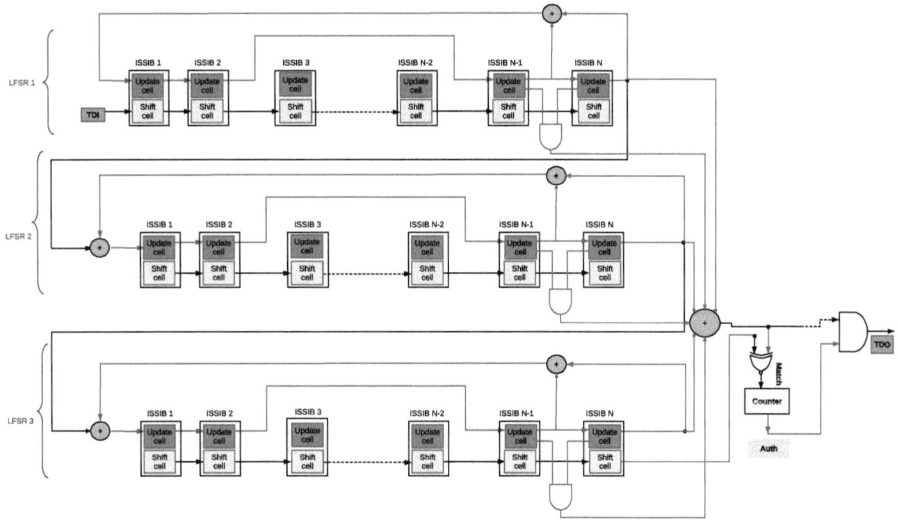

Fig. 6. Secure IJTAG Network with NLFSR

instigated by the attacker with insider information. It is noteworthy that the shift cells of $LFSR_i$ are connected to $LFSR_{i+1}$. However, these signals are not shown in Fig. 6 for the sake of brevity and analyzability. Additionally, the *Auth* signal generated by the counter is connected to all ISSIBs that are used to form NLFSR, albeit not represented in Fig. 6 for visual clarity.

4 Experimental Results

In order to validate the functionality of the proposed ISSIB, the IJTAG network shown in Fig. 2 is implemented in Xilinx Vivado using VHDL. In the implementation, ISSIB is used for reconfiguring the IJTAG network rather than standard SIB. In the example IJTAG network, four out of six ISSIBs are used to form the LFSR. Here, a 4-bit LFSR, $1+x+x^4$, is used for key generation, as explained in Sect. 3. A key sequence of 8-bit should match for authorization, i.e., the counter value is set to 8. The key used for authorization is "11000101", which is generated by LFSR after n cycles.

4.1 Design Validation

The simulation waveform generated by the Xilinx Vivado tool illustrates the authorization process using ISSIB, as depicted in Fig. 7. Initially, when Reset is high, the *Auth* signal is deasserted and ISSIB is initialized in Authorization mode. Furthermore, the LFSR (update cell of ISSIBs) is initialized with the seed value "1010". Subsequently, the TAP controller transitions to the shift state, with signal details omitted for clarity. Once it reaches the shift state, the user then begins to shift in the key sequence through the scan path, starting with the Most Significant Bit (MSB), while the LFSR concurrently generates the key. Notably, the TDO port is gated with the *Auth* signal, preventing any data from passing through it during the authorization process. A logic low value ('0') is visible at the TDO port until the authorization process completes successfully. In this instance, the user's sequence takes four cycles to reach the last ISSIB after *ShiftEn* is asserted, as shown by SIB4_SO signal (red colour) in Fig. 7. In the same clock cycle, the key bit generated by the LFSR comes out from the last ISSIB as shown by SIB_feed_out signal (magenta colour) in Fig. 7. It should be noted that there is a delay of half clock cycle between the SIB4_feed_out signal and SIB4_SO signal. This is because the shift cell operates as a positive edge triggered flip flop while the update cell operates as a negative edge triggered flip flop [11]. Therefore, both bits are compared using a logical XNOR operation in the next rising edge of the clock to generate a *Match* signal. Whenever the *Match* signal is at logic '1', i.e., the user key bit matches with the LFSR key bit, the counter decreases. However, if the *Match* signal is at logic '0', the counter resets itself and the user needs to reinsert the complete key sequence again. When the counter value (counter signal in Fig. 7) reaches zero, it means all the user key bits are matched with the LFSR key bits. It takes eight cycles to verify all the eight key bits. Once all the key bits are matched, the *Auth* signal is set to logic '1', as shown in Fig. 7, which means authorization is successful. The data at the TDO port, which was gated using *Auth* signal, starts passing through it. Now, ISSIB switches from authorization mode to standard mode and functions as a standard SIB for reconfiguring the IJTAG network.

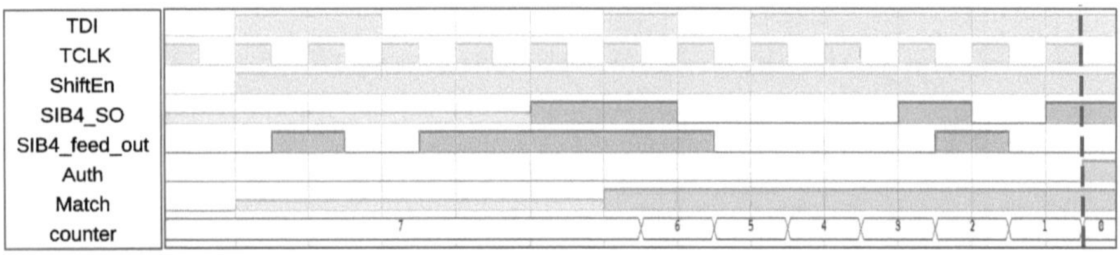

Fig. 7. Simulation Waveform for Design Validation (Color figure online)

4.2 Security Analysis

The security of the proposed scheme depends upon LFSR and the counter size (K). Further, the security of the LFSR is dependent upon its feedback polynomial and seed. The feedback polynomial of LFSR is a primitive polynomial which is decided during the design phase. The sequence generated by primitive polynomial is a maximum length sequence, i.e., $2^L - 1$ (L is the degree of the polynomial). For the example IJTAG network shown in Fig. 4, the primitive polynomial of degree 4 is $1 + x + x^4$. The seed is also fixed at design time. In order to initialize the LFSR with a predecided seed at reset/power-up, ISSIBs with set/reset feature can be used. This is because the set/reset feature is available in standard SIB [11]. The security analysis of the proposed scheme that is based on the value of the counter K and degree of LFSR (L), is discussed in the following subsections.

***K* and *L* are Known.** In this case, it is assumed that both the parameters (K and L) are known to the intruder. There are two possible cases in this scenario, as described below:

Case 1: $K < 2^L$

The probability of successful authorization of an intruder using random patterns will be

$$Prob\ (\text{Authorization when } K \text{ and } L \text{ are known}) = \frac{1}{2^K}$$

Case 2: $K \geq 2^L$

The probability of successful authorization of an intruder using random patterns will be

$$Prob\ (\text{Authorization when } K \text{ and } L \text{ are known}) = \frac{1}{2^L - 1}$$

This is because of the fact that LFSR can generate a sequence with maximum length of $2^L - 1$. Selecting $K \geq 2^L$ has no significant impact on the security, because after $2^L - 1$ cycles, the pseudorandom pattern generated by LFSR starts to repeat. However, if $K \geq 2^L$, it will increase the computational cost of the attack. In the above expressions, '-1' accounts for 'all zeros' invalid state of LFSR. The K and L are chosen as per the required security level.

In both the aforementioned cases, the computational time required to mount the brute-force attack depends on the counter value (K) and initial scan path length (n). To apply every possible sequence, the intruder has to control the TAP controller and pass through some fixed states (5 cycles), as shown in Fig. 8. Each possible sequence takes K cycles as the sequence length for authorization is K bits and n cycles to fill the scan path with the sequence bits. Therefore, $K + n + 5$ cycles are required to try a single random key sequence. The total possible key sequences are 2^K. Thus, the total number of cycles required for authorization using random patterns in an exhaustive manner will be

$$cost\ (\text{Authorization when } K \text{ and } L \text{ are known}) = 2^K(K + n + 5) \text{ cycles}$$

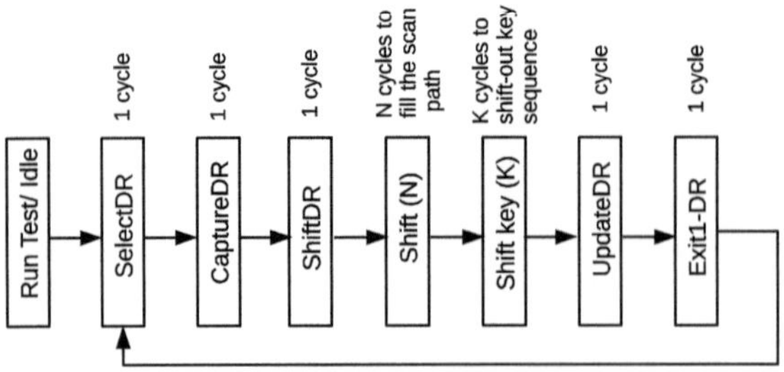

Fig. 8. Number of cycles to apply a single sequence using TAP controller

***K* and *L* are Unknown.** If the counter value (K) and degree (L) are unknown to the intruder, then the intruder needs to brute force the counter value first and then brute force the exact required key sequence. In this scenario, if $K \geq 2^L$, then the LFSR sequence repeats after $2^L - 1$ cycles. Since K and L are unknown to the intruder, (s)he does not know when to repeat the LFSR sequence. Hence, the security of the IJTAG network depends on the value K. The value K can be chosen from a few hundred to a few thousand. However, it is observed from the experiments that the $K \geq 128$ makes it secure against brute-force attack. Consequently, the probability of successful authorization by an intruder, in this case, will be

$$Prob\ (\text{Authorization when } K \text{ and } L \text{ are unknown}) = \frac{1}{\sum_{i=1}^{K} 2^i}$$

Also, each possible sequence takes $K + 5$ cycles as the sequence length is K bits and n cycles to fill the scan path with the sequence bits. Therefore, number of cycles required to apply a single key sequence is $K + n + 5$. The total possible key sequences, in this case, are also 2^K. However, the value of the counter (K) is unknown to the intruder. The intruder needs to brute-force the value of K. Thus, number of cycles required for authorization using random patterns will be

$$cost\ (\text{Authorization when } K \text{ and } L \text{ are unknown}) = \sum_{i=1}^{K} 2^i (i + n + 5) \text{ cycles}$$

The authorization is a one-time activity for every test session. Hence, for an authorized user, the value of K could be in tens of thousands, which makes it highly resistant to brute-force attack. Moreover, the number of SIBs in the IJTAG network which could be replaced by ISSIB varies from 50 to 400 as shown in Table 1. Therefore, a very large size LFSR can be used to generate the authorization key. Furthermore, due to the large number of ISSIBs, various configurations explained in Subsect. 3.4 can be employed to enhance the security. The expected time required for authorization by brute-force, considering that the attacker can apply at a rate of 2 GHz frequency for different values of K, is given in Table 2. Additionally, for Table 2, the degree of LFSR is considered to be 32. It can be observed from Table 2 that a counter value of 128 (7 bit counter) with 32 bit LFSR is strong enough to make the brute-force attack impractical. Hence, a small size LFSR could be used to elevate the security of the IJTAG network and make it computationally infeasible to break. However, the size of the LFSR is restricted by the number of ISSIBs in the IJTAG network.

4.3 Area Overhead

To compare the area overhead, the proposed ISSIB, along with other types of SIBs, are implemented using VHDL in Cadence Genus tool with 45 nm library. The area overhead of an ISSIB over a standard SIB is constant as it does not have any key-size dependent structure. A comparison among the area of LSIB, SSIB, eSIB and the proposed ISSIB is shown in Table 3. While calculating the area, it is considered that the IJTAG network consists of only one type of SIB at a time. For example, while considering Locking SIB, a 32-bit key is used to unlock it. Similarly, for the proposed ISSIB, a 32-bit key sequence should match for successful authorization, i.e., the counter is set at 32. It can be observed from Table 3 that the proposed ISSIB has an area overhead of 21.62% over the standard SIB, which is negligible with reference to a complex SoC. It should be noted that the area overhead of the proposed ISSIB is least among all other Secure SIB structures. The LSIB overhead increases with the increase in the key size because of the AND gate which is used for gating the update signal. The SSIB and eSIB have an area overhead approximately equal to the area of the standard SIB. This is because of the extra two flip-flops used for creating the secure path. Moreover, columns 4 and 5 represent the area overhead of various SIBs with respect to TreeFlat and Mingle benchmarks. It can be seen from Table 3 that the proposed ISSIB incurs area overhead of 0.97% and 1.11%, for TreeFlat and Mingle benchmarks, respectively, which is minimal as compared to the existing secure SIBs.

4.4 Security Analysis vs. Overhead Evaluation

In order to break the proposed scheme, the attacker needs to shift in the correct user key sequence via TDI port. When this user key sequence matches with the

Table 1. Number of SIBs in ITC'16 Benchmarks [22]

Benchmarks		Number of SIBs
Basic	TreeflatEx	57
	Mingle	13
	TreeFlat	13
	TreeBalanced	43
Classic	t512505	160
	p22810	283
Advanced	NE1200P430	381
	NE600P150	207

Table 2. Expected time for authorization using brute-force

Counter Number (K)	Expected Time (sec) (K known)	Expected Time (sec) (K unknown)
64	6.73×10^{11}	1.32×10^{12}
128	2.33×10^{31}	4.62×10^{31}
256	1.52×10^{70}	3.05×10^{70}
512	3.44×10^{147}	3.46×10^{147}

Table 3. Area overhead for various SIBs over standard SIB

SIB Name	Exact Area μm^2	% Area overhead (w.r.t. Standard SIB)	% Area overhead (of 13 SIBs w.r.t. TreeFlat)	% Area overhead (of 13 SIBs w.r.t. Mingle)
LSIB [8]	46.816	58.56	2.64	3.0
SSIB [1]	55.328	87.38	3.94	4.46
eSIB [18]	57.988	96.39	4.34	4.96
ISSIB	**35.910**	**21.62**	**0.97**	**1.11**

LFSR key, which is generated on-the-fly, then only the attacker is authorized and can access the on-chip instruments. If the user key bit matches with the LFSR key bit, the counter is activated and subsequently decremented to keep track of the correct key bits. For successful authorization, all the K bits of the user key should match with the LFSR key so that the counter remains enabled for K cycles and reaches zero. If any user key bit mismatches with the LFSR key, then the counter is reset, indicating unsuccessful authorization. Additionally, the chosen key size can be adjusted as per the required security level, balancing security and hardware overhead considerations. If the key size is sufficiently large, then the authorization time (number of clock cycles) required for brute force by the attacker to get authorized increases exponentially while the area overhead increases linearly. In order to validate our claim, we have implemented various basic benchmarks such as Mingle, TreeFlat, TreeFlatEx, TreeBalanced and classic benchmark t512505. Figure 9 presents a comprehensive analysis, illustrating the authorization time and percentage increase in area for different counter sizes.

For instance, Fig. 9a highlights that in the Mingle benchmark circuit, if the chosen key size is 256 bits, i.e., the counter size is 8 bits, then the authorization time taken by the attacker to access the IJTAG network is $1.56 * 10^{70}$ clock cycles. In contrast, if the chosen key size is 512 bits, i.e., the counter width is 9 bits, then the authorization time taken by the attacker for successful authorization escalates to $3.53 * 10^{147}$ cycles. This exponential increase in authorization time for unauthorized users is due to the necessity to attempt all possible key combinations, and to try a single key sequence, there is a fixed cost (in terms

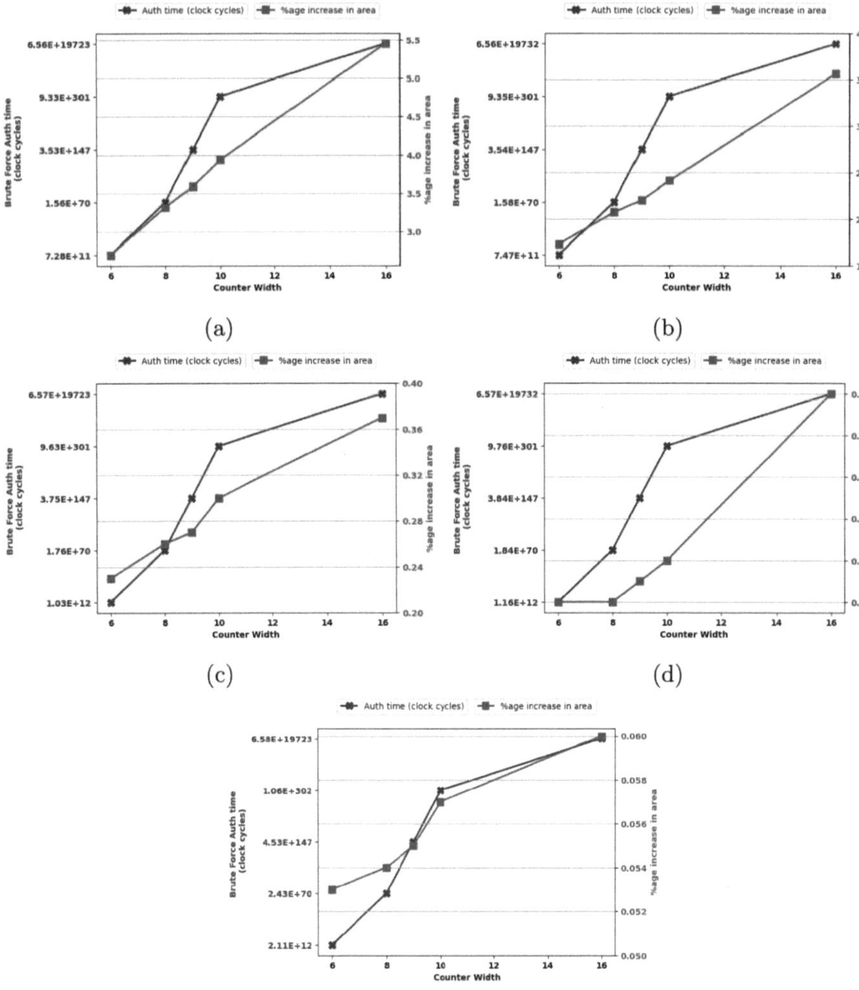

(e)

Fig. 9. Authorization time and area overhead vs. Counter width (a) Mingle benchmark, (b) TreeFlat benchmark, (c) TreeBalanced benchmark, (d) TreeFlatEx benchmark, (e) t512505 benchmark

of clock cycles) of K+n+5 clock cycles, where K is the length of the key, n is the number of ISSIBs in the scan path. Thus, to try all possible combinations, the authorization cost for the attacker increases exponentially, with the increase in the counter size. On the other hand, the authorization cost in terms of cycle time for the authorized user is K+n+5 only. Also, it can be observed from Fig. 9a that the area overhead gets increased by 3.32% and 3.59% for the key size of 256 bits and 512 bits, respectively. It is important to emphasize that the percentage increase in area is specifically in relation to the IJTAG network. In the context of

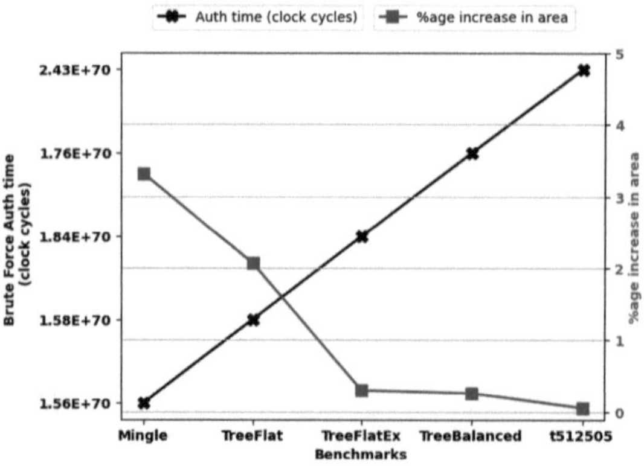

Fig. 10. Authorization time and area overhead for various benchmark circuits

a complex System-on-Chip (SoC), where the IJTAG constitutes only a fraction of the total area, the resulting area overhead from replacing the SIB with the ISSIB would be negligible. Therefore, the area does not increase substantially with a significant increase in key size. This is because the area is unaffected by the key size and solely depends on the counter size. Consequently, increasing the counter width from 8 to 9 results in only a minor area increment, as it involves adding only a single sequential element (flip-flop) while significantly enhancing the challenge for the attacker.

In the case of the TreeFlatEx benchmark circuit (Fig. 9d), the authorization time is $3.84 * 10^{147}$ clock cycles for a key size of 512 bits (counter width is 9 bits). The authorization time increases to $9.76 * 10^{301}$ cycles for the key size of 1024 bits (counter width is 10 bits). Intriguingly, the corresponding %age increase in area is only 0.31% and 0.32%, respectively, as shown in Fig. 9d. This trend is consistent across other benchmark circuits like TreeFlat and TreeBalanced, illustrated in Figs. 9b and 9c, respectively. In the case of TreeFlat benchmark, the authorization time is $3.54*10^{147}$ clock cycles for a key size of 512 bits (counter width is 9 bits), which increases to $9.35 * 10^{301}$ cycles for a key size of 1024 bits (counter width is 10 bits). However, the area overhead increases to 2.20% to 2.41% for the key size of 512 bits and 1024 bits, respectively. Furthermore, in the case of TreeBalanced benchmark, the authorization time is $3.75 * 10^{147}$ clock cycles for a key size of 512 bits, which increases to $9.63 * 10^{301}$ cycles for a key size of 1024 bits, while the increase in area overhead is 0.30% and 0.27%, respectively. Since TreeFlatEx is very large in terms of area compared to the Mingle benchmark, the area overhead of the TreeFlatEx benchmark circuit gets increased by a lesser amount as compared to the Mingle benchmark. It can be observed in Fig. 9e that for the classic IJTAG network t512505, which is the largest benchmark in terms of the area, the increase in the area overhead is 0.057% and 0.055% for the key size of 512 bits and 1024 bits, respectively. However, the authorization time increases exponentially for all the benchmark circuits, regardless of the size of the benchmark circuit, as shown in Fig. 10.

It is evident from Fig. 10 that for large benchmark circuits such as Tree Balanced, TreeFlatEx and t512505, the area overhead is minimal, while the authorization time is too high for the key size of 256 bits. To have a fair comparison among all the benchmarks, counter size is kept constant, i.e., counter size is 8 bits in Fig. 10. It can observed from Fig. 10, the area overhead for Mingle benchmark and t512505 are 3.32% and 0.054%, respectively. However, their authorization time for the attacker varies from $1.56 * 10^{70}$ clock cycles to $2.43 * 10^{70}$ clock cycles. Thus, as the size of the IJTAG network circuit increases, the %age increase in the area with the proposed ISSIB decreases, which makes our proposed ISSIB scalable and practically viable solution against unauthorized users. The same trend can be observed for all other benchmark circuits, reinforcing the scalability and practical viability of the proposed ISSIB against unauthorized users. It is noteworthy that all the SIBs are replaced by the ISSIBs in the benchmark circuits in order to have a fair comparison of the area.

5 Conclusion

In this work, an inherently secure SIB (ISSIB) based security mechanism is proposed to prohibit unauthorized access to the IJTAG network. The proposed scheme brings testability/functionality and security together in the design of IJTAG network. The proposed ISSIB is area efficient, scalable and provides a very strong level of security. Further, the security level can be enhanced with a negligible area overhead.

Acknowledgements. This work has been partially supported by the project number IHUB-NTIHAC-/2021/01/14.

References

1. Baranowski, R., Kochte, M.A., Wunderlich, H.J.: Fine-grained access management in reconfigurable scan networks. IEEE Trans. Comput.-Aided Design Integr. Circuits Syst. **34**(6) (2015)
2. Biryukov, A.: Known plaintext attack. In: Encyclopedia of Cryptography and Security (2005)
3. Das, A., Touba, N.A.: A graph theory approach towards IJTAG security via controlled scan chain isolation. In: IEEE 37th VLSI Test Symposium (VTS), pp. 1–6 (2019)
4. DaSilva, F.: IEEE standard testability method for embedded core-based integrated circuits. IEEE Std 1500TM-2005 (2005)
5. De Canniere, C., Preneel, B.: Trivium. In: New Stream Cipher Designs: The eSTREAM Finalists, pp. 244–266. Springer (2008)
6. Dworak, J., Conroy, Z., Crouch, A., Potter, J.: Board security enhancement using new locking SIB-based architectures. In: International Test Conference (2014)
7. Dworak, J., Crouch, A.: A call to action: securing IEEE 1687 and the need for an IEEE test security standard. In: IEEE 33rd VLSI Test Symposium (VTS), pp. 1–4 (2015)

8. Dworak, J., Crouch, A., Potter, J., Zygmontowicz, A., Thornton, M.: Don't forget to lock your SIB: hiding instruments using P1687. In: IEEE International Test Conference (ITC) (2013)
9. Elnaggar, R., Karri, R., Chakrabarty, K.: Security against data-sniffing and alteration attacks in IJTAG. IEEE Trans. Comput.-Aided Design Integr. Circuits Syst. (2020)
10. Gupta, S., Crouch, A., Dworak, J., Engels, D.: Increasing IJTAG bandwidth and managing security through parallel locking-SIBs. In: IEEE International Test Conference (ITC), pp. 1–10. IEEE (2017)
11. IEEE Standards Association and others: IEEE standard for access and control of instrumentation embedded within a semiconductor device. IEEE Standard (2014)
12. IEEE Standards Association and others: IEEE standard for test access port and boundary-scan architecture. IEEE Std **1149** (2013)
13. Kan, S., Dworak, J., Dunham, J.G.: Echeloned IJTAG data protection. In: 2016 IEEE Asian Hardware-Oriented Security and Trust (AsianHOST), pp. 1–6. IEEE (2016)
14. Kumar, G., Riaz, A., Prasad, Y., Ahlawat, S.: On attacking IJTAG architecture based on locking sib with security LFSR. In: 28th IEEE International Symposium on On-Line Testing and Robust System Design (IOLTS), Torino, Italy (2022)
15. Kumar, G., Riaz, A., Prasad, Y., Ahlawat, S.: On attacking locking SIB based IJTAG architecture. In: Proceedings of the Great Lakes Symposium on VLSI 2022, GLSVLSI 2022, pp. 105–109. Association for Computing Machinery (2022)
16. Larsson, E., Xiang, Z., Murali, P.: Graceful degradation of reconfigurable scan networks. IEEE Trans. Very Large Scale Integr. (VLSI) Syst. **29**(7), 1475–1479 (2021). https://doi.org/10.1109/TVLSI.2021.3076593
17. Liu, H., Agrawal, V.D.: Securing IEEE 1687-2014 standard instrumentation access by LFSR key. In: 2015 IEEE 24th Asian Test Symposium (ATS), pp. 91–96 (2015https://doi.org/10.1109/ATS.2015.23
18. Maistri, P., Reynaud, V., Portolan, M., Leveugle, R.: Secure test with RSNs: seamless authenticated extended confidentiality. In: 2021 19th IEEE International New Circuits and Systems Conference (NEWCAS), pp. 1–4 (2021).https://doi.org/10.1109/NEWCAS50681.2021.9462778
19. Paar, C., Pelzl, J.: Understanding cryptography (2010). https://doi.org/10.1007/978-3-642-04101-3
20. Elnaggar, R., Karri, R., Chakrabarty, K.: Securing IJTAG against data-integrity attacks. In: IEEE 36th VLSI Test Symposium (VTS), pp. 1–6 (2018)
21. Thiemann, B., Feiten, L., Raiola, P., Becker, B., Sauer, M.: On integrating lightweight encryption in reconfigurable scan networks. In: 2019 IEEE European Test Symposium (ETS), pp. 1–6. IEEE (2019)
22. Tšertov, A., et al.: A suite of IEEE 1687 benchmark networks. In: 2016 IEEE International Test Conference (ITC), pp. 1–10 (2016). https://doi.org/10.1109/TEST.2016.7805840
23. Valea, E., Da Silva, M., Di Natale, G., Flottes, M.L., Rouzeyre, B.: A survey on security threats and countermeasures in IEEE test standards. IEEE Design Test **36**(3), 95–116 (2019). https://doi.org/10.1109/MDAT.2019.2899064
24. Yang, B., Wu, K., Karri, R.: Scan based side channel attack on dedicated hardware implementations of data encryption standard. In: 2004 International Conference on Test, pp. 339–344. IEEE (2004)
25. Zygmontowicz, A., Dworak, J., Crouch, A., Potter, J.: Making it harder to unlock an LSIB: Honeytraps and misdirection in a P1687 network. In: Design, Automation & Test in Europe Conference & Exhibition (DATE) (2014)

Author Index

Published by Springer Nature Switzerland AG 2024
I. (Abe) M. Elfadel and L. Albasha (Eds.): VLSI-SoC 2023, IFIP AICT 680, pp. 319–320, 2024.
https://doi.org/10.1007/978-3-031-70947-0

MIX
Papier aus verantwortungsvollen Quellen
Paper from responsible sources
FSC® C105338

If you have any concerns about our products,
you can contact us on
ProductSafety@springernature.com

In case Publisher is established outside the EU,
the EU authorized representative is:
Springer Nature Customer Service Center GmbH
Europaplatz 3, 69115 Heidelberg, Germany

Printed by Libri Plureos GmbH
in Hamburg, Germany